Brain-Based Learning

Eric Jensen

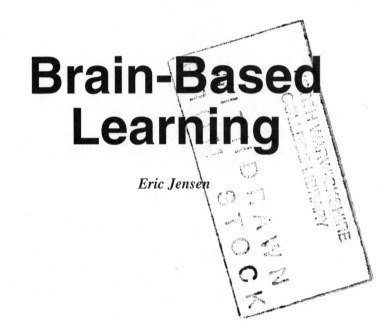

Printed in the United States of America
Published by Turning Point Publishing
Del Mar, CA, USA

Brain-Based Learning
Eric Jensen ©1996

Dedicated to my wife Diane
for her incalculable love & support
Illustrations by Gary Johnson
Cover Art by Mike Warter
Editing by Melissa Fraser

Printed in the United States of America
Published by Turning Point Publishing
Del Mar, CA, USA

ISBN #0-9637832-1-1

 0046603

For additional copies, contact:
Turning Point Publishing
Box 2551
Del Mar, CA 92014 USA
(619) 546-7555 phone
(619) 546-7560 fax

Preface

There's an explosion in brain research that threatens the existing paradigms in learning and education. New and dramatic theories may force all of us to take a closer look at what we are doing. We may even have to stop altogether and redesign what we do and how we do it. The new paradigm is emerging with spellbinding implications. It's a marriage of many powerful concepts and discoveries in neuroscience including the role of emotions, patterns, survival, environments, rhythms, positive thinking, assessment, music, gender differences and enrichment.

In addition, amazing theories by top scientists assert that when we are learning something, we may only be discovering something that has already been genetically built-in or "pre-programmed" into our brains. In addition, our brains *may not at all be designed for formal instruction,* but rather, only *the learning necessary* for survival. New systems theories tell us how to successfully restructure our schools as a complete learning organization. If these postulates hold true, many of our conventional educational models will be shattered like glass. And some would say, it's about time.

After all, knowledge about the brain and standard education practices have traditionally been in different worlds. It's time for a marriage. The visionary author-scientist H.G. Wells said, "Civilization is a race between education and catastrophe." Indeed, there is an urgency to our planet that we've never before collectively experienced. At both local and global levels, we lack the luxury of being able to weather continued "Dark Ages" in learning. There is too much at risk. Time is running out and we must act on these problems now.

> *Present problems cannot be solved*
> *with the same level of thinking and*
> *by the same tools that created them*

This book calls for the initiation of a educational paradigm change. The implications of these "brain-based" discoveries are going to be widespread and profound. Shortsighted priorities, outdated teacher education programs, visionless leaders, the "program of the week," clumsy systems, budgetary bottlenecks, hierarchical in-fighting and professional jealousy all contribute to the problem and have to stop. Furthermore, we need to quit playing "victim" and quit the "helplessness" mentality. We can make the changes needed in education if we collectively make it important enough to do so. Nearly every change suggested in this book is either free or can be done simply at a surprisingly affordable cost.

Let's make an important distinction between core problems and symptoms of problems. Solving core problems gives you a ten, twenty or fifty-fold return on your time, money and energy. Solving symptoms creates a net loss. That means that for every symptom you "solve," you not only miss the real problem, but you create more symptoms to solve later. And those take more time, money and effort. As a result, you can dig yourself deeper and deeper in a hole.

When an organization is designed to be antagonistic to the natural and effortless way the brain can learn, you will get a mind-boggling array of symptomatic problems, each creating more and more difficulties and costs. Each wears down an already over-burdened staff. And they all miss the larger and more core problem. Schools have to be designed and run around a simple concept: "How does the brain learn best?" and "How can we create a successful learning organization?"

Why is now the time for a shift in thinking? The research on what works is both compelling and comprehensive. We are all great natural learners, so it's increasingly critical to understand how we, as human beings learn best. Secondly, when students are provided with a learning environment that is optimal for learning, graduation rates go up, most learning difficulties disappear, most discipline problems are reduced by 90%, students love learning and most schools find that they can focus on the real issues, not the distracting peripheral ones.

The first thing that "brain-based" advocates
got from others was indifference... that was followed
by ridicule, opposition... now, finally, respect

In short, designing an organization around the way the brain learns best may be the simplest and most critical core reform to be initiated. In fact, of all the changes that can be made and are being made, nothing will give you a better return on your time, effort and money as the developing "Brain-Based Learning." In the last 30 years, every single reform that has come and gone were examples of brain-antagonistic learning.

This is no fad, no trendy gimmick. This is neuroscience. It's now tested and classroom-proven. Isn't how the brain learns fundamental to all that we do? The current research on how the brain learns is both compelling and comprehensive. It is now possible for nearly every challenge to be solved at the core level, with what we currently know. In fact, it's being done, as you read this, worldwide. In learning organizations across the globe, determined individuals, cooperating teams and whole communities have successfully implemented brilliant, innovative, low-cost, brain-based solutions.

It's imperative we share what we know works as quickly and as effectively as we can. It's no longer a question of "Can we?" Let's admit we <u>do</u> have the resources needed to do the job now.

Teaching, training and learning provide a major source for the preservation of humanity. We must become a world of learners and begin to value learning as much as freedom, shelter, health and justice. We are obliged to take this assignment seriously - our collective future depends on it. I invite you to start now. If you can't do it by yourself, get some support to bring together resources. Start a network. Determined people like Joan Caulfield, Bobbi DePorter, Dee Dickinson, Sara Dinsdale, Launa Ellison, Barbara Given, Wayne Jennings, Penny Kelly, Jan Spralding and Judy Stevens have all done it. They simply said "Let's get all these people talking to each other and see what comes of it." When they started sharing what works, they realized that their results were far beyond those of the typical educator.

You *can* make a significant difference. You are a unique, one in a trillion, biological event. Your parents could conceive test tube babies for a lifetime and never have another like you. This planet gets one opportunity, just one chance for your singular, powerful contribution to humanity. Can you step up to the challenge and accept the unique opportunity of your historical role? Turbulent times demand that all of us be our best. Find other, like minded people, and organize to increase your impact. As Margaret Mead once said,

"Never doubt that a small group of
concerned citizens can change the world.
It is, indeed, the <u>only</u> thing that ever has"

This book examines the initial stages of an entirely new paradigm in education. I am proposing a model in which we promote learning the way the brain is best and biologically designed to learn. In this crucial time in history, it seems that more of our future hangs in the balance than ever before. As a result, we must share what we know works as quickly and as effectively as we can. Let's all pull together and make it happen. We have the knowledge, the resources and motivation. If not now, then when? If not you, then who?

Acknowledgments

All of us in the field owe a debt to the giants of a more brain-based learning approach. These individuals have either provided critical research or publicly promoted better ways to learn: Dr. Jane Bancroft, Dr. Ron Brandt, Dr. Tony Buzan, Dr. Renate Nummela Caine, Geoffrey Caine, Dr. Joan Caulfield, Dr. Barbara Clark, Dr. Antonio Damasio, Dr. Marion Diamond, Dee Dickinson, Gorden Dryden, Dr. Gerald Edelman, Marilyn Ferguson, Dr. Michael Gazziniga, Dr. Jane Healy, Dr. Jean Houston, Dr. Georgi Lozanov, Dr. Lyelle Palmer, Joseph Chilton Pearce, Dr. Robert Ornstein, Dr. Paul MacLean, Dr. Paul Messier, Sheila Ostrander, Dr. Richard Restak, Colin Rose, Dr. Steven Rose, Dr. Arnold Schiebel, Lynn Schroeder, Dr. Peter Senge, Dr. Robert Sternberg and Dr. Robert Sylwester. I am indebted in particular, to trailblazing by brain-based learning pioneer Leslie Hart. Many thanks to Susan Kovalik, for her leadership and editing feedback.

Every one of these are professional practitioners and strong supporters of brain-based learning. They have have all contributed to the field in their unique way: Among them are: Rob Abernathy, Frank Alessi, Nancy Bently, Chris Brewer, Stephanie Burns, Annette Cam, Bruce Campbell, Don Campbell, Linda MacRae Campbell, Glen Capelli, Phillip and Libyan Cassonne, Dr. Joan Caulfield, Dr. Frank Clement, Dr. Charles Connolly, Christine Culling, Bob Cunningham, Bobbie DePorter, Dr. Lynn Dhority, Sarah Dinsdale, Kay Distel, Glen and Janet Doman, James Doran, Nancy Ellis, Launa Ellison, Norm Erickson, Dr. Ron Fitzgerald, Anne Forester, Mary Francis, Nancy Gallagher, Michael Gelb, Barbara Given, Lonnie Gold, John Grassi, Michael Grinder, Nancy Harkrider, Carole Helstrom, Ronald Hering and Paul Hobbs.

Other contributors and supporters include: Dr. Wayne Jennings, Sue Jorgensen, Mike Kelly, Penny Kelly, Dr. Jeff King, Dr. Jim King, Peter and Syril Kline, David Lazear, Charlotte Lettecha, Don Lofland, Sandy MacGregor, Luis Machado, Nina Malm, Nancy Maresh, Laurence Martel, Ron Maxfield, Doug McPhee, Linda MacRae Campbell, David Meier, Greg Meyer, Twyla Moshel, Ann Nevin, Nancy Omaha Boy, Karen Olsen, Robert Owen, Gary Phillips, Pedro Portes, Barbara Praschnig, Allyn Pritchard, Pamela Rand, Mark Reardon, Charles Reinhart, Anthony Robbins, Bob Samples, Charles Schmid, Don Schuster, Hideo Seki, John Senatore, Karen Sliwka, David Sousa, James Smith, Jan Spralding, Wayne Stead (& colleagues Ken, Allie and Ann), Judy Stevens, Nina Sunday, Edgar Thomas, Marshall Thurber, Larry Van Etten, Roberta Verey, Deborah Voosen, Jeannette Vos, John Wade, Dr. Win Wenger and Pat Wolfe.

Table of Contents

Chapter 4   Brain-Based Environments

Chapter 5   Preparing the Learner

Chapter 6   Sex, The Brain & Learning

Chapter 7   The Learning Climate

Chapter 8   Getting Attention & Keeping It

Chapter 9   Unlocking the Code: Learning Styles

Chapter 10   Enrichment, Activation & Movement

Chapter 11   Better Thinking Strategies

Chapter 12   Strategies For Understanding and Meaning

Chapter 13   Memory & Recall

Chapter 14   Music With A Purpose

Chapter 15   Threats, Rewards & Praise

Chapter 16 Making Sense of Discipline

Chapter 17 Motivation & The Brain

Chapter 18 Rethinking Assessment

Chapter 19 From Course Planning to Learning Planning

Chapter 20 Interdisciplinary Brain-Based Frameworks

Chapter 21   Building a Learning Organization

Chapter 22   A Systems Approach: The Learning Community

Chapter 23   The Next Step

Appendix

Introduction

*"If we learned to use our brain
the way it was naturally designed to work,
we would astonish ourselves everyday"*

How does our brain learn? And more importantly, once we know that, what do we do about it? The ability to learn, both individually, in groups, in organizations and as a country is now more critical than ever. In *The Learning Imperative,* editor Robert Howard emphasizes how dramatically Xerox, Shell Oil, Levis, Motorola and dozens of other Fortune 100 Corporations have made learning a priority. In *The Fifth Discipline: The Art and Practice of the Learning Organization,* author Peter Senge says that nothing less than *the very survival of an organization* depends on how well it learns. And how can we become purposeful and skilled at learning unless we truly understand *how* we learn? We can't.

This book provides a summary of the principles of "brain-based learning." It is an approach to learning which favors the brain's best natural operational principles, with the goal of attaining maximum attention, understanding, meaning and memory. In short, it means learning smarter, not harder. The brain is a complex organ that has hundreds of "rules" for learning. Some of these rules are simple: the brain likes oxygen, glucose, amino acids, adequate rest and moderate stimulation. Other rules are complex and require a great deal of explanation and qualification. For example, we know that rewards and punishments can be detrimental to some types of learning, but what exactly qualifies as a reward? Approval? Material rewards? And what is punishment? A frown? A loss of privileges?

While there are still many unanswered questions, much is known. In fact, enough is known to start using brain-based learning as a framework for redesigning teacher education classes, course curriculum, staff in-services, lesson plans, schools and corporate trainings. The incentives for getting started are quite strong. When brain-based learning is occurring, the learner is likely to:

- understand the subject better & feel relevantly connected to it
- be intrinsically motivated
- enjoy the process
- feel more competent as a learner
- become interested in the subject
- want to return to the activity again

- remember it longer
- be able to generalize the learning productively into other areas

This book is written for those who want to know not only just "what works," but also why it works and what specifically to do about it. It's written for the novice in the hope that it will get you off to the right start. When you form positive habits from the beginning, the job is significantly easier. It's also written for the more experienced in the hope that it will validate much of what you intuitively know works.

This book is also intended to be non-technical. At the end of each section, I have included "How You Can Follow Up" and additional resources. If you don't find something in a chapter, check the index. Many items may be referenced under several chapters. For more details on the research, use the author's name to reference the source material in the bibliography.

I share these principles only after vigorously applying them in my own teaching and training, first hand. Certainly, there are hundreds of other implications for "brain-based" learning. But even if only a few were thoroughly applied in schools, homes and businesses, I am convinced there would be a significant, lasting and positive impact on our world. Use these book's suggestions *as the ideal,* since you'll have specific limitations due to scheduling, rules to follow, time constraints, curriculum mandates and budgets to follow.

These principles work because they are based on the way our brains learn best - not just the brains of certain learners, employees, primary schoolers, middle schoolers, special education students, high schoolers, preschoolers, collegians and adults, but also the brains of "low kids," the aged and elderly, Asians, Anglos, Germans, Blacks, Kiwis, Indians, the disadvantaged learners, Indonesians, Japanese, Maoris, the discouraged learners, the English, Israelis, Africans, Chinese, the so-called "gifted," the Arabians, Latinos, the "at-risk," Australians, Hispanics, Native Americans or Europeans. In short, these strategies work on all of us. When we respect and utilize how the brain works best, we get miracles... consistent, common miracles.

By the way, this book has enough ideas to last you for years. *Add one strategy per week* and you're more likely to make lasting changes than trying to do it all overnight. You officially now have the author's permission: start with one, simple, easy-to-implement step. Just do what you can. Over time, you'll be pleasantly surprised at how many positive changes you've made. If you make a mistake, forgive yourself, learn from it and move on. *That's what learning is about.* Now, go ahead, enjoy the book and join us all for a global learning revolution.

Brain-Based Learning

Eric Jensen

In a gentle way you can shake the world
Ghandi

1

1
The New Brain Research

It's a Jungle in There

How can we understand something as complex as the human brain? Sometimes analogies, examples or metaphors can help. Common 20th century brain metaphors have included a telephone switchboard, a computer and a massive city. The good thing about metaphors is that they can give you a framework for understanding. The bad thing about metaphors is that an inappropriate one can steer you in the wrong direction. Since this book is about learning, based on the way the brain naturally learns best, an easy way to begin is with a metaphor.

Given what we now know about the brain, one of the best metaphors for understanding it is a rain forest jungle. The jungle is active at times, quiet at times, but always teeming with life. The brain is similar: it is very active at times, much less at others, but always alive and busy. The jungle has its own zones, regions and sectors: the underground, the streams, the ground cover, the low plants and shrubs, the air, the taller plants, the trees, etc. The brain has its own sectors; for thinking, sexuality, memory, survival, emotions, breathing, creativity, etc. And while the jungle changes over time, one constant remains true: the law of the jungle is survival *and no one's in charge!*

We'll come back to this theme later, but keep in mind that the brain is best at learning what it *needs to learn* to survive; socially, economically, emotionally and physically. From your typical learner's point of view, keep in mind that somewhere about 53rd on its list is "academic success."

3

The analogy of the jungle is especially important when we consider classroom learning. A jungle has no "presenter" or "trainer." It is simply a rich, evolving system. The jungle has no short or long-term goals with one exception: the genetic goal is survival. It simply does everything it can to exist; systematically and ecologically. In fact, it is messy, overlapping and inefficient in many ways. Our brain is similar - we have huge amounts of useless information stored, extinct programs running and yet it still manages to help us survive. Just as no animal (not even a lion or Tarzan!) runs the jungle, Damasio reminds us that *no single region in the human brain is equipped to run our brain.* Everyone and everything participates to make the "jungle production" happen. A plant may not communicate with a bird or monkey, but it is used by them for housing, food or survival. It's a mutual reliance club. This, after all is a jungle - the most appropriate metaphor for understanding the human brain.

The jungle is very different depending on the time of day, the weather and the month of the year. The brain also has its own timetables and inner clock. The jungle is also very much dependent on the totality of both the biological and animal life to maintain itself, just as is the human brain dependent on the connectedness of each part of itself to the other parts. The jungle is constantly evolving, growing more complex as it ages, just as the human brain does. The jungle is also responsive to change and can even weather a natural disaster. The human brain also is quite resilient and can grow and change over time with stimulation. Considering the amazing complexity of the rain forest jungle and the human brain, both are extraordinarily impressive.

Changing Paradigms:
From Psychology to Biology

In the 50's and 60's the dominant theory of human behavior (and resulting educational paradigm) came from the doctrines of B.F. Skinner. Skinner's behaviorist theories went something like this: "We may not know what goes on inside the brain, but we can certainly see what happens on the outside. Let's measure behaviors, and learn to modify them with behavior-reinforcers. If we like it, reward it. If we don't, punish it." The educational system of the Western world "bought into" these theories on a grand scale. As a result, schools have continued to increase the measuring, defining and recording of behaviors. Today, in most schools, you can find some kind of assessment for nearly anything and everything. Neuroscientists see the problems quite clearly as this:

Most of what we can measure now,
behaviorally, is neurologically immaterial
to the optimal development of the brain

4

This realization is fueling a massive and urgent movement worldwide in redesigning academic assessment. What we thought was important in the past, may not at all be important. It may have simply been *more measurable!* In other words, what if Skinner was wrong? You can have the most efficient oil rig in the world, but if you're digging in the wrong area, you'll still not strike oil.

During the 80's a whole new breed of science was quietly developing. By the 90's, it had exploded into dozens of mind-boggling sub-disciplines. Suddenly, seemingly unrelated disciplines were being mentioned in the same science journal articles. Readers found immunology, physics, genes, emotions, pharmacology seamlessly woven into articles on learning and brain theory. The new cutting-edge voices in the field of neuroscience featured names like Alkon, Gazzaniga, Rose, Damasio, Calvin, Restak, Herbert, Sachs and Edelman. Drawing from a wide multi-disciplinary body of technical knowledge about the brain, there's a new, paradigm-shaking, proposition:

The brain is poorly designed for formal instruction
It is not at all designed for efficiency or order...
Rather, it develops best through selection and survival

The importance of this paradigm to those who teach or train is stunning - it's no less than the destruction of our old Skinnerian model of instruction. What Nobel-Prize contender Edelman says is that our brain, biologically and functionally, does primarily whatever it has to in order to survive. He suggests much of our brain is neurologically pre-wired to learn. We have a predetermined genetic "menu" to select from, which we got from our parents. This includes the capacity to learn the 52 sounds of universal languages, their intonation and syntax. It also includes the ability to write, sing, create and play music, to think, plan, draw, problem-solve, sculpt, act, learn and a thousand other talents, each of which can be nurtured to various degrees. Another Nobel-Prize contender Gazzaniga, says "...acquiring the capacity to speak French or English... or for that matter, any capacity - may reflect *little more than a specific environment guiding one of dozens of built-in systems to arrange and process information...*"

The Biology of Learning

It may be that biologically, we are evolving a better brain every generation by natural selection. Throughout recorded history, in every instance where we thought the environment (instruction) was presenting the organism, some feature of the organism may have, in fact, *been merely stimulated to grow*. It's a sobering thought about the role of the presenting profession. San Diego bioanthropologist Willis asserts that "...(the new model)...demonstrates by cold and incontrovertible mathematics that most evolutionary change is not driven by natural selection at all.

Instead it can be explained more simply, cleanly, and convincingly by random events–mere throws of genetic dice." In either case, through instruction or selection, the older behaviorist model is dead.

Neuroscientists today propose a stunning corollary to the earlier paradigm of the brain being designed to survive. Gazzaniga puts it best (you might like to read this next statement twice): *"Learning may be nothing more than the time needed for an organism to sort out its built-in systems in order to accomplish these goals."* There's more; he also argues that from a biological perspective, *"...all we are doing in life is catching up with what our brain already knows."* Now, try and figure out implications for THAT in today's educational climate. You might have guessed that this book is just the start.

> ***Nature's biological imperative is simple:***
> ***No intelligence or ability will unfold until***
> ***or unless given the appropriate model environment***

The bottom line is, our brain is pre-wired to learn *what we need to learn to survive.* The brains that are "poorly-wired" (have considerable learning difficulties), would, in the past, have had a lower chance, genetically, for survival. When we are talking about survival at a larger "systems" (school or life) level, all processes are instructive. When we are talking about instruction (the presenting, classroom level), all processes are simply selective mechanisms. In other words, nature is evolving the best brains through natural selection. The "jungle" has no "Special Ed" programs for plants that need extra fertilizer or for birds that sing poorly. They survive or they don't.

Now, you might respond by saying, "That's cruel. Hopefully we are a bit more caring, sophisticated and culturally advanced than a jungle population." Yes, generally we are. But from a biological perspective, the fact that our brain, like our immune system, is designed solely for our survival, is important information. It implies dramatic changes in the way we organize formal education and training. As you continue this book, keep a mental note of the Edelman paradigm: "The brain is designed for selection survival, not instruction."

What This Means To You: For starters, begin to think of presenting as "learning to get out of the way of the learner." The brain is trying to learn, in order to survive. Design learning so that it is more based on learner needs for reaching social, economic and personal agendas. Many programs designed to incorporate this need to survive are in place already. They are usually community service, sports, apprenticeships, music, clubs and art. Perceived learner survival forces learning on many levels.

Our Astonishing Learning Potential

Learners are far more capable than ever imagined. Each successive study of the brain's potential has documented that the previous ones were often too modest. Estimates by Huttenlocher, Edelman and Ornstein verify that the brain has almost countless cells. It is the most complex organ known to humans. For the sake of comparison, let's compare the number of brain cells in a few different organisms: a fruit fly has a hundred thousand, a mouse has five million, and a monkey has ten billion.

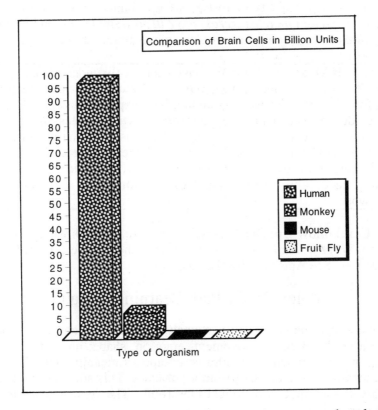

Extraordinarily enough, humans have about one hundred billion (100,000,000,000) cells! When all linked together the number of connections our brain can make is variously estimated by the above researchers to be from 10^{14th} power (a hundred trillion), 10^{800th} power, to as much as ten followed by millions of zeroes (more than the estimated number of atoms in the known universe, which is estimated to be between $10^{80th\text{-}100th}$ power).

Some researchers say that our brain begins to lose cells starting at birth. Others say cell deterioration begins about age twelve. It's not so significant how much we lose; we are born with so much, we can afford the loss of a few million cells. Research by Jernigan has revealed that there is evidence of slightly increasing brain volume in subjects aged 25-39 years old. We know that the brain's plasticity continues as one ages.

One professor said, "We can show that *each of the ten billion neurons* in the human brain has a possibility of (establishing) connections with others *up to a figure with twenty-eight noughts (zeros) after it!* If a single neuron has this quality of potential, we can hardly imagine what the whole brain can do...."

> **What This Means To You:** We have been vastly underestimating the capacity of the learner. In fact, our expectations may have been too low for all types of learners. Maintain high expectations regardless of the evidence. Teach in many different learning styles so that the potential of every learner is tapped. Then use alternative forms of assessment to provide avenues for those who learn differently. Provide a climate where every learner is respected and nourished. Avoid homogeneous ability grouping. Utilize multi-status and multi-age teamwork.

How You Can Follow Up: Read *The Amazing Brain,* by Ornstein; *The Brain* by Restak; *The Three Pound Universe*, by Teresi and Hooper; and *The Learning Brain,* by Jensen. See Appendix for listings.

Complex, Multi-Path Learning Is Natural

Hart says that the brain simultaneously operates on many levels, processing all at once a world of color, movement, emotion, shape, intensity, sound, taste, weight, and more. It assembles patterns, composes meaning and sorts daily life experiences from an extraordinary number of clues. This amazing multi-processor can be starved for input in a typical classroom. The typical response is often frustration or boredom.

Caine and Caine also remind us that the brain is processing on many paths, modalities, levels of consciousness, and meaning levels. It's designed to process many inputs at once. In fact, it prefers multi-processing so much, a slower, more linear pace actually reduces understanding. In short, many instructors, trainers and presenters actually inhibit learning by the way they teach.

The work of Botella and Eriksen also verifies the parallel processing methods used by the brain in RSVP (rapid, serial, visual presentation) tasks. We all learn in random, personalized, often complex patterns that defy description except in the most reductionist terms. In fact, the brain seems to thrive immensely by pursuing multi-path, multi-modal experiences.

A terrific analogy about the brain's processing comes from University of Oregon professor Robert Sylwester. He says we are multi-processing in a manner much like a jazz quartet. It's a blend of four different instruments, four personalities, with no overt communication and they still make great music. Anytime presenters think that they can get great learning by presenting consistently to just one "musician" in the quartet, is going to be disappointed. What our brain does when used best, is to make great music (metaphorically and literally)!

Some scientists say that there is very little learning that the brain does best in an orderly, sequential fashion. In fact, Nobel Prize winning scientist and co-discoverer of DNA's double-helix formation, Francis Crick, says that the functions of the brain "are usually *massively parallel* (author's emphasis). For example, about a million axons go from each eye to the brain, all working simultaneously."

We learn about a city best from the full multi-path, sensory experience of it, rather than from sequential information in a book. We learned our neighborhood as a child from scattered, random input, not from a manual or guidebook. Learning is best when it provides many options and inputs. Keep in mind the metaphor of the jungle. The capacity of the brain is so incredibly complex that something as simple as crossing a street is processed in five different areas of the brain - visual pattern movement, shape, velocity, sounds and feelings. And for a 15-year-old, crossing the street is usually quite mundane. A typical classroom could have double and triple the input and you'd still get no complaints from the learners. In fact, your discipline problems would probably cease forever.

We are quite used to the "fact" that we do things **one at a time**. We think of a thought, then another thought, then another one. We get up, shower, get dressed and eat, all apparently in sequence. But these illusions are far from the reality of our brain's true operations. Biologically, physically, intellectually and emotionally, we are constantly doing many things at once, says Ornstein. In fact, the brain can't do less than multi-process! It is constantly registering perceptions (over 36,000 visual ones per hour), monitoring our vital signs (heart, hormone levels, breathing, digesting, etc.) and it is continually updating our reality (matching new learning with representations from the past). In addition, the brain is attaching emotions to each event and thought, forming patterns of meaning to construct the larger picture and inferring conclusions about the information acquired.

The brain is designed for survival, not instruction. The brain learns to survive so that it can live another day. But it also learns, becomes "smarter," so that it can meet its destiny - survival. Traditional presenting is incompatible with the brain's natural design. We like to learn individually and often with others. But we learn so differently that group learning needs to be dramatically minimized. Hart said:

> *"[A]ny group instruction that has been tightly,*
> *logically planned will have been wrongly planned*
> *for most of the group, and will inevitably*
> *inhibit, prevent or distort learning"*

Learning is generally too individualized and complex to get much value out of traditional group instruction. Five senses are taken in and each is individually prioritized. The body's hormones are being released at specified periods. Learning is all multi-processing - the learner is immersed in sensory input and the brain makes meaning out of it. In short, any lock-step, sequenced presenting ignores the real complexity of the brain.

> **What This Means To You:** Provide complex, multi-sensory immersion environments. Reduce or avoid lock-step whole class instruction. Offer options for learning: in one part of the room, play a video. In another, set up a reading area, in another, arrange a discussion group or study session. Make the room rich with colorful posters, pictures, charts, mobiles and mind maps. Use mastery learning centers, grouping by interest levels or learning centers. There may be some low volume music being played and large projects going on with multi-status, multi-age cooperative groups. We learn the most from rich, multi-modal influences such as field trips, simulations, excursions, discussions, real-life projects and personalized activities for your learners. Provide richer environments for learning.

How You Can Follow Up: *Human Brain and Human Learning*, by Hart; *The Learning Brain,* by Jensen. See Appendix for details.

Human Brain - Unique As A Fingerprint

Teaching to the human brain means greater choice for learners and diversity in instruction. Why? Scientists have verified that just as with our fingerprints, no two brains are alike. In research by Edelman, the huge variability of retinotectal maps (thinking & perception) is emphasized. He says that not only are the maps not fixed, but in some brain areas, "there are major fluctuations in the borders of maps over time." Moreover, each individual map is unique. The variability of maps depends on signal input (your experience). "In the visual system alone there may be over 30 interconnected brain centers, each with its own map."

Learning occurs when these "maps" all over the brain (not just in visual), talk to each other. They are often referred to as neural networks. The more connected they are to each other, the greater the "meaning" you derive from the learning. Each of these may have from 50-100,000 neurons in them. They represent life as you know it. In fact, if you don't have a representative neural network for something out there in the real world, it simply doesn't exist. That's why totally new concepts are so difficult to grasp at once; there are no networks to create the associations. It's almost as if all of your experiences are stored in a library (the cortex) full of books (stacked neurons) and the books with common bibliographies are all related (neural networks). The dynamics all result from your individualized life experiences and chemistry.

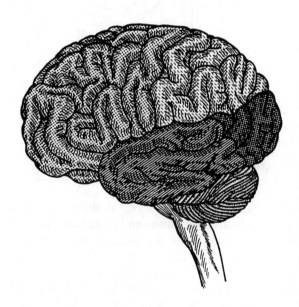

However, each of these "micro-universes" is quite different. As an example, brain size and weight among humans can vary as much as 50%. While Einstein had an average sized brain, the writer Balzac's brain was almost 40% larger. Our brain's internal wiring is quite different, too. Two people are both at the scene of an accident. Each reports on it in such a different way, it's hard to believe that they are describing the same thing. Our perceptions are different, our filters and biases are different. Genetics and nature mold our brains into distinctly individual organs.

Lock-step, assembly-line learning violates
a critical discovery about the human brain:
each brain is not only unique, but is also
growing on a very different timetable

In addition to the "in the moment" differences in physiology, neural wiring and biochemical balance, every brain is on a different timetable of development. For some brains, the "normal" time to learn to read is age two. For another, the "normal" time is age five. There can be, in fact, *a spread in differences up to two and even three years in completely normal developing brains,* says Healy. This discovery has dramatic implications for the organization of learning worldwide.

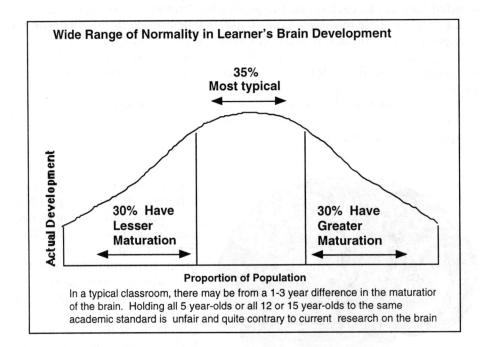

Wide Range of Normality in Learner's Brain Development

35%
Most typical

Actual Development

30% Have Lesser Maturation

30% Have Greater Maturation

Proportion of Population

In a typical classroom, there may be from a 1-3 year difference in the maturation of the brain. Holding all 5 year-olds or all 12 or 15 year-olds to the same academic standard is unfair and quite contrary to current research on the brain

All 5-year-olds should NOT be expected to perform at the same level academically, physically or socially. Statewide curriculums and frameworks which include specific grade-level performance standards are biologically inappropriate. All 13-year-olds may not be neurologically ready for algebra or geometry. The human brain is capable of an enormous amount, IF the neurological groundwork (environmental exposure) has been laid or the presenter has extraordinary flexibility. Doman discovered he could teach babies under three to read. On the other hand, when the groundwork is not laid (typically) the learner may simply become frustrated. Ultimately, some learners simply conclude they're stupid and leave school.

What This Means To You: Find ways to allow for more differences in what is expected for each learner each school year. Lobby for less structured age-based assessments. Add more variety. Some may need to learn or express their learning with sound, mind maps, song, role play, journals, models, movement, pictures; others may want to combine their learning into special projects. Reduce whole-class instructional practices. Utilize more "learning stations" and partner-oriented and individualized mastery learning. Add more choice to your presenting: many learners on many timetables mean that it's difficult to please all of them at the same time. Establish small localized learning groups.

How You Can Follow Up: Read *Maps of the Mind*, by Charles Hampden-Turner.

The Left-Right Brain Theory Revisited

Is there more to our brain than simply left-right side? Yes, in fact our brain is very spatially oriented; there is an amazing relationship between physics and our brain function. Today's neuroscientists have discovered an astonishing parallel between models in physics and in our brain's own organization. While those models were designed to explain the universe, our brains also seem to have their own micro-universe. Einstein developed the relationship between energy, mass and light in the equation $E=MC^2$. His Unified Field Theory brought together for the first time, in a theoretical "weave," time, space and matter. However, our brain also moves and relates energy, space, mass and time in a very coherent way.

The energy in our brain moves up and down on a **vertical axis,** from the brain stem to the cortex and back down again. Our brain is designed to process spatially, from small particles to larger spatial relationships from **left-to right** hemisphere. It gets even more interesting. We process time in our brains, from the **back to the front,** from our past to future. And the mass, the movement of particles, is throughout - with blood flow and neurochemical reactions. Our brain is, in fact, a micro-universe.

Let's turn to the neo-cortex for a moment. It's reassuring to know that much of the original work of Nobel Prize Laureate Dr. Roger Sperry, who discovered the functioning differences between left and right brain hemispheres, remains valid. The controversy since then has been created by overly zealous enthusiasts who insist on creating a "them vs. us, bad-good, super-logical vs. intuition" war. Books have appeared which draw up the battle lines over the "old left-brain way" and the "updated right-brain approach."

What we can safely say about each hemisphere is that
the left side processes "parts" (sequentially) and
the right side processes "wholes" (randomly)

However, updated research by Levy has confirmed that *both sides of the brain are involved in nearly every human activity.* It's all a matter of timing and degree of involvement. Gazziniga says that "...events occurring in one hemisphere can influence developmental events occurring at the same time at very remote parts of the other hemisphere." It is best to leave the hemispheric puzzle as simple and unbiased as possible. Use the two sides more as a metaphor for understanding how we process instead of pigeon-holing all behaviors into either left or right brain as a blueprint for a reductionist model.

Listening to another speak may seem like a left hemisphere activity, since it is the side that processes words, definitions and language. In fact, the female brain processes both language and feelings at the same time far more efficiently than the male brain. Ross' evidence suggested the right hemisphere processes the inflection, tonality, tempo and volume - which are actually more critical to the *meaning* of the conversation. But how function-specific is each side of the brain? Only moderately, it turns out. Iaccino claims that although each hemisphere does have some clear-cut specialization, each side "still requires the other to complement its overall functioning."

The corpus callosum, the largest of the hemisphere's interconnecting nerve fibers (which also includes the anterior commissure) develops at a slow rate, causing the two hemispheres to develop unequally. While some researchers, such as Levy, believe the corpus callosum copies the messages from one side to another. Pribram says the brain operates through patches or pocket holograms called neural fields. Cook describes the role more as topological inhibition. That means that an excited neuron *on one side* sends a generalized, contextual message *to the other.* And the message simply calls on related programs to prompt further understanding. It's like a politician in a helicopter dropping leaflets onto a nearby neighborhood to spark interest. This model explains how we "turn on" our ideas, like a sparkler throws out sparks on New Year's Eve.

In short, we are using both sides of the brain, most of the time. In fact, it's hard to shut them off. Sternberg of Bell Laboratories found that even when we come up with the appropriate answer to a question, the brain continues to process alternative prospects of the question, non-consciously. It literally *practices thinking* even when you are not aware of it! So much of our brain's work is, indeed, outside of our conscious awareness.

Our Asymmetrical Brain

Originally it was thought that the left brain controlled the right 50% of the body and the right brain controlled the other 50%. But researchers now know that our brain is asymmetrical. Iaccino asserts that *the left brain is in charge "in a majority of cases, regardless of body side."* Considering how much else in the body is asymmetrical, that's no surprise. Humans have functional preferences for handedness, eyedness and earedness. The body is not equal; Robin & Shortridge report breast, kidney, ovary, nasal and testes tumors occur more on the left-side of the body.

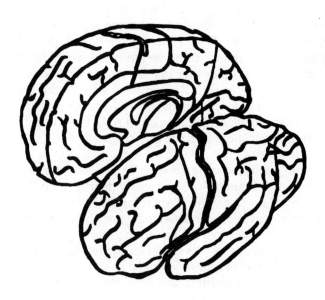

There's a greater number of motor fibers in the nerve pathways from the left hemisphere to the right side of the body. This may indicate a biological preference to right-handedness. The right hemisphere's frontal and central regions are wider, as are the left brain co-occipital lobes. The major lateral groove, the sylvian fissure, is longer on the left side. The left temporal planum is also larger than the right, as is the parietal operculum. In the prefrontal area, the left areas are smaller then the right side, but more hemispheric "folding" may compensate. Blood flow is unequally distributed: it often depends on which appendages are in use.

In the learning context, both left and right brain learners can have their advantages. It totally depends on the presenter. Some of the characteristics of each learner type are listed on the next page.

Left Brain Dominance	vs.	Right Brain Dominance
prefers things in sequence		comfortable with randomness
learns from part to whole		learns whole first, then parts
phonetic reading system		whole language reader
likes words, symbols, letters		wants pictures, graphs, charts
rather read about it first		rather see it or experience it
unrelated factual information		relationships in learning
detailed orderly instructions		spontaneous, go with the flow
prefers internal focus		more likely external focus
wants structure, predictability		open-endedness, surprises

Left Brain Creativity

The notion that one side of the brain is logical and the other side is creative, is outdated. We can become very creative by following and using logical options, patterns, variations and sequences. The work of DeBono on lateral thinking reminds us that one can use "left-brain systems" to be creative. For years he has articulated processes to arrive at creative solutions through sequential methods. Is music a right brain experience? Think again! Researchers discovered that *musicians* process music *more in the left hemisphere* and *non-musicians* process it more in the *right* one. So much for the old adage that music is a right brain activity! Musicians, it seems, tend to analyze music more than the novice.

PET (positron emission tomography) scans give specific locations for brain activity, telling us which part of the brain is used during specific activities. Maguire reports that in research by Yale researchers Ahern and Schwartz, it was found that the *right side of the brain* was the most activated when the learner was *feeling depressed, negative, or stressed.* But when the learner was feeling a healthy optimism about life and the future, most activity was found on the left hemisphere. However, an excessively "Pollyanna" view of reality is linked to right hemisphere activity, as is those who overestimate good feelings and deny negative ones says Mandell.

Learners may be much more effective if taught how to process negative moods or events which could impact their learning. Make sure that the skills needed for thinking things through and learning optimism are part of the learning. Learning optimism comes from conflict-resolution skills, goal-setting skills, a sense of belonging and acceptance, visioning activities, developing a sense of value and purpose in life, and physical vitality.

Right Brain Logic

The right side of the brain can understand and do many logical things. Drawing, composing and painting may seem like a right hemisphere activity, yet artists show bilateral activity. In the planning of artwork, they follow their own logic and rules about shapes, colors and sounds. An artist can express anything on canvas, clay, glass, metal or paper. But to be acceptable to the masses, it needs to follow very specific, certain (though unwritten) rules of proportionality, complimentary color schemes, balance and order. The right brain, it seems, does prefer its own kind of holistic order.

In the 70's and 80's, there was an emphasis on presenting more to the "right brained learner." Current brain research tells us that we generally use both sides of the brain, most of the time. The right brain emphasis was simply an important "pendulum swing" to create awareness in an area that was under-represented.

Not surprisingly, one researcher, Efron, even wrote a book called *The Decline and Fall of Hemispheric Specialization.* Although some of his thesis is valid (the brain has much bilateralization and some asymmetrical), his research is inconsistent. In addition, his reliance on traditional research puts many of his other conclusions out of date. The newer evidence from brain scans and other computer generated metabolic assessments provide exciting and dramatic possibilities for the future.

The prevailing research in neuroscience
avoids the definitive left-right brain labels.
They now use the term "relative lateralization"

That means relatively speaking, there is more activity in one hemisphere than another. It's time for us to insure that BOTH types of learning and presenting are represented. We can now focus our efforts on "whole-brained" learning and drop the "left vs. right" argument.

> **What This Means To You:** Both parts and wholes are important to learning. Neither should be emphasized at the cost of the other. Some of those who are promoting "right-brain thinking" might do more good by promoting "whole-brain thinking." Provide learners with global overviews. Provide them with a sequence of steps that will be followed. If you use an overhead transparency, first show all of it, or all of your overheads for the day or for the whole course. Then you can sequence them, one idea at a time. Alternate between the "big picture" and the details. Validate that we are "whole-brain learners."

Best Bet Resources: For technical research, read *Left and Right Brain Differences,* by Iaccino, Evolution's End by Pearce. For personal usage, read *Learned Optimism,* by Martin Seligman and *Strategies of Optimism,* by Vera Pfeiffer. Other excellent books on hemisphericity (which side of the brain is being used dominantly) include: *Righting the Educational Conveyor Belt,* by Grinder; *The Creative Brain,* by Herrmann; *Use Both Sides of Your Brain,* by Buzan; and *Unicorns are Real,* by Barbara Meister Vitale.

Handedness and Learning

Researchers have been unable to determine conclusively the origins and percentages of handedness throughout history. The best generalization is that most early tools seem to have been made for the right hand. Among Americans, 90% are right-handed, 8% are left-handed and the remaining are ambidextrous. There are many degrees of handedness based on hand preference surveys and handedness inventories. Is it inherited? No. Annett's study found 84% of left-handers had two right-handed parents. Among identical twins, 25% of pairs had BOTH a left and right-hander.

It's a right-handed world: Halpern and Coren report left-handers are five times as likely to die of accident related injuries than right-handers. The Porac and Coren life span study of 5,147 subjects, showed a complete and total absence of left-handers over age 80! The life stresses may be too much: schools, books, pens, tools, appliances are all designed primarily for right-handers.

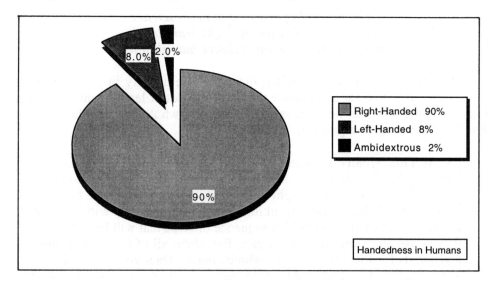

8.0% 2.0%

Right-Handed 90%
Left-Handed 8%
Ambidextrous 2%

90%

Handedness in Humans

Overall, spatial processing in left-handers is impaired seriously, says Iaccino. Levy cites deficits in both visual-spatial and verbal tasks. Among clinical pathological populations there is a higher incidence of left-handers. There is greater incidence of dyslexia, a weaker immune system and maturational delays.

Many reviews indicate a left-handed superiority in listening tasks. There is less lateralized ear superiority, so either ear can process instructions well. This can be of benefit in attentional areas. There is less head turn when asked to solve verbal or spatial problems, resulting in longer attentional sets say Gur & Gur. In general, right-handers show a consistent right-ear comprehension superiority. Iaccino and Calvin have discovered that the majority of left-handed learners process language in the left hemisphere, while from 5-40% use both sides equally for language. Right-handers process language dominantly in the left brain.

Chapter Questions

1. What was novel, fresh and new? What was familiar or "old hat"?
2. In what ways do you already apply the information in this chapter?
3. What three questions can you now generate about this material?
4. How did you react emotionally to this information?
5. In what ways can you translate the key three or four theories and discoveries presented here into practical everyday useful ideas?
6. How did you react cognitively when you were reading the ideas of this chapter?
7. If these things are, in fact, true about the brain, what should we do differently? What resources of time, people and money could be redirected? In what ways do you suggest we start?
8. What was the single one (or two) most interesting or valuable insights you had?
9. Plan your next step, the logical practical application of what you've learned.
10. What obstacles might you encounter? How can you realistically deal with them?

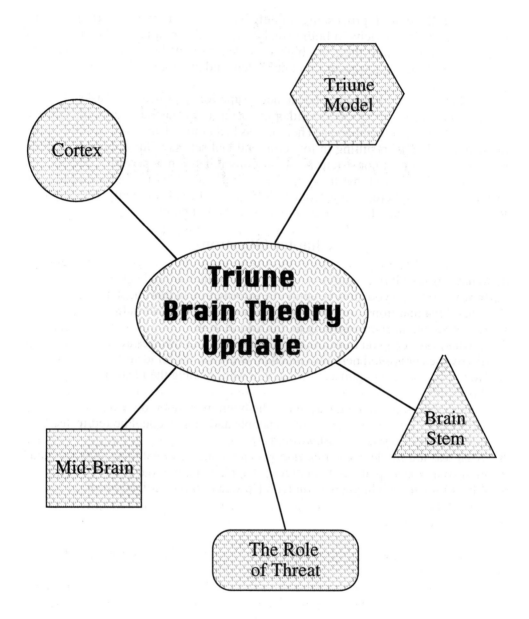

Cortex

Triune
Model

Triune
Brain Theory
Update

Mid-Brain

Brain
Stem

The Role
of Threat

2
Triune Brain Theory Update

The Evolution of Brain Theory

Dr. Paul MacLean was the former Director of the Laboratory of Brain and Behavior at the United States Institute of Mental Health. In 1949, MacLean proposed that our brain acts as if we actually have three brains in one: the R-Complex (reptilian: includes the brain stem and cerebellum), the mid-brain (limbic area: amygdala, hippocampus, hypothalamus, pineal gland, thalamus, nucleus accumbens) and the neomammalian (cerebrum & neocortex). Now, nearly 50 years later, is the triune brain theory still true?

In general, it's not. Its beauty is its simplicity. Its drawback is that recent discoveries tell us that much of the brain is involved in most every function. Emotions are not just in the limbic area. Renowned neurobiologist Antonio Damasio reports evidence of emotions in the prefrontal cortices (frontal lobe) and even the cerebellum. The so-called primitive "reptilian brain" may in fact, not be the oldest, anthrobiologist Willis says. Part of our vision links up with our emotions. Our survival functioning is not just the "reptilian" brain stem, but the reactive mid brain area, especially the amygdala which may store intense memories like rage, fear and surprise.

Most of us like metaphors because they are simple and prescriptive for understanding complex things like the brain. In this case, a better metaphor may be that of a pharmacy, an electrochemical soup, a submarine or a rain forest jungle. Each of which is much more complex than a triune model. MacLean was certainly helpful in furthering our understanding. But to continue to use the triune brain model is outdated, stereotypical and in some cases, dead wrong. As a way to help us understand certain functions of the brain, we'll talk about the upper, middle and lower areas. But a word of caution: these are only generalizations and should be used only as such.

21

About the thickness of your middle finger and coming up from the spinal cord, is the brain stem area. It monitors and presents the physical world. It is instinctive, fast-acting and survival-oriented. Researchers say it's the part of the brain that's responsible for learner behaviors such as:

- social conformity... common hairstyles, clothes, etc.
- territoriality... defending "my stuff, my desk, my room"
- mating rituals... flirting, touching, attracting another
- deception... often forms of subverted aggression
- ritualistic display... trying to get the social attention of peers
- hierarchies... the dominance of leaders, "top dog" behaviors
- social rituals... the repetitive & predictable daily behaviors

The mid-brain area contains the amygdala, hippocampus, thalamus, hypothalamus, pineal gland and some scientists believe, other critical areas. It is the part of the brain most responsible for:

- attention and sleep
- social bonding and attachments from parental bonding
- our hormones, feelings of sexuality
- sense of space and location
- our emotions, both positive and negative
- what is true, valid and what we feel strongly about
- the formation of memories
- immediate expressiveness
- long-term memory

The cerebrum and the neocortex covering it are the bulk of the brain. It used to be called our "thinking cap." But it includes much more. It includes the frontal, occipital, parietal and temporal lobes and provides us with the following:

- thinking, reflection, consciousness
- some processing of emotions
- problem-solving, computations
- language, writing and drawing
- long-range planning, forecasting
- visualizing, envisioning
- reading, translating and composing
- creativity in art, music and theater

Each of the three areas of the brain influences the other. There is no one single part of the brain in control; living is the consensus of a big neural committee.

22

The Impact of Threat

Remember the metaphor of the brain as a jungle? The prevailing "law of the jungle" is survival. The brain is hard-wired to survive and may be run more by natural selection than instruction. As an infant, you learned fastest what you *had* to learn to survive (eating, walking, etc.). A significant part of your brain will insure that you learn, react and adapt primarily for survival. The survival instinct will dominate your behavior under negative and is most responsive to any threat. The brain wants to make sure that when the negative stress is strong, creativity is set aside in favor of the faster, easy-to-implement rote, tried-and-true behaviors which may help you survive. As a result, under moderate to strong stress or threat, you'll get very constricted, predictable behaviors. Usually, you'll get just a ghost of our real human potential.

Brain Activity in States of:

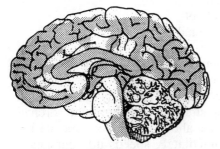

High Challenge, Low Stress

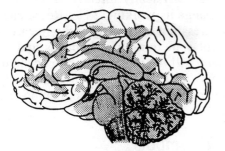

Stress, Anxiety, Threat or
Induced Learner Helplessness

Computer generated images show very clearly that under threats, anxiety, negative stress and induced learner helplessness, the brain operates differently. There is an altered blood flow and electrical activity pattern in the brain. That means the brain has "minimized." You get more predictable, rote, knee-jerk reaction behaviors when the brain senses any threat that induces helplessness. Survival always overrides pattern-detection and problem-solving. This fact has tremendous implications for learning. Stress, threat and induced learner helplessness have got to be removed from the learning environment to achieve maximum potency.

Learning theorist Leslie Hart referred to it as "down-shifting." Since all areas of the brain are still being used (it's simply a matter of degree), the expression "minimized" may be much more accurate than "downshifted." It is less capable of planning, pattern-detection, judgment skills, receiving information, creativity, classifying data, problem-solving and other higher-order skills. It's as if your open, receptive arms suddenly close down to much new information. The brain is likely to "minimize" under the following conditions:

- potential physical harm
  from classmates, staff, family, others
- intellectual threats (ideas being attacked, your potential)
  a test or essay returned with derisive comments
  lack of information to meet the task requirements
- emotional threats (feelings or self-esteem under criticism)
  potentially embarrassing moments
  reward systems that threaten withdrawal if not achieved
- cultural-social threats (disrespect)
  isolation from peers, working by oneself
  inability to pursue personal values at school
  limited chance to utilize meaningful personal life
- resource restriction
  constricting time deadlines for performance

When your brain perceives "alarm" or "danger," the body reacts instantly. In these types of intense, stressful or threatening situations, the hormone adrenaline is released from the adrenal glands. They are right above the kidneys and are injected into the bloodstream immediately. That immediately speeds up your heart rate, depresses your immune system, gets your body ready to fight or flight. You know the feeling, when your brain causes you to feel physically threatened. Does the brain have to have a serious assault on it to change its workings? No. Researchers have found continued exposure to moderate stress not only triggers the release of glutocortoids and which inhibit attention, but something else happens and it's deadly to learning. Constant stress can actually kill neurons in the hippocampus. That's the area of the brain thought to help us "package" our learning into long-term memories. In short, stressful living or learning can increase the likelihood of losing your mind!

Learning, Icons & Symbols

Part of our brain is "wired up" to respond to partial representations. And our response to these is nearly instantaneous. The brain has a tendency to make more out of the symbols than what's there. In other words, what the brain isn't given, it makes up. The symbolic information asks little of the brain: contrasts of light and dark, outlines and edges, no spatial dimension or depth. Our culture is full of symbols: the heart, the eye, mountains, the sun, a mother, icons in computer programs, the ocean, a can of Campbell's soup, jeans, the golden arches, a soccer ball, the stop light, international picture signs, and more. Each of these symbols has come to represent larger meanings, ranging from hunger, success, happiness, and love, to freedom, independence, power, sex, and satisfaction.

Interestingly enough, this part of the brain is our body's brain; our way of acting out in the body-world. It stores all of our various learning from the higher cortical systems and turns them over to "auto-pilot." This part of the brain embodies our sensory-motor system and provides our body-awareness.

> **What This Means To You:** The influences on learners are more far-reaching and powerful than first thought. The posters and peripherals in a learning environment may be more important also. In fact, in one study by Lozanov, peripherals were found to have an increased effect over time, while much of the direct instruction was forgotten. Our opportunities to reach learners may be greater than we first thought. Increase the use of learning symbols and images in the learning environment. Utilize learner input to create new messages about learning. Could they draw, design or build "learning icons," such as a human brain, to represent curiosity? Inspirational posters of mountain climbers, teamwork and great discoveries may help. Make them on poster paper and post them up high. Let them become a part of the peripheral learning environment.

Reactive Responses May Have Biological Basis

Have you had your "hot buttons" pushed by another? Those are the automatic, usually negative, responses which are concerned with the immediate protection of your body, your physical property, intellectual property and emotional property. They are often put-downs, threats, withdrawals or sarcasm. These response-behaviors are the same, regardless of whether you're 6 or 60. Fortunately, they can be altered with awareness and practice.

As an example, a participant makes an inappropriate comment or behaves improperly. You react immediately by snapping back with a quick reaction or a clever verbal comeback. A hot button is pushed once again. The learner reacts intellectually, emotionally and physically. A defensive posture is taken. That "threat-response" posture continues to be reinforced.

Since survival is the most important function of the brain,
survival behaviors dominate our brain in
our everyday lives more ways than we can imagine

You rarely ever get angry for the reason you think you do. Each time you react, it's the re-triggering of an earlier, stored reaction. The trigger may be nearly insignificant. Nevertheless, your brain says, "React! This is horrible!" Over time, your body becomes a storehouse of defensive postures. If physically threatened by a learner, let your brain stem act for you instantly. It is designed to save your life. If the threat is, in fact, insignificant, pause for a moment, take a slow, deep breath and relax. After you've allowed yourself a moment to calm down, then you can act more appropriately.

All Of Our Behaviors Need Expression

Many so-called annoying, strange or inappropriate behaviors are simply a way for the brain to express itself. These rituals may be playful or taunting games, compulsion to follow daily routines, tropistic behaviors (fads, cliques), preening for better attractiveness, informal debates over meaningless subjects, competition for approval, informal role-plays, a learning environment which is "nested" like an animal's home, the "It's my stuff," and "I'm top dog" type behaviors, learners flocking in teams, flirting with each other and adhering to group fads. Traditionally, presenters invest a great deal of energy combating the ever-evolving counter-productive rituals. But there are alternatives.

Rituals can fill the needs of the learners without being counterproductive to learning. Brain-based learning environments and presenting strategies avoid problems. They focus on understanding the brain and working with its natural tendencies instead of constantly suppressing and conflicting with them. You might focus on the following:

- Creating a brain-affirming learning climate
- More personally meaningful projects of choice
- The use of productive rituals
- An absence of threat, rewards and artificial deadlines
- Provide resources needed for learning
- Allow participants multi-status learning with self-assessment

> **What This Means To You:** Some behaviors are going to occur regardless of what you do. Many of them can be destructive. Accept the necessity for these needs and rituals, but not always the content of them, especially if they are negative. But you have the power to provide alternative productive outlets for what are basically powerful, biological expressions. Examples include:
> 1. Establish new, positive and productive rituals such as: arrival and beginning rituals (music fanfare, positive greetings, special handshakes, hugs, etc.),
> 2. Special organizational rituals (team or class names, cheers, gestures, games, etc.)
> 3. Situational rituals (e.g., applause when learners contribute), and closing or ending rituals (songs, affirmations, discussion, journal writing, cheers, self-assessment, gestures, etc.).

How You Can Follow Up: For a source booklet on learning rituals: *Rituals for Learning, Teaching & Training* . See Appendix for how to order.

The Mid-Brain Area

The mid-brain is not one, but actually composed of several related areas: amygdala, hippocampus, thalamus, hypothalamus and the pineal gland. Some say it also includes the top of the reticular formation. It's "complex, widely distributed, and error-prone" says Sylwester. Combined, these regulate our immunity, hormones, our sleep cycles, our appetite, our sexuality, our emotions and more. Our mid-brain area may be the glue that holds our whole system together. The carriers of our emotions are peptide molecules which are composed of a chain of amino acids (shorter than one of protein). *There is a far greater number of neural fibers extending FROM the mid-brain into the neocortex than there are going from the neocortex INTO the mid-brain.* From an survival viewpoint, this makes sense - when your feel strong fear, the brain places a priority on that emotion over any other information. This is important evidence that:

Emotions are more important and powerful
to the brain than higher-order thinking skills

This brain area is the seat of all emotional bonds, is the healing capacity, intuition and immune system. This area ties all three parts of our brain together, directing attention where it is needed.

27

The **reticular formation** is at the top of the brain stem and the base of the limbic system. This is the part of our brain that integrates incoming sensory information. Using peptide receptors, it regulates our general level of attention. It also regulates our focus-diffusion cycle and internal-external shifts in awareness. The **amygdala** has a similar task and is critical to linking memories and emotion. It processes the *emotional content* of information and memory. It's made up of two nut-sized structures which are highly connected to most other brain areas. It regulates breathing, circulation and other automatic body functions. Like the reticular formation, it is most concerned with our survival and the emotional flavoring or interpretation of feelings in a situation.

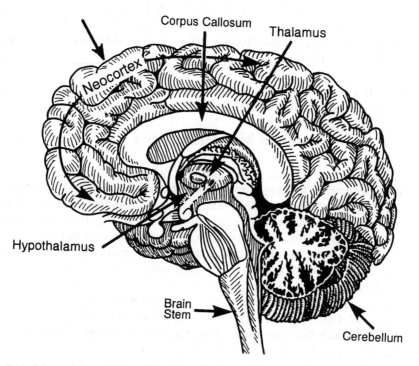

The **hippocampus** is critical to the formation and storage of our memories. The content of our experiences are processed by the hippocampus while the emotional flavor of our experiences are processed by the amygdala. Calvin says that "The overlap of frontal lobe sites for emotion and visceral function is particularly promising because of the link to higher cognitive processes - spinning all those 'what if' scenarios that contribute to anxiety, worry and suffering." Kandel and Kandel suggest that this part of our brain is responsible for suppressed memories. The **thalamus and hypothalamus** (walnut and pea-sized respectively), also help regulate our emotions and safety. The thalamus regulating external processes and the hypothalamus monitoring internal information.

Learning and meaning is driven by feelings;
The brain is virtually a "box of emotions"

Maybe the most amazing thing about this part of the brain is: while all of us can be presented with evidence that something is true, it is not verified in our own world until we *feel* that it is true. In spite of all we have learned from reason, science, logic or common sense, we do not feel that anything is true until our mid-brain, the limbic portion, which deals with emotions, says that it is true.

The Role of Emotions in Learning

In *Descartes' Error; Emotion, Reason and the Human Brain,* Damasio argues that the brain, mind, body and emotions form a linked system. He criticizes the typical neurologist's narrow-mindedness regarding the role of emotions: "...uncontrolled or misdirected emotion can be a major source of irrational behavior...(but)..a reduction in emotion may constitute an equally important source of irrational behavior." He adds, "...certain aspects of the process of emotion and feeling are indispensable for rationality." Emotions he says, are not separate, but rather enmeshed in the neural networks of reason.

Many other researchers including McGaugh, Pert, MacLean, O'Keefe and Nadel have written about the critical role of emotions in learning and the link between cognitive data and emotions. MacLean says that the most disturbing thing about the way the brain is "wired up" is the limbic system which insists that ultimately the learner must *feel that something is true before it is believed.* MacLean says with puzzlement:

"The limbic system, this primitive brain that
can neither read nor write, provides us with
the feeling of what is real, true and important"

The work of Bandler reveals that our brain has three criteria which must be filled in order for it to "know what it knows." These criteria give the brain its "self-convincers," and they vary from person to person. Learning is one thing; the brain must get verification for it in order to truly believe it. The brain requires three criteria and they are:

1) **Modality.** The learning must be reinforced in your dependent modality: it must be in either visual, auditory or kinesthetic. You must see it, hear it or feel it. Examples include a written test score, a compliment, holding a trophy, a smile on a another's face, peer assessment in a discussion or performing a play.

2) **Frequency:** You must get reinforcement a certain number of times, from 1-20 depending on the person. For example, you might re-look at a test score over and over or listen to another tell you about it again.

3) **Duration:** Finally, you must have the validation process last for a certain length of time, from as little as two seconds to as much as several hours. Or you might hold a returned test, a birthday card or some momento in your hands for a few minutes. Even though you've already read twice!

Once we have had any kind of reinforcement about what we have learned in our preferred modality, the right number of times and for the right length of time, we will feel that it is now true. We believe it and have a gut feeling for it. Until then, it's data, but not a "felt meaning."

When each of these three things occur, in your preferred combination, you have a feeling that *what* you know, you REALLY know. As an example, let's say you leave the house and go for a drive. Ten minutes away, you suddenly wonder, "Did I lock the door? Did I unplug the iron? Did I turn on my answering machine?" This is no memory problem. It is a case of, "I don't know whether I did or I didn't." Similarly, when you write or type out a familiar word, you sometimes look at it and wonder, "Is that word spelled right?" Do you believe yourself or not? And all of these self-convincers are contextually driven. What is a self-convincer in one context may not work in another context.

We've all heard someone say, "I'll believe it when I see it." That's a case of a visual learner who HAS to see it. Another might say, "I saw it, but I just don't believe it." They call their neighbor first and find out whether they get agreement, then they decide. And a third might say, "If I can touch it, hold it or be there first hand, I'll believe it." These three examples represent modality variables: visual, auditory and kinesthetic. In addition, a frequency variable defines how much repetition, ranging from one to ten times, each learner requires before believing something. And a duration variable indicates the length of time learners need for affirming information, ranging from as few as a couple of seconds to an entire minute.

Self-convincers are especially critical when it comes to changing beliefs. If a learner already believes that he or she is going to succeed, it takes only "maintenance reinforcement" to preserve that belief. But if a learner believes that he is a failure and you want him to convince himself that he is a success, all three of his criteria must be met. Otherwise, the belief stays the same. Emotions, beliefs, fears, worry, they are all intermingled. Calvin even goes so far as to say that since wide areas of the cortex interact with the limbic system, your personality is in your hypothalamus and limbic area.

> **What This Means To You:** There are far-reaching and profound implications. Many learners access the self-convincer state on their own. They simply know how to convince themselves of what they know. They tend to have more self-confidence, often even arrogance. But many learners simply do not know what they have learned. A learner must "know what he knows," or he'll leave the room thinking he has learned nothing. He goes home and someone asks, "What did you learn today?" And he says, "Nuthin," although he actually did learn a lot. Brain-based learning says we must learn to elicit this state.

In general, hard-to-reach, slow, discouraged, or low-level learners often have inappropriate self-convincer strategies. In other words, they don't know what they know and have little self-confidence. They may self-convince too easily, meaning they give up on learning the more in-depth levels. On the other hand, the so-called "gifted" learners are often more accurate at self-convincing. As a result, they tend to have more self confidence.

Multiply that scenario over a thousand times and you have learners with little or no self-confidence, motivation or love of learning. Too easily self-convinced and you are gullible. Too hard to self-convince, and you're a skeptic.

To make sure that all your participants leave in a state of "knowing what they know," provide activities that give them a chance to validate their learning. It's actually quite easy. The activities should use all three modalities, last for several minutes and ideally, with several persons or several times. They might teach a peer, put on a role play, write in their journal, do self-assessment or teamwork. Do these activities at the end of the learning, so that participants can discover what they know and if what they know is "right."

Learners not only need to learn but also need to know that they know

For those who "self-convince" too easily, and think they "know it all" long before they really do know it, there's another solution. These are usually the more contextual-global learners. Give them a checklist of the specific criteria for what is to be learned. Tell them that they are ready for assessment when they have completed each of the items on the checklist. That will help insure more in-depth, true learning.

In a learning context, the engagement of emotions at the end of an activity can help the brain to "know what it knows," to give the needed stamp of approval. Listen for expressions that let you know that others are processing the veracity of an experience. Someone says that "It just doesn't feel right." Another says, "I'll believe it when I see it." A third says, "Wait 'til he hears about this." These phrases indicate an attempt to feel convinced about something. Only then will there be actual belief.

Increased learner self-confidence follows, along with intrinsic motivation for future learning. Many rituals that celebrate the learning can do more than just make the learning fun, they can also seal the information and experiences in the brain as real and worth remembering.

Include simple opportunities for learners to engage emotionally after a learning experience. It could be learner enthusiasm, "high fives," acknowledging their partner, drama, role-plays, quiz shows, debates, impactful rituals and simple celebrations. It could even be as simple as an enthusiastic learner conversation about the topic. The key is simple, but critical: engagement of emotions leads to learners "knowing that they know it." And that leads to self-confidence and motivation to learn more.

How You Can Follow Up: *The Learning Brain,* by Jensen; *How to Boost Learning by 30%;* or the book *SuperTeaching*, by Jensen. See Appendix for details.

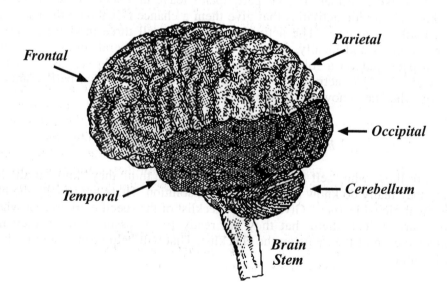

Key Functions of the Cerebrum

When you see a picture of the brain, or a brain in a jar, the bulk of what you see is mostly the wrinkled cortex wrapped around the cerebrum. It has four dominant areas.

1. Frontal lobe: problem-solving, will power, planning
2. Parietal: reception of sensory information
3. Occipital: primarily deals with vision
4. Temporal: deals with hearing, language & some memory

This part of the brain is split into two halves, the left and right hemisphere. The cerebrum is covered by the cortex (often called the neocortex). This "thinking cap," about the size of a rumpled up newspaper, is 1/8" thick and covers the cerebrum. The work of Hart has highlighted one of the key characteristics of the neocortex: the ability to detect and make patterns of meaning. This process involves deciphering cues, recognizing relationships and indexing information. The clues that the brain assembles are best recognized in a Gestalt format, not in a digital, "adding up" process. In short, the brain is not very good at handling isolated, sequential bits of information. Of course, many presenters offer a great deal of that. That is both boring and frustrating to the learner.

*The brain's capacity and desire to make or
elicit patterns of meaning is one of the
keys of brain-based learning*

Hart reminds us that "...pattern recognition depends heavily on what experience one *brings to* a situation" (emphasis added). These patterns must continually be revised, altered or updated as new experiences add information, insights and corrections. In fact, Hart says that learning is the extraction of meaningful patterns from confusion. In other words, figuring things out *your way*. Humans never really cognitively understand or learn something (certainly there is much motor and procedural learning as a infant) until they can create a personal metaphor or model. This point is quite important about the brain, so we'll repeat it and then come back to it in a later chapter.

*We never really understand something
until we can create a model or metaphor
derived from our unique personal world*

33

In a study of readers, Bower and Morrow found that comprehension increased when readers created a mental model or pattern of the material while reading. The readers would make patterns, connections, relating the actions of the characters to their goals. The readers also focused attention on the character's movements, visualized locations for several seconds and related them to the model or pattern they were building in their minds. This activation resulted in the reader's undiscovered recall speed and comprehension.

Edelman says that "learning in any species results from the operation of neural linkages between global mappings and the value centers." Learning is achieved when behavior leads to synaptic changes in global mappings that satisfy set points. Let me translate that: you are learning when you can relate the knowledge from one area to another, then personalize it. Three essentials of higher brain functions are categorization, memory and learning. The last depends on the first two; the second depends on the first. Perceptual categorization is essential for memory. The value centers are located in the hypothalamus and mid brain.

Let's take an example. When you arrive in a new city, you not only want to know how to get where you're going, but also where you are in relationship to where everything else is located. In other words, the spatial, contextual relationships are the patterns which help you understand and get around in a city. You link up information ("Where are the hotels, entertainment and McDonald's?") with personal meaning ("Why am I here?").

> **What This Means To You:** Learners are left with two options: 1) the unit of knowledge, understanding or experience, and 2) the pattern. Facts may provide the answer on a test, but the pattern helps bring about real meaning. Before beginning a new topic, ask your participants to discuss it orally or make it graphic in a mind map. Post up a mind map of the patterns of your topic before you begin. That gives the brain "addresses" at which to store key information and make relationships. Reduce the amount of "piecemeal" learning. During a course, continually have participants make maps, story boards, graphic organizers or paintings of the material. At the end of the course, ask them to make a video, a play or a larger, mural-sized map of their learning. They key is that it has to be related to their own personal life. If it's not, it's not brain-based learning.

Cortex Learning Is Automatic

Researchers Pfurtscheller and Berghold verified that as early as two seconds prior to an actual activity or movement, your brain has already decided what body parts to activate and which side of the brain to use. This means you are already acting on something before you are truly aware that you are even thinking about it. Your non-conscious mind acts before your conscious one does!

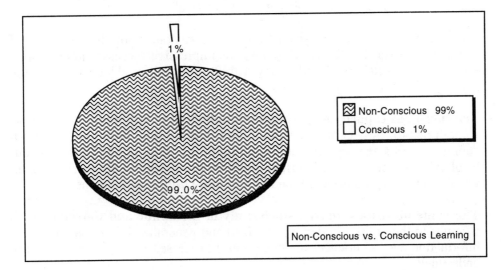

1%

Non-Conscious 99%
Conscious 1%

99.0%

Non-Conscious vs. Conscious Learning

Dr. Emanuel Donchin, at the Champaign-Urbana campus of the University of Illinois, documented something even more profound. He says that *more than 99% of all learning is non-conscious.* Your participants are learning without knowing it. They are constantly picking up learning from visual cues, sounds, experiences, aromas and other environmental cues that far exceed any content from a lesson plan or course outline.

Most of what's learned in your class is <u>not</u>
in your lesson plan - in other words,
there is a documented, enormous and profound
difference between presenting and learning

As an example, you drive from one city to another. You arrive safely and check into a motel or stay with a friend. Someone asks you about something. You say you can't quite recall it. Then they mention the company's name and suddenly a light goes on. "Yes," you say, "I did hear of that company. Weren't they on a billboard somewhere on the road? Oh, yes, now I remember. They are the ones who...." You actually learned that information hours ago; but at the time, you were not conscious of it.

Or, let's say your participants are working on a project in cooperative teams. In their view, they are learning the content. They are also learning about each other and acquiring collaborative skills. In fact, that may be the majority of the learning.

This is an example of non-conscious learning. It means we simply absorb the experience and our brain adds it to our perceptual maps. Learning is going on all the time. The question is whether or not we're aware of it.

The power of the nonconscious in learning was one of the fundamentals of Bulgarian researcher, Dr. Georgi Lozanov. His impressive successes in presenting foreign language (often 500 words a day with 90%+ recall weeks later) were built on a foundation of three key principals:

- **The enormous capacity of a receptive mind.** He says that everything suggests something to our complex minds and we cannot NOT suggest. All communications and activities are occurring on a conscious AND nonconscious level at the same time. It is critical to train presenters in the world of non-verbals: how to avoid negatives and how to make useful implications.

- **The value of visuals, music, stories, myth, metaphor and movement.** All stimulus to the brain is coded, symbolized and generalized. In other words, all information and experiences are being multi-processed in ways we have yet to understand.

- **Our perceptions, biases and barriers must be addressed before the learning can be accelerated.** Once we understand and act on them, one can achieve dramatic results.

Because of the nearly unlimited capacity of the human brain, and it's natural predisposition to sort, label and code things, all the so-called "unimportant influences" turn out to be very important. And Lozanov discovered, over and over, that in a well-orchestrated, positively suggestive learning environment, the quantity and quality of the learning possible is literally astounding.

> **What This Means To You:** Learners are aware of what you're not focusing on. While you put up an overhead transparency, they are listening, too. When you have something clever, articulate and important to say, they are watching your facial expressions and other non-verbals. You may want to become more aware of your non-verbal messages, since research verifies that it is being absorbed by the non-conscious minds of your learners. Practice your presentation in front of a mirror to improve the non-verbals. Or, videotape your presentation and critique yourself. You may also want to get some "coaching" from a colleague. Create a learning environment rich with positive suggestions. Use more congruent body language. Set higher standards for yourself and your environment. Involve your learners in meeting those standards.

Your learning climate and environment are very important. So are your dress standard and your nonverbal messages. Those are all "learned" by your participants even though you may not be "presenting" any of them. How you treat your participants, what you say, how you say it, the temperature, the room set-up is all influencing the learner and being processed either consciously or non consciously.

What About Subliminal Learning?

Taylor and Silverman say that subliminals can and do affect the brain. *This does not mean that all subliminal messages are effective.* The best body of research says that **when** done in the appropriate medium, using the right message, which fits the subject's belief systems, many subliminals can consistently affect behavior.

A subliminal is defined as a stimulus perceived **below the threshold of awareness.** In other words, the auditory or visual trigger must be able to be perceived, but you're not aware of it at the moment it's happening. For example, a whisper a block away is well below our threshold of perceptiveness unless you have electronic listening gear. But *it's not subliminal* because no neural activity is triggered. A poster in a classroom that is out of normal awareness (off to the side, in the back of the room) **is not** a subliminal, either. All a learner has to do is turn his head to see it. You can't put up a "subliminal poster."

Visual subliminals fall into three categories: 1) Altered light levels, 2) High speed flash projection, and 3) Variable insertion. Altered light levels mean that a lower wattage message may be shown on a screen continuously during the time a brighter message is being consciously perceived. The high speed flash projection is similar to tachistoscope and movie theater projection where a message is flashed at 1/100th to 1/3000th of a second continuously. The variable insertion is like adding a flashcard to a deck of cards and flipping it like an old-time movie screen.

How Much of Our Brain Do We Use?

Although many say we use only two, five or ten percent of our brain, it's a moot issue. We "use" most of our brain on any given day. The real question is how much do we develop of our brain's capacity? In general, very little. British neuroscientist Lorber found 150 adults with virtually NO neocortex (they had 5% or less because of childhood hydrocephalic disease). They had normal basal and limbic structures, but the neocortex area was 80% water. Now, here's the shocker: these "brainless" people had IQs ranging up to 120. Many held advanced professional degrees, got along well with others and had normal lives. That should tell you something about the importance of the neocortex compared to the limbic and lower brain areas!

While some maintain that these studies validate the "holographic brain model" postulated by Pribram, there's more to it. Pribram said the brain operates through patches or neural networks. He never stated that the entire brain works as a single hologram, with every part of it functioning for any other part. What Lorber's studies tell us is that the brain is quite remarkable, even when just 5% of the neocortex is used. Additionally, that more functions than we earlier thought are handled by the subcortical regions.

Learning is Holistic

For years, scientists gathered information about the role nutrition, exercise, attitude, lifestyle, posture and emotions play in learning. There are studies by Tert, McGaugh, O'Keefe and Nadel on the role of emotions in learning. There is research on the role of exercise and stimulation by Diamond and Greenough. Learning is linked to our hormones and biochemical rhythms say others. Connors and Healy remind us about the role of nutrition. The compilation of that research is persuasive and compelling:

All learning involves our body, our emotions,
our attitudes and health. Brain-based learning
says that we must address those variables
more comprehensively

Holistic learning means that we are learners with feelings, beliefs, food cravings, personal problems, attitudes and various levels of learn-to-learn skills. While the old academic model addressed primarily the intellectual part of learners, the prevailing model says we learn with our minds, heart and body. It also says that the better we deal with all of the issues, the more effective we'll be in presenting and learning.

Our entire triune brain system works together, as one. It's chemically, electrically fueled to produce the illusion of one brain. Brain researcher Cloniger has an interesting way to summarize the brain chemically. He says three neural systems run our lives. They are: 1) the neocortex's **quest for novelty**, 2) the limbic's **hunt for pleasure** and 3) the R-complex reptilian brain's **desire to avoid harm**. That's a perfect summary of our daily lives. Try new things, seek pleasure and avoid getting hurt. Each of these is run by the brain's chemicals and each of them is working for the overall survival of the "system."

What This Means To You: First develop a greater awareness of all the factors influencing your learners. Secondly, take the time to influence as many of the variables as you can. You cannot control all the variables, but you can influence many of them. You can set a good example and role model the benefits of exercise, nutrition and stress management. You can send home handouts and suggestions with your participants, on how to better manage their bodies and mindset. You can teach relaxation, offer more stretch breaks and better manage your learner's states.

Chapter Questions

1. What was novel, fresh and new? What was familiar or "old hat"?
2. In what ways do you already apply the information in this chapter?
3. What three questions can you now generate about this material?
4. How did you react emotionally to this information?
5. In what ways can you translate the key three or four theories and discoveries presented here into practical everyday useful ideas?
6. How did you react cognitively when you were reading the ideas of this chapter?
7. If these things are, in fact, true about the brain, what should we do differently? What resources of time, people and money could be redirected? In what ways do you suggest we start?
8. What was the single one (or two) most interesting or valuable insights you had?
9. Plan your next step, the logical practical application of what you've learned.
10. What obstacles might you encounter? How can you realistically deal with them?

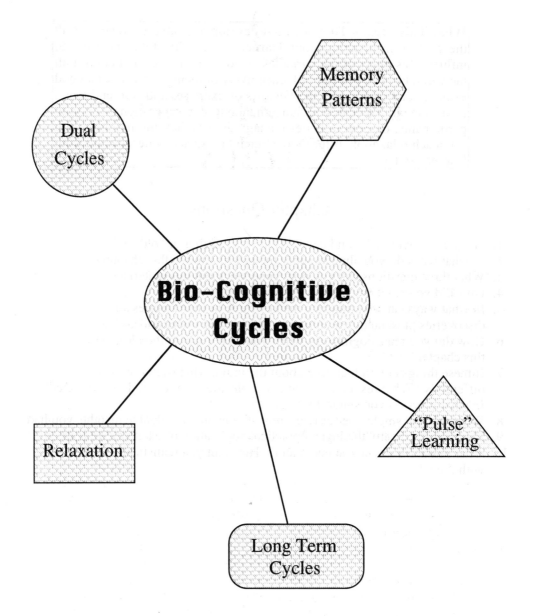

3
Bio-Cognitive Cycles

Brain's Clock Runs Our Learning

Recent brain research suggests we are far from a "learning machine." Instead, our learning and physical performance are dramatically affected by our biological rhythms. Orlock says that we have temporal cycles of the mind and body that correspond to lunar and solar cycles. We have a 24-hour solar cycle and a 25-hour lunar cycle that affect us in countless ways, including cell division, pulse rate, blood pressure, mood swings, concentration and learning ability. In addition, these cycles influence memory, accident rate, immunology, physical growth, reaction time and pain tolerance.

Our brain's electrical rhythms (cycles) range from 1-25+ per second. Our heart beats about once a second. We breathe about 15 times a minute and blink from 5-15 times a minute. Our skeletal muscles have 4-6 minute cycles of strength. Overall physical strength and our body's temperature peak in the afternoon.

Hormones are released into our bloodstream every 2-4 hours and can dramatically alter learning. Women are better learners the two weeks after their period is over. Sleep and alert cycles are predictable. The middle peak hour of one's nightly sleep would be the same time and peak of daytime drowsiness, 12 hours later.

Haus says that we also have 7-day (circaseptan) rhythms. Organ transplant patients have the highest rejection episodes 7, 14, 21 and 28 days after surgery. Even rats and unicellular organisms have these same seven-day rhythms. That's because our brain and body periodically change the immune levels and white blood cell counts.

41

Even our breathing has cycles. On the average, we breathe through one nostril for three hours. The tissue then becomes slightly engorged, then we tend to switch to the other side. This has profound influences on the brain of the learner since it affects which hemisphere of the brain we use. Left nostril side, means right brain learning. These cycles are the same, day or night. We are simply more alert during the daytime cycles. And the learner may want to know how best to take advantage of them.

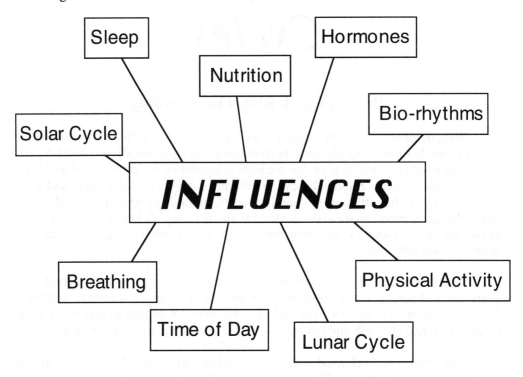

Researcher Englund found these rhythms in his tests that included psychomotor tasks, intellectual tasks, affective states tasks and physiological function tasks. His research tells us that overall intellectual performance (thinking, problem-solving, debating) is greatest in later afternoon and early evening. Although comprehension increases as the day progresses, reading speed decreases.

Scientists have found that our levels of minerals, vitamins, glucose and hormones can vary as much as 500% in a given day. That profoundly affects the brain's efficiency and effectiveness. In general, short-term memory is best in morning, and least effective in the afternoon. Long-term memory is best in the afternoon.

Halberg and Cornelissen say that each person has a different time profile, a "chronome," which is a map of our internal rhythms. This personal knowledge, they say, is critical; it is not only *what we do, but when we do it* that counts. For example, the potency or toxicity of your household medications and prescription drugs vary dramatically, depending on when you take them. For maximum effect, take them two hours before the peak of your daily blood-pressure rhythms. You'll need the lowest dose and you'll get the best effect from them.

Our normal daily cycle is more likely to be 25 hours, not 24. This can cause problems for our brain as a learner because it means that every day, you "rotate" your efficiency an hour later in the day. But the rest of the world doesn't change for you, so you may be "out of sync."

We may be underestimating the ability of participants if we test them at the wrong times of the day

Two Canadian researchers, Klein and Armitage, discovered that there is an alternating period of efficiency for each side of the brain. In other words, when spatial is high, verbal is lower. This alternating efficiency oscillates on 90-100 minute cycles. In other words, learners switch from right brain to left brain dominance throughout the day. The day, for our brain, is defined by 16 cycles lasting 90 minutes each. Every 90-100 minutes, your brain is at the strongest left hemisphere dominance and 90 minutes later, it peaks with right hemisphere dominance. When verbal skills are high, spatial skills are lower. Naturally, very few presenters want to work with participants during the "low" times of the afternoon, from 1-3 p.m.

This discovery fits in well with the earlier discovery that all humans have ultradian rhythms known as the "B-R-A-C" cycle, the "basic rest-activity cycle." These cycles are the alternating periods of REM (rapid-eye-movement) which corresponds with our dream time and our non-REM light rest periods. This nighttime cycle is continued throughout the daytime also.

Orlock says that these 90 minute cycles also coincide with hormone release into the bloodstream, regulating hunger and attention span. She cites experiments in isolation where the subjects consistently "headed for the refrigerator or the coffee pot about every ninety minutes." Sensitivity to pain, appetite and learning varies because the brain is changing continually. She also quotes a study on the hemispheric dominance switches that occurred on learning, thinking, reasoning and spatial skills tests. Once again, the switch-over occurred every 90 minutes.

Another researcher, Maryland gerontologist Morton Leeds, suggests that this 90 minute cycle may be the perfect time for suggestion and affirmation. Why? The changeover may be a time when the body is switching gears and entering a neutral time highly receptive for change and healing. Caffeine actually disrupts the body's own natural cycles, says Ehret. Your body increases its own levels of norepinephrine throughout the day to increase alertness. Therefore, it may be best to drink decaffeinated coffee or tea.

At the Hermann Center for Chronobiology and Chronotherapy in Houston, Texas, the staff helps patients track their biorhythms to aid treatments. One man had a 26-hour daily cycle and was driving him and others around him crazy. With dramatic solar therapy, he was re-synchronized to a normal life. An elderly woman's daily pattern was entirely redesigned by exposing her to four extra hours of bright light each day for one week. Researcher Czeisler says that her temperature and cortisol rhythms were actually reset as a result of this therapy.

> **What This Means To You:** Brain-based learning means taking into consideration how the brain learns best. The brain does not learn "on demand" by a school's rigid inflexible schedule. It has its own rhythms. Problems in learning may be a result of lateralization. Learners who are at the peak of the right or left hemisphere dominance may need cross lateral activation to "unstick" them. Dr. Paul and Gail Dennison suggest cross lateral physical activity that moves one side of the body across over to the other side, which can stimulate both sides of the brain and energize thinking.
>
> Options for assessment at varied times could increase learner performance. Vary your presentation hours to suit the ideal timetable for the brain. Provide diversity of activities to suit different learners. Englund even recommends that testing of participants be offered at various times of the day to account for these differences. A brain-based school might have exams on a rotating schedule.

How You Can Follow Up: Dr. Michael Smolensky at the Hermann Center for Chronobiology and Chronotherapy in Houston, Texas; Dr. Franz Halberg, Director of the Chronobiology Laboratories of the University of Minnesota; *Inner Time,* by Carole Orlock; *Brain Gym,* Presenter's Edition, by Paul & Gail Dennison or *Rhythms of Learning,* by Brewer and Campbell. See Appendix.

Dual Cycles Run Our Learning Brain

Our brains are constantly running on two learning cycles, says Thayer. The first is a "low to high energy" cycle and the second is a "relaxation to tension" cycle. These two cycles dramatically affect our learning and perception of ourselves, he says. Thayer says learners can focus better in the late morning and early evening. Yet they are more pessimistic in middle to late afternoon. Our thinking can get unrealistically negative at certain low times and quite positive during high cycles. These patterns, or "rhythms of learning," coincide with the ultradian cycles described by Brewer and Campbell.

Can these patterns be modified, and are they consistent? Yes, to both. Learners were taught to modify the rhythms by varying their sleep, exercise, diet and exposure to sunlight. In addition, differences in personalities can result in pattern variations. Introverts reported higher tension during the first two-thirds of the day; extroverts, during the last two-thirds.

> **What This Means To You:** Presenters and learners may have much more influence over the quality of learning than previously thought. By understanding patterns and fluctuations, one can better learn to take preventive action. Help your learners to become aware of their own best times for learning. Use the influence you have to encourage your learners to manage or stabilize any of their awkward rhythms. They can do that through nutrition, rest and activity.

Even Memory Varies By The Clock

University of Sussex researcher Dr. Oakhill conducted experiments to discover whether the time of day affects memory. She found that we incorporate two different types of memory into our learning: literal and inferential. In the morning we seem to favor literal memory and in the afternoon our brain is better at integrating knowledge with what we already know.

Brewer and Campbell say that from 9-11 a.m., the brain is 15% more efficient for short term memory. Semantic cerebral process is generally more efficient in the afternoon. Campbell says that 9 a.m.-12 noon is the best time for rote learning, spelling, problem-solving, test review, report writing, math, theory, science. Noon to 2 p.m. is best for movement-oriented tasks, paperwork, manipulatives, computer work, music, singing & art. The time from 2-5 p.m. is best for studying literature and history, and for doing sports, music, theater and manual dexterity tasks. Because some of us are "morning people" and others are "night people," there is a 2-4 hour variance among learners for optimal timing.

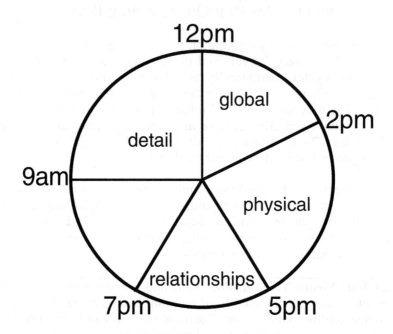

A Duke University study conducted by Cynthia May took 42 learners and showed that how well you recall depends as much on your age as on the time of day. May reports that young adults do best on memory recall in the afternoon or evenings. Older people performed significantly better in the morning and worse when they were tested in the afternoon.

Given all of the variations in people types, research tells us that no matter when you present a particular topic, it is likely to be out of sync, or the wrong time, for about one-third of your learners, according to Freely, Price, and Virotsko. In fact, Carruthers and Young demonstrated that when adolescents were allowed to learn subjects at their preferred time of day, the motivation, behavior and mathematics scores improved.

> *The question now arises: "If we know what*
> *time of the day learning can be optimized,*
> *what can or should we do about it? "*

As an example, if a standardized test is always given at a certain time, some will consistently underperform. If test material is read early in the day, learners are better able to recall exact details; names, places, dates, facts. However, more meaningful information is grasped better in the afternoon.

> **What This Means To You:** It seems that literal memory may decline across the day, forcing learners to pay closer attention and relate more of the information to personal experience. Present new information earlier in the day. Use the afternoon to integrate what's already known. The morning is best for sourcing information; the afternoon, for synthesizing and applying it. Do reading, listening, watching activities in the morning; role-playing, projects, drama, and simulations in the afternoon.

How You Can Follow Up: Read *Rhythms of Learning,* by Chris Brewer and Don Campbell. The Duke University study was reported in *Psychological Science,* available from 40 W. 20th St. New York 10011.

Learning Cycles Alternate Relax-to-Energize

Lozanov says the activation and suppression of cerebral/limbic structures is key to the success of a presenter. He says the relaxing effects of a positively suggestive learning climate are key to "reducing the vigilance intensity to an optimum by activating the serontonin-energetic systems or suppressing the catecholaminegetic systems." Translated, that means the brain stays alert and relaxed for learning but not anxious and hyper-stressed.

Lozanov adds that the whole brain is a system that needs to be simultaneously satisfied. By purposely activating both the more structured, sequential educational content and the more emotionally satisfying experiences (left and right hemisphere, cerebral and limbic), the system "accelerated... in all levels...." In fact, Lozanov believes that by satisfying the "optimum functional needs of the central nervous system... [presenting and training can become] a factor in the accelerated development of the personality." In other words, the richer the learning experience, the more individual and personal benefits there are to the learner aside from the intended content.

> **What This Means To You:** Any presenting process which is 90-100% lecture or 90-100% any methodology could be more effective if designed better. A simulation/role-play followed by a discussion would fit the activity-rest cycle in learning. Many participants who are not succeeding now may be impaired by the methodology used. Make sure that your learning is sequenced to appeal to the abstract/cerebral and emotional/limbic parts of the brain. Alternating formats of activity and rest, instruction and discussion or exploration and de-briefing make the most sense.

"Pulse" Style of Learning Is Best For The Brain

Hobson reports that the ability to maintain learning attentiveness is affected by normal fluctuations in brain chemistry. These fluctuations occur in cycles of approximately 90 minutes across the entire 24 hour day. At night we all experience periods of "deep sleep," REM time, and light sleep. During the daytime, *these cycles continue, but at a level of greater awareness.* Even animals have these periods of basic rest and activity (Jacobs). The brain seems to have a natural learning pattern of a pulse.

Learning is best when focused, then diffused,
focused, then diffused. Constant focused learning
becomes increasingly wasted over time.
In fact, the whole notion of "time on task" is
biologically wrong and educationally irrelevant

How long is best for a focused activity like a lecture? Take the age of the learner, and add two minutes. The maximum, even for adults, is about 20-25 minutes, say researchers. French researcher Pieron found that the brain learned best when the learning was interrupted by breaks of 2-5 minutes for diffusion or processing.

Optimal Learning Pattern for 10 Year Old Students

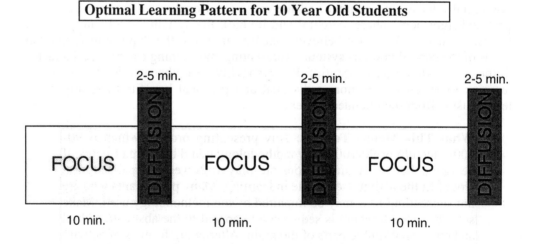

48

Campbell says that the break should consist of a diffusion activity, a total break from the content or an alternate form of learning the content. Consider a peer presenting session, mind-mapping or project work. He also found that deep breathing and physical relaxation were especially useful in sustaining the learning.

> **What This Means To You:** Never expect constant full attention from learners. The brain simply doesn't work that way. Many times what looks or sounds like learner apathy or fatigue is simply the down side of a predictable attention cycle. After a half hour or more, the audience is restless, inattentive and frustrated. The learning rate goes down and the presenter wonders why. You can influence the cycle. If you are working with young learners, you may want to limit your lectures and activities to 5-10 minutes at a time. For adolescents, limit lectures to 10-15 minutes and with adults, 15-25 minutes. After that focused time, have a diffusion activity. It could be something physical, something fun, a stand-up sharing with partner time or learner-generated ideas, teamwork, applications or personal development.

Gender Learning Cycles

Is there a best time for women to learn? Researchers Kopera, Messant, Rossi, and the teams of Kimura and Hampson and Meleges and Hamburg think so. In addition, Elizabeth Hampson of the University of Western Ontario discovered that women's learning and task performance levels changed throughout the menstrual cycle, varying with the levels of estrogen.

According to the research on hormonal influences on the brain, a woman's 28-day menstrual cycle may explain why some learning succeeds and some doesn't. During the first 14-day half of the menstrual cycle, estrogen alone is present. Estrogen specifically promotes more active brain cells, increases sensory awareness and increases brain alertness. The brain, flooded with this hormone, experiences feelings of pleasure, sexual arousal, well being, enthusiasm and self-esteem. Researchers suggest this may be the optimal time for female learning.

During the second half of the cycle, progesterone is present with the estrogen. Progesterone induces a profound reduction in cerebral blood flow, oxygen and glucose consumption, and produces sluggish, unmotivated behavior. It is also responsible for a sense of calm and acceptance. But in the five final days before menstruation, both levels drop. In this state, there is little estrogen to promote well-being and little progesterone to calm the moods.

As a result, females often experience mood swings, aggression and depression. Learning is negatively affected by depression, lower self-confidence and irritability. Females who do not experience such fluctuations may have more of a "male brain," meaning that there is more hemispheric laterality and higher levels of testosterone. After all the variance from men to women in testosterone levels can be as much as twenty times. That can to create quite a difference in behaviors.

Interestingly, these variations are matched in men. Spatial ability is higher when testosterone is lower. So is musical ability. Margaret Henderson, a research physiologist and endocrinologist, says that men appear to have a temperature cycle that is synchronous with the menstrual cycle of their cohabiting partner. Researchers have already verified that temperature changes are known to affect sexuality, attention, immunity and learning. It's common to have one week where your learning seems like "high performance" and the next week it seems like you've gone "brain dead."

> **What This Means To You:** There are over a dozen structural differences between male & female brains and entirely different hormonal swings. As females and males grow up, their timetables remain different. We want equal opportunity for both sexes, but equal treatment may be inappropriate. In spite of all of today's awareness about stereotyping, boys and girls still do things at their own respective paces. Let's acknowledge differences.

Our Brain Needs Deep Rest

Horne has discovered that the brain can become more easily fatigued when conditions for learning are weak. To get the brain's best performance, it needs deep physiological rest, the kind in which you are "dead to the world." Students from abusive families, areas of high crime, those with high stress parents, those in overcrowded homes, or affected by divorce, the death of a loved one, violence or poor nutrition are impacted.

Learners who live under stress, anxiety or a constant
threat of some kind never get this all-important brain rest...
without it, learning & thinking is impaired

How dramatic is the impairment? At the Three Mile Island nuclear power plant, sleep loss and exhaustion led to failure to recognize the loss of coolant water. That, in turn, led to a near catastrophic melt-down of the reactor, says Mitler. He also says sleep loss was a significant contributing factor in the faulty decision-making leading to the 1987 space shuttle Challenger explosion and the disastrous Chernobyl accident. Without adequate sleep, decision-making is impaired and new learning is practically absent.

How much is enough? We all know that different learners need different amounts of this deep sleep. While some adults insist on 8-10 hours per night, others seem to function perfectly for years on 4-6 hours a night. The brain has its own particular cycles of functioning and requires deep, non-threatening rest so that it can utilize the REM stages properly for dreams and down-time processing.

Accordingly, learners who are short on sleep may perform well on short quizzes requiring rote memorization. But learners who are deprived of sleep score lower on extended performance testing and those requiring creativity and higher-level problem-solving.

Sleep Time Assists Long-Term Memory

Research at the University de Lille in France indicates that sleep time may affect the previous day's learning. By cutting nighttime sleep by as little as two hours, your ability to recall may be impaired the next day. The rule holds truer for complicated and complex material than it does for familiar or simple material. Some scientists speculate that sleep gives your brain time to do some "housekeeping" and rearrange circuits, clean out extraneous mental debris and process emotional events.

Hopfield suggests that the real reason for this may be a concept called "unlearning." Using complex mathematical and computer modeling, he discovered that neural networks can become much more efficient when certain memories are "unlearned." It's much like your computer "cleaning up the desktop." In fact, in his research, the role of REM sleep was critical for the brain to process the days events. By eliminating unnecessary pathways or information, the brain becomes much more efficient. The fact that you have trouble remembering dreams may indicate how effective dreams are in "cleaning" your cerebral "house."

Every year researchers discover more and more things, events and processes that impact our learning. The old way was to treat each learner as, "That's the way he or she learns." Today's more brain-based approach asks different questions. We are more responsible and likely to ask:

"What is the optimal environment for learning"
"What are some of the things that have the highest impact at
 the lowest cost?"
"How can I increase staff interest in these changes?"
"What are the best ways to find the money to provide these?"
"What one simple step can all of our staff take immediately?"
"When will I take the first step?"

In short, be proactive in using more brain-based learning strategies. Find the things you can control and start with those. The effects will be lasting and powerful.

What This Means To You: Many of your learners may either need more sleep or better quality sleep. Let your participants know of the importance of physical rest and dreams. Learners may also need day-time, down-time for optimal brain performance. The Latin tradition of an afternoon "siesta" from 12-2 p.m. may have a useful biological basis to it. Encourage your learners to get adequate rest at night.

Chapter Questions

1. What was novel, fresh and new? What was familiar or "old hat"?
2. In what ways do you already apply the information in this chapter?
3. What three questions can you now generate about this material?
4. How did you react emotionally to this information?
5. In what ways can you translate the key three or four theories and discoveries presented here into practical everyday useful ideas?
6. How did you react cognitively when you were reading the ideas of this chapter?
7. If these things are, in fact, true about the brain, what should we do differently? What resources of time, people and money could be redirected? In what ways do you suggest we start?
8. What was the single one (or two) most interesting or valuable insights you had?
9. Plan your next step, the logical practical application of what you've learned.
10. What obstacles might you encounter? How can you realistically deal with them?

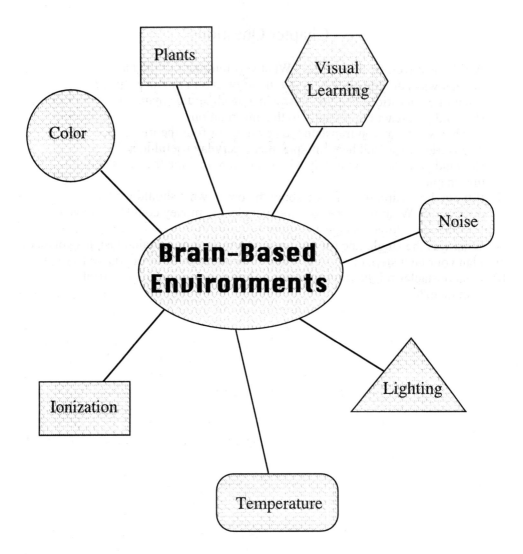

4

Brain-Based Environments

Brain Dominant In Visual Learning

Light is simply one form of electromagnetic radiation. It's a pattern of waves (or a stream of photons, depending on the model) that range from about 400 through 700 nanometers in length. Over 90% of all information that comes to our brain is visual. The retina accounts for 40% of all nerve fibers connected to the brain. Our eyes can register 36,000 visual messages per hour. We may want to be taking much better advantage of this enormous capacity.

Researchers Treisman and Gormican discovered the primary aspects of vision - what the brain is designed to see soonest and easiest. They identified the building blocks, the essentials of how our eyes actually compose meaning from our visual field. These essential elements are contrast, tilt, curvature, line ends, color and size, and are perceived before the learner actually understands what was seen. This provides a framework for the ways we can best attract and keep a learner's attention. While there is far more to learning than getting and keeping attention, the principles of brain-based attention-getting are still useful.

Attract the brain with movement, contrast and color changes

Our brain responds fastest to wavelengths of color, lightness and darkness, motion, form, and depth. We blink every 2-10 seconds, either as a nonconscious habit to keep the eye moist or clean, or as a signal from our brain that we have just understood or received a "bite" of information. By observing blink rates, you'll be able to get clues about how the learner is accepting the new information. Each blink is the brain's way of saying "I got it." In fact, if you watch participants in focused states of anticipation or curiosity, the blinks can be withheld for over a minute until the brain gets the "Ah-ha" needed for the confirming blink rate.

Treisman also discovered that the brain is wired to identify objects more quickly when they differ from the rest of the objects in basic features. These differences are analyzed in parallel by the brain so that while the learner may be observing location, the brain may also be processing changes from one object to another. This certainly gives us a survival edge.

There are many ways to access the brain's inherently fast response to color, shape and size. For example, in labeling stored boxes, it makes sense to color code them by types of content instead of labeling them with words only. Another interesting study was done by Backman on the relative value of using verbal cues versus color cues in learning and memory. He found that when memory for verbs and memory for colors were tested, learners recalled color better. And when objects were tested against color, once again, color memory was stronger. Even an intention to remember did not affect the outcome of the experiment.

What's the best way to convey motivating information to your learners? Is it through discussion, reading material or computers? None of the above, say the research teams of both Fiske & Taylor and Nisbett & Ross. The most powerful influences on your learners' behaviors are *concrete, vivid images*. Neuroscientists might say that it's because 1) the brain has an attentional bias for high contrast and novelty; 2) 90% of the brain's sensory input is from visual sources; and 3) the brain has an immediate and primitive response to symbols, icons and strong, simple images.

Savvy advertisers and political strategists have known this for years. Many people recall quite vividly the Zapruder's amateur movies of the JFK assassination, the 1988 "Willie Horton" commercial, the CNN shots of SCUD missile attacks in the 1990 Gulf War and starving children in 1992 Ethiopia and Somalia. The pictures of the starving children got the U.S. to send relief aid to Somalia, but the sight of an American soldier (Michael Durant) shot and dragged through the streets of Mogadishu was a prime motivator for American policy changes.

What This Means To You: We may have been under using some of our brain's visual system's best qualities. Utilize more visuals, more motion in the visuals and more changes in location in visuals to get and keep attention. As a presenter, a lot of talking, lecture or speeches may deliver content, but not be compelling or particularly memorable. For maximum impact, change the medium. Use impactful videos, strong posters, mind maps, vivid drawings and symbols. Bring in things to show and tell. Ask participants to generate the most evocative images they can, either through visualization or in the form of posters or murals.

Color in the Environment

You might wonder, "How could color affect our brain?" It's simple. Color is part of the spectrum of electromagnetic radiation. Other electromagnetic radiation forms includes x-rays, infrared, heat and microwaves. And we could likely all agree that those can affect us dramatically. Dr. Robert Gerard of UCLA did extensive testing on the physiological affects of color on anxiety, pulse, arousal and blood flow. His findings are consistent with Faber Birren of the University of Chicago. Every color has a wavelength. And every wavelength, from ultraviolet to infrared, red to blue, affects our body and brain differently.

Should you paint your learning environment? Maguire also says that different colors affect your moods and learning. But the research clearly shows that how a color affects you depends on 1) your personality and 2) your state of the moment. If you are highly anxious and stressed, red can trigger more aggressiveness. But if you're relaxed, it can trigger your engagement, with positive emotions (like buying a product!)

Red *is an engaging and emotive color best for restaurants. It is considered more disturbing by the anxious subjects, and more exciting to those who are calm. Triggers the pituitary gland, adrenal gland and finally, adrenaline is released. Blood pressure may elevate, increased breathing, stronger appetite and smell.*

Orange *has the characteristics halfway between red and yellow.*

Yellow *is the first color a person distinguishes in the brain. Associated with some stress, caution and apprehension.*

Blue *calmed the tense subjects, increased feelings of well-being. Researchers say sky-blue is the most tranquilizing color. When you see blue, your brain releases 11 neurotransmitters that bring relaxing calmness to the body. The effects can lower body temperature, reduce perspiration and appetite.*

Green *is also a calming color. The body reacts in many ways: blood histamine levels are elevated, less sensitivity to food allergies, antigens are stimulated for overall better immune system healing.*

Darker colors *lower stress and increase feelings of peacefulness.*

Brown *promotes a sense of security, relaxation and reduces fatigue.*

Brighter colors *such as red, orange and yellow spark energy and creativity. They can also increase aggressive and nervous behavior.*

Gray *is the most neutral color.*

Lighter colors *are best for optimal learning, choose yellow, beige or off-white. Those colors seem to stimulate positive feelings.*

Walker says that your preference for colors say a great deal about you. He also says that color preferences are "innate." As an example, you walk into a room and immediately feel comfortable. In another room, you feel happy and inspired, and in yet another, you feel "heavy" and depressed enough to want to leave. The colors may be responsible. When asked to identify a person, we say "the white guy" or "the girl with the orange jacket." We remember colors first, content next.

What This Means To You: We may be vastly underutilizing the potential of color in learning. Use colored handouts, color your overhead transparencies, use colorful posters and encourage the use of color in mind maps.

How You Can Follow Up: Read *Office Biology: Or Why Tuesday is Your Most Productive Day,* Edith Weiner, MasterMedia Limited, 17 E. 89 St. New York, NY 10128. *The Power of Color,* by Dr. Morton Walker. See Appendix for details.

Peripherals Impact Learning

Researchers Lozanov, Nadel, and Rosenfield have verified that the brain learns from both the traditional, focused kind of attention and from surrounding peripherals. They discovered that colors, decoration, sounds, smells and other stimuli are processed by the brain at a more subtle, nonconscious level. Yet they do influence the learner.

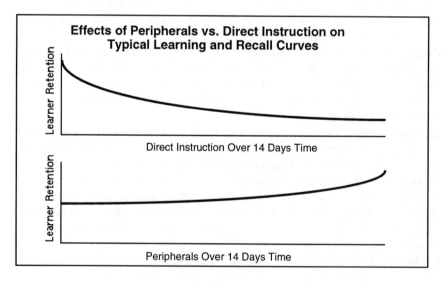

Rosenfield quotes a study done by Lozanov which used visual suggestion by color-coding key items. Five hundred subjects showed much greater recall than subjects who did not get the color-coded material. Time had positive effect: consciously learned material went from 80% to 50%; the peripherals went from 85% to 91%. Even when the audience knows it's being used, the method works: scores from 600 people were 93% and 96%.

Using direct instruction (lecture), the audience recall drops quickly - but research shows peripherals create effortless, subject-specific, longer-lasting recall

Quiet background baroque music is being played. The learners may not notice it, but the music can quietly evoke positive states of relaxation. Inspiring or relaxing posters or quotations on the walls of the room can also peripherally create a relaxing effect.

> **What This Means To You:** A purposeful plan should be made for positively influencing the learner in ways aside from the traditional lesson. In the learning environment, assess what influences you have right now. Are they positive? What's the reaction of the learner to your environment? Could it be better? A passive approach to surroundings on the part of the presenter can actually detract from the learning, making it less enriching than if an effort was made to enhance the visuals and/or audios.

Also, the use of music can be quite powerful. Make the room a happy, pleasant place to be in. Colors affect learner moods, too. Peripherals in the form of positive posters, learner work and symbols of expression, change, growth or beauty can be powerful. Make sure the furniture is arranged in a way so that learners can see each other, which usually provides the most interesting visual enhancement of all.

Type of Lighting Influences Learning

Dr. Wayne London's 1988 experiments caught worldwide attention. London, a Vermont psychiatrist, switched the lighting in three elementary school classrooms half way through the school year. He was curious about whether the type of lighting mattered to the participants. During the December Holiday break, he changed the current fluorescent lighting to Vitalite full spectrum lighting. Although the experiment was not a double blind one, no one expected any particular result.

The results, however, were amazing. London found that the participants who were in the classrooms with full-spectrum lighting missed only 65% as many school days as those in the other classrooms. London was not surprised. He said, "Ordinary fluorescent light has been shown to raise the cortisol level in the blood, a change likely to suppress the immune system."

Dr. Harmon studied 160,000 school-age children to determine which, if any, environmental factors influenced their learning. The results of his research were shocking: By the time they graduated from primary school (age 11-12), over 50% had developed deficiencies related to classroom lighting! To test the hypothesis, changes were made in the student's learning environment and the same children were studied six months later. The results of the change were equally dramatic: visual problems reduced 65%, fatigue reduced 55%, infections decreased 43%, and posture problems dropped 25%. In addition, those same participants showed a dramatic increase in academic achievement.

The positive impact of a quality learning environment
with strong natural lighting is both dramatic and lasting

The experiments have since been repeated with similar results. What about bright versus dim lights? Many participants relax, focus and actually perform better in low-light situations, say Krimsky, Dunn and Dunn. Brighter lights, especially fluorescent, seemed to create restless, fidgety learners. Low-level lights seemed to have a calming effect, especially at the younger ages.

Have you gotten any complaints about lighting? It may not be just an irritable learner. Lighting can affect the brain and learning. Some learners seem to prefer certain seats simply because of the lighting.

> **What This Means To You:** Many learners may be underperforming simply because the lighting is difficult on their eyes. Soft, natural lighting is best for learning. Provide a variety of lighting in your room. Give your learners some choice in where they sit.

Seasons Can Impact Learning

Can sunlight affect our learning? Definitely, says Orlock. The length and brightness of daylight affects our body's melatonin and hormone levels and influences the release of neurotransmitters. A portion of the hypothalamus (located in the mid-brain area), which scientists call the SCN, gets direct information from the eyes and sets our bodies' clocks. This affects our alertness, responsiveness and moods. Each of these, in turn, affects our learning.

A lack of exposure to sunlight during the winter months creates a specific condition which was identified and labeled as Seasonal Affective Disorder (SAD) in 1987 by the American Psychiatric Association, which officially recognized this as a biomedical problem. Walker says that women are more affected by this than men.

Orlock says that residents closer to the equator face less than a two percent chance of being affected by SAD, but those farthest from the equator face up to a 25% chance. Researchers say *the best time* for learning is when the hours of the day are longest: from June to August in the Northern Hemisphere and December to February in the Southern Hemisphere. For most schools, these are when *the least number of days and hours of learning are scheduled.*

Researchers have found that a small amount of artificial or sunlight therapy can alleviate the symptoms if the dosage of light is strong enough. Phototherapists measure light in lux units. Typical outdoor light measures between 10,000-80,000 lux units. Successful light therapy requires a whopping 2,500 lux to be effective. To put that in perspective, a typical indoor light has 500-700 lux, and 1,500 lux only works partially. Treatment sessions can last from 30 minutes to four hours a day. In one case, a woman who was suffering from SAD got light therapy treatments of an hour a day for six weeks. Her anxiety and depression ended. Research shows that 85% of SAD learners respond positively to similar light therapy.

Carbohydrate cravings may be triggered by SAD and premenstrual syndrome (PMS), says Wurtman. She says that the brain neurotransmitter serotonin may be involved in regulating eating habits and diet successes or failures. She also adds that eating a high carbohydrate dinner may alleviate some of the PMS symptoms.

What This Means To You: We may be able to improve learning by simply improving the lighting during those darker winter months. Explore your options for improving the lighting in your environment during periods of low sunlight. Ask others if they have witnessed the SAD symptoms or if their participants have experienced them.

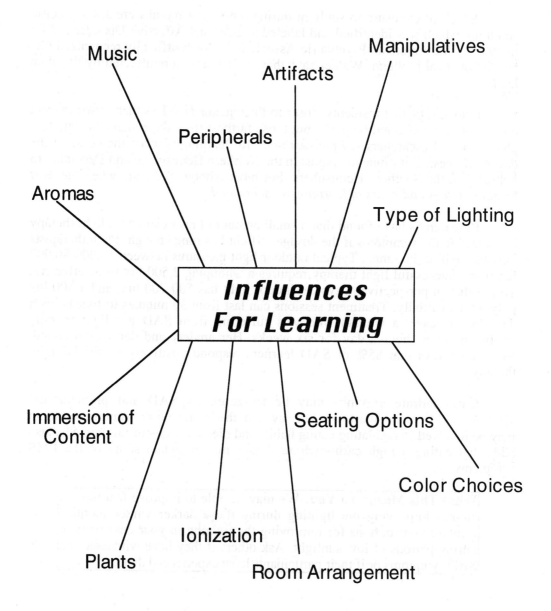

Music

Artifacts

Manipulatives

Peripherals

Aromas

Type of Lighting

Influences For Learning

Immersion of Content

Seating Options

Color Choices

Ionization

Plants

Room Arrangement

Optimal Temperature For Learning

In U.S. Defense Department studies, Taylor and Orlansky report that heat stress dramatically lowers scores in both intellectual and physical tasks. In combat tests where special protective clothing was worn, Taylor found that high temperatures were responsible for decreases in performance requiring accuracy, speed, dexterity and physical acuity. While many types of obstacles and barriers are known to reduce or impair learning, heat stress is one of the most preventable.

Ornstein speculates that it was evolutionarily beneficial for humans to become upright and begin walking. He says that development helped to keep the brain cooler, since the air temperature is a bit cooler at two meters off the ground than it is at just one meter. A "rise of only 1-3 degrees centigrade in brain temperature above normal is enough to disturb brain functions," says Ornstein. In fact, anthropologist Dean Falk says that as brain size has increased over the last two million years, one of the most important adaptations was the cooling mechanisms. Our very survival is vested in keeping the brain at the right temperature.

Choice may be the most important variable in the temperature of the learner's environment. There is a wide variety of perceptions, say Dunn and Dunn, in what constitutes a warm or cool room. The optimal is NOT always 68-72 degrees Fahrenheit for all learners, says Murrain. There are differences among ages, peers, and genders which can change with seasons, moods, and other miscellaneous factors. Having said that, it is a great baseline or standard temperature to start off a learning environment.

As an example, a room that's cool for you may be hot for the learner. They complain, and you're perplexed. Some researchers (Della Valle, Hodges, Shea, Kroon) have found that the environment (seating choices, comfort levels, lighting) and learning styles (global, sequential, concrete, abstract, etc.) are a significant factor in determining the success of participants.

> **What This Means To You:** We may be creating learning environments that are too rigid. Provide choice. Give options for learners to sit where it's cooler or warmer, which may improve their learning. Be more responsive to the temperature. It's better to be too cool than too warm. But it is best to be neither of these.

Dehydration Hurts Learning

Researchers Dennison, Ward and Daley assert that the average learner is often dehydrated. This dehydration leads to poor learning performance. Hospitals report that patients improve when they are encouraged to drink up to 20 glasses of water a day. Athletes boost water consumption for peak performance. Theater performers keep a pitcher of water nearby for the same reason. More and more educators have found that pure water does help learner performance.

Learning specialists recommend from 8-15 glasses per day, depending on your body size, weather and your activity level. Nutritionists recommend pure water to insure that it is free of contaminants. It's also better to have pure water than coffee, tea, soft drinks or fruit juices. This is because the caffeine and alcohol found in many of them serve as diuretics and your body needs even more water to make up the deficit. Presenters have found that in classrooms where participants are encouraged to drink water as often as needed, behavior improves, as does performance.

> **What This Means To You:** Students who are bored, listless, drowsy and who lack concentration may, in fact, be dehydrated. Talk to your participants about dehydration and the value of water. Remind learners to get a drink of cool, fresh water before entering a class. Allow learners to bring a container of water into the learning area. If you have tests or classes which last over 45 minutes, allow participants to bring water or leave the room to get water. Let them leave to get a drink if they feel dehydrated.

How You Can Follow Up: Read *It's All in Your Head,* by Barrett; *Learning to Learn,* by Ward and Daley.

Can Plants Affect Learning?

Scientists at the National Aeronautics and Space Administration have discovered that the use of plants creates a better scientific, learning and thinking environment for astronauts. Could their same research apply to learners indoors? Dr. Wolverton, who headed the Environmental Research Laboratory, says that certain plants have improved life for the astronauts and his own personal life at home. He says that they remove pollutants from the air, increase the negative ionization and charge it with oxygen. In fact, according to the Federal Clean Air Council, studies discovered that plants raised the oxygen levels and increased productivity by 10%. The ideal is between 60-80% humidity.

A single plant can often affect 100 square feet of space. Learners in a sterile, stark classroom or hotel room are often much more unresponsive than those in an environment filled with plants. It was found that participants exchange between only 10% and 25% of their lung's capacity with each breath taken. That's bad because stale air starves the brain. For optimal learning, provide your learners with fresh, uncontaminated, highly oxygenated air. Encourage your participants to breathe in more deeply.

> **What This Means To You:** We have underestimated the impact of walls, wood, concrete and glass. Wolverton recommends 4-8 small (or two large) plants for a typical 900 square foot (9 meters square) classroom. We also have been unaware of all the positive benefits of certain plants. The best plants for optimal pollutant reduction, fresh oxygen and enhancement of indoor learning environments are: gerbera daisies, yellow chrysanthemums, ficus benjamina, philodendrons, dracena deremensis, peace lilies and the bamboo palms.

Aromas May Boost Attention & Learning

There's a strong link between the olfactory glands and the autonomic nervous system. Olfaction (the neuroscience of smell) drives the human basics such as anxiety, fear, hunger, depression and sexuality. It also can be used for learning. Weiner reports that Professor Baron at the Rensselaer Polytechnic Institute in Troy, New York found that when certain aromas are used, participants set higher goals for themselves, took on more challenges and got along better with colleagues.

In experiments on neonatal rats, Sullivan et al., found that conditioned odor stimulation and tactile stimulation "are addictive in their effects on learning." The positive learning effects came from a peppermint odor injected into various norepinephrine receptor blockers, a procedure which allowed researchers to rule out other causes for the change.

Dr. Alan Hirsch, a Chicago neurologist, has found that certain floral odors increase the ability to learn, create and think. Working with recovering patients, he used thinking and creative puzzles with control groups and with those exposed to a flowery scent. Those with the scent consistently solved the puzzles 30% faster.

Dr. Lewis Thomas, President Emeritus of the Sloan-Kettering Cancer Center in Ohio, says, "The act of smelling something, anything, is remarkably like the act of thinking.... [Y]ou can feel the mind going to work...." McCarthy says that some scents are effective in re-triggering specific optimal learning states. Lavabre agrees that specific aromas are highly influential and consistent in triggering specific bodily reactions.

Harry Walter, former Chairman of International Flavors and Fragrances, has been researching the psychobiology of aromas. He says, "Brain input from smell and taste receptors are known to affect vital brain functions – reproductive behavior, learning, memory and emotional states." Smells can regulate stress and alter our flight or fight response. The current chairman, Dr. Eugene Grisante, claims aromas may be potent enough to boost learning, decrease food intake, increase productivity, and aid relaxation.

The olfactory regions are also rich receptors for endorphins, signaling the body's response to feelings of pleasure and well-being. The human brain's ability to detect changes in the environment are well documented. "People can distinguish odors with tiny variations in the chemical structures of the odor molecule." Get one aroma and test it out. Not every day, but once a week. Gauge the reaction. If it's positive, try a new aroma. Put the smell of fresh baked bread in a classroom. You walk into it and immediately feel positive, happy, almost like at a special home meal.

Twenty years ago you could hardly find a presenter who used music in learning except a music presenter. Now, it's becoming common around the world. Many schools even provide music resources for their presenters. Today, the use of aromas is thought of as strange among many educators. But they simply don't know the potential positive impact on learning. Within twenty years, aroma learning will be common.

> **What This Means To You:** Smell is an important sense that we have been underutilizing in learning. Attention to the influence of aromas could be a very powerful strategy to reach many types of learners. Start simple. Current research says that for mental alertness, try using peppermint, basil, lemon, cinnamon and rosemary. For calming and relaxation, use lavender, chamomile, orange and rose.

How You Can Follow Up: Read *Aromatherapy Workbook,* by Shirley Price; *The Complete Book of Essential Oils and AromaTherapy,* by Valerie Anne Worwood; *The Aromatherapy Handbook,* by Daniele Ryman. Or, contact: International Flavors and Fragrances, 521 West 57th, NY, NY 10019, (212) 765-5500.

Impact of Negative Ionization

What is negative air? The air around is electrically charged from cosmic rays, the friction of air movement, radioactive dust, ultraviolet radiation and atmospheric pressure changes. If you are feeling groggy, lethargic, sleepy or depressed, it may be the electrical charge in the air. You may have discovered that when you stand in front of a waterfall, or step outdoors just after a rain, or stand atop a mountain or just get out of a shower, you often feel fresher, inspired and energized.

In areas of higher population, the atmosphere's healthy balance of positive to negative ions is disrupted. Human activity, destroys negative ions which in turn affects the oxygen that we breathe and the functioning of our mind. It seems that when it comes to air, the more negatively charged it is, the better. Smoke, dust, smog, pollutants, electrical emissions, heating systems, coolers and traffic are all culprits. The air becomes more highly electrified (too many positive ions) and humans react. Studies suggest between 57-85% of the population is strongly affected and can gain dramatically from more positive ions.

The impact of negatively charged air on the body is powerful. Originally, it was found to speed recovery in burn or asthma patients. It was later discovered to affect serotonin levels in the bloodstream, to stabilize alpha rhythms and to positively impact our reactions to sensory stimuli. The greater levels of alertness can translate to improved learning. Studies by Minkh in Russia, Hansell in the USA, Sulman in Israel and Hawkins and Barker in England suggest improved well being and enhanced human performances on mental tasks.

There are over 700 research papers on the various effects of ionized air. Dr. Hansell, a researcher at RCA Laboratories, first stumbled on the "ion effect" in 1932 through his work with electrostatic generators. Dr. Kornblueh of the American Institute of Medical Climatology was among the first to demonstrate the dramatic effect that the electrical charge in the air has on our behavior. His work at Pennsylvania Graduate Hospital and Frankfort hospital in Philadelphia led him to make them a permanent part of hospital treatments. Many corporations, including ABC, Westinghouse, General Electric, Carrier, Philco and Emerson now use ion generators in the workplace.

> **What This Means To You:** Many lethargic or underperforming learners may simply be very highly susceptible to the ionization changes in the air. You may want to purchase an environmental ionizer. Be sure to get one powerful enough for the size of the room you're using. They can help boost alertness and learning.

How You Can Follow Up: Read *The Ion Effect,* by Fred Soyka. Order an ionizer for optimal learning, available by calling 800-382-IONS.

Environmental Noise Alters Learning

Price says that many learners understand and recall better when music is being played. The percentage of learners who fall into this type of category varies dramatically. Among musicians, you would get a different response than from more visual learners. Learner preference for some low-level background music (such as Baroque, in a major key) will run from a low of 20% to a high of 75-80%. Variables include the cultural background of the learner, the learning styles, the circumstances, the way the music is used, the volume, the type of music and carrier of the music. Best results have come from experimenting.

Some learners perform better in a noisy, busy environment; others need total silence. In one study, (Carbo, Dunn and Dunn), one-fifth (20%) of learners preferred a noisy environment to a quiet one. On the other hand, some participants need so much silence that only earplugs can filter out enough noise for their tastes. McCarthy says that even the amount of neatness and clutter in the learning environment varies by learner.

The computers used in the classroom may be causing some women anxiety. Sutter reports that researchers at the University of Evansville discovered some VDTs give off a high frequency tone than induces stress and impairs learning. The women in their study had an eight percent loss of productivity because the tones are at about a 16kHz level and men rarely hear above 15 kHz.

> **What This Means To You:** We may be causing our learners anxiety by stressing uniformity in the environment. We may want to have either separate environments or to rotate the type used. Many of our learners are underperforming because the environment does not suit their own, best learning style. Add variety to the learning environments you create. Over a span of two weeks, vary your lighting, use music, provide silence, provide earplugs and encourage cooperative learning as well as individual learning.

Chapter Questions

1. What was novel, fresh and new? What was familiar or "old hat"?
2. In what ways do you already apply the information in this chapter?
3. What three questions can you now generate about this material?
4. How did you react emotionally to this information?
5. In what ways can you translate the key three or four theories and discoveries presented here into practical everyday useful ideas?
6. How did you react cognitively when you were reading the ideas of this chapter?
7. If these things are, in fact, true about the brain, what should we do differently? What resources of time, people and money could be redirected? In what ways do you suggest we start?
8. What was the single one (or two) most interesting or valuable insights you had?
9. Plan your next step, the logical practical application of what you've learned.
10. What obstacles might you encounter? How can you realistically deal with them?

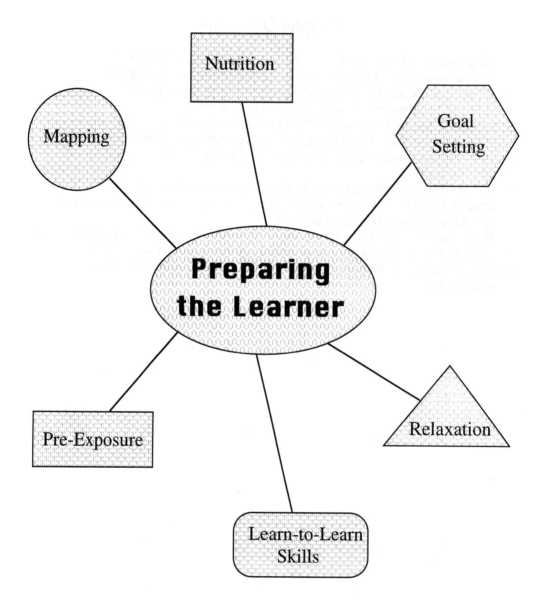

5
Preparing the Learner

Learning Impacted By Six Barriers

Building partly on the work of Ford and Lozanov, there are powerful beliefs which affect learning. In the positive, these beliefs can be almost tsunami-like in strength to aid learner success. In the negative, they are crippling to the learner.

- **Intuitive-Emotional... our fears, concerns and emotions**
  Learners worry about being embarrassed, not looking good, looking too good, succeeding, not succeeding, how they'll do and dozens of other concerns. These worries induce stress which inhibits learning and restrict the courage to try new behaviors.

- **Critical-Logical... the "taken-as-true" reasons, facts and authority**
  Learners have built up a whole set of capability beliefs which shape their success. A capability belief might be some well-meaning parent, relative or presenter saying, in a fit of frustration, "You'll never learn this... and furthermore, you'll never amount to anything!" These false beliefs are often paralyzing for a lifetime unless identified and reversed.

- **Ethical-Moral... family values, religion and the community**
  Surprisingly, many hold beliefs which deter rapid, effortless learning. Some ethical values say, "Learning only happens with struggle, anything quick cannot be sound!" It means that participants who learn something in ten minutes that they expected to take an hour, will often discount the learning... "We didn't really learn anything." Some parents will not believe their teen is "done" until a certain amount of time has been spent on homework.

71

- **Biological-Medical... nutrition, biochemistry and disabilities**
  Learning is very biochemical and biological. Food affects learning, as do medication, drugs and of course, any neurological diseases. There are bio-sexual differences between girls and boys (girls develop language and reading earlier, among many other differences).

- **Cultural-Social... gender, peers, ethnic and learning styles**
  There's another whole set of behaviors that can be impaired or expressed depending on the culture (Many Asians may value spending more learning time on homework). Socially, boys express more anti-social behavior and girls may not be encouraged in math and the sciences. Racism is prevalent among educators and presenters often form first impressions based on skin color, not potential. Peer pressure may encourage or discourage some from achieving the highest level of excellence. There are dozens of learning styles and the research is conclusive: kinesthetic (haptic-tactile) learners are at a significant disadvantage at the middle school and secondary levels.

- **Institutional-Physical...financial stoppers, barriers of access, discrimination and hierarchy**
  Learners face discrimination if they are different, poor, have extended health problems, are in a wheelchair, have AIDS, or if they get pregnant. They also face problems of getting the best education if they live in a depressed area or the school is unresponsive.

> **What This Means To You:** Instead of judging the potential of learners by their behavior, one might first assess, as best as possible, the many invisible barriers to learning. Many learners underperform because of barriers, not ability or will. Make a purposeful effort to counter the effects of the negative barriers. For example, use positive posters, oral affirmations and start with immediate hands-on successes in learning.

The Role of Nutrition in Learning

Proper nutrition can definitely boost thinking and learning. Your brain's most critical need is for oxygen. Beyond that, Dr. Judith Wurtman of MIT says that amino acids set the stage for you - either positively or negatively. The ingredients in protein are critical to the brain. Tyrosine and tryptophan are two examples. The first enhances thinking; the latter slows it down.

Your brain uses tyrosine to make the neurotransmitters dopamine and norepinephrine, two electrically charged chemical messengers that are critical to alertness, quick thinking and fast reactions. These neurotransmitters can help your brain to perform calculations, increase attention span and increase conscious awareness. Tyrosine is found in proteins.

Proteins can partially counteract the negative effects of sugar. Wurtman says, "Eating protein either alone or with some carbohydrate will result in an increase of the alertness chemicals dopamine and norepinephrine if your brain is using up your current supply and needs to replace them." Is more protein better? No, it's not. Obviously, if your brain already has enough, too much is just overkill and has no beneficial effect. But how much is enough? It depends on your weight, age and activity levels, but 15-30 grams per day is sufficient, say the experts.

Unfortunately, many low-income learners typically have carbohydrates for breakfast (toast, breads, cereals) which may impair thinking. Middle and upper-income learners often have the more costly yogurt, eggs, cottage cheese, fresh fruits or lean ham, which provide nutrients that can enhance learning.

It's time to take learner nutrition more seriously
Influence what the school lunches serve and
what's put inside the vending machines

In a well-designed, rigorous study, Benton and Roberts reported that 90 teens (12-13 year-olds) who took multivitamin supplements showed a significant increase in visual acuity, reactive time and intelligence over those who took a placebo. Maguire reported that at the Maudsley Hospital in London, Dr. Richard Levy experimented with Alzheimer patients to boost memory. In his study, over half of his patients showed significant memory improvement after drinking two milkshakes daily containing 35 grams of lecithin, an acetylcholine-booster.

In recent studies in Germany, Finland and the University College in Wales, England, folic acid and selenium were discovered to reduce depression and boost learner performance. Folic acid are found in dark leafy greens. Selenium is a mineral found in seafood, whole grain breads, nuts and meat. The best sources are white meat tuna and brazil nuts.

Tucker, Connors and a recent study by the U.S. Department of Agriculture reported that boron, iron and zinc supplements improved mental activity. The trace mineral boron is found in broccoli, apples, pairs, peaches, grapes, nuts and dried beans. Zinc can be found in fish, beans, whole grains and dark turkey meat.

The other foods eaten at the same time as iron-rich foods (dark-green vegetables, meat, beans, fish, poultry, eggs, grains and rice) make a difference in the amount of iron actually absorbed into the bloodstream.

Vitamin C sources (like orange juice, broccoli and bell peppers) enhance the iron absorption, while phytates (cereals, bran and soybeans) and tannin (found in tea) inhibit absorption. In fact, **five times as much** iron is absorbed into the bloodstream with a breakfast of orange juice, fruit and eggs as it is with cereal or bran, coffee or tea.

At the University of Toronto, Dr. Greenwood found that although the brain needs fats in order to be at its best, the kind of fat eaten is important. In one of her studies, animals on a diet of polyunsaturated fats learned 20% faster than those on a saturated fat diet. And they also retained the information longer. If you've made lots of suggestions about nutrition and none have helped, maybe the problem is related to fats in the diet. Most learners have no clue about the effects nutrients can have on the brain and learning. As a result, many participants underperform in relation to their actual capabilities. Be aware of the dietary sources of saturated and unsaturated fat. Diets rich in polyunsaturated fats include safflower, sunflower or soybean oils. Encourage your learners to be attentive to the kind of fat that is in the foods they eat.

How much does our eating affect our brain and thinking? Researchers say, "Plenty!" The basic cellular reaction involves sodium and potassium. Your alertness, memory and problem-solving is affected by many nutrients including glucose, lecithin, magnesium and tyrosine. The source of all these? Your diet!

A study by Jenkins et al. published in the *New England Journal of Medicine* took subjects with normal eating habits and divided them into two groups: One group ate the traditional three meals a day; the other had the identical food, but spread it out over 17 snacks per day. The subjects followed the diet for two weeks. The results were that the "nibblers" maintained a better insulin level, had lower cortisol levels and better glucose tolerance. These indicators can lead to better cognitive functioning, fewer discipline problems and an enhanced sense of well-being.

In another study in Mexico, Cravioto reported that well-fed learners rated higher in communication skills and did better in the classroom. The participants on even marginally deficient diets produced 300% more "poor" performances. This study was interesting because the diets were only slightly worse. Yet, the performance was much worse.

In MacMurren's research, adolescents were given a choice of either snacking and nibbling during a test or not eating at all. Those who were permitted to eat the snacks (popcorn or raw vegetables) achieved "significantly higher" scores than the group that was not allowed to nibble.

> **What This Means To You:** You or your learners may be underperforming if the foods eaten are slowing down the brain. To boost your alertness and mental performance, include a natural source of tyrosine in your diet by eating protein. The best foods high in protein are eggs, fish, turkey, tofu, pork, chicken, and yogurt. Eat just three to four ounces, since eating more than that does not further increase alertness. Keep saturated fats low, iron levels normal. Eat carbohydrates late in the day, not early. Eat a "nibbling" diet of many meals a day, not the traditional three. Too much time in between eating can cause loss of concentration and decreased alertness. Allow for appropriate foods in the classroom. Make sure your learners are given several opportunities to eat nutritious snacks throughout the day. Talk to your learners about the positive role nutrition can play in performance, thinking and testing. Many important nutrients are often not found in your typical learner's diet.

How You Can Follow Up: *Managing Your Mind and Mood Through Food,* by Wurtman; *Feeding the Brain,* by Keith Connors; *The "Almost Genius" Diet,* see Appendix for details.

Learning Study Skills Has Positive Effect

When learners are taught learn-to-learn skills, their ability to process new information can rise substantially. Researchers Weinstein and, in another study, Segal et al., confirmed the importance of what we knew: that presenting learn-to-learn skills can have a significant positive impact on the learner. Futurist and business guru Peter Drucker says, "We can predict with confidence that we will redefine what it means to be an educated person...(it) will be somebody who has learned how to learn and who continues to learn..." If we fail to teach these skills to our learners, who will prepare them for a fast-changing global society?

What are the key ingredients in study skills mastery? Here are ten of the top sources, including *Becoming a Master Student* (Ellis), *Study Skills Program* (NAESP), *How To Study* (Standley), *SuperStudy* (Wade), *Dancing With Your Books* (Gibbs), *Mastering the Information Age* (McCarthy), *Getting Straight A's* (Green), *Use Both Sides of Your Brain* (Buzan), *30 Days to Bs and As* (Jensen). Most of these sources suggest that learners:

- Get proper nutrition & a good environment
- Set a goal, develop a purpose
- Browse the material, build "perceptual maps"
- Develop maps on paper and ask questions
- Read for best comprehension, writing & thinking
- Summarize what's been learned or reflect on it
- Act on the learning, make tapes, build models, projects

What This Means To You: The reasons study skills programs can boost learning are clear: 1) participants can learn to work better with their own best learning style 2) they gain confidence in learning and that improves self-concept 3) they've become more proactive, in control, and that helps, also. A worthwhile investment in time would be to make sure that your learners have the learn-to-learn skills necessary to succeed. Make sure that your learners have access to either the actual instruction or the resources to become excellent learners.

How You Can Follow Up: *Student Success Secrets,* by Jensen; *30 Days to Bs and As*, by Jensen; *Quantum Learning,* by DePorter. See Appendix for details.

Faster Learning With Pre-Exposure

Does prior exposure to information speed up the learning? Researchers say yes. Ornstein says that pre-exposure to information makes subsequent thinking go more quickly. He likens this phenomenon to pre-consciousness. Donchin found that the greater the amount of "priming" stimulus, the more the brain extracted and "compartmentalized" (lateralized) the information. He thinks the brain has a way of putting information and ideas into a "buffer zone" or "cognitive waiting room" for rapid access. If the information is not utilized over time, it simply lays unconnected and random. But if the other parts of the puzzle are offered, the understanding and extraction of meaning is rapid.

Gazzaniga reports that in experiments done at Stanford, prior exposure to sentences led to quicker responses. Bower and Mann also found that learning and recall increased when a pattern was provided prior to exposure to the learning material. He also found that providing "post-organizing clues" was useful. The clues related to past learning and provided a framework for recall.

In my own workshops, the participants recount, as part of an exercise, all of the forms of pre-exposure provided. They get workshop content and process from the following sources:

1. Course description mailed out prior to attending
2. Talking to other past participants
3. Reading one of my books
4. Watching a video on the course
5. Colorful peripherals in the courseroom
6. Transparencies in the first few minutes that re-previewed
7. The workbook to browse through
8. My own specific "previews of coming attractions"

Advance Revelation With Mapping is Helpful

Would it help if you put up poster-sized graphic organizers, mind maps or webbing? Yes. Luiten examined 135 studies of the effects on learning of advance stimulation and organizers. He studied both acquisition and retention. His conclusions were that some form of "advanced organizers" are consistently positive. Mapping our ideas gives learners a way to conceptualize ideas, shape thinking and understand better what they know. But most importantly, it solidifies the learning as "mine."

The research of Weil and Murphy says that the use of some kind of pre-exposure is very powerful. They say, "Advance organizers are especially effective for helping participants learn the key concepts or principles of a subject area and the detailed facts and bits of information within these concept areas [the advance organizer idea]... is a highly effective instructional strategy for all subject areas where the objective is meaningful assimilation...."

When it comes to learning, limit the surprises.
Constant and varied pre-exposure will
encourage quicker and deeper learning
far better than any surprise value

Lozanov used pre-exposure with positive visual suggestion by color-coding key items. Five hundred subjects showed much greater recall than subjects who did not get the color-coded material. By preparing the mind, it learned on its own clock, in its own way. It's the essence of "ownership."

Mind mapping can serve as pre-exposure to a topic. These spider web-like drawings are a graphic, creative visual display of the topic and the key relationships, symbols and buzz words that create meaning to the learner. Through the use of color, drawings, use of contrast and making them personal, they can serve as the perfect way to create "mental maps." Once made on paper, they can be shared with others to increase their meaning and to reinforce context and details.

What This Means To You: Many participants who seem like slow learners may simply need pre-exposure to lay the foundation for better comprehension and recall. Pre-expose learners to your topic before officially starting it. Visually, you can prepare them with a note before the course begins, then posted mind-maps two weeks before beginning the topic or with preview texts and handouts. You can also get them ready with oral previews, examples and metaphors. Kinesthetically, you can offer role plays with similar experiences, simulations or games.

Learning Boosted With Prior Knowledge

When prior learning is activated, the brain makes many more connections. Learning, comprehension and meaning increase. The research of Anderson revealed that the importance of discovering and relating to previously learned material is much greater than earlier thought. Additionally, "[i]t is a better predictor of comprehension than is... an intelligence test score...."

Let's say you're a learner attending a new class. The instructor immediately starts in on new material. You're lost and overwhelmed in the first ten minutes. By the end of the first class, you're already worried about how you'll do in the class. It would have helped to first find out what you already know, and tie that into the course material.

> **What This Means To You:** Many learners who should do well in a subject actually underperform because the new material seems irrelevant. Unless connections are made to their prior learning, comprehension and meaning may be dramatically lessened. Before starting a new topic, ask the participants to either discuss, do role plays or skits, or make mind maps of what they already know.

Goal-Setting Increases Performance

There are many types of goals that you may have for your participants. Some are directed by an external agency (state standards for outcome-based learning, as an example. Others may be your own goals ("I want them to develop a real love of learning"). Student goals are certainly critical to a more brain-based learning approach. The optimal goals are learner-generated goals which are continually increased as the challenge of the work increases.

Two researchers, Locke and Latham, surveyed nearly 400 studies on goals, and the results were definitive. They found that specific, difficult goals lead to better performance than easy, vague ones. They add that these "results are based on studies conducted in the U.S. and seven other countries... [on] more than 40,000 subjects, 88 different tasks, time spans ranging from one minute to three years, and many different performance criteria, including behavior change, quantity and quality outcomes and costs."

However, a few other criteria for goal setting are necessary, says Ford. First, the target has to be at an optimal level of difficulty – "challenging, but attainable." Then the goal-pursuing process will only be effective if the learners have: 1) ample feedback to make corrections; 2) capability beliefs to sustain pursuit in the face of negative feedback; 3) the actual skills needed to complete the task; 4) an environment conducive to success.

However, if goals are given too much attention, they can be counter-productive, according to Baumeister. Learners report that they feel self-conscious, make simple mistakes, and sometimes experience test anxiety and "choke" on material, forgetting things they should have known.

There are two types of "PABs" (personal agency beliefs). They are capability beliefs ("I think I could graduate from the university") and context beliefs ("Now that I'm carrying a full load at school, getting good grades is harder than I thought"). Both of these PABs are activated once the goal is set, and not before. There are three keys to learner goal acquisition, says Ford. They are learner beliefs, goals and emotions.

An instructional leader may have no idea that these PABs exist within any particular learner. The effects on a learner's progress are very contextualized. It takes special circumstances to trigger them. In fact, unless there is a particular goal in place, no one else around them would know that they hold those beliefs.

In a long-term study of 250 participants, ages 12-15, researchers Meece, Wigfield and Eccles found that the single best advance predictor of success in mathematics was *their expectancy* of future math success. In other words, their PABs. Once these participants were in the classes, the best predictor of their likelihood of continuing in math classes was *its importance* to them. This fits in with many presenters' experiences of participants who first say, "I can't learn this stuff," and then, when they do learn it, say, "What's the point?"

When the learner does not have the PABs to succeed in a particular context, there is a solution. Co-establish, with significant learner input, "controllable short-term goals," says Barden and Ford. By doing this, the long-term outcomes may be in doubt, but with successes, the PABs of the underconfident learner may be enhanced in increments.

Goals are best when:
1) created by the learner
2) concrete & specific
3) have a specific due date
4) when self-assessed often
5) and re-adjusted periodically

Do beliefs affect the presenter or trainer? Yes, powerfully. The research by Rosenthal was one of many compelling arguments for why the instructional leader must always have high expectations. Rosenthal discovered that participants will turn out, not coincidentally, just about how you expect them to turn out.

Commonly, you are able to engage some learners with simple, short goals ("Here's what we can get done today"). Other learners want larger, more challenging goals ("Let's design a better health care system and get it in the local news").

> **What This Means To You:** In the proper context, goal setting serves a function. Let participants generate their own goals. Have them discover whether their own beliefs can support them. Ask them about the learning environment. Is it supportive to achieving the goals? Do they have the resources to reach their goals? Most learners who want to succeed are capable of succeeding, though they often lack the beliefs to do so. Ask learners to set their own goals for today's class. Make sure the goals are positive, specific and obtainable by the end of class. For example, a goal could be as simple as wanting to learn two new interesting things. You then need to provide the resources and learning climate to help your learners reach their goals. Then hold them accountable. Check back later to assess results and celebrate, if appropriate.

How You Can Follow Up: Read *Creating Your Own Future,* by Tad James; *Motivating Humans,* by Martin Ford. For presenting middle-school learners ages 10-15, get *Classroom Magic,* by Linda Harper.

Pre-Visualization Boosts Learning

An Oxford University study found that thinking before a learning activity improved learning. Elementary school children were asked to practice visualization, imagery and make believe. Then their performance was measured. The group that did the visualization first, then learned, scored higher than the group who didn't.

Before you went to your last job interview, chances are you rehearsed the interview in your mind many times over. This kind of practicing accesses the information, rehearses it and, in a sense, "pre-exposes" your mind to it.

> **What This Means To You:** In some cases, your learners may not be unmotivated, they may just need mental warm-ups. A few minutes invested early in the class could produce a big payoff later. Create a daily routine for your participants. Before you start, have them do both physical stretching and mental warm-ups, such as mentally rehearsing a role-play, asking questions, visualizing, solving problems or brainstorming.

How You Can Follow Up: Order *How to Boost Visualization Skills,* see Appendix for details.

Relaxation & De-stressors Boost Learning

Many studies have shown that stress can lower your learner's intelligence. Ostrander and Schroeder report that in one of the studies, Dr. Bernard Brown of Georgetown University discovered that increased stress impaired learning, thinking, memory and problem-solving in over 4,000 participants. In fact, increased stress even slashed their IQ scores by fourteen points! Brown says that chronic stress robs ones' ability to think.

Most presenters have seen this over and over. The more the stress, the more participants tighten up and underperform. Murphy and Donovan say that lowered learner stress through meditation may reduce the release of hormones linked with threat, while keeping those linked with the ability to meet a challenge. In other words, a relaxed nervous system is best for learning.

The work of O'Keefe, Nadel and Spielberger reminds us of the devastating effects of stress on the brain. They use descriptors like "rigidity of behavior, stereotyped behavior," and "repeated use of particular responses." In other words, you'll get an uptight learner who behaves more like a rat or a robot.

> **What This Means To You:** Take the time, before beginning each and every class, to relax your participants. Here are some of the best ways to relax them: 1) slow stretching 2) laughter and humor 3) music 4) games and activities 5) unstructured discussion and sharing 6) low-stress rituals 7) visualization.

Chapter Questions

1. What was novel, fresh and new? What was familiar or "old hat"?
2. In what ways do you already apply the information in this chapter?
3. What three questions can you now generate about this material?
4. How did you react emotionally to this information?
5. In what ways can you translate the key three or four theories and discoveries presented here into practical everyday useful ideas?
6. How did you react cognitively when you were reading the ideas of this chapter?
7. If these things are, in fact, true about the brain, what should we do differently? What resources of time, people and money could be redirected? In what ways do you suggest we start?
8. What was the single one (or two) most interesting or valuable insights you had?
9. Plan your next step, the logical practical application of what you've learned.
10. What obstacles might you encounter? How can you realistically deal with them?

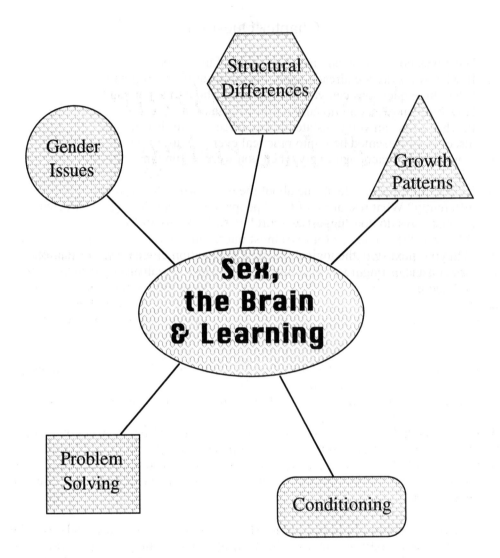

6

Sex, The Brain & Learning

Gender Issues Extremely Complex

Many researchers have documented pervasive demotivating influences on females in academics and subsequent career pursuits in technology, mathematics, science and computer-related fields. The most common solutions are often one-dimensional (such as single-sex schools). But Miura says this problem requires more complex and integrated solutions. Gender inequities are expressed in the following ways:

1. Personal goals. Until females have clear objectives that include technology, disadvantages will be dismissed as "peripheral."
2. Emotional arousal. There's a need to eliminate all variations of "technophobia" and any other related fears, concerns, etc.
3. Capability beliefs. Questions arise such as "Can I?" or "Is it hard?" These represent issues of self-confidence and skill assessment.
4. Context beliefs. There are a host of issues that surface when females enter technological fields. These include peer disapproval and "responsive environment" issues.

The research on gender inequities shows that progress is being made. But the rate of progress could be greatly enhanced by a more comprehensive program. Ford concludes by adding that "interventions designed to address just one aspect of this problem would probably yield disappointing results." Encouraging girls (who otherwise wouldn't) to take up a math, science or computer class is a great idea. But unless you address the issue of peer pressure, increase the capability beliefs, support the context beliefs and jump-start the emotions, there's little chance for success.

As an example, many girls are encouraged to take higher level math. But girls don't stay in the math programs for long. Something causes them to leave. There's a 13-to-1 ratio of males to females in higher level math classes.

> **What This Means To You:** To get more females into technological fields, we must address the less obvious underlying problems. Beliefs, emotions, and goals all need to be aligned. Handle the problem systemically. Interview girls. Find out what interests them, what would encourage them to pursue studies and maintain interest in technology programs.

There are distinct, measurable, structural differences between male and female brains

After years of persuasive research by Kimura and dozens of other eminent neuroscientists, including Butler, Levy, McGlone, Nyborg and Whitleson, the conclusions are profound: the male and female brain not only act differently, they are structurally different. And these verifiable physical differences may explain vastly different processing methodologies by male and female brains.

Barrett says that the male brain, on the average, weighs 49 ounces and the female brain, 44 ounces. There is still some dispute over the scope and magnitude of other differences. LaCoste at Yale and Holloway at Columbia reported corpus callosum differences. Some studies confirmed this; others did not. In those that did (particularly in Levy's work), the female corpus callosum was found to be heavier with greater number of connections. Allen and Gorski also found conflicting data. Denenberg at the University of Connecticut has stated that the differences are still unclear.

Yet, Diamond at Berkeley, Stewart of Concordia in Montreal, Kolb of the University of Lethbridge in Alberta, Canada, and LaCoste all reported clear-cut male-female brain differences. Kimura says, "Taken altogether, the evidence suggests that men's and women's brains are organized along different lines from very early in life." Variances within the same sex do exist, but certainly not to the same extent as the differences found between men and women.

While each brain will have different amounts of sexually differentiated characteristics, the generalizations about differences still hold

The list below of sexually determined differences makes a strong statement. It seems that post-conception hormonal influences are the primary difference-maker. Not all women are five foot five and not all men are five foot nine. But on the average, men are taller than women. The range of the differences listed below is more like a continuum. In the same spirit of averages, neuroscientists have found many physical differences. Examples of sexually determined differences include:

• length of the nerve cell connectors
• nucleus volume in hypothalamus
• pathways that the neurotransmitters follow
• density of nerve cell strands
• shape of the nucleus in the hypothalamus
• thickness of left and right side of the cortex control centers
• the number of vasopressin neurons in hypothalamus
• thickness and weight of the corpus callosum
• location of control centers for language, emotions & spatial skills

Growth Patterns Vary
Between the Sexes

Healy, Epstein, and other scientists and developmental specialists have found that in the early years, brain growth rates may vary from as little as a few months to as many as five years. And there are definite differences in how the female and male brains develop. Therefore, assessing and grouping children chronologically is as ridiculous as it would be to group presenters or business persons chronologically by age in their jobs.

Whitleson says that boys show a much earlier specialization of the right brain than girls do. In a study of 200 right-handed children, the boys outperformed the girls on spatial tasks. But linguistically, the girls show earlier dominance than the boys. Boys often have trouble, because of right brain specialization, in learning to read early in life. Since reading is both spatial and linguistic, it makes sense that girls generally learn to read earlier than boys.

Developmentally, girls learn to talk and read earlier,
on the average, than boys do... does this make it right
to label the boys "slow learners" or "hyperactive?"

The brain not only grows differently, it decays differently. We now know that the right brain of females has longer plasticity than that of males. This means it stays open to growth and change for more years in girls than in boys. Wree

87

reports that the degeneration of nerve cells in the male brain precedes that of females by 20 years. Although the rate of loss by females is greater than that of males, it is still not enough to overtake them. The researchers say that their estimates of cell loss are conservative.

There may be a reason why adolescent boys are more physical than adolescent girls. That part of the brain is much more developed in males at that time in their life. For females, the part of the brain used for interpersonal skills is more developed and plays an integral role in teenage girl culture.

Gender-Differences in Brain Sensory Intake and Thought Processing

Researchers Garai and Scheinfield, McGee, McGuiness, and Bracha say that the female brain is very different from the male brain with regard to sensory perception. Males and females almost live in a different world created by the processing of very different sensory information. Women often report having experiences that men don't understand, such as intuition, food cravings or social interaction clues. Literally hundreds of studies have been done to eliminate cultural biases from experiments so that researchers can really understand the true differences, not what has been socially programmed.

While there are documented functional differences between females and males, there are still biases which affect the early brain development of infants, which, in turn, change to respond to the bias. Nature or nurture? it's both. Here is a summary of some differences between males and females:

Hearing: The female ear is better able to pick up nuances of voice, music and other sounds. In addition, females retain better hearing longer throughout life. Females have superior hearing, and at 85 decibels, they perceive the volume twice as loud as males. Females have greater vocal clarity and are one-sixth as likely as a male to be a monotone. They learn to speak earlier and learn languages more quickly. Three-quarters of university participants majoring in foreign languages are female. Women excel at verbal memory and process language faster and more accurately. Infant girls are more comforted by singing and speech than males. In contrast to this summary of research, however, Klutky says females showed no significant auditory advantage in his own studies.

Vision: Males have better distance vision and depth perception than females. Women excel at peripheral vision. Males see better in brighter light; female eyesight is superior at night. Females are more sensitive to the red end of the spectrum; excel at visual memory, facial clues and context; have a better ability to recognize faces and remember names. In repeated studies, women can store more random and irrelevant visual information than men.

Touch : Females have a more diffused and sensitive sense of touch. They react faster and more acutely to pain, yet can withstand pain over a longer duration than males. Males react more to extremes of temperature. Females have greater sensitivity in fingers and hands. They are superior in performing new motor combinations, and in fine motor dexterity.

Activity: Male infants play more with objects, more often, than females. Females are more responsive to playmates. The directional choice, called "circling behavior," is opposite for men and women. In other words, when right-handed males walk over to a table to pick up an object, they are more likely to return by turning to their right. Right-handed females are more likely to return by circling around to their left.

Smell and Taste: Women have a stronger sense of smell and are much more responsive to aromas, odors and subtle changes in smell. They are more sensitive to bitter flavors and prefer sweet flavors. A "significant advantage" in olfactory memory was found by Klutky. Differences in the brain also relate to the effects of contaminants from beauty products. By using neuroradiological imaging to assess brain shrinkage, Harper and Kril found that women are "more susceptible to the damaging effects of alcohol than males."

Cultural or Genetic?
Problem-Solving Differences

Kimura says that males and females have very different ways of approaching and solving problems. She has been a pioneer for decades on the anatomical and functional differences between the sexes. Here is a summary of the research on differences in problem-solving, broken down by gender. In general, females do better than men in the following areas:

1) Mathematical calculation
2) Precision, fine-motor coordination
3) Ideational fluency
4) Finding, matching or locating missing objects
5) Use of landmarks to recall locations in context, maps

The problem-solving tasks that favor men are:

1) Target-directed motor skills (archery, football, baseball, cricket, darts, etc.)
2) Spatial: mentally rotating objects
3) Disembedding tests (locating objects, patterns from within another)
4) Mathematical reasoning, word problems
5) Use of spatial cues of distance, direction in route-finding

So, are these differences environmental or genetic? There is considerable research going on to determine this. So far, the consensus is that the answer indicates both factors play a role.

There are many activities in which females excel over males: assembly, needlework, precision crafting, micro-production, communication, sewing, nursing, pharmacy and many of the arts. On the average, developmentally, girls read earlier than boys. If we actually accounted for differing brains, we'd suddenly find that up to 75% of all boys who are now considered "developmentally slow" would immediately be reclassified as normal. Think of the ones in which males excel: gross motor skills like sports, mechanics, construction and sculpture.

> **What This Means To You:** We may want to consider whether we have gone overboard in trying to make education "gender-bias free." Equal education does not mean that everything should be done the same; it means providing equal opportunity. There are real, physical differences between the sexes. Many male-female behaviors make much more sense when considered in the context of brain development.
>
> Eliminate groupings by age or grade. They tend to cause feelings of inadequacy. Learners are being measured against those with developmental advantages instead of by effort. Change expectations. Keep participants in age clusters, such as ages 2-4, 5-7, 8-10, 11-13, 14-17.
>
> Become informed. Learn the differences between culturally reinforced stereotypes and real physical differences. Keep expectations high and avoid stereotyping. Change some expectations about behavior and learning. Be holistic and ecological, using a "systems" approach to insure greater success. Educate others about the differences. Many problems may not be problems at all. They may simply be an expression of the "natural" way in which one sex or another really operates. Open up discussions with your colleagues about the research and its implications.

How You Can Follow Up: Order *Insider's Guide to Learning Styles* or *Brain Sex,* by Moir & Jessel. Or, request *"Understanding the Opposite Sex"* a **Free** Bulletin. Simply send a self-addressed stamped envelope to address in Appendix. Get *Men are From Mars, Women are From Venus,* by John Gray; or *You Just Don't Understand,* by Deborah Tannen at local bookstores.

Chapter Questions

1. What was novel, fresh and new? What was familiar or "old hat"?
2. In what ways do you already apply the information in this chapter?
3. What three questions can you now generate about this material?
4. How did you react emotionally to this information?
5. In what ways can you translate the key three or four theories and discoveries presented here into practical everyday useful ideas?
6. How did you react cognitively when you were reading the ideas of this chapter?
7. If these things are, in fact, true about the brain, what should we do differently? What resources of time, people and money could be redirected? In what ways do you suggest we start?
8. What was the single one (or two) most interesting or valuable insights you had?
9. Plan your next step, the logical practical application of what you've learned.
10. What obstacles might you encounter? How can you realistically deal with them?

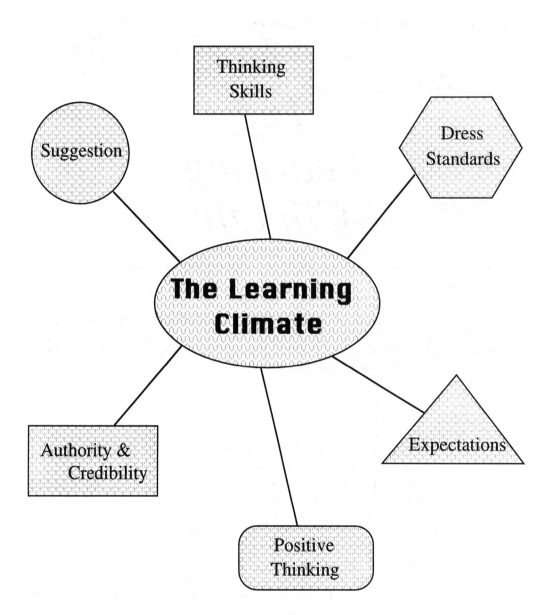

7

The Learning Climate

Learner Attitudes Impact Learning

There has been so much research about learner attitudes and perception that it scarcely bears repeating (Marzano, Silver & Marshall, et. al.). But what strategies are there, realistically, for presenters to use to positively impact paralyzing learner beliefs about a subject to be learned? Here are several:

1. Presenter states how much she or he enjoys & uses the information
2. Positive posters, peripherals in classroom, school
3. Use of positive role models, cult idols, guest speakers
4. Cite authority figures, videos, CDs, on that topic
5. Tell success stories of previous participants who succeeded
6. Have an initial positive experience with that topic
7. Make the topic "cool" to learn and peer popular
8. Point out negative stereotypes and myths in that subject area
9. Provide the skills so that learners who want to, can succeed
10. Hold learner discussions to air fears, feelings and concerns about learning
11. Provide sufficient resources to learn a topic
12. Allow learners to learn it in a personally meaningful way
13. Maintain a positive and receptive climate for questions & answers (group work, wait time, learner-generated Qs, rephrasing, restating)
14. Provide an atmosphere of physical and emotional safety
15. Insure participants of acceptance, respect and welcome them each class

Authority and Credibility

The more "positive authority" and credibility the presenter has with the participants, the stronger the learning. Lozanov's research on the power of "presenter authority" was extensive. The studies of Dr. Lozanov indicated that a great deal of learning took place simply because of the presenter's prestige and authority in the subject taught. Some might call this a variation on the "placebo effect." Research has consistently documented that if you believe that a particular drug or other medicine will help you, it's much more likely to work.

Although his orientation was Eastern European (translate: stronger respect, male dominated and authoritative cultural positioning of the presenter-role), much can be learned from his insights. Since research has documented that the student's opinion of the presenter is critical in the learning process, the prudent path for presenters is to be more attentive to what raises or lowers their authority or credibility. It is pointless to say that in today's society, learners won't give presenters the respect they deserve or even the time of the day. Real life experience has taught us that thousands of presenters around the world create on their own, a tremendous sense of positive authority and credibility every day. Their participants refer to them as "role models."

While "authority" sounds more heavy-handed in the Western role, the usage here is more in the sense of "looking up to," as in "one worthy of respect." Also, it is more defined by strength of character, presence, charisma, confidence and competency. It is definitely **not** "authority" in the case of a police officer or security guard. There is nothing to "authorize" as in "having control over." It simply means, in this context, "one who is worth listening to" as in being "an authority on the subject."

Credibility implies believability, but there's more. It means, in this context, that your actions as well as your overt academic message are imbued with purpose and pedagogy. It means that others want to do what you ask them to do, because you are credible.

What This Means To You: Become more aware of the things you do that increase or decrease your authority. Here are some specific examples:

1. Let others know the number of years of experience you have in your profession & how many in a particular field or specialty.
2. Did you say which school, university or graduate program you attended?
3. Tell others who were your mentors. Were they eminent in their field? How long did you work as an understudy?
4. Have you been published in newsletters, bulletins, books, articles, videos, or CDs?
5. Say what your degree is in? Did you graduate with honors?
6. What innovative or important state-wide or national projects did you work on?
7. Are there articles on you in newspapers, have you been interviewed on TV?
8. Do you attend key conferences, or speak at them if possible?
9. Do you do what you say you will? Do you keep your promises?
10. Do you use positive language, never use any vulgarity, profanity, racist or sexist remarks?

How You Can Follow Up: For a **free** bulletin on *"How to Build and Maintain Sky-High Credibility,"* simply send your request, along with a self-addressed stamped envelope to the address in the Appendix.

Congruency in Words and Body Language Key In Learning

Research on the brain and our senses has shown that we are able to be conscious of only one incoming sensory message at a time. In other words, while you watch a movie, the sounds are reaching the nonconscious. While you are listening to a concert performance, the sights are reaching the nonconscious. European learning pioneer Lozanov describes presenter and trainer congruency as "dual plane messages," messages that are received by your learners on two levels, the conscious and the paraconscious. Your learners are aware of both your verbal and nonverbal communication, and are being influenced by messages that you, the presenter, may not even be aware of sending.

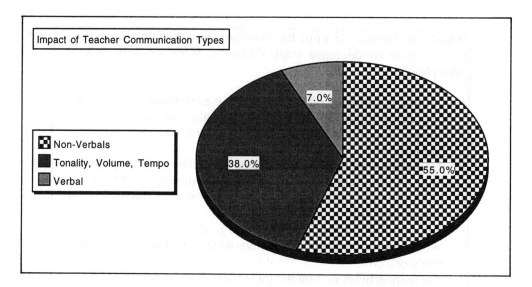

Impact of Teacher Communication Types

Non-Verbals
Tonality, Volume, Tempo
Verbal

7.0%
38.0%
55.0%

Let's say that, as an example, you say to your learners, "I am very happy to be here today." But actually, your head is shaking from side to side as if to say, "I'd rather be elsewhere." While both messages are being received, the second one will have the greatest credibility.

What This Means To You: Your learners are receiving a lot of mixed messages which undermine the content of your desired message and reduce your credibility. Lozanov calls this a loss of prestige and authority with respect to the course you are offering. Learners will learn more when the presenter communicates more congruently. You may want to practice your non-verbals. Videotape yourself and review it. Find the two or three areas you can improve the most and work on just those. Get feedback from others. Take an acting class. Practice in front of a mirror.

How You Can Follow Up: *Present Yourself*, by Michael Gelb. See Appendix for details.

Learning Affected By Dress Standards

We know from the Pygmalion experiments that presenter expectations of the learner's ability affects learning. But what about the reverse? Do learner expectations about presenters affect how they learn? Yes, according to clothing consultant John Malloy. He set up experiments to discover whether learner perceptions of presenter clothing impacted their learning. Malloy summarized the conclusive results:

"The clothing worn by the presenters
substantially affected the work
and attitudes of the pupils"

He claimed that presenters who were better dressed had participants with fewer discipline problems, better work habits and who learned more. He added that at different socio-economic levels, learners responded differently to the various types of clothing. Some attribute this to the "placebo effect."

Let's say you go to a conference or workshop and the presenter is very casual or sloppily dressed. There's a different reaction in your mind than if the presenter is professional and businesslike, with good grooming. It's well known that one of the strongest influencers in sick patients getting better is the belief that the doctor knows best. Studies done where the doctor did not wear the white coat and tie showed patients took longer to heal.

What This Means To You: Your clothing conveys powerful messages about yourself, the organization you work with, and what you think of the job and your customers (or participants). Dress professionally. Look like you are a professional of status and pride. We may not like it but others judge us by what we wear, consciously or nonconsciously.

Positive-Thinking Impacts Achievement in Learning

Should a presenter give more positive affirmations and reduce or eliminate fault-finding in participants? An article in the New England Journal of Medicine suggests so. Dr. Rozanski reported that *sarcasm, criticism and put-downs increased abnormalities in heart rate.* These aberrations were as significant and measurable as those from a heavy workout or pre-attack myocardial chest pains.

The fact that negative comments may pose
a health risk to their participants is stunning
new evidence of the importance of
positive presenter & learner comments

Do the positive or negative emotions of the presenter affect the learning of the participants? Yes, according to Mills. He says that learners pick up on the particular emotional state of the presenter/trainer/instructor and it impacts their cognition. Presenters who use humor, give warm smiles, have a joyful demeanor and take genuine pleasure in their work will have learners who outperform those who do not. It does seem that the days you are in a better mood, your learners mirror it back to you.

The Positive Climate

The author of *Pygmalion in the Classroom,* Robert Rosenthal indicates that *the single greatest influence* on learners is the learning climate. But where's the biological "proof?" In a climate typified by positive challenge and joy, the body releases endorphins, the peptide molecules that elevate our feelings and cause us to feel good. Research by Levinthal and Sylwester suggest that this "positive learning climate" promotes better learning, stronger problem-solvers and higher quality learning. In short, when we feel good, we learn better!

Learners in positive, joyful environments
are likely to experience better learning,
memory and feelings of self-esteem

Many factors contribute to a positive climate. It includes many things: our dress, our positive comments, our enthusiasm and values. As presenters, our beliefs and attitudes are inextricably intertwined with *how we teach.* Because of the power of suggestion, we nonconsciously "suggest" that learning is hard or easy, homework is valuable or it's not, school is important or it's not. We also suggest to our participants that they may find things easy, fun and challenging, or we suggest that things will be hard, boring and frustrating. Your smile, or lack of it communicates to your participants. Your conversation, your clothes and handouts all add up the impact of the "collective whole."

What This Means To You: You may want to invest some time each day to make sure that you are at your best before presenting others. Regardless of the science of *how* it works, we know it does work. Presenters who are happier and more pleasant to be around bring out the best in their learners. Take a few minutes each day for de-stressing. Listen to music that will help to put you in a great mood. Put up some kind of humorous cartoon or positive affirmation around your presenting area. Get into a good learning state before you start.

Your Learner's Expectations
Strongly Influence Their Learning

Gratton and fellow researchers were interested in finding out why, when, and how the learner's brain responds to visual and auditory information. They questioned if it matters whether or not the learner thinks that the material is going to be useful later on. The answer was "yes" to each of these. The results of their experiments indicate that "expectancies about the relative utility of the information was *the key determiner* in how successfully they responded."

Popper's attacks on the supposed "science" of scientific reasoning are well known. He continually pointed out how prior beliefs, presuppositions and prejudices made much of what was discovered or not discovered predetermined. His lecturing ploy which made the point beautifully, was to ask the audience to please "observe." Their reply was typically, "Observe what?" To which he said, "Exactly my point." Observation does not occur in a vacuum; it is strongly influenced by what we are looking for.

Can you send a note to the participants before the course begins to generate positive expectancy about the value of the course? Have participants generate their own high expectations of the learning: What's the best that they could learn, how could it help them, how easy will it be to learn? As the instructional leader, you can help set up the learners to learn more with your own enthusiasm and positive expectations.

> **What This Means To You:** Because your so-called "top" learners often expect to get the most out of a class, they usually do. Those who learn less often expect to learn less. You may want to affect your learner's expectations about your course or class. How much learners get may be affected profoundly by how motivated you get them, how much relevance the material has for them, and how much they think they will learn.

How You Can Follow Up: Order **free** *How to Get Yourself Motivated to Go To Work,* send simply send your request along with a self-addressed stamped envelope to the address in the Appendix.

Learning Adversely Affected By
Forced Silence & Class Inactivity

Many learners are asked to remain in their seats and to remain quiet for optimal learning. But research by Della Valle et al. says that may not be a good idea. Among adolescents, 50% of the learners needed "extensive mobility while learning." Of the remaining 50%, half of those (25%) needed occasional mobility and the remaining needed minimal movement opportunities. As an example, you're talking to a group and the majority of them begin to get drowsy and listless. Is it your fault or the audience's? It doesn't matter; let them get up and move around.

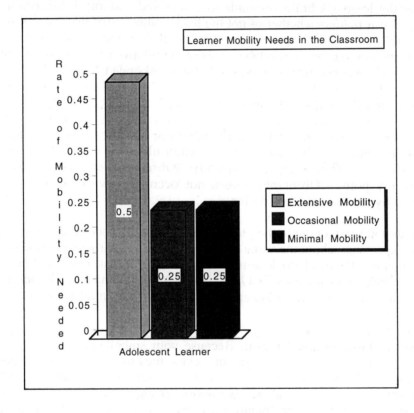

The work of James Asher on TPR (Total Physical Response) reminds us of the power of activity and motion in learning. While it's true that much learning can occur without ever leaving a seat, it's also true that most of what you think is important in your life, what you "really know," you have learned through experience, not from a chalkboard or textbook. In addition, the research on the power of physiological states is conclusive: the body remembers as well as the mind... in many cases, it remembers better!

What This Means To You: Some learners are paying little attention to your message. Others seem low in energy or curiosity. Both of them may need some mobility. What may seem like a boring topic or bad time of the day may simply be a product of learners who are restless and need some activity.

Schedule a "stand up and stretch" break every 20 minutes. Create a diversity of activities so that learners get to move into teams, go outside, work with partners or do simple activities that get the circulation going and keep active learners happy. You may want to do cross-lateral movements, offer water, create a more active learning process or simply let them stretch and take in some deep breaths.

The Skill of Thinking Boosts Learning

The old model of presenting as "filling a container" is long out of date. The learners have brains of unlimited potential and it's a disgrace to treat the learner's brain as a wheelbarrow. The brain requires work, and work is thinking and problem-solving. Learning is an interactive process that occurs on many levels. The learning has to be input, filtered, associated, processed, evaluated and stored. It has to be reframed, generalized and contextualized. It needs usage and feedback, then reshaping. Over time the learner feels a kind of meaning and sometimes expertise. This takes time and it takes a knowing presenter to coach the learner through the process. An upcoming chapter goes into this in more detail.

How You Can Follow Up: Read *A Different Kind of Classroom: Teaching with Dimensions in Learning,* by Robert Marzano. Available from ACSD at 703-549-9110.

Daily Manipulation
Slows Most Learning

Caine and Caine report that excessive control by presenters actually reduces learning. They say that learners "must have choice and variety." It all comes down to this simple concept that Caine explains so well: "If participants are to be predominately self-motivated, they must be given the opportunity to focus on *their* areas of interest and to participate in activities *they* find interesting" (my emphasis).

In brief, unless learners have a real vote in determining the content and method of their learning, the learning becomes forced, rote, mechanical, short-lived and, eventually, distasteful. And, as Glasser notes in *Control Theory*, the more learners feel controlled, the more resentful they get. And resentment is either expressed or suppressed. It is expressed in the form of frustration, anger, rebellion, or lack of discipline. It is suppressed in the form of detachment, sabotage, apathy and cynicism about learning. Harter suggests that participants who lack perceived control on an assigned task will hold back and give less than their best efforts. It makes sense. Unless you feel like you control your destiny, why invest in someone else's destiny?

You've had a manipulative and controlling presenter before. How did it feel? Presenters who enrich environments their way, use music their way, do their kind of stretching, and design learning stations their way, can create a state of resentment and helplessness among their learners.

The Secret of the SAT Method

Overall, there are seven basic auditory forms that are universally used to alter a learner's behavior. As a presenter, you'll want to use the best ways to get the learners to do what you want them to do *without manipulating or controlling them.* The letters SAT (#'s 3,4,5 below) refer to the first letters of the optimum ways for classroom communication. Let's talk about each of them:

1. **Hope:** The request is never made, nor is it even "talked around." It is simply assumed that the learner will figure out what you want & comply. The thought is actually outside the awareness of the learners. Since the learner doesn't know about it, there is NO perceived choice by the learner with this strategy.

2. **Imply:** The literal request is never made, it is talked around, the hope is that the learner will infer from the implication. Because there is no overt recommendation made, there's minimal perceived choice unless the learner successfully makes the proper inference

3. **Suggest:** The request is made in a way that illuminates preferred options... there IS strong perceived choice. If you like the options you're likely to choose one. "You might like to use a colored pen for taking notes."

4. **Ask:** The request is made in a way that encourages one to follow... there IS some perceived choice in this method. "Would you please use a colored pen for your notes?"

5. **Tell:** Acceptable instructional level – to simply give them a directed statement in an expectant tone they have minimal perceived choice, they are strongly encouraged to do it. "Using a colored pen, write this down..."

6. **Demand/Threaten:** The second strongest (also a poor choice) is to absolutely order in a way that they have minimal or NO perceived choice. To choose otherwise would be unsafe or wholly inappropriate

7. **Force:** The strongest way (acceptable only in an emergency) of changing behavior in others is physical authority or physical presence or extreme coercion. Learners have NO perceived choice, you make no other option available to them. This is unacceptable unless lives or property are at stake.

The ideal rapport with your learners is this: sometimes you ask, sometimes you tell and sometimes you suggest. Too much of any can create problems. The presenters who have the toughest time with discipline or motivation are consistently the ones who have a poor balance of S-A-T. Usually they are way too high in telling and that creates a bad working relationship.

What This Means To You: Even the best planned presenting can fail if it's too controlling. In the long run, all controlling presenter strategies will backfire. Learners will give you less than their best effort, will feel resentful and learn to dislike the very subject you wanted them to like. It's better to get learner input or elicit learner responsibility for creating aspects like the environment, music, goals and activities.

Provide more options for learners, more choices in what they learn and how they learn it. Give participants choices about the learning environment, the methods of instruction and types of assessment. Have discussion groups on the best types of learner input. Utilize suggestion boxes, teams and expression areas. Students buy into and take pride in doing activities which they have helped to define and over which they have some control.

How You Can Follow Up: *SuperTeaching,* by Jensen. See Appendix for details.

The Real Power of Suggestion
Is Dramatically Under Used

Research by Lozanov and many others has confirmed that the use of positive suggestion in a learning environment can bring dramatic results. What a presenter wears, what the environment is like, how the material is presented and hundreds of other simple acts all suggest something to the mind. In this entire book, the most important concept may be:

Suggestion is everything and everything is suggestion...
In fact, you cannot not suggest. The question is,
"What are you now suggesting?"

Bulgarian-born Lozanov was the first presenter who carefully and purposely organized all levels of suggestion. His use of suggestion included the use of peripherals, positive verbal suggestions about learning ability, the power of memory, the ease of mastery, the joy of learning and powers of the mind. It worked. How? While conscious, directed, focused, content-level learning drops off over time (see graph on the Ebbinghaus Curve of Forgetfulness), the use of suggestion actually increases learning over time. Research in Lozanov's courses demonstrated that all the positive, suggestive messages became more powerful over time. In *Super Memory,* the authors report that on the tenth day after a Lozanov exposure suggestion, the learner recall was five times better than the first day!

Lozanov also said that since suggestion is affecting the biases (beliefs, limiting thoughts, attitudes, etc.) of the learner, there can be no suggestion without de-suggestion. In other words, all positive suggestions are simply a "counter" to another negative belief. In that sense, we are always countering the prior negative conditioning. If none of that existed, the need for positive suggestion would drop dramatically. In Lozanov's words,

"There is no suggestion without de-suggestion,
without freeing the paraconscious from
the inertia of something old"

Suggestion in Verbal Messages

Everything is a source of suggestion, purposeful or not. Some of these are positive, some are not. Read each statement and decide if you like the message that it gives or that a learner might infer. In what ways might a learner interpret what you say?

"If the instructions are not clear to you, start paying more attention."

"While I don't expect to make scientists out of you, I do expect to provide you with the basics."

"What part of the word 'No' do you not understand?"

"You might dislike this subject now, but by the time we're done with it, you'll definitely learn an lot and appreciate it more."

"Don't forget to do your homework."

"I know I have a reputation for not being an easy grader. But you're likely to enjoy this class and learn much more than you thought possible."

"Have a Merry Christmas!"

"Forget about Spanish and enjoy the holiday break."

"Hey, guess what? Only 45 days 'til school's out!"

"I hope you will gain an appreciation for the power, simplicity and elegance of this material."

"If you fail to complete any of the four basic requirements, you can expect an F for the course. In case you're wondering, there are no exceptions."

"Don't be late or your grade will drop."

"This upcoming section is the hardest one in the book so don't let your mind wander. That could be a disaster."

"I know that you might be a bit nervous or uptight about the upcoming test. But don't worry about how you'll do. You won't fail."

The pioneering work of Lozanov reminds us that suggestion in many forms is always operating. Suggestion is operating at both the conscious and nonconscious level. It is also the single greatest untapped influence you have with your learners. Lozanov has discovered:

1) if the learner is confident, learning goes up
2) if the learner believes in the presenter, the learning goes up
3) if the learner thinks the subject is important, learning goes up
4) if the learner believes it will be fun and valuable, learning goes up etc., etc.

How do you get the learner to believe these things? Use the power to influence through the artful application of positive suggestion. You can influence (but not control) what your participants believe about themselves, you, the topic, learning, etc. And, in fact, you already influence them in those areas. You simply may have underestimated the power of that influence. You could say, "This upcoming chapter is the hardest in the book, so everyone bear down!" Or, you could say, "This upcoming chapter is my favorite, so get ready for a great experience."

As an authority figure, the presenter carries far more influence than ordinarily thought. It's a common experience to have had a presenter who told us that we were "bad" in math or English. A portion of those told actually believed it. Naturally, that subject became nearly impossible to master. This bias is just one of many that we all carried throughout out learning life.

All learning is affected by our own personal history; we have a lifetime of experiences, beliefs, values and attitudes about each subject and our capability and probability in learning it. Lozanov calls these "biases." Since he believes that all learning is heavily influenced by all of the biases, should we try to change those, or simply "do our job" and simply "teach?" You may have guessed the answer. The overwhelming evidence is that the presenters who influence the biases are much more successful. In other words, we can change the behaviors in the classroom, or we can change the biases (or both).

The shortest route to learner success is not by simply
changing the biases about ourselves or the topic,
but to change the behaviors AND the biases at the same time.
In fact, changing biases will eventually and
automatically change the learner behavior

> **What This Means To You:** It is useful, powerful and ethical to use positive suggestion in every way you can. Put up positive messages on posters ("My success is absolutely assured"). Suggest to your learners how easy they might find the learning of this material ("Learning is fun, easy and creative"). Suggest that they might enjoy further studying it on their own. Suggest that they might find new ideas popping into their mind at just the right time. Suggest that learning is relaxing and enjoyable. For every hour of presenting and learning, it is recommended that you orchestrate at least twenty positive messages.

How You Can Follow Up: *The ACT Approach,* by Dhority. See Appendix for details.

Environmental Options: Offer Seating Choice For Best Learner Success

Two researchers, Shea and Hodges, did studies to determine the effects of "formal" (hard-backed chairs facing the front of the room) and "informal" (seated on pillows, lounge chairs, floor, according to learner choice) seating in the classroom. Shea found that participants who preferred "informal" seating arrangements performed "significantly" better on language (English) comprehension tests. Another group scored much higher in mathematics when they taught and tested in the seating of their choice.

The New York Times of July 15, 1992 reported on a study done at a midwestern university. Students (120 undergraduates) were assigned either a crowded exam room or an uncrowded exam room. The chair distance from others was the determining factor. The subjects with less personal space had higher anxiety and lower test scores than those in the other group.

Dunn and Dunn say that at least 20% of learners are significantly affected, positively or negatively, based just on the type of seating options. To be at their best, they need to have choice. Some participants need the floor, a couch or beanbag furniture to be at their best in learning.

Does location matter? Can you position your learners for maximum learning success? Wlodlowski says that circles, U shapes and V shapes are best. When given a choice, good spellers tend to sit on the right side of the classroom. This may be related to handedness (hemispheric dominance), or left-brain-right field of vision, or the fact that visual creativity is dominant on the upper left side of the eye pattern range. Some environmental researchers (Della Valle, Hodges, Shea, Kroon) have found that the environment (seating choices, comfort levels, lighting) and learning styles (global, sequential, concrete, abstract, etc.) are a significant factor in determining the success of participants.

As an example, let's say you go to a seminar and sit on the left hand side of the room. You change the seating at the break and sit on the right hand side. You'll discover that it's almost a different seminar just by switching seats.

> **What This Means To You:** We may accidentally reduce motivation and learning by keeping a traditional seating pattern. Change seating patterns often. Provide choice and make it easy to change types of seating arrangements.

Optimal Learning Climate
Likely to Require These Keys

Ford researched optimal motivating environments and found that four factors were critical to what he calls "context beliefs." These are the functional elements that are "in vitro," meaning embedded within the learner's situation. According to Ford, all of them must be present to create an optimal environment:

1) The environment must be consistent with an individual's personal goals. This means that the learning environment must be a place in which the learner can reach his or her own personal goals.
2) The environment must be congruent with the learner's bio-social and cognitive styles. This means that if abstract learning is taking place in a crowded, competitive room with fluorescent lighting, it will be a problem for a concrete learner who needs space and works cooperatively.
3) The environment must offer the learner the resources needed. In addition to materials, advice, tools, transportation and supplies, another key resource is time and affordability.
4) The environment must provide a supportive and positive emotional climate. Naturally, trust, warmth, safety and peer acceptance are critical.

As a child, you found yourself naturally and effortlessly engaged in learning. Why? So many of the qualities that are motivating were naturally a part of the environment.

> **What This Means To You:** Many participants whom you thought of as being unmotivated may be very motivated - if you provide the right conditions. Make a big poster featuring the four conditions of the optimal learning environment. Post it in the back of the room you work in the most often. Let it be your guide for how to motivate learners.

How You Can Follow Up: *Optimal Learning Environments,* see Appendix for details.

Chapter Questions

1. What was novel, fresh and new? What was familiar or "old hat"?
2. In what ways do you already apply the information in this chapter?
3. What three questions can you now generate about this material?
4. How did you react emotionally to this information?
5. In what ways can you translate the key three or four theories and discoveries presented here into practical everyday useful ideas?
6. How did you react cognitively when you were reading the ideas of this chapter?
7. If these things are, in fact, true about the brain, what should we do differently? What resources of time, people and money could be redirected? In what ways do you suggest we start?
8. What was the single one (or two) most interesting or valuable insights you had?
9. Plan your next step, the logical practical application of what you've learned.
10. What obstacles might you encounter? How can you realistically deal with them?

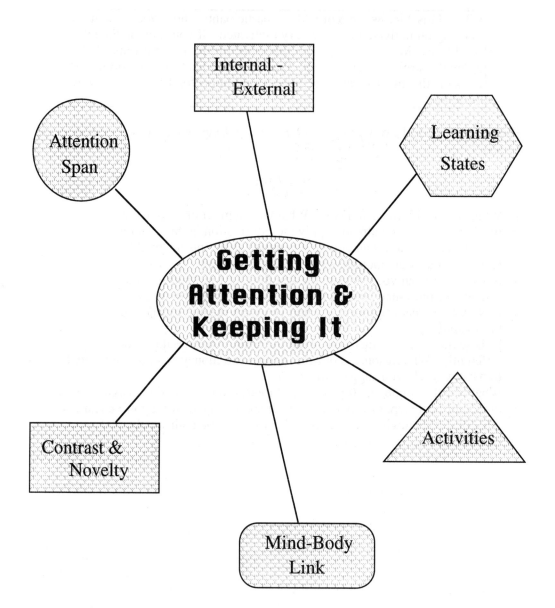

Internal - External

Attention Span

Learning States

Getting Attention & Keeping It

Contrast & Novelty

Activities

Mind-Body Link

8

Getting Attention & Keeping It

How to Hook the Brain's Attention

Researchers Sylwester and Cho say the brain has a built-in bias for certain types of stimuli. Since our brain isn't designed to consciously attend to ALL types of incoming stimuli, it deletes that which is less critical to our survival. To the brain, contrast, emotion and novelty win hands down. "Giant Two-Headed Baby Born to Siamese Dwarf," screams the tabloid headlines. And, "Double murder near you with a shocking twist - news at eleven," teases another. What gets your attention on television is the "shock effect." Even commercials are playing into our brain's bias for high contrast and novelty. We know that a passing glance over any crowd of people will pick up what's different (any familiar faces), any sudden changes in movement, familiar voices or emotional overtones.

*Any stimuli introduced into our immediate
environment which is either new (novel) or of
sufficiently strong emotional intensity (high contrast)
will immediately get our attention*

Funny thing is, you only want attention for a short period of time–just enough to get a quick "learning bias." First, the brain is not designed for extended periods of attention. Changes in amine levels, hormones, nutrition, emotions and course content limit attention levels. Second, attention means your participants are "externally" processing. But the only way they can make the learning meaningful is to break from the attention and "go internal." Attention is particularly useful for openings, closings, key ideas, safety and special instructions. But, in general, you'll be wanting the learner's attention no more than about 20-30% of the time.

What This Means To You: Your learners can become jaded and "over-shocked" by television and tabloid-type constant high contrast stimuli. As a result, in a sedate learning environment, learners may become bored, listless and detached. Presenters who capitalize and use this part of the brain's tendency can get and keep attention longer. But that's only useful for the short term.

It makes more sense for the presenter to be less of the "show." Capturing the learners' attention then becomes less of an issue. Giving the learners more control and allowing them to choose complex, interesting life-like projects will focus their attention on their learning instead of on their daydreams.

Use the brain's bias for high contrast - be outrageous and different. But also focus more on designing learner-generated projects so that you don't have to be a shock-show to run a class. Then the novelty and variation of other learners provides much of the attentional bias needed.

Role of Laughter & Learning

Dr. William Fry at Stanford University has discovered that the body reacts biochemically to laughing. Fry inserted catheters into the veins of medical participants who were watching and listening to a comedian. He and his associate Lee Berk of the Loma Linda Medical School wanted to measure the changes in blood chemistry. They found *an increase in white blood cell activity* and changes in the chemical balance of the blood which may boost the body's production of the neurotransmitters needed for alertness and memory.

How could this happen? For one thing, a good laugh can lower stress - and a low stress brain and body makes for a better learner. In the classic book *Anatomy of an Illness,* Dr. Norman Cousins revealed his laughter therapy which, he stated, was instrumental in his battle with cancer. So, does laughing change the chemistry of the brain? Many scientists now think so. Dr. Arthur Stone at the State University of New York says that having fun may be good for you. To summarize, he says pleasant experiences "improve the functioning of the body's immune system for three days–the day of the fun and two days after. "

Let's say your participants are feeling stressed, and one of them tells a joke. The whole room erupts with laughter and they now seem ready to learn something new. Research on the body and the brain tells us that the laughter is good for learning.

What This Means To You: Maybe humor and jokes do have more of a place in learning environments, provided, of course, that their use is tasteful and respectful of the time available. Be tolerant of learner contributed humor. At times, having a two minute joke session may be an appropriate way to deal with stress.

Brain Awakens With Cross Lateral Activity

Most of us would say we feel better when we are healthy, exercise a bit or work out. But are our brains actually better? In a study on rats by Isaacs, et al., research found that vigorous physical activity increases blood flow to the brain and increases synaptic and associated neuropil volume change.

Dennison goes further. He says that the use of cross lateral repatterning motions can have dramatic effects on learning. For participants who are "stuck" in their learning, cross lateral movements can be the perfect and simple antidote to engage both sides of the brain for full advantage. This is particularly effective for participants who are sleepy, overwhelmed, frustrated or experiencing a learning block.

Cross laterals are arm and leg movements that cross over from one side of the body to another. Since the left side of the brain controls the right side of the body and vice versa, engaging the arms and legs in cross over activities forces the brain to "talk to itself." A brain which is fully using more than just a small part is far more efficient and effective.

What This Means To You: When you go for a brisk walk or work out before coming to work, you feel better, happier. That's no coincidence. Learners who are active tend to also be more alert and learn more. Building some physical activity into your daily learning schedule may be preferable to leaving the activity up to the learner to do in a separate physical education class or on his or her own.

Take two minutes when you start your class to activate your learners. A short stretching, a brisk walk, some cross-lateral movements - all would do some good. Then make sure that you have some short but effective and well-timed breaks throughout the day. It will boost learner motivation. Your participants will enjoy it, too.

How You Can Follow Up: Read *Brain Gym: Presenter's Manual*, by Dennison. Available by catalog - details in Appendix.

113

Attention Drifts From External to Internal

Research about the brain and its attention-processing mechanism suggests that it is critical to understand the E-I (external-internal) shift. Sylwester and Cho say that our brain frequently shifts its focus between external learning events and our internal stored memories and present interests. This shifting of focus seems to be a critical element in: 1) maintaining understanding; 2) updating long-term memories; and 3) strengthening our neural networks. The brain needs time to "go inside" and link up the present with the past and the future. Without it, learning drops dramatically.

Implementing current brain research
means the whole concept of "on task"
or "off task" has become irrelevant

This shift can happen non-consciously or consciously, through recalling and telling stories. When we do recall or retell our memories, they serve to enhance and enrich our own brain's networking system. The best and simplest way to describe this learning pattern is that learners alternate their focus between the external source of learning and their own internal processing. Some participants need equal time for external and internal time and others may need a 5-1 ratio, meaning they have a longer attention span. Let's say you see a good learner in the class who is not paying attention. It may be that something he just learned has triggered his internal memories or has shifted to internal processing.

> **What This Means To You:** It may be that this "on-task" notion is an inappropriate (and insane) way to measure learning. Keeping students' attention 100% is a moot issue. We shouldn't have their attention all the time. Maybe they need more time than we think to internalize information. The learner who we think is not focused may be simply re-thinking things in light of new information. Provide thinking time and group and partner discussion time. Avoid long lectures. Give frequent breaks. Provide end-of-class reflection time.

Does It Matter How You Listen?

Many researchers, including Gordon, Mills & Rollman, Schwartz and Talall have suggested that the right ear is superior for listening. In fact the more complex the listening the better the right ear. It's access to the left brain makes it "...more capable of processing the internal structure of very complex tones... (and)... its unique ability to analyze temporally ordered inputs."

Researcher Asbjornsen wondered if it matters whether learners use their left or right ear for listening to instructions. His staff conducted research with 40 right-handed females undergoing 36 trials with four different instructions. To insure complete data, he varied head and eye turns, together and separate, for both left and right sides, and he varied directions toward and away from the source of the voice. The results were a significant and clear *right ear advantage in all groups* during all conditions.

Dr. Albert Tomatis, one of the pioneers of sound, acoustics and hearing, says that our right ear is the best ear for listening, learning and language. In fact, his studies show that normal readers became dyslexic when they could only listen with their left ear. Conversely, he has successfully treated thousands of dyslexics by using sound therapy to improve their ability to hear high frequencies. Actors and singers who monitored themselves with their right ear improved voice quality and memory.

Music pioneer Don Campbell says that "half the people in the world change their voice response depending on which ear receives the information." He adds that if you have sequential, detailed information for your learners, position yourself so that you can address their right ear. That's the ear that has the superior path to the left side of the brain.

In "Brain-Mind Bulletin," a report of research done at Cal State Fullerton in Los Angeles, California, explains that the ear choice used for listening was important. The study showed that when music (low volume baroque) was played into the opposite ear of the preferred hand used, learning increased. For right-handers, this meant music was played into the left ear.

Watch your learners. You may have noticed that some of your learners constantly tilt their ear one way or another. It may be because they are appealing to the opposite side of the brain for best understanding.

What This Means To You: Just as there are right and left handers, there are also ear dominances. It is unrelated to handedness, however. Some listeners may do better if they change position, if they "cup" their dominant listening ear, or if the person talking changes position in the room. Make sure that you move around the room as you speak. You might redefine the "front" of the room. Have participants move into groups and teams each day or sit in different locations each week so that no one is disadvantaged.

How You Can Follow Up: *100 Ways to Improve Teaching Using Your Voice & Music,* by Don Campbell.

Research Once Again Verifies
Mind-Body-Feelings Link

Researchers Campbell & Grossberg discuss how the structure and function of hippocampal and infero-temporal processing may be linked. Learning areas such as categorization, attention, memory, novelty recognition and memory search all work together at different stages of development.

While researchers have known that the infero-temporal cortex can recognize both specialized and abstract information, Campbell proposed a link between this ability to recognize and lesions in hippocampal formation. This proposed link may verify the relationship between how we feel and how we learn. Dr. Candace Pert, chief of brain biochemistry at National Institute of Mental Health, says, "The emotions are not just in the brain, they're in the body... this may explain why some people talk about gut feelings." We are more driven by emotions than logic. Sylwester says that because the limbic portion of the brain tells our cortex how to feel about things, *it is actually implying what you might want to do* in the future.

> **What This Means To You:** The emotional state of your learners is at least as important as the intellectual-cognitive content of your presentation. Never avoid emotions; deal with them. Allow negatives ones to be processed out and positive ones to be drawn out. Make sure you put your learners in a good emotional state before you present the material. Allow your learners time to de-stress first, then make the learning enjoyable with amusing activities so that the emotions are positively engaged.

Specific Learning Conditions
Suggested For Maximum Success

Kenyon, Csikszentmihalyi, Caine and Singer suggest that there are optimal states for the learner. The ideal learning takes place when the following conditions are met:

- High challenges, intrinsically motivated
    (not too easy, not too hard, your own relevant choice)
- Low stress, general relaxation
    (not NO stress, just minimal stress)
- Immersed "flow" state: attention on learning and doing
    (not self-conscious or evaluative)

Very little learning goes on when learners are in poor learning states. In fact, since learning is so "state-dependent," it may be more critical than ever previously suggested to consciously read and elicit the optimal states. Given the extreme importance of states in learning, it is quite safe to say:

***The presenter's top priority is managing
states - read and elicit, read and elicit***

When you keep your learner in the appropriate states for learning, they will naturally do better. Noted University of Chicago psychologist Mihaly Csikszentmihalyi says the optimal learning requires a state of consciousness known as "flow." This uninterrupted state in which one "loses oneself" in the performance is well known as a timeless, pleasure-producing absorption in the experience. Children, teenagers and athletes often get into this state more easily than adults.

Csikzentmihalyi defines this as a pattern of activity in which individual or group goals emerge (as opposed to being mandated) as a result of a pleasurable activity in interaction with the environment. When your skills, attention, environment and will are all matched up with the task, it's "flow." In other words, a situation where learners "go with the flow," enjoy themselves and increase their own challenges as they see fit. This philosophy allows learners to discover what standards they want to achieve as they incrementally improve and enjoy. Another benefit of this type of experience is that creativity and learning are maximized.

***The best learning state is in between boredom and anxiety -
a relaxed, happy concentration... not a forced one***

You can't just "will" yourself into flow. Millions have tried. There are some ways to make it more likely, though, such as starting with an easy task and upgrading the challenges until it's just right. Your performance anxiety can be reduced by switching your focus to a particular part of the task.

Let's say that you start out learning to play an instrument, speak a new language, ice skate, play golf, jog or use a computer. At first, it seems a bit difficult. You are making an effort. Then, in time, mysteriously, it seems that you are not only getting better, but you are having fun! Time passes without your awareness, skills improve and you seem to learn without struggling. It's the perfect combination of your personal skill level increasing at the same time that the challenge of the task seems to increase. It's the way a child in the snow, at the beach or at the lake can get engrossed in playing and lose all track of time, learning for hours. The graph on the next page brings this concept together.

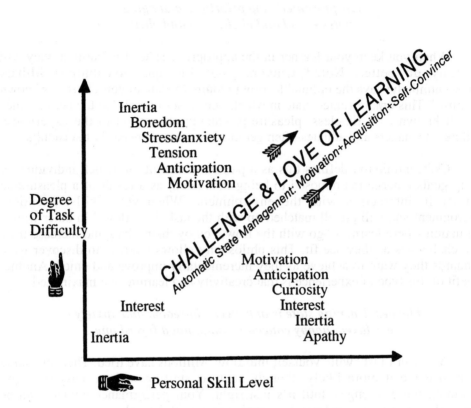

THE PERFECT LEARNING STATES

Studies done on task difficulty at the National Institute of Mental Health in Maryland showed greater brain activity when the tasks increased in complexity and difficulty. Even when the learners were unsuccessful on very challenging experiments, the brain continued to be actively engaged. You play much better in a game of tennis than your partner. You get bored and want to quit; but then a Wimbledon Champ invites you to play and you experience anxiety.

As an example, you get a new computer, open it up and start it. You begin to play around with it, getting used to it. Time passes, you keep learning new things. At a certain point, the phone rings or you realize it's dark outside. You discover you've been at it for almost three hours, but it felt like a half hour! That's being in a state of "flow."

> **What This Means To You:** Getting and keeping your participants in a state of "flow" may be one of the most important roles you have. In that state, learning is enjoyable and learners are highly internally motivated.

Mandated, step-by-step instruction can work well for the initial stage of learning. It can create focus, belief and motivation. But once beyond that stage, learners can be stifled by it. Assist your learners to get into the "flow" state by setting up favorable conditions for it. Set the challenge high, but keep stress low. Let the learners set the pace, then provide support to help them to continually improve and re-set goals. This is probably the same way you learned to ride a bike, use a computer, ski, swim, talk, use chopsticks or fix a household item.

The Magic Learning State

Csikszentmihalyi says that we can get into this "magical state" everyday. The formula is simple, he says. When "[C]hallenges that are greater than your skills, that's anxiety. When your skills exceed the challenges, that's boredom." But match up the challenge and skill levels, and whamo! Jackpot! You get the perfect learning state, or "flow." It is fairly easy to get learners into optimal learning states if you remember what gets *you* into that state. Have your learners design a complex project that is relevant to them, and then vary the resources to keep the task appropriate to their ability levels. Make it exciting, use teams, simulations, technology, and deadlines, but without too much pressure.

Researchers on brain states will give you differing viewpoints on the titles for those states. EEG (electroencephalogram) readings can measure brain activity for each identified category. The activity produces chemical reactions which produce electrical fields, each having a quantifiable CPS (cycles per second).

Delta	0-4Hz	deep sleep/no outer awareness
Theta	4-8Hz	twilight/light sleep/meditative
Alpha	8-12Hz	aware/relaxed/calm/attentive
Beta	12-16Hz	normal waking consciousness
High Beta	16-30Hz	intense outer-directed focus
K Complex	30-35Hz	the "Ah-ha!" experience
Super Beta	35-150Hz	extreme experiences psychic/out-of-body states

Which state is best for learning? It all depends on *what type* of learning and for how long. In general, the best learning is orchestrated from one state to the next, either by the presenter or the learner. Different states are better for different types of learning:

Delta is useless for any type of learning, as far as researchers know.
Theta is the state that we all go into and out of right before falling asleep and waking up. It can be great for sleeplearning (if you're auditory) and free association of creative ideas. It's passive and poor for direct instruction.
Alpha is great for listening and watching. More alertness, still fairly passive.
Beta is great for typical thinking, asking questions, problem-solving.
High Beta is ideal for intense states such as debates, drama & performance.
K Complex is difficult to orchestrate; you'll need to set up the circumstances for it and simply allow it happen on its own course.
Super Beta is such an intense state, it is highly inappropriate for schools, classrooms and formal education

Reading & Eliciting States Is
Your Key to Motivation

Since all motivation is dependent on the learner's state of the moment, it's critical to be able to read their states. Once you have done that, ask yourself if you like the states you are seeing. If so, continue. If not, you may want to change their states to a more useful one. You won't have an EEG to measure brainwave activity in a classroom. That's overkill. But you can make some simple observations about where each learner is at. Here are a few examples of common bodily reactions (states) and how you might read them.

What Learner's Feel:	What You Might See:
Fear	restricted breathing tightened muscles a closed body posture
Anticipation	eyes wide open body leans forward breath held
Curiosity	Hand to head facial expression head turned/tilted
Apathy	relaxed shoulders/posture slowed breathing no eye contact
Frustration	fidgeting/movement tightened muscles shortened breathing
Self-convinced	breathing shift body rocks/tilts/rolls

What can put learners into the optimal learning states? Hundreds of stimuli can do it - it depends on what's appropriate for the context you have. Some of the most commonly used strategies to change states are:

1. **Activities:** change from one to another, intensify, stretching, energizers, go from individual to group work, change locations and do role play.
2. **Environment:** change lighting, use aromas, music, ionizers, fresh air, change the temperature of the room, change seating, etc.
3. **Multi-media:** change to video, computers, overheads, music, slides, etc.
4. **People:** change presenters, have a guest speaker, learner teaches, switch rooms.
5. **Tone:** change theme, time allowed, goals, resources, rules, opinions.
6. **Focusing:** breathing exercises (inhale & exhale slowly, nostril breathing, use of visualization, key imagery).
7. **Student input:** learners get very motivated to learn when they have control over their learning, creative input, frequency of feedback, positive social bonding, good nutrition, proper learning styles and safety.

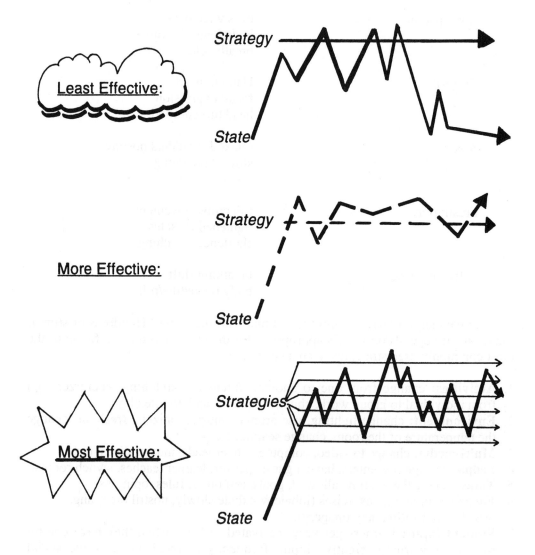

> **What This Means To You:** As a catalyst, an instructional leader, a priority goal is to manage states. You are always reading the states you see and comparing them to the target state. If there's dissonance, change the state of your learners. You can do that through a number of strategies. Use music, a change of activities, a shift in voice, a change in your location, a change in lighting, move participants to a new location or any other hundred or so possibilities.

How You Can Follow Up: *Flow: The Psychology of Optimal Experience,* by Csikzentmihalyi; or *Brain States,* by Kenyon. See Appendix for details.

Our Body Learns: Physiological States Hold Information

Stanford University psychologist Gordon Bower and Howard Erlichman of New York City University confirm that each mental, physical and emotional state "binds up" information within that particular state. In other words, states like anxiety, curiosity, depression, joy and confidence also trigger the particular information learned while in that state. It's almost as if you visit a library and check out a resource while in each state.

Bower says, "It is as though the two states constitute different libraries... a given memory record can be retrieved only by returning to that library, or physiological state, in which the event was first stored." Learners who hear a lecture while a certain baroque music composition is playing will test better if that same music is re-played at exam time.

Maguire confirms this "state-bound knowledge" brain research, also. How and where we learn is as important to the brain as what we learn. In experiments with color, location and movement, Kallman says the recency effects are enhanced by identifying the stimulus at the time of the state change. In other words, pause and take notice of the circumstances of your learning and it will trigger more easily later on.

Shields and Rovee-Collier have also documented the particular context to be critical to the memory of infants. Infants better remembered faces and sounds when they were triggered again by the same contextual (location) cues. You may have had the experience of hearing a favorite song. The melody or words triggers a memory of you being in a particular location, years ago, with your sweetheart. Each physiological state is a moment in time that locks together two elements: that state and the circumstances (sights, sounds, feelings, location, etc.)

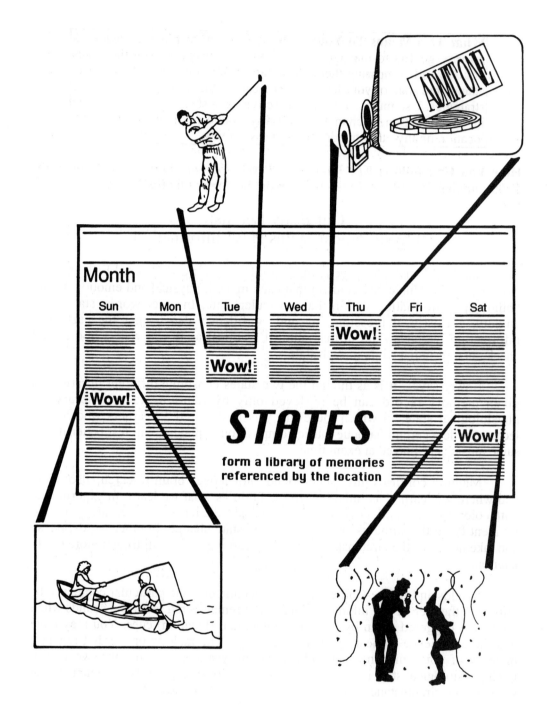

Studying and cramming for a final exam presents a problem. If your participants study in a hyped-up state with coffee to keep awake, that's a specific psychological state. The next day, while more relaxed and calm, they may forget much of that same information.

Or, let's say you're in one room of your house and decide to go get a book in another room. You walk three-quarters of the way there and you forget what you wanted to get. So what do you do? You walk back to the original room and stand in the same place, and let your brain remember what it was you were supposed to get. Then, confidently, you stride back to the other room and retrieve the appropriate book.

What This Means To You: There are hundreds, if not thousands, of inferences. Many learners may actually know the material they are being tested on, but may not demonstrate it well during exam time. If they study under low stress, then take an exam under high stress, their brain will not retrieve as much as if they study AND take the exam BOTH under moderate stress. Obviously, it's unlikely that an exam would be a low stress experience; studying that way is less useful.

The fact that information is "state-bound" also lends credibility to role plays, simulations and acting out learning. This may explain why the physical, concrete learning done when learners act out the learning better prepares them for the actual event. Pilots use simulators for training, the military creates mock war situations and theater groups do rehearsals. In formalized learning situations, an increase in the amount of role playing may increase the applications of the learning.

Role playing is most productive when the same physiological, emotional and mental states are rehearsed that would be needed for the real situation. Fire drills, safety and health emergencies may be best rehearsed under deadlines. Business and social role-plays may be best done with the same intensity as real-life. Learners may want to coordinate their study time, environment and state of mind with the exact time, place and state that may be present at the final exam.

How You Can Follow Up: Read *Brain States,* by Thomas Kenyon. See Appendix for details.

Helplessness Triggers Poor Learning States

Helplessness can devastate even the best learners. Giving the learner control over his environment, however, can definitely improve his attitude, according to Breier. There is evidence showing that giving learners control can boost their learning. And this effect happens whether the control is real or illusory. In an experiment on noise and control, two groups were put into a noisy room. The subjects used were in good mental health. One group had no control over the noise and the other had a placebo control knob that they thought gave them control over the loud noise. The subjects reported their moods before and after each 100 decibel session.

Neither group actually did have control over their environment, but one of them had the perception that it did. After the group who perceived no control ended their sessions, subjects reported increases in depression, anxiety, helplessness, stress and tension. After the other group's session ended, with exactly the same level of noise, they reported being affected very little.

For the moment, let's assume your learning environment is cold. But you give the learners control over monitoring the temperature. Their perception of having some control changes their attitudes about learning. On the other hand, if you ask a learner to complete an assignment, and he doesn't know how to do it, he experiences induced helplessness.

The state of helplessness is a common one for participants who do poorly in school. It's common for participants in schools where the administration or presenting staff is controlling, manipulative and coercive. Since the natural state of the brain is curiosity and motivation, schools and staff have to ask themselves hard questions such as, "What are we doing that makes learners feel powerlessness? In what ways might our behavior create helplessness and how can we change?"

What This Means To You: Participation and motivation are boosted by inclusion, ownership and control. They are impaired by autocratic insistence. Think of three aspects affecting your learners that they can control. For example, it could be temperature, sounds, teammates, the content of their work or the learning style. Rotate the emphasis, so that they get to control one factor at any given time. You'll find that participation and motivation goes up.

Chapter Questions

1. What was novel, fresh and new? What was familiar or "old hat"?
2. In what ways do you already apply the information in this chapter?
3. What three questions can you now generate about this material?
4. How did you react emotionally to this information?
5. In what ways can you translate the key three or four theories and discoveries presented here into practical everyday useful ideas?
6. How did you react cognitively when you were reading the ideas of this chapter?
7. If these things are, in fact, true about the brain, what should we do differently? What resources of time, people and money could be redirected? In what ways do you suggest we start?
8. What was the single one (or two) most interesting or valuable insights you had?
9. Plan your next step, the logical practical application of what you've learned.
10. What obstacles might you encounter? How can you realistically deal with them?

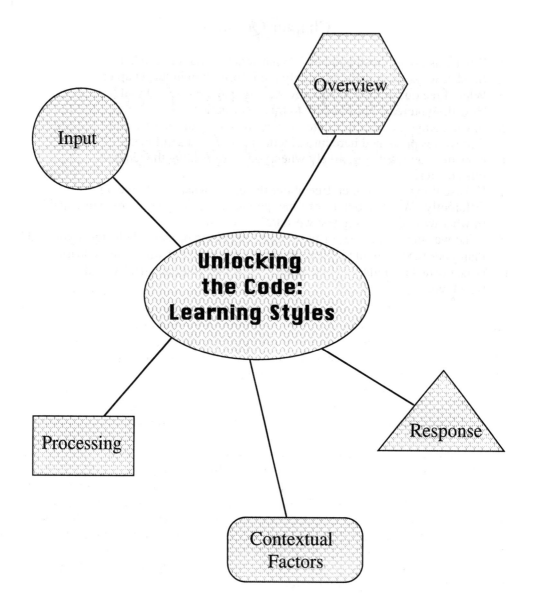

Input

Overview

Unlocking
the Code:
Learning Styles

Processing

Response

Contextual
Factors

9

Unlocking the Code: Learning Styles

A New Way of Thinking
About Learning Styles

There are countless studies which verify that learners have preferences for different kinds of input and learning experiences (Shipman and Shipman, Carbo, DeBello, Della Valle, Hodges, Shea, Virotsko, White, Kroon, Douglass and Trautman). Mayberry and Sinatra say we now know that *the way we learn* can affect the structure of the brain. For the moment, let's take learning styles out of the social and educational behavior category and assess it in terms of current neuroscience. After all, just because you can identify and measure a behavior, doesn't mean that the behavior is neurologically or biologically valid. In other words, the fact that we all seem to have favorite ways of learning (that we can name and teach to), does not make every learning style brain-based.

While there is a substantial body of research that defines and justifies the variety of ways to learn, what is the evidence from neuroscience about learning styles? Edelman says that activating different parts of the brain can automatically activate other parts of the brain. Restak says that, "The dynamic interplay of neural activity within *and in between systems* is the very essence of brain function." Pribram says that the brain has "holographic" tendencies and that many functions, including sensory input (read: learning styles) *work in parallel concert*. In short, the research on the brain does not validate that we are singularly processing input or learning with a single sensory input.

*The whole notion of learning styles
becomes irrelevant when we consider the
variety with which the brain works.*

129

For example, were you taught to present things in a logical, sequential order? That's the "kiss of death" for many learners. Why?

Seventy-five percent of presenters
are sequential, analytic presenters
that's how their lesson is organized...
Yet 100% of their participants
are multi-processors

Many studies have been done that the learning styles of certain participants will virtually guarantee school success and others will doom a learner to failure. Blackman reports that the learners who are field-independent and have a reflective, cognitive style are far more likely to succeed in a traditional school context. Start with a more global overview, and then go to the sequential style. In order to reach both global and sequential types of learners, one must use both approaches. While doing this, remember that the brain is multi-processing.

There are many learning style profiles available today. Each of them have their strong points. The reason that they are so different is that they are assessing different things. Like the story of the six blind men and the elephant, each has a different opinion of what they are holding. Some are assessing the input process, others the cognitive filters, others the processing and others the response styles. The learners below exemplify many different styles... to reach them all, do you try to always use every single learning style? No. *Simply provide variety and choice.*

The human brain does not just have a single "learning style." Humans are far more complex than that. Our brain is a complex multi-processor. To get a more accurate understanding of how we actually learn, it makes more sense to sub-divide the learning process into four appropriate categories comprising a more realistic, global learning choices profile. They are the following:

1. CONTEXT. The **circumstances surrounding the learning** provide important clues about what will happen during the learning. For example, are temperature, social conditions or relationships important? The learning style profile that does this best is Rita and Kenneth Dunn's Profile.

2. INPUT. All learners have to have some **input to initiate the learning.** But we only have five senses. The input is most likely either visual, auditory, kinesthetic, olfactory or gustatory. Although all two month-old babies are gustatory learners, less than 1% of all child, adolescent or adult learners use it as their dependent or preferred source. The same can be said for olfactory input (Dogs are great olfactory learners!). The input has to be either external (from an outside source) or internal (you create it yourself, in your own mind). Visual external would be you looking outward, visual internal would be you visualizing.

Samples says that we have many other senses including the vestibular (repetitious movement), magnetic (ferromagnetic orientation), ionic (electrostatic atmospheric charges), geogravimetric (sensing mass differences), proximal (physical closeness) and others. He suggests that infants may actually possess all of these senses. But early conditioning tells them which ones are "socially correct" or "culturally appropriate." Maybe in other societies, we would all be using different senses or a wider range of them. The model that is the most useful for this information is the Bandler-Grinder model.

3. PROCESSING. This is the function where the way you handle it and the actual **manipulation of the data** comes in. You can process globally or analytically, concrete or abstract, multi-task or single-task etc. This is the relative hemispheric dominance, either right or left side. There are several options when it comes to HOW you process the learning. The two models that do this well are the Ned Herrmann Brain Dominance model and the Gregorc/Butler model.

4. RESPONSE FILTERS. Once you have taken in the information, and processed it, you're likely **to do something** about it. But your mind's response filters will be your very first, nearly intuitive "reasoning" behind what you do. You'll react based on time, risk assessment, internal or external referencing. The models drawn from here are the partially 4-MAT and Meyers-Briggs.

Brain-Based Distinctions
in the Learning Process

Traditional	The "Hard to Reach"

Context for Learning

Traditional	The "Hard to Reach"
Field independent	Both field dependent & independent
Structured environment	Flexible environment
Independent	Independent and interdependent
Content driven	Learner driven

Input Preferences

Traditional	The "Hard to Reach"
Authority driven	Learner driven
Choice narrowed	Multi-sensory, multi-modal
Less A/K at higher levels	Visual, auditory & kinesthetic

Processing Format

Traditional	The "Hard to Reach"
Sequential	Global-sequential-global
Abstract	Concrete to abstract
Curriculum mandated	Learner-driven

Response Filters

Traditional	The "Hard to Reach"
Externally referenced	Both external & internal
Match	Both match & mismatch
Reflective	Both reflective & experimental
Curriculum driven	Learner driven

How Do We Learn?

Always In Context:
Field dependent
Field independent
Flexible environment
Structured environment
Interdependent
Independent
Dependent
Relationship driven
Content driven

With Input Preferences
Visual external.
Visual internal
Auditory external.
Auditory-internal
Kinesthetic-tactile
Kinesthetic-internal

By Processing It
Contextual-global
Sequential-detailed/linear
Conceptual (abstract)
Concrete (objects & feelings)

Then Reacting to It
Externally referenced
Internally referenced
Matcher
Mismatcher
Impulsive-experimental
Analytical reflective

Contextual Factors

Here are the variables you can offer for creating the circumstances of learning. You will want to provide all of these for maximum success. How? Rotate which ones are used each day and offer learners many more choices.

Field dependent... prefers contextual cues, learning presented in natural contexts like field trips, experiments, real life, a street learner, not artificial. Learns best in situations where the learning would naturally occur. Learns about science by going to museums, doing outdoor experiments, and field trips.

Field independent... learns in irrelevant contexts, uses computers, textbooks, audio tapes, books, classrooms, can learn in libraries and is comfortable with second-hand and third-hand learning.

Flexible environment... can learn well in a variety of different environmental conditions. The variables include: lighting (natural or fluorescent), sound, temperature and furniture design, the noise of others talking or music played, sitting in chairs or on the floor, standing or choice.

Structured environment... prefers a more structured environment. Has very particular needs for exactly how to learn with minimal tolerances for variations. Prefers learning with more certainty from rules, conformity & authority.

Independent... prefers to learn alone... possible to learn with others, but effectiveness is lessened.

Dependent... prefers to work with pairs, partners, groups and teams... can work alone but is less effective... works best in a busy, noisy talkative environment with others, where interpersonal relationships are valued.

Interdependent... likes being involved with other learners in helping them and works well alone. Their success is tied into the success of all.

Relationship driven... prefers to like the presenter... WHO delivers the information is more important than WHAT the information is. It means one must build a relationship of trust, credibility and respect BEFORE learning.

Content driven... prefers valuable content... it's MORE important than the source of the information. Even if the learner dislikes the presenter, learning will still go on, as scheduled.

Input Preferences

Visual external... prefers visual input, keeps eye contact with a presenter, posture is upright, creates mental pictures, talks fast in monotones, wants handouts, uses visual terminology like, "See what I mean?" A visual learner is usually a good speller, would rather read than be read to, enjoys writing, prefers neatness, is organized, chin is up, less distracted by noise. Do you get the picture? They have a "personal space" and don't like others standing too close. If asked, "Are you hungry?" They might check their watch to "see" if it's time for them to be hungry!

If we were to describe visual habits, we'd say they likely prefer colorful, thinner clothes. They love handouts, books, computers, overheads, art and photos. They buy a car based on its looks, not the feel. If you're in another room talking to them, they want to come into the room to see you as they talk. They are good at visualization and have trouble with verbal instructions.

Visual internal... prefers to "see it" in the mind's eye first. They want to visualize the learning before it's presented. They tend to daydream, imagine and let their mind make many mental pictures prior to more formal learning.

Auditory external... prefers input to be auditory, talks constantly, either to self or others, they are easily distracted, they memorize by steps and procedures, head bobs, eyes move to side, greater use of tempo, tonality, pitch and volume... answers rhetorical questions, wants test questions to be put in order learned, can mimic sounds of other's voices, they talk to themselves at night and before they get up in the morning, they often replay conversations in their head.

Math and writing is more difficult. They speak rhythmically, like class discussion, dislike spelling, like to read aloud, enjoy storytelling, remember what was discussed, often mimic tone, pitch, tempo and pace of the presenter. They like social occasions more than others and often are better at recalling jokes and conversations.

Auditory internal... prefers to talk to him or herself before learning about it. "What do I know? What do I think about it? What will this mean to me?" They often hold nearly endless conversations with themselves and have difficulty making up their minds. They are also very strong in metacognition.

Kinesthetic tactile... prefers physical input. They want to learn by doing. They're a "hands-on," try it first, jump in and give it a "go" type of learner. They have a commitment to activity or comfort, in touch with feelings, physical body, minimal facial expression and talking, measured words with pauses, slower breathing, likes

135

action novels, Can be very active, but area is often a mess where they are. Uses words like "This feels good" or "Let's get a handle on this." More likely to be a big eater. May like active events a lot. This learner is more likely to be relatively right hemisphere dominant. Proximity and personal attention has greater impact. This means learning by doing the task is more interesting than reading about it or hearing about it.

Kinesthetic internal... prefers inferential, intuitive, TV, stories and movies or those with a great deal of "heart" and feeling in them. Strong non-verbal communications valued (tonality, tempo, posture, expression, gestures). Greater emphasis on HOW something is said than on WHAT is said. It also means they need to have positive feelings about the task first. Kinesthetic internal learners are less verbally expressive, more physically expressive, less likely to be first to raise their hand in class (because they need to go "internal" to check out their answers before offering them).

Preferred input could also be kinesthetic internal (as opposed to external). That means the learner prefers to first experience feelings about something before learning about it or doing it. They want to experience them on their own, first. You can either feel your way into doing or act your way into feeling. These would be the former.

Processing Format

Contextual global... prefers the big picture, an overview first, key concepts only, relates with all pieces together, holistic, gestalt. This learner wants the relevance, the thematic vision & purpose first. More likely to prefer multi-tasking... means learner prefers to work on many problems and tasks at the same time... attend to one for a while, then switch to another, then back to the same or even another. More likely to be inferential and intuitive... infers meaning, uses kinesthetic internal cues to relate, prefers simple and quick approximation to measure, asks the question, "Why be so exact?" They often have a "feeling" for the information.

This learner is often referred to as a "right-brain" learner. A more visual right-brain dominance means a preference for processing in pictures, symbols, icons and themes. This learner has external focus tendencies, with a high degree of distractibility. That encourages the mistaken "at-risk" label; in truth, the learner simply needs to be reached with more multi-tasking, non-verbals, global overviews and stronger relationships in learning.

Sequential detailed/linear... prefers things sequenced, small steps at a time, do one thing, then asks "What's next?" Also wants a menu, formula, list of upcoming events, subject material. More likely to be a single task learner... prefers to stay focused on a single problem or task... can work on several tasks only if done in order. More likely to be analytical and word-based, measuring, analyzing, asking Qs, compares, contrasts, knows why and how, wants to fully understand something before doing or deciding on it. Words have specific meanings and the presenter will usually be held to what is said, word for word.

This learner is often referred to as left-hemisphere dominant. It means that they prefer the world of the written word, want clear, detailed instructions and want structured lessons. They tend to focus internally, meaning a lower level of distractibility. They are oriented for the long-term and prefer to know what's coming up each day, hour by hour. These learners excel in math, language, computers and other sequential work.

Conceptual (abstract)... prefers the world of books, words, computers, ideas, conversations, this learner enjoys talking or thinking but not much "doingness," very much "in the head." This learner often goes into more abstract professions such as writing, accounting, or becoming a college professor.

Concrete (objects & feelings)... prefers the world of the concrete: things that can be touched, jumped over, handled and manipulated. Also wants specific examples given, use of hands-on experiential, learns by doing an activity, wants to try things out, wants action, games and movement. This learner prefers to use their hands or body for work: dancer, sculptor, truck driver or actress.

Response Filters

Externally referenced... responds primarily based on what others think. The question often asked is "What are others expecting me to act like, think or say?" They use society's norms and rules for sources of their behavior. Before responding, they ask themselves questions on topics like etiquette and family values.

Internally referenced... responds using him or herself as the primary judge or source for behaviors. Their own set of rules may or may not be the same as those of society. Very independent because they themselves are the sole judge.

Matcher... responds by noting similarities, agrees more easily, likes consistencies, finds sameness in relationships, prefers things that belong, go together, make sense and enjoys consistency, habits. This learner will more likely approve of something that has been done before, that fits into an overall plan and that is generally consistent with the rest of the learning.

Mismatcher... responds by noting differences, what's off, missing, wrong or inconsistent. They say "But... why not?... or, what if?" They find flaws in the arguments, prefer variety and change; not negative, simply contrarian. More likely to sort incoming information by differences. Mismatchers tend to want to discover exceptions to the rule, find out what's missing, discover what's wrong, off or different. As a result, rules and laws are less potent and "testing" the rules is more common. Mismatchers are skeptical of words like "always, everyone, all, never and no one." Hence you'll hear more responses like, "Yes, but... " This learner wants more variety, enjoys experimenting and abhors traditional lesson plans, predictability and doing what everyone else is doing.

Impulsive experimental... responds with immediate action on thoughts, trial and error, experiential, the pattern is do it, then keep doing it until it is figured out. This learner is more likely to be present oriented.

Analytical reflective... responds internally, take in information, processes it reflectively, a pragmatist, stay at a distance, the classic passive, "stand back and watch" learner. More likely to be past or future referenced. Wants to reflect on the possibilities.

Each of the other parts of the Global Learner Choices™ are your variables for presenting and learning the way the brain is naturally inclined to learn. Using it as a model will provide valuable insight for both instruction and assessment.

Learning Styles: Preferences or Labels

In experiments by Torrance and Ball, learner learning styles were assessed, and then the participants were put through a course to expose them to other methods. Through exposure to right-hemisphere, non-linear learning strategies (imagery, intuition, brainstorming, metaphors, etc.), the learners were able to make more use of their existing capabilities and extend into new areas. The results also showed that the participants were able to "change their preferred styles of learning and thinking through brief but intensive training." All of us have altered our own learning style in cases where we simply had to in order to learn. While our dependent input would stay the same, we can be taught to utilize a greater variety of methods to input, process and respond.

Learners often change preferences for how information is presented to them based on the time of day. In a study by the University of Sussex in England, researchers found that detailed and literal learning was better in the morning, when performance was better on tests involving details and exact, precise information. In the afternoon, global learning improved, as did inferential and contextual material.

While you might use several styles, your preferred (or dependent) style will likely stay with you for most of your life. Why? It's the one that you learned to use for survival as an infant, so your brain always gives it first priority whenever survival is threatened later on in life, too.

Let's use this example: a fire breaks out in a room. Your immediate, first reaction will be one of the following: 1) visual (quickly size up the situation, looking for exits, others in need, etc.); 2) auditory (start yelling "Fire" or giving directions or screaming); or 3) kinesthetic (start running for the exits or grabbing others to help them out). While you may do all three, one will be an instinctual first reaction. That's your dominant, dependent input preference.

Learning preferences are age-dependent. As a baby, up to six months, all of us were gustatory. Then, as an toddler, ages 2-5, most of us became more kinesthetic. All preferences are learned early in life; researchers believe ages 2-5 seal in our dependent profile. As a young child, ages 5-9, most of us became more auditory. About 40% of learners develop into visual learners by secondary schools. Those learners that remained kinesthetic often fell behind in instruction or became a behavior problem. Those are often labeled as "developmentally delayed" or hyperactive. More often than not, their brain is NOT delayed. It's just fine, there is simply a great range of what is normal for development.

All learning styles are culturally reinforced. While this does not guarantee that anyone in that culture will have those same characteristics, it does speak to the bulk of the bell-shaped curve. In other words, the majority will have that learning style. Women are more likely to be auditory than men. So are Southern Europeans. Northern Asians are more likely to be matchers, as are Midwesterners. Research suggests Native Americans are strongly right-hemisphere dominant as are a high percentage of blacks. A higher percentage of Hispanics are kinesthetic, rural learners tend to be more field dependent. Israelis and Australians have a higher-than-usual percentage of mismatchers. Northern Europeans and Asians are more likely to prefer visual learning. These are merely generalizations and you will want to deal with each learner on an individual basis only. The book *SuperTeaching* can provide you with much more information on cultural differences in learning.

> **What This Means To You:** Many learners who seem apathetic would be very enthusiastic if the learning was offered in their preferred style. There are many ways to learn, so provide continual variety and expose them to many other styles so that they may become flexible learners. Create options for your learners so that they can learn in the style of their first choice.

We know that each different learning style uses a different sequence and different area of the brain. But does that justify assessing, grouping and organizing lessons around an individual's learning style? No.

In brain-based learning, we recognize the
brain as a multi-path parallel processor.
Many senses and sensory patterns are being
processed simultaneously.

Many presenters and trainers have delighted in identifying their learners with one profile after another. It's as if the grouping of the learner will solve the learning. It won't. The keys to a successful brain-based learning styles approach are simple: offer both variety in what you do so that the learner is exposed to many styles (this book is rich with examples), *and* offer choice (the learner will pick the one he or she is most comfortable with using.

Unless there is damage to the brain,
you cannot have biologically-based
learning style. Most of the brain
is involved in every act of learning

In short, it's useful to know about learning styles. They can provide you with a smarter, more streamlined approach when dealing one-on-one. In a larger group setting, offer learning with variety and offer choice. It will save you a lot of stress trying to constantly figure out, "Who is what kind of learner?" Plus, the learners will learn to be more responsible to learn in the way that they learn best.

How You Can Follow Up: Books: *SuperTeaching* by Jensen, *Righting the Educational Conveyor Belt*, by Michael Grinder; *Teaching and Learning Styles*, by Katherine Butler; *The 4-Mat System*, by Bernice McCarthy; *The Creative Brain*, by Ned Herrmann. For *Cultural Differences in Learning Styles*, See Appendix for details.

Chapter Questions

1. What was novel, fresh and new? What was familiar or "old hat"?
2. In what ways do you already apply the information in this chapter?
3. What three questions can you now generate about this material?
4. How did you react emotionally to this information?
5. In what ways can you translate the key three or four theories and discoveries presented here into practical everyday useful ideas?
6. How did you react cognitively when you were reading the ideas of this chapter?
7. If these things are, in fact, true about the brain, what should we do differently? What resources of time, people and money could be redirected? In what ways do you suggest we start?
8. What was the single one (or two) most interesting or valuable insights you had?
9. Plan your next step, the logical practical application of what you've learned.
10. What obstacles might you encounter? How can you realistically deal with them?

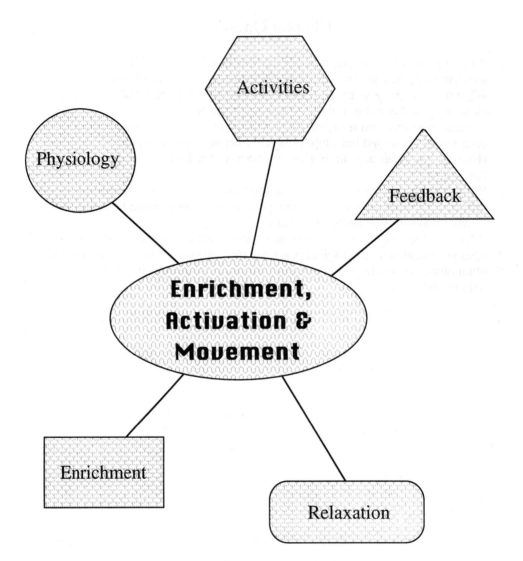

10

Enrichment, Activation & Movement

Enriched Environments Build Better Brains

In groundbreaking research by UC Berkeley pioneer Dr. Marion Diamond and, separately, by University of Illinois researcher William Greenough, an amazing plasticity to the brain was discovered. The brain can literally grow new connections with stimulation, even as you age. The fact that we can "grow brain," means nearly any learner can increase their intelligence, without limits, using proper enrichment. This discovery was first done on rats, then the findings were extended in human studies. Calvin says cortical area growth does have something to do with "being smart," although the internal efficiency of your "wiring" and connections make a larger difference.

Many types of rat groups were studied in various conditions. They divided the experiment into three groups: control groups, those in impoverished environments and those in enriched environments. Time and time again, for over 30 years of varied experiments, the rats in enriched environments grew better brains. Greenough found that he could increase the number of connections in animal brains by 25% by exposing them to an enriched environment. Dr. Diamond summarizes the data:

"[W]ith increasing amounts of environmental enrichment, we see brains that are larger and heavier, with increased dendritic branching. That means those nerve cells can communicate better with each other. With the enriched environment we also get more support cells because the nerve cells are getting bigger. Not only that, but the junction between the cells - the synapse - also increases its dimensions. These are highly significant effects of differential experience."

Most importantly, the research of UCLA
neuroscientist Bob Jacobs confirms
that this research on brain enrichment
translates directly to human brains

He found that in autopsy studies on graduate participants, there were up to 40% more connections than with high school dropouts. The group of graduate participants who were involved in challenging activities, showed over 25% more overall "brain growth" than the control group. Yet education alone was not enough. Frequent new learning experiences and challenges were critical to brain growth. The brain of graduate participants who were "coasting" through school had fewer connections than those who challenged themselves daily. Jacob's research on cortical dendrite systems in 20 neurologically normal right-handed humans (half male and half female) evaluated:

- total dendritic length
- mean dendritic length
- dendritic segment count
- proximal vs. ontogenetically later developing distal branching

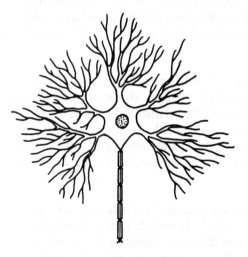 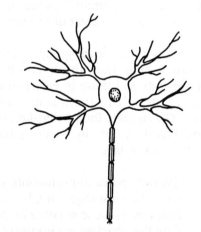

Extensive dendritic branching
from active, challenged minds

Brain in deficient environment
shows sparse dendritic branching

144

These variables have been known to relate to the complexity of the brain, the ability to solve problems, and overall intelligence. Jacobs' measurements investigated several independent variables: gender, hemisphere and education. The results of his research uncovered the following:

Gender: Females had greater dendritic values and variability than males.
Hemisphere: Left hemisphere had greater overall dendritic measurements than right, but the results were not consistent with each individual.
Education: Level of education had a "consistent and substantial effect" on dendritic branching: the higher the level, the greater the measurements.

Challenges must engender learning, not just exercise. The work of Greenough and Black confirmed this. They used complex environments to grow better brains. When Black isolated other factors, such as aging and stress, from complex environments, he affirmed that it was the learning, not simply the motor activity, that caused the optimal brain growth.

Why Novelty is Critical
To Brain Enrichment

Dr. Arnold Scheibel, director of the brain research Institute at UCLA says, "Unfamiliar activities are the brain's best friend." The fact that the brain is so stimulated by novelty may be a survival response; anything new may be threatening the status quo (potential danger). Once we have grown accustomed to an environment or situation, it then becomes routine. Over time, the reticular formation operates at progressively lower levels and the brain gets less and less stimulation. Do something new, and once again, the reticular formation is alerted. This starts the brain growth; more messages are carried by nerve cells and novelty encourages more dendritic branching. That branching triggers new connections, called synapses. It's as if you can almost "grow" your brain at will.

The most astonishing research may have come from Wallace et al. They discovered that *in just four days, there are significant "structural modifications"* in the dendritic fields of cortical neurons. The measurements were made in the visual cortex and were done on dendritic length and total number of branches. Sirevaag and Greenough found that brain enrichment happens in stages, from surface level to depth growth. The research draws three important conclusions:

1) Rats in enriched environments actually grow heavier brains, with more dendritic connections that communicate better. They also show increased synapses, greater thickness in sensory areas, increases in enzymes and more glial cells (the ones that assist in growth and signal transmission).

145

2) Enriched environments need to be varied and changed often (every 2-4 weeks) to maintain the positive differences in rat intelligence. This meant other rats, more toys and frequent challenges (same for humans, too).

3) Rats of any age could increase their intelligence if they were provided challenging and frequent new learning experiences.

4) The real world, outside of the cages (even the enriched ones) provided one of the best environments for brain growth .

For growing a better brain, provide frequent challenges, continual novelty and dramatic feedback

In working with children, Craig Ramey at the University of Alabama found that he could increase intelligence with mental stimulation. Ramey's intervention program worked with children of low IQ parents who were divided into two groups. The children who were exposed to the enriched environment had significantly higher IQs than the control group. They were, in fact, 20 points higher. And the stronger results lasted; when the children were retested after 10 years, the effects of early intervention had endured. That's quite an endorsement of active, challenging learning environments.

Have you ever noticed that when learners talk with motivation, passion and meaning, many times it's about the real-world experiences they have had – much more so than the "book learning" they get. That's why the best educators promote variety. It can include the use of field trips, varied work environments, home environments, the park, on-the-job training, the zoo, a convention, a rally, a vacation or *anything rich and varied* that would naturally occur in life.

> **What This Means To You:** Reduce "contrived" learning. Get your learners into the real world for as much as possible. Create a more multi-sensory environment. Add posters, aromas, music and more engaging and relevant activities. Increase social interaction. Use different rooms and, if possible, larger rooms, too. Change the environment often (something minor daily, something major every 2-4 weeks) to create novelty and challenge.
>
> Encourage participants to explore and create new things. Give them quality, trusted adult time for learning and practicing critical skills like categorizing, counting, labeling, language, cause and effect, and thinking. Give plenty of positive feedback and fun celebrations with each accomplishment. Provide a rich use of several languages in a variety of contexts. Reduce all forms of severe negative experiences and disapproval. And most of all, find ways to get your participants outside the classroom as often as possible!

Exercise & Activities
Boost Learning

Aerobic exercise can improve thinking and learning, says Dienstbier. His research confirms that "physical exercise alone seems to train a quick adrenaline-nonadrenaline response and rapid recovery." This adrenal response is critical to facing and coping with challenges. Wlodlowski recommends "energizers" to increase circulation, attentiveness and interest. In one study, researchers found that those who exercised regularly were "far better" at remembering than their peers who did not exercise. Aerobic exercise improved mental functioning by increasing oxygen flow to the brain. Dr. Hermann suggests that even a brisk 20 minute walk can be enough to serve both the body and the mind. "The main thing is to get out and move your body around," he said.

In another study, Dustman, a Utah psychologist, divided groups into three categories: vigorous aerobic exercisers, moderate non aerobic exercisers, and those who did no exercise at all. The results were clear cut: "The aerobic exercisers showed an improvement in short-term memory, had faster reaction times and were more creative than the non aerobic exercisers."

A study done by Dr. Kushner at Scripps College in California also divided groups into the same three categories. Each had various levels of exercise or none at all. Then the researchers spent three hours testing memory, reasoning and reaction time. The results were that "[t]he exercisers scored significantly higher on working-memory tests, reasoning and reaction time." Increased blood flow to the brain does help you to think better and be smarter.

Stimulation of the Body
Can Stimulate the Mind

Many researchers have verified the plasticity of the brain and the positive effects of tactile stimulation including Kosmarskaya, Kanter, Bennett, Clark, Rosenzweig and Wilson. The work of Dr. Jean Houston confirmed that stimulation of the whole or parts of the parts of the body can stimulate the brain. Later, Kandel and Hawkins reported on the effects of digital manipulation on the brain. Using an owl monkey, researchers set up a study. The brain areas that related to the digits were measured and recorded. The monkey worked manipulatives for an hour a day for three months. By having the monkey use certain digits, they were able to measure the contrasting effects with those digits *not* used for manipulation. After 90 days, the area of the brain representing the stimulated fingers in the brain had increased (in size and connections) substantially.

As an example, concert pianists are often highly articulate and are able to stay sharp well into old age. The constant playing and manipulation of the fingers seems to stimulate the mind as much as the hands. Elderly who play cards, chess, shuffleboard, golf or swim all have a greater chance of staying sharp than those who only do gross motor activities such as walking. Learning does, indeed, grow a better brain in humans. And while our life's goal may not be to grow a better brain, we need better thinking and problem-solving skills in today's world.

French researcher and neuroepidemiologist Jean-Francois Dartigues says that non-intellectual are more likely to face senility later in life. Apparently, if you don't want to lose your marbles, you'd better use them throughout your life. Dartigues did a study of 3,700 people over the age of 65 in which he correlated their intellectual functioning with their former occupations. Then he adjusted for variables such as age, sex and even environmental and toxic risks. He found that the subjects who performed best on the tests were not those with the greatest formal education, but those who had the most intellectually demanding careers.

In Dartigues' study, after retiring, former farm workers were *over six times more likely to become mentally impaired* than those who were in more intellectual occupations, such as presenters, trainers, executives, managers and other white collar professionals. But for farm managers, whose job forced more challenging thinking, the rate is only 2.9 times that of intellectual occupations.

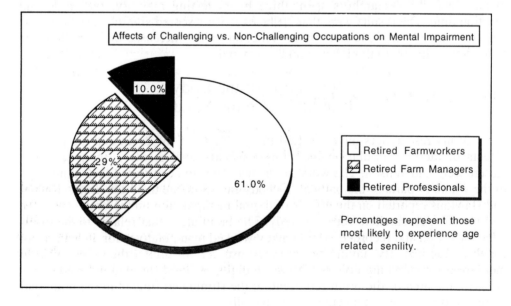

Affects of Challenging vs. Non-Challenging Occupations on Mental Impairment

10.0%

29%

61.0%

☐ Retired Farmworkers
▨ Retired Farm Managers
■ Retired Professionals

Percentages represent those most likely to experience age related senility.

Never assume that your learners will get sufficient exercise elsewhere. At the very least, encourage physical activity for your learners away from the classroom and in class, a few moments of stretching or deep breathing. Although it's not officially part of the curriculum or your lesson plan, giving your learners exercise and movement can be very productive.

While primary school presenters have been doing this for years, now it's more obvious why it works. Secondary and upper level staff may want to start using these "brain-compatible" strategies. Three easy enrichment areas are: 1) positive, engaging, social contact (use of partners, teams, cooperative projects), and 2) high-challenge, low-stress novelty exercises (continual variations of learner-generated experiences) and 3) real-life experiences in novel situations (travel, cultural events, etc.).

What This Means To You: Use more: 1) slow stretching and breathing to increase circulation and oxygen flow to the brain 2) Use energizers every 20 minutes 3) Make sure that some of your planned activities have a built-in component of physical movement (going outside to do a project, working on jigsaw puzzles, etc.) 4) The hand manipulatives are useful for the brain, let participants hold, mold, and manipulate clay or other objects. This could actually stimulate the brain! Give your participants permission to get up on their own to move around, stretch or do an errand, so that they can monitor and manage their own energy levels 5) Have your participants move, manipulate and exercise their hands each day. Use clapping, dancing, puzzles, manipulatives. Invent new ways to shake hands or greet another.

How You Can Follow Up: Read *Enriching Heredity,* by Diamond.

Physiology and Learner Posture
Known To Affect Thinking

Presenters have long known that posture affects the learner. A contracted, slumped over learner will learn less than an alert one in an upright posture. But how much does learner physiology affect the learning? A great deal, it turns out. The human body, as represented in the brain, says Damasio, is the indispensable frame of reference for the neural processes we call thinking. It is, in fact, the one grounding reference point of reality for our ability to make sense of the world.

When it comes to posture, many of the learners who are having difficulty are sitting in slumped-over postures, getting insufficient oxygen and blood flow. At test time, allow participants to move their chairs away from other participants. Then let their eyes rove around. Provide leadership by conducting "stand and stretch" breaks every 20 minutes. Offer stretching, "Simon says" or movement activities. Keep your learners alert with movement, stretching and water breaks.

Dr. Max Vercruyssen of the University of Southern California discovered how your body's posture affects learning. His research showed that, on the average, standing increased heartbeats by 10 extra times per minute. That sends more blood to the brain, which activates the central nervous system to increase neural firing. Psychologically, he says, standing up creates more attentional arousal and the brain learns more. "Standing speeds up information processing 5-20% compared to sitting down," he says. Even changing posture can assist in increasing blood flow and oxygen. Overall, there's a 10-15% increase in blood flow (and oxygen) to the brain while standing up (versus sitting down). While sitting, you are more likely to get bored and lose focus. But while standing and listening to another, your focus is stronger.

Students who are standing may
be much more alert and ready to learn
than those in a poor sitting posture

Researchers at a Florida University have found that dolphins (oxygen breathing mammals) exchange nearly 90% of their lung's capacity each time they surface. That means most all of the "stale" air is exhaled and replaced with fresh oxygen. That may not seem like a great deal until you compare it with humans. In one study, it was found that classroom learners exchange between 10% and 25% of their lung's capacity with each breath taken. The human brain, which thrives on oxygen, is often starved for it!

What This Means To You: We are wasting learning time by having participants sit too much. When the group energy seems to lag, ask your learners to stand up. Then you can either continue to talk for 1-3 minutes while they stand, or give them a diffusion activity, an energizer, or ask them to start a relevant discussion with a partner.

150

How Relaxation Affects Learning

Researchers at the Stanford University School of Medicine did a study on 39 men and women. Members of one group were taught to relax every muscle in their body, from head to toe. The other group was simply given a lecture on positive attitudes. Then, each group attended a 3-hour memory training course. The researchers then tested the two groups. The group that had consciously practiced relaxation before the test scored 25% better than the other group.

According to Gelb, threats (even a simple verbal remark) affect our physiology. And this change of posture affects motivation, learning and attitudes. The reptilian portion of our brain is designed to respond quickly to threats. But threats can be so subtle that only the non-conscious mind reacts. Here's an example:

"I'll just stand here and wait until YOU
decide you're ready to learn!"

This is one of many common threats given by unknowing presenters. This same presenter would swear that she NEVER threatens her participants. Yet, that's a thinly disguised threat: "I'll withhold my wisdom, the class and test information UNTIL you behave the way I want you to behave." Threats like these affect the learner on a continuous basis, impairing learning and reducing the presenter-learner relationship to that of parent-child or master-servant.

Gelb says the work of Alexander has shown him a person's posture reflects a lifetime of threats and learning fears which are constantly re-activated and stimulated in a stressful learning environment. A slumped-over learner breathes poorly, often constricting circulation. A learner with bad posture can create new tensions and cause the body to compensate laterally with another equally poor posture. With any threat, the body stiffens up and the "fright" posture is re-triggered. Learning potential again decreases.

Let's say your participants are worried about an upcoming test or some tension around the school or at work. They underperform. Maybe it's you that is tense, stressed and uptight. You rush off to a meeting or a class in a state of stress. Your performance is a bit below your usual high standards.

> **What This Means To You:** Reduce or eliminate threats. Physical relaxation may be more important to learning than just having the will to learn. Teach your participants about the benefits of relaxation. Even better, make it part of the daily routine.

The Contributions of James Asher

To millions of presenters around the world who are pleading with participants to please sit down and be quiet, Asher is a rebel. He's the developer of TPR (Total Physical Response) and was a pioneer in second language learning. Asher's hypothesis is "teach the body - it learns as well as the mind." He maintains that learning on an immediate, physical, and gut-level, speeds acquisition dramatically. His approach requires the following conditions to be successful:

- Presenter creates strong positive rapport & relationship with participants
- Learning climate is cooperative, playful, active and fun
- Presenter has developed respect from participants
- Students listen to presenter's statements/commands
- Students respond rapidly without analyzing

The instructions are in the imperative form, telling the learners to follow along, but not in an authoritative way. It's more of a "strong invitation, one you can't refuse." Asher might be presenting Spanish and he simply stands up, and says the word in Spanish. Then he points to a chair, and says the word for it (they point), he says walk, and starts walking (and the participants follow). It's all very simple, much like what a parent might do when presenting an infant. This approach can be used in many types of subjects and classes. Use TPR to learn vocabulary, to role play new behaviors, learn cultural geography, language, collaborative skills and teamwork.

Role-Playing & Game Shows Enhance Meaning

Making learning physical is "old hat" to most primary presenters. And the whole idea of taking academic learning and embedding it within creative expression or entertainment is also centuries old. But does the method of re-contextualizing the learning really work? Does brain-based learning research support this type of learning? Yes, according to Bandura, Brophy, Malone and Leper, Bergin, and Csikszentmihalyi.

It allows the brain to make complex perceptual maps. It has a high likelihood of engaging emotions. Being physical is much more naturally engaging, motivating and likely to keep the learning going. The stress and threat to learn is usually low, which helps creativity. Since knowledge is "state bound," what is learned *during* a role-play may be accessible during that same situation later on.

Most important to participants is the fact that in these contexts, learning becomes more enjoyable, learners exercise more choice and creativity, and there is minimal negative, evaluative pressure. There is little time for negative inner thoughts as long as all are kept busy in the planning, production, rehearsal and marketing of a play. It would be interesting to find out how many people have learned history through a Jeopardy game show format.

Another positive reason is that these creative presentations afford the opportunity for participants to reach multiple goals (social, artistic, emotional, academic, etc.). A learner might think, "I don't care about the content of the play, but I like hanging around that person, so I'll do it."

> **What This Means To You:** Primary school participants learn much more than they can consciously know when they work together to put on a school play. Many presenters and professors think that active, physical response learning and role-plays are, well, elementary. Brain research says otherwise. Activate the brain through presentations, skits, mock debates, "Jeopardy" shows, and humorous treatments of commercials. Include creative and/or entertaining activities as a regular part of the learning process. Ideas include re-doing a popular commercial, presenting a debate, or role playing.

How You Can Follow Up: *99 Energizing Activities,* a practical booklet for presenters and trainers. See catalog on Appendix for details.

Active Multiple Roles
Can Enhance Learning

Research by Cohen at Stanford University, Pintrich and Garcia suggests that taking on many roles enhances learning. The optimal environment is one in which learners are at different times; partners, teammates, individuals, and presenters. This diversity of roles provides for greater contextual, real-life immersion learning, and better ensures that the learning is integrated as real-world learning should be. By designing the learning so that there are many roles and status levels to fill, instructors can insure that all learners will be able to find at least one contextually suitable activity that they can strongly invest in.

A learner who thinks of himself as smart outside the classroom might find himself getting average or below average grades. He becomes frustrated by his lack of status, his self-image suffers, and he wants to drop out of school. Lozanov advocates alter-egos as the solution to low learner self-concept in specific subjects. In language classes, his participants assumed another name, occupation (with full character) from the first day. The advantage was that this character could then take risks, make mistakes and have fun in a way that they (their other real character) could never do. While this method takes careful, thoughtful and creative planning to get the full benefit, Lozanov claimed his participants could learn *hundreds* of new words in a single day.

> **What This Means To You:** You may have many very smart learners, but in the absence of favorable circumstances, these learners may not be readily apparent. All of us are gifted; the context provides the evidence. There are many ways to utilize multiple status roles. Change the learner's status through the use of teams, alter-egos, peer tutoring, study buddies, multi-age projects, and multi-grade projects. Involvement in the community or with co-workers, learner-presenter partnerships and projects are other approaches. Involve siblings, too.

Why Introduce Wide-Ranging Activities

The research from genetics, biology and neuroscience tells us that there's a powerful rule from mother nature: *no intelligence or ability will blossom until it's given the appropriate environmental "need" or model for developing.* Further, Pearce adds, "We are born into a world like a garden that has been sown, but the seeds must be nurtured and nourished..." In short, the greater the variety of activities offered to your learners, the greater the chance of learning.

This provides dramatic impetus for using Gardner's multiple intelligences in the learning process. It reminds us about the value of providing second and third languages before age 12, when the brain loses some of its language-learning capacity. It also gives much greater validation to novel, activity-based learning.

Which is Best: Competitive Or Cooperative Learning?

The answer to the headline above is that both have their place. The world is highly competitive and it's important to know how to compete. At the same time, the brain learns poorly under the negative stress caused by excess anxiety and fear of loss. But what's fearful to one can be good, clean fun to another. We are all stressed by different things, so generalizations are difficult.

In the last several years, there's been a deluge of research about the advantages and disadvantages of competition in the classroom. Kohn argues strongly in his book, *No Contest: The Case Against Competition,* that competition has vastly undermined educational and business systems. Ames argues that the typical competitive learning environment is strongly detrimental to the learner. He summarizes:

> *"[T]here is little, if any, viable evidence that*
> *a competitive goal structure in the classroom*
> *is associated with outcomes that are indicative of*
> *positive self-worth, continuing motivation,*
> *or quality of task engagement"*

So, does the cooperative learning model fit for everyone? Among the pioneers of cooperative learning, Slavin and Johnson et al. found that when positive cooperative structures were in place, *some inter-group competition could exist without reducing motivation.* In fact, the more you use cooperative groups and individual learning contexts, the competition can work. Only in balance can it provide legitimate learning opportunities. Yet so many schools use only the competitive model.

The grading system of a "curve" is a competitive model. The system is a win-lose. In order for someone to win, another must lose. The model compares one learner with another. What in the world does one student's evaluation and assessment have to do with another's? Either you have a certain level of understanding and mastery in that area or you don't.

How You Can Follow Up: Order *TeamWork,* by Alyce Cornyn-Selby, *The New Circles of Learning: Cooperation in the Classroom and School,* by Johnson, Johnson and Holubec.

Feedback Spurs Fastest Learning

While enriched environments and both mental and physical activity are important, something else is equally critical. Research by noted brain expert Santiago Ramon y Cajal has emphasized that the brain needs feedback from its own activities for best learning and growth.

> *The absolute best feedback is*
> *immediate, positive and dramatic*

Other researchers such as Moore, Anderson and Wenger have verified that one of the best ways to boost thinking and intelligence is by describing your own perceptions and recording your own observations onto audio tape or CD. This examination of one's own thinking, sensing and organizing language provides a powerful vehicle for the brain's development as a problem-solver and thinker.

Since different areas of the brain process different activities, the question is: what does one area of the brain do with the activity once it processes it? If it does nothing with it, some of the potential is lost. Intelligence is often the ability to bring together many diverse bits of information to create new thinking, to maximize potential and provoke solutions. The brain needs a large number of circuits and connections to make the best possible decisions. These are called "phase relationships" because they tie together simultaneous stimuli. By providing more consistent feedback, better quality feedback and tying it all together, the brain integrates the information into higher quality relationships and patterns.

To do this, it takes a strategy known as "pole-bridging." This word, coined by Wenger, describes the way the brain connects information and processes both the front and back and the left and right side of the brain. To "pole-bridge," simply talk about what you do while you do it. While you *can* write it down later in a journal, the best results have come from recording it "in the moment." By talking deliberately, perceptively and purposely, you'll find that the learning and thinking go up dramatically. Studies collected by Wenger have documented gains from one to three I.Q. points *per hour* of "pole-bridging" practice. Some have increased intelligence up to 40 points in 50 hours of work.

Most "great" thinkers of history like Leonardo Da Vinci have kept elaborate journals of their work. That was their self-feedback. As a child, you had plenty of environmental stimulation, but you also got the all-important feedback. When you first learned to ride a bike, you experienced immediate and conclusive feedback: either you stayed up or fell down. Imagine trying to learn to ride a bike *without knowing how you're doing until a month later.* You'd go nuts, and still be trying to learn how to ride the bike!

What This Means To You: We may impede and retard thinking, intelligence and brain growth, and ultimately create "slow learners," by the lack of feedback and the large lag time built into the typical learning environment.

Here are ways to increase the frequency and value of feedback. 1) Greet them at the door. 2) Comment about the previous learning. 3) Allow them to peer-teach reviews daily or weekly. 4) Have them talk themselves through their thinking. 5) Learners keep score charts for their team and post the results. 6) Encourage the use of a journal. 7) Have them make up and take "mock tests" that don't count. 8) Have them pair up with other learners and prep for a test. 9) They correct their own homework, quizzes, tests. 10) Learners present to the group and get oral or written feedback.

How You Can Follow Up: Best contact person for individualized intelligence growth through "image streaming and pole-bridging" is Win Wenger. For more information on these techniques, call (301) 948-1122 or write to him at: Project Renaissance at Box 332, Gaithersburg, MD, 20884-0332.

Chapter Questions

1. What was novel, fresh and new? What was familiar or "old hat"?
2. In what ways do you already apply the information in this chapter?
3. What three questions can you now generate about this material?
4. How did you react emotionally to this information?
5. In what ways can you translate the key three or four theories and discoveries presented here into practical everyday useful ideas?
6. How did you react cognitively when you were reading the ideas of this chapter?
7. If these things are, in fact, true about the brain, what should we do differently? What resources of time, people and money could be redirected? In what ways do you suggest we start?
8. What was the single one (or two) most interesting or valuable insights you had?
9. Plan your next step, the logical practical application of what you've learned.
10. What obstacles might you encounter? How can you realistically deal with them?

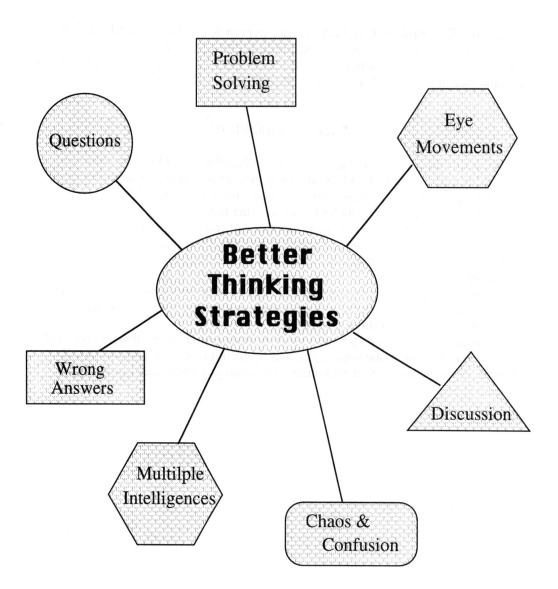

158

11
Better Thinking Strategies

Thinking Processes Are
Brain's Representations

How does our brain think? When you or I say "I am thinking," what we are really saying is, "I'm trying to manipulate internal symbols in a meaningful way." Thinking is composed of accessing prior or creating new modal representations. All representations fall into these categories:

1. Visual. These include pictures, symbols, words or "internal movies."
2. Sounds. This includes voices, music, nature or technology.
3. Feelings. How you feel about something is part of the thinking and decision-making process; feelings are just as cognitive as any other sense.
4. Others: It's certainly possible to think using other senses. Since they comprise such a small percentage of our thinking, we'll set them aside for the moment.

As we learned earlier, our mind, body and feelings are all an integral part of learning and processing. There is no separation. As a result of this, it will come as no surprise that *how* you are thinking can often be discerned by observations of our body. When we are tense or happy, we can say nothing and another can pick up all the needed clues. And, just like our body, our eyes provide some of the best thinking clues.

How Eye Movements Provide
Clues To Learning & Thinking

Our brain is designed so that our thinking style can often be determined by particular shifts in eye movements. Where your eyes are positioned actually better enables the brain to access certain senses. There are seven basic eye movements that related to thinking. These are useful for 90% of right-handed learners, and reversed for many (but not all) left-handers.

The best way to determine the particular eye (and thinking) pattern for a learner is to observe that person in a "real-life" no stress situation. Controlled, laboratory testing has yielded inconsistent results (Trevarthen, Galin & Ornstein, Rosenberg). But the relationship between eye movements and cognitive functioning has been well documented. Cognitive activity occurring in one hemisphere *does* trigger eye movements in the opposite hemisphere. In other words, take each learner individually, the information below is a useful generalization, but each learner is unique.

1. Visual thinking of stored picture memories. Looking up and to the left allows you to access stored pictures (visual recall). Questions you can use to verify: "What car was parked next to yours in the parking lot? Describe your bedroom. Walk me through the clothes in your closet. "

2. Visual thinking of created new pictures. Looking up and to the right is where your eyes usually go to create new images. Questions you can use to verify: "How would you look with a radically different haircut? What would you do to rearrange your living room? What would a dog look like with a cat's legs?"

3. Auditory thinking, recalling sounds. Eyes go to the left; that's the usual way we accesses stored sounds (what was said or heard). Questions you can use to verify: "What did the other person say, right at the end, of your last phone conversation? What's the 9th word of the 'Happy Birthday' song? When you were a kid, how did your mother call you when she was mad at you?"

4. Auditory thinking, creating new sounds. Eyes go off to the right, creating new sounds. Questions you can use to verify: "How would a dog sound if it has a voice like a pig? What sound do you get if you heard a siren and a rooster at the same time?"

5. Internal dialogue (talking to yourself). Eye direction most common is looking down and to the left. When you see another walking down the street talking to him or herself, notice where their eyes are.

6. Experiencing feelings. This is down and to the right. If you know another person failed to complete a task, you can ask them, "Did you complete the task?" In many cases, before answering, their eyes will go down (meaning "I feel badly about it"), then go back up to continue the conversation.

7. Digital; for memorized information. Eyes will go straight ahead for this interaction. You are asked, "How are you?" Your polite answer is, "Fine, thank you." You probably kept your eyes straight ahead the whole time because you did not need to search for or rehearse the answer.

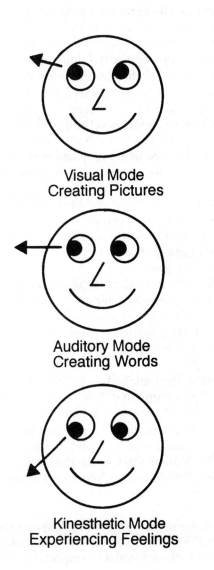

Visual Mode
Creating Pictures

Visual Mode
Recalling Pictures

Auditory Mode
Creating Words

Auditory Mode
Remembering Words

Kinesthetic Mode
Experiencing Feelings

Auditory Mode
Talking to Yourself

How to Use Eye Accessing Cues
To Promote Better Learning

You cannot use this information about eye accessing cues to determine if another person is telling the truth or lying. Experienced liars will rehearse their answer so much that they can say it without having to access or create the information on the spot. But you can use this information to help understand why many participants underperform.

As an example, a learner whose eyes are roving at test time may actually be searching within his brain for the answers. Eyes to the side means he is trying to recall or construct sounds. Eyes up and to the side mean he's trying to recall stored images (maybe a text, computer, chart, etc.) or he's creating new images (assembling thoughts). It takes eye movement to get the internal information.

Students who have trouble spelling are very likely unaware of the value of putting their eyes in the appropriate positions. Here's an example of many possible success strategies:

1. Start with their eyes looking down to access feelings
    (Student should access a positive feeling prior to start)
2. Eyes up and to the right to create a new image
    See the new word, in full or chunked down
    If learner is auditory, say the letters by looking to right
    If learner is kinesthetic, trace the letters with finger
3. Eyes closed, looking to the left
    recall the stored image... if correct, then
4. Eyes on paper, write out the correct spelling
    check your work, looking up to left
5. If correct, look down and feel good, then celebrate
    if incorrect, chunk down word, repeat correctly

The implications of the brain's eye accessing patterns are enormous. When participants create posters, art projects or murals, the best placement is shoulder high or above for best recall. When you put learner work up on the wall, put it low if you want them to access feelings, head high for discussion and overhead for storing the pictures.

When you present new material, stand to your learner's right (on the right side of the classroom from their point of view). When you review, stand on the left side (from their point of view). This simple strategy allows your learners to learn the information easier.

At test time, let participants move their eyes around. A learner who is constantly told to "Keep your eyes on your own paper," may actually be moving his eyes to get a picture or sound in his brain. It's detrimental to say to him or her "Keep your eyes on your own paper!" Usually, that accesses the "Bad dog!" feelings, his eyes go down and he forgets what he was thinking of. Ask participants to spread out their desks so that they have greater personal space at test time. This lowers your own stress about the possibility of them cheating.

> **What This Means To You:** Where you put things on the walls does matter. Students who are poor spellers can be helped. Test-taking instructions and strategies ought to be made more brain-compatible.

The Importance of Thinking

Biologically, the brain learns to solve problems to advance survival chances. The best thing we can do, from the point of view of the brain and learning, is to teach our learners how to think. Thinking takes many, many, forms. Those forms include:

- learning to gather information
- flexibility in form and style
- how to ask better quality questions
- the ability to weigh evidence
- how to understand & create metaphors and models
- strategies to conceptualize
- the ability to deal with novelty

What makes learning to think and thinking to learn complex is that there are so many different forms of thinking. Additional ones include:

- how to generate possible strategies
- discussion and brainstorming skills
- being effective at finding mistakes and discrepancies
- how to generate alternative approaches outside the usual domain
- strategies to test hypotheses
- generalizations: what can be said that is "in common" with all the parts
- thinking of new meanings for things

We don't know how easily or quickly thinking can be taught. We do know it is valuable and it can be taught. For example, you might want to offer these thinking skills:

- the ability to identify and organize information, values, events
- learning about something and learning to describe it objectively
- sequencing: the ability to figure out the logical or natural order of events
- problem-solution: assess the apparent problems and potential solutions
- thematic/concepts maps: grouping, thematic information based on defining characteristics such as age, location, function, culture, value, etc
- thinking for creativity; a twist, a turn, a new approach
- the ability to step outside your role or culture
- composing or creating new thinking

Sometimes the best way to teach thinking is to do thinking. That is, walk through your own thinking steps out loud so your learners can learn from you. You might teach the following steps:

- learning to "reframe" the problem so that it is not a problem
- learn to discover the course of the problem to prevent reoccurrence
- how to deal with life's difficulties
- process/cause: discover the flow, the process and speculate on causes
- thinking about thinking (metacognition)
- how to alter your own styles of thinking
- applying your thinking skills to add value & joy to your own life
- application of thinking to enhance the lives of others

Creativity, life skills and problem-solving are the primary skills in the presenting of thinking. These are all part of intelligence. Remember, intellect asks the question "Is it possible?" but only intelligence asks the question, "Is it appropriate?" Can intelligent thinking be taught? Absolutely yes. It not only can be taught, it should be a significant part of any school curriculum. It's part of *the* essential skills package needed for survival in today's world.

Being especially good at problem-solving
does not guarantee success in life.
But being poor at it does guarantee failure

What is the best way to teach problem-solving, creativity and thinking? In brain-based learning, it is with real world problems, with real people under real conditions. Put the brain under the conditions of relevant, challenging "survival" (real or imagined, but with positive stress) and it will excel in learning. The brain loves to think and learn. For children, games are all about inventing new ways of thinking. For adolescents, school survival requires thinking skills. Adults need thinking skills to deal with their daily challenges. In a way, it all may turn out to be a moot issue: what we are really after in our learners is not intellect, but intelligence. Intellect asks, "Is it possible." Intelligence asks, "Is it appropriate?"

How To Help Your Learners
Learn to Think Better

How do you get your learners to "grow" their learning skills? There are many ways to learn thinking skills. Since thinking is obviously internal, the trick in presenting and learning it is to make it external so that others can discover and "coach" the process. Here are some of the best ways to teach others to think better:

1. Use examples or stories imbued with personal meaning.
   Give relevant examples of how others solved problems.
2. Set up team projects, where everyone feels safe to use metacognitive options. Allow learners time to think about and discuss thinking.
3. Role-model, "walk" your participants through the process.
   Use a well-guided facilitation or a checklist of ideas & questions.
   You and your participants work to solve a problem together, out loud.
4. Students learn through debate, meaningful dialogue or discussion.
   Set up a coach, a listener and a thinker to learn the process.
5. Develop thinking skills through introspection, reflection & feedback.
   Utilize journal-writing, partner feedback and steps to follow.
6. Create large challenging projects (with deadlines) for public display.
   (Here's where the learners are forced to learn, to "survive.")
7. Use mapping or graphic organizers so you can visually see the models of thinking, the patterns, the sequences, the extent of detail.
8. Honor the feelings. Feelings are neither intangible or elusive, they are a legitimate part of the thinking process. No, this is not a New Age belief, today's neuroscientists have validated the critical role of feelings in thought.

Today's forward thinking learning catalysts now talk about how to turn *any topic or situation into a creative-growth learning experience.* Here's a paraphrased example of brain-based classroom presenting and thinking from "Turning Learning Inside Out."

Fletch Coolidge asks his high school science class to brainstorm a list of world problems. Working in small study groups, they narrow the list to ten. Then they brainstorm how the science topic of the week (weather) could impact, illuminate or solve the problems. Overpopulation would be impacted by a natural weather disaster or flooding could slow down tanks in a war. The class discusses these impacts. Then other academic areas are discussed and their relationship to the topic of the week. Does physical education relate to an army at war? How about home economics or math? Finally, participants are asked to take these concepts home for discussion with family and assess the personal impact.

Today's presenters are providing all subjects, topics and experiences with the parallel thinking and learning processes, strategies and insights built-in. No need for a special course on thinking. Gardner and Sternberg both believe that this ability, the skills to relate learning to our lives is one of the keys to intelligence. They also suggest that dealing with moderate novelty provides learners with critical and valuable life skills. Too much novelty and you are testing only creativity. Too little and you're not testing problem-solving enough. You may want to vary the amount of novelty you offer until you feel you have the right blend for your learners.

Chaos & Confusion Valuable to Learner

Should all the learning and thinking be sequential and orderly? Researchers Prigogine and Stengers, Gleik, and Doll have postulated that the learner climate of suspense, surprise, disequilibrium, uncertainty and disorder can lead to a richer understanding of the content. Prigogine even says that the brain is designed for chaos. He says, "Instability creates purposeful activity and direction."

In fact, these researchers say that the behaviorist, reward-punishment, super-ordered systems attempted in most learning contexts are actually the least likely to produce the desired results. Why? The most effective learning is either real-life or patterned after real-life. And real life can be suspenseful, surprising, uncertain and disorderly.

Green and associates found that when discrepant phonetic information is delivered both orally and visually, the brain creates a whole new encoding for it. A typical experiment would feature the subjects watching videotapes of female presenters with a male voice dubbed over it. The reverse was also used. Even though there was an obvious gender incongruence, the learner was not only able to understand the material, but also created whole new meanings for it. In other words, it was so incongruent that it became novel and, hence, powerful.

Some researchers postulate that
learning only occurs at "impasses"

Brown and Van Lehn say that we simply repeat stored "programs" most of the time. And that's not learning, that's replication of a habit. The brain runs programs and patterns all day. But only when we are stopped in our tracks by a problem or situation and forced to rethink it is there the possibility of new learning. Naturally, many times, learners, even at an impasse, will choose a prior "tried and true" path and no learning occurs. But the point here is this: the experience of chaos and confusion may be one of the few ways to naturally trigger new learning.

Sylwester says *we cannot really tackle a huge new idea head on.* In *The Structure of Scientific Paradigms,* Thomas Kuhn argues that we have to either go into chaos and confusion first or "nibble" at the idea over time until we have built up a new paradigm.

Does this mean that excess chaos is good? Hardly. Paradoxically, the more routine and ritual you provide for the learners, the more chaos they can handle. Presenters who have sloppy lessons, with scattered thinking and poor preparation will find that their participants may begin to reflect the excess chaos. Learners with presenters who over-structure, manipulate and control the learning may find that learners resist by creating disruptions or detachment. The optimal is an orchestrated learning environment: reinforced by the structure of positive rituals and infused with choice, novelty, chaos and challenge.

According to Bigge, learner involvement "is at its best" when the learner is perplexed and confused, but not yet frustrated. He uses what he calls "positive dissatisfaction" to engage learners at peak levels of motivation and understanding. The designer of a computer-based program called HOTS (Higher Order Thinking Skills), Stanley Pogrow of University of Arizona, says that he purposely puts participants into a state of "controlled frustration" in order to develop better quality thinking, patience and mental toughness. And it works. Students report gains in math, language, problem-solving, logic and thinking skills.

Let's use this example: learners are working on a play. An interpersonal conflict develops and two participants want to quit. Instead of the instructional leader jumping in to "save the day"" and solve the problem, the learners are simply encouraged to solve it for themselves in a way that everyone is happy. The chaos and controlled frustration becomes a learning tool instead of a way for the presenter to "take charge" and show how much he or she knows.

> **What This Means To You:** We need to allow for more variety and reality in our learning contexts. This does not mean that we should embrace thoughtless chaos, but rather that we should encourage a sort of "orchestrated disequilibrium" much more often. Utilize learner-generated role-playing, simulations, theater, songs, experiments, field trips, extemporaneous speaking and meaningful project work in which chaos can occur. Allow the activity to run its natural course when possible. Minimize time-regulated intervention.

Questions May Be Better Than Answers

Sternberg at Bell Laboratories says when asked a question requiring a yes or no answer, an amazing thing happens: Even after we come up with the appropriate answer, *our brain continues, nonconsciously, to process alternatives to the answer.* Questions generate sustained, enriching, brain activity, Pearce reports.

Berliner reports that the better the quality of the questions asked, the more the brain is challenged to think. The Socratic Method may have more than history going for it; it may be best for our brains. In study after study, (Redfield), learner performance scores improved when the questions asked of the learners improved in depth.

Instead of asking participants questions which require a statement of fact or a "yes" or "no" answer, ask more thought-provoking ones. Instead of: "What is it called when things keep falling back towards the earth?" ask, "What theories are there about gravity, which ones do you think are true, and why?" And, as mentioned earlier, the HOTS computer program succeeds precisely because it is *not* a quickie, or "math facts" type of shallow thinking. It succeeds because it asks questions that stimulate thinking and discussion. And that shapes lifelong patterns of meaning-making, and eventually, character.

The Power of Restating Questions

The research of Wicker et al. discovered that the best way to help learners solve a problem may be to restate the problem. When they provided re-thinking training for 200 participants in two separate studies, they found that flexible thinking was significantly more useful in problem-solving. By reframing and restating the problem, more creativity is unleashed and solutions arise that might otherwise have remained dormant.

Let's say, participants are asked to design a clock with no moving parts and no face. By visualizing, they may get stuck and come up with no answer. By re-framing the problem and asking new questions, however, they may come up with other solutions, such as a talking clock.

Restating questions can lead to creativity and self-confidence. Typically, a presenter asks a question like "What was the Berlin Wall?" or "What brought it down?" A more empowering question would be to ask learners "What interesting questions could we ask about the Berlin Wall?" Get learners involved in being a part of the problem by asking the question in different ways. If participants say a class is boring, ask them, "In what legal, free ways could we make it interesting?"

The New Paradigm of Emotions & Logic

A top neuroscientist, Damasio, makes a powerful case for the role of emotions in our thinking process. He says that excessive or undisciplined emotions can harm our rational thinking. However, he adds, a lack of emotion can make for equally flawed thinking. Here is the evidence:

1) The critical networks where feelings reside are not only in the limbic system, but also prefrontal cortices and "most importantly, the brain sectors that map and integrate signals from the body." Damage to the limbic system (primarily the amygdala and anterior cingulate) impairs primary emotions (innate fear, surprise, etc.). But, "...damage to the prefrontal cortices compromises the processing of secondary (our feelings about thoughts) emotion," says Damasio.

2) The body experiences primary emotions and the brain "reads" these as part of our world. Our body serves as a critical frame of reference for the internal creation of our reality. In other words, the body generates the sensory data, feeds it to the brain and integrates it with feelings and intellect to form a "thinking triumvirate" for best thinking. Too much or too little of any of the three variables may impair thinking quality. He adds,

> *"While uncontrolled or misdirected emotion*
> *can be a major source of irrational behavior...*
> *(a) reduction in emotion may constitute an*
> *equally important source of irrational behavior"*

Our thinking is not contaminated by emotions; that's the design of the system. There are no integrated brain sites, like a central processing computer to insure that your thinking is always non-emotive and logical. The reason for this is two-fold. First, emotions can speed thinking by providing an immediate response to possible choices to make. The ones that make you feel badly or feel good are selected faster. Secondly, your values in life, those which you hold most dear, are all "emotionally charged." Any time your values are being challenged or ignored, you'll have an emotional reaction. That stronger, more chemically-fortified reaction is a survival benefit to preserve that which is important to you.

Let's summarize the role of emotions and feelings in our thinking. Feelings are under the control of both subcortical (limbic and reptilian) brain AND neocortical (prefrontal cortices). Emotions are just as cognitive as any other form of data to the body. We honor what we see, what we hear and what we smell and taste. Just as importantly, the cognition of our own physiological, visceral and musculoskeletal state is "hard data" to the brain. Feelings let us mind our body's physical reaction to the world. Because they give us a "live" report at all times on the body's response, they are given a privileged status in our body's system. We all, like it or not, are a feeling, emotive being. The influence of feelings on our behavior is immense.

169

> **What This Means To You:** Most of the question-answer interactions in a typical learner environment are of minimal, if any, benefit to the learner. Have your learners make up the test questions instead of just answering them. Let participants do all of the lower-level quizzing of each other on simple-answer questions. As the presenter, you can put more attention on the more complex and provocative questions.
>
> We have for so long stressed the importance of the role of logic, fact and intellect. Brain-based learning says that notion is outdated. We must include the role of emotion in our thinking. This does not mean to ignore logic, but biologically we are designed to use emotion for better quality thinking. So it makes sense to integrate it into our learning process. Asking participants how they feel about a topic and why may be just as valuable or more so than a list of recalled facts. Thinking means integrating with emotions.

Answer Patterns Provide Key Clues

A Canadian researcher, J. W. Powell, says that by analyzing a learner's "wrong" answers, we can discover meaningful information. Often the wrong answers fit a pattern or reveal something important about the type and style of the learner's processing. Because presenters often listen for the expected answer, they can miss out on the more interpretive and qualitative possibilities. Powell discovered that "profoundly informed people often read more ambiguity into a question than had been intended."

As an example, a learner completes a multiple choice test. Wrong answers usually get a zero and are 100% wrong. Yet the learner may have a more profound understanding of the topic than the single answer possibility indicates. What if the learner made the same type of mistake 10-15 times? Does your feedback indicate that? The learner would love to know if they are just one or 15 answers off!

A physics presenter has a test question: "Using a barometer, how can you tell the height of this building?" The "proper" answer is to say, "Measure the air pressure at the bottom of the building and then compare it with the air pressure at the top of the building. Then use a prescribed formula to compute the difference in feet or meters." But a learner who got the answer right was marked wrong because he found other, more creative, ways to calculate the right answer.

After all, you could: 1) Tie a string onto the barometer and throw it off the top of the building. Then when it lands, measure the length of the string needed. 2) On a sunny day, use the shadow cast by the barometer and the building as a comparison and compute the ratio. 3) Go to the stairwell of the building. Using the barometer as a ruler, count how many times you need to flip it end over end to get to the top. Multiply that number by the length of the barometer. 4) Take the barometer to the building inspector, engineer or architect. Offer to trade the barometer to that person in exchange for the exact height of the building... etc.

> **What This Means To You:** We have been missing out on a huge opportunity for learning about our learners from the in-depth diagnosis of so-called wrong answers from the assessment instruments. Allow learners to work in groups to self-assess their tests. Let them formulate rules for the patterning and understanding of the experiences and information. Have them share and shape their discoveries instead of being evaluated by a "superior" who tells them what is right and what is wrong.

It's one thing to say, "Be more responsive." It's quite another to provide realistic alternatives. Here are some suggestions on how you can handle asking questions and dealing with all types of answers:

> **Before you ask questions, use these options to create a better climate of success. Pick the one(s) you're most comfortable with using:**

Provide a mistakes OK, "safe" classroom climate for questions & answers.
Assert that there may be multiple answers to your question.
Check in before asking questions to insure learner readiness.
Everyone may get a partner or learning buddy to serve as consultant.
Utilize mini white-boards, learner response cards, hand signals, private cues.
Give a multiple choice menu with the question.
Ask who is ready and has a possible answer.
Provide more wait time - respect the more kinesthetic learning styles.
Be more selective in calling on participants... only those that know it.
Utilize team and group cooperative responses.
Use a learner-presenter signal to let you know they're ready.
Role reversal, have learner check your work on board or in book.
Do a drawing for learner names from a globe or hat.
Tell & show them at start of class all the questions to be asked.
Do Jeopardy turnaround - participants have answer, ask you the questions.

When you get the answer you like, choose any of the following responses that you're comfortable using:

Repeat it in their words to validate what was said, avoid improving on it
Can they tie the answer into what other classmates have said?
Can they ask the learner to expand on what was given?
Always acknowledge and thank the learner for the contribution

When the answer was different than expected, choose any of the following responses that you like:

Prompt them for a better answer... Do the "hotter & colder" game
Ask the learner to say more about their answer to clarify what they mean
Ask for a follow-up comment in 5 min... check back then
Give more non-verbal or verbal clues to coax the learner
Class rule: no answers are incorrect, all are just possibilities
Walk them through the steps of learning or logic to get a better answer
Say your answer is "a good contribution" or "good effort" & move on
Change the question to make problem more understandable
Put the answer on hold & ask if others would like to add or comment
Change *your question* to make their answer right
Give the correct answer indirectly within 20-90 seconds, but only after
     attention is switched away from learner
Make humor out of the situation... but never, never, never at the learner
Use confirmatory phrases such as "so your answer is... are you sure?"
Do a "break-of-stress state" to shift the attention away from learner
Class rule: all answers are temporary until we validate them
Give credit for speculating, for simply suggesting any answer
Have learner find others who agree with his answer & re-contribute
Re-assign the problem again, change one variable
Give partial credit for giving the process of how they got the answer
Always acknowledge and thank the learner for the contribution

Predetermined Questions & Answers
Can Limit or Impair Learning

Research suggests that there's very little point to the typical presenter query. Presenter asks a question and participants try to get the "right" answer. If there is a single right answer, and the presenter already knows it, why ask it? Is the presenter trying to find out what the participants already know? A simple signal system will do that job. Once again, we have the old model of education at work, "I teach, you cough it up on cue," it says. In brain-based learning, alternatives to the traditional question and robot-answer might be the following:

- Students generate the questions to be asked
- Presenter asks the participants to link ideas to other subjects
- Students ask each other questions
- Students write up their own test
- Students relate ideas & questions to personal lives
- Students brainstorm as many questions as they can in 5 min.
- Students try to generate the "Ultimate" question for that topic

The more we discover about learning and the brain, the more it becomes evident that our old model of a classroom and the "factory-model" school has done a great disservice to the magnificent minds that learners bring to us. We are given as participants, budding Einsteins, Mozarts, Robert Frosts and Helen Kellers. The methods currently used are often turning them into bored, frustrated and disillusioned dropouts who never get a chance to experience their own greatness.

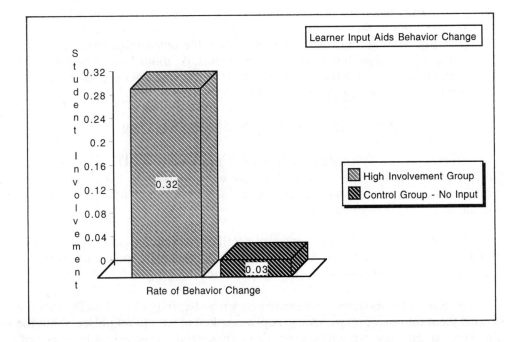

Thinking and Unguided Discussions
More Likely to Lead to Behavior Changes

Lewin, in USDA experiments, discovered that learners are more likely to integrate the learning and implement changes when lecture is followed by discussion. One group, the control group, was simply lectured to, then allowed to leave. About 3% of them actually changed their behavior based on the lecture. But in the other group, which stayed and discussed the lecture information informally, 32% changed their behavior. Research has documented, over and over, when participants make the learning *their own,* when they get to talk about it *their way,* without being manipulated and controlled, learning increases.

When done poorly, class time consists of a presenter lecturing for 45 minutes until the bell rings and the participants leave for their next class. When done well, there's discussion and thinking time built in to every class session. To produce better learning, share information, problem-solve and discover, then discuss.

> **What This Means To You:** Teaching more or faster is not the solution. The problem is that the learner has not *made the information his or her own.* The discussion of the information may allow the learner time to integrate, trouble-shoot and "buy-in" to more of the learning. Provide consistent opportunities for learners to stop and discuss what they have learned. Let them talk about how it might affect them and what they could do about it. Many shorter discussions are just as powerful as single long ones.

Brain Activated By Problem-Solving

University of Wisconsin psychology professor Dr. Denney says that "[p]roblem-solving is to the brain what aerobic exercise is to the body." It creates a virtual explosion of activity, causing synapses to form, neurotransmitters to activate and blood flow to increase.

Her studies indicate that your brain will stay younger, smarter and more useful by working out with these mental weights. Especially good for the brain are challenging, novel and complex tasks requiring multi-tasking and think time.

At Harvard University, a researcher conducted a study of the elderly. First he divided them into two groups. One group was asked to sit and reminisce about the old days, when they were younger. The other group was asked to play act, pretending to be in the year 1959. They listened to old radio programs, watched old speeches, watched old TV shows, and did activities they used to do. They acted, thought, talked and role-played being years younger. The results were spectacular. After just one week, the role-playing group showed a dramatic increase in their scores on intelligence and reaction times. The other group showed no improvement.

Dr. Schaie, Director of Pennsylvania State University's Gerontology Center, confirms that these results are duplicated in countless other studies. She says that withdrawal from the world and reduction of stimulation will be certain to bring on senility; and that activity, challenges, novelty and stimulation are best.

In class, many learners want it all done for them. They have not been taught to think, have forgotten how to think or are out of the habit. Heavy television watchers and drug users are less interested in learning than those who purposely challenge their minds.

> **What This Means To You:** Learners who spend all of their free time "doing nothing" can get out of shape - not just physically, but mentally. Television is not exercise; active thinking and problem-solving is. We, as instructional leaders, have to set the example and provide the climate to make it happen.
>
> You might want to get some resources that can provide a variety of mental "workouts." Make sure that you are not just presenting or training, but that you are "growing better brains." Use visualization, problem-solving, debates, projects and drama. Reduce lecture time, seat-work and other rote activities. Challenge your students' brains, and also give them the resources to meet the challenge.

How You Can Follow Up: *Turning Learning Inside Out,* by Leff and Nevin (Zephyr Press); *A Different Kind of Classroom,* by Marzano (ASCD); *Lateral Thinking* or *Six Hats of Thinking,* by DeBono (Harper & Row); *Mind in Context,* by Sternberg and Wagner (Cambridge University Press); and *How to Be Twice As Smart,* by Witt (Parker Publishing).

Shifting the Paradigm:
Learning and Intelligence

In order to boost learning and intelligence, it's useful to know what it is. Dr. Robert Sternberg says, "Intelligence boils down to your ability to know your own strengths and weaknesses and to capitalize on the strengths while compensating for the weaknesses." He says that when we think of intelligence, we are really talking about our ability to react intuitively, creatively and constructively to a wide range of experiences. In other words, being "street smart" is just as, or more important than, being "book smart."

The work of Harvard Graduate Professor of Education, Howard Gardner led him to the conclusion that there is not just one way to be smart, there are over 200 ways! Gardner researched the nature of intelligence and defined it as the ability to: 1) use a skill, 2) fashion an artifact, or 3) solve a problem in a way that is valued by the particular culture of that individual. In other words, a Wall Street stockbroker and an Australian Aborigine can both be considered highly intelligent... in their own culture. If they switched roles with each other, both would have a difficult time surviving (although I suspect the Aborigine might last longer).

Gardner grouped the array of human intelligences into just seven categories. He purposely included what some refer to as "abilities" because he wanted them to get the respect they deserve. Instead of having one single figure or mark that assesses our intelligence, he says that each of us has our own unique combination of these intelligences and that they can and do change over a lifetime. Here are the two models; the old and the new.

Old Way:
    a standard, fixed, out of date model
    IQ as a thermometer
    intelligence as fixed for life
    labels on learners as slow or smart
    linguistic-verbal & math-logical bias
    grades and ability as bell-shaped curve
    zero sum, win-lose game:
    more of one takes away from another

New Way:
    intelligence as a multi-faceted expression
    use of multiple assessments
    use experiences & background as a strength
    teach in all seven intelligences
    all types of intelligence appreciated & nurtured
    avoids labelling of "low" or "high" learners
    win-win game, all can succeed

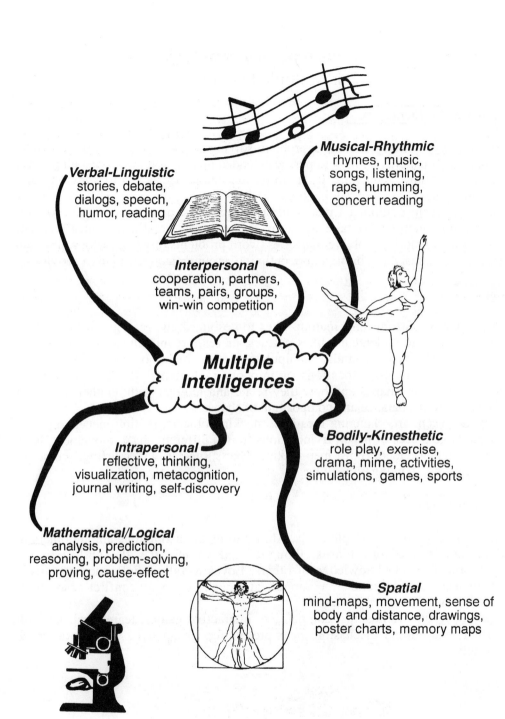

Musical-Rhythmic
rhymes, music,
songs, listening,
raps, humming,
concert reading

Verbal-Linguistic
stories, debate,
dialogs, speech,
humor, reading

Interpersonal
cooperation, partners,
teams, pairs, groups,
win-win competition

Multiple Intelligences

Bodily-Kinesthetic
role play, exercise,
drama, mime, activities,
simulations, games, sports

Intrapersonal
reflective, thinking,
visualization, metacognition,
journal writing, self-discovery

Mathematical/Logical
analysis, prediction,
reasoning, problem-solving,
proving, cause-effect

Spatial
mind-maps, movement, sense of
body and distance, drawings,
poster charts, memory maps

How To Recognize and Nurture
Our Multiple Intelligences

Logical-Mathematical

Recognize by: Strong at math & problem-solving skills. Ability to discern logical or numerical patterns. Ability to pursue extended lines of logic and reasoning. Asks "why" and "how" questions, wants to reason things out, wants to know "what's coming up next" - sequential thinking.

Ways to reach: computer time, writing applications, programs, objects to sort, classifying, gadgets to take apart or fix, magnets, math, science, reading, discussion, exploring, solving mysteries, word problems, breaking codes, museum trips, riddles, analyzing information, outlining, grouping and calculation activities.

Spatial

Recognize by: Strong imagination, likes to design, draw, read graphics, posters, needs pictures to understand, likes puzzles, mazes, organizing space, objects and areas. Has ability to mentally manipulate forms, objects or people in space or transfer them to other locations or into other elements. It's the capacity to recognize forms, shapes and how they relate and interact with another. It is also sensitivity to the balance and composition of shapes.

Ways to reach: art, changing locations, stacking objects, putting pieces together, sports, large pieces of paper, trying things from a different angle, movement, likes mind-mapping, video, films, map making, charts, theater, wind-surfing, sculpture, roller blading, drawing & painting.

Interpersonal

Recognize by: Strong people skills. Ability to make distinctions among others in their moods, feelings, biases, thoughts and values. It's the ability to act appropriately using knowledge of others. Loves to talk & influence, usually a group leader, an organizer, communicates well, good at conflict resolution, listening, negotiating & persuasion.

Ways to reach: friendships, competition, interactive games, teams, pair up with partner, one-on-one discussion, peer presenting, group work, collaboration & empathy.

Bodily-Kinesthetic

Recognize by: Ability to handle objects skillfully, either fine or gross motor movements. Also the ability to control your own movements for function or expression. Desire to move! Constant movement or commitment to comfort. Wants to get up, move around, tap, touch, fiddle with things & do things. Ways to reach: Stretching, role play, Simon Sez games, new games, building models, demonstrations, changing seating, drama, exercise, body sculpture, crafts & hobbies, dancing, games & sporting events.

Verbal-Linguistic

Recognize by: Use of core operations of language. Sensitivity to the meaning, sound, inflection and order of words; loves language, reads and loves to talk. Constant talking, a good memory for dates & names, likes to tell stories, likes to listen to stories, likes a variety of voices & remembers jokes. Enjoys reading.
Ways to reach: presentations, speeches, role-play, dialog, interactive games, writing, group work, doing reports, discussion, listening to tapes and reading - especially books with dialog.

Intrapersonal

Recognize by: Enjoys solitude, likes thinking, happy to work alone, has a good understanding of strengths and weaknesses, good at goal-setting & is comfortable being alone. The ability to develop successful working models of oneself. A way to learn and develop new behaviors based on self-knowledge.
Ways to reach: thinking strategies, imagery, journal writing, relaxation, learning about one's self, focusing and concentration exercises, self-assessment, metacognition practice, reflection and time to be alone and process.

Musical-Rhythmic

Recognize by: Appreciation of sounds, sensitivity to rhythm, pitch, timbre; making music or rhythm. Constant humming, tapping & singing.
Ways to reach: allow for rhythm, give them a musical instrument or let them make one, making fun sounds, learning with music, a Kazoo, use background or environmental music, singing, piano, musical performances.

Here's an example of a typical learner profile for a 14-year-old male. This is not a statistical average, it's merely typical. There would be various strengths in each of the seven intelligences. It might look like the following graph.

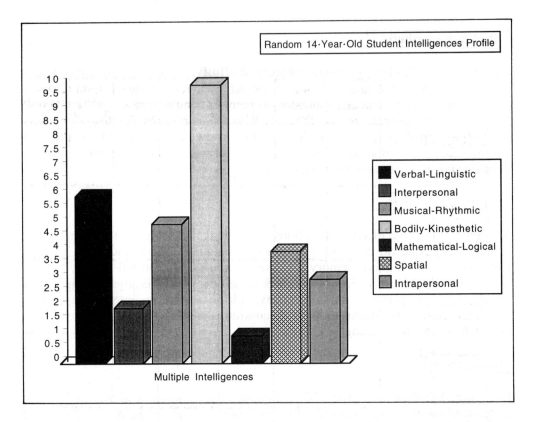

In the example above, it's NOT done in a pie-chart for a reason. A pie-chart is, once again, a fixed, zero-sum formula. More of one part of the pie means less of another part of the pie. Multiple intelligences are unrelated to each other. If you are stronger in intrapersonal ability (being on your own, reflection), you may or may not be strong in interpersonal (being strong in "people skills"). In the bar graph above, a 14-year-old boy who plays for a school football team is described. He's extraordinary at bodily kinesthetic (maybe even a bit too high). He's average at verbal, lowest at mathematical-logical and interpersonal. This profile can and will change; especially over the next ten years of this young man's life. Over an entire lifetime, there may be many changes in it, though probably none as dramatic as from ages 10-20.

It is more difficult to assess participants using multiple intelligences, but much more rewarding and accurate. There are many, many ways to do it. One of the more challenging aspects is determining exactly what is high or low quality in any area. If you want to take a moment and assess your own M.I. profile, you might use a rubric like this:

	Verbal-Linguistic	Inter-Personal	Musical-Rhythmic	Bodily-Kinesthetic	Math Logical $E=MC^2$	Spatial	Intra-Personal
5-Extraordinary Able to consistently go beyond peers Mistakes are rare Effortless grace							
4-Strong Unconscious Competency Usually gets what one wants or needs							
3-Intermediate Conscious Competency- Succeeds thru concerted effort							
2-Occasional Conscious Incompetency Struggles usually Often frustrated							
1-Beginner Consistent difficulty Constant problems and frustration or Major avoidance							

In a mathematics class, a learner who is average in mathematical-logical intelligence, but low in interpersonal or verbal-linguistic skills, may be poor at explaining or expressing what he knows. Yet if he is strong in intrapersonal skills, he may be able to assess his own progress and troubleshoot for mistakes. If he's strong in spatial, he may be able to make a graphic of what he knows. And if he's strong in musical-rhythmic, he could express ideas with sound. Each of your participants has a unique combination of intelligences and having one is unrelated to another. You could be high interpersonal and high intrapersonal, too. The power of this model is that the questions have now changed.

"How smart are you?" is now irrelevant.
A more powerful new question is,
"How are you smart?"

If you have decided you are going to test, it makes sense to test in ways that reflect the real learning going on. The old out-dated notion of testing and intelligence is like a thermometer. In the old model, you were either smart and high up on the thermometer, or in the middle (average) or lower (below average intelligence). Yet most educators have known for years that's a very narrow view of human intelligence. Not only is this model NOT brain-based, it's very narrow in terms of the wide range of human talents, abilities and intelligences. Refer to the chapter on assessment for a better way to test what we really know.

In addition, research from genetics, biology and neuroscience reminds us of a powerful rule: *no intelligence or ability will blossom until its given the appropriate environmental "need" or model for developing.* Pearce says, it's as if we are, "...like a garden that has been sown, but the seeds must be nurtured and nourished..." In short, the greater the variety of activities offered to your learners, the greater the chance of learning.

What This Means To You: Many intelligent learners have been labeled as stupid, average or slow because: 1) the presentation style of the presenter did not tap into all seven intelligences; or 2) the assessment was so narrow that it never allowed the learner to demonstrate what he really knew. We now know that is a tremendous loss of talent and ability. We must teach and assess in the seven intelligences to reach all learners, not just give lip service to the concept of equality.

Learn more about multiple intelligences. Two areas for immediate action are presentations and assessment. Use all seven intelligences in your instructional design at least once every five to seven hours. For assessment, make sure that your learners have choices on how to express their knowledge.

How You Can Follow Up: *Multiple Intelligences in the Classroom,* by Thomas Armstrong; *If The Shoe Fits,* by Carolyn Chapman; *Seven Kinds of Smart,* by Armstrong; *Seven Ways of Teaching,* by Lazear; *Teaching and Learning Through the Multiple Intelligences,* by Campbell; *Multiple Intelligences Made Easy,* by Jensen; *Evolution's End* by Pearce and *The Theory of Multiple Intelligences in Practice* and *Frames of Mind* by Gardner. See Appendix for details.

Chapter Questions

1. What was novel, fresh and new? What was familiar or "old hat"?
2. In what ways do you already apply the information in this chapter?
3. What three questions can you now generate about this material?
4. How did you react emotionally to this information?
5. In what ways can you translate the key three or four theories and discoveries presented here into practical everyday useful ideas?
6. How did you react cognitively when you were reading the ideas of this chapter?
7. If these things are, in fact, true about the brain, what should we do differently? What resources of time, people and money could be redirected? In what ways do you suggest we start?
8. What was the single one (or two) most interesting or valuable insights you had?
9. Plan your next step, the logical practical application of what you've learned.
10. What obstacles might you encounter? How can you realistically deal with them?

184

12
Strategies For Understanding and Meaning

Facts Versus Deep Meaning

There's an enormous difference between memorizing a few key facts and having an authentic grasp of the material. It's the difference between eating a meal at Taco Bell™ and living in Mexico for a year. It's the difference between being able to answer a true-false or multiple choice test versus being able to hold a substantial discussion about a topic. It's the difference between reading or hearing about hospitals and being hospitalized for a week. It's the difference between memorizing a few "math facts" and being able to tutor another learner in mathematics.

The emphasis on memorizing trivia, names, facts and formulas must stop. It's a poor use of precious educational time. The brain is not very good at learning isolated information except through an enormous amount of rote learning, games or rap. It rarely brings joy or meaning to any subject. In fact, it's quite likely to turn many participants off to nearly any topic. Memorizing lists of information has little to do with true learning. It's a "throw-back" and "hang-over" from mid-20th century schoolrooms.

Brain-based learning and presenting means that education is organized around the basic principles of how our brain learns best. The truth is, our brain does not process information the way we used to think it does. Sensory data is categorized as information, then codified and constructed, into meaning. The goal of our brain is constant: turn data into meaning.

185

The truth is, our brain is not designed to learn information very well in traditional classroom settings. "Input-output" is better suited to a computer. The learner needs to acquire information on his own time schedule, make perceptual maps, analyze, sort, and make it meaningful. The brain is designed to seek meaning. Until we provide learners with the resources (time, context, other learners, materials, opportunities) to discover meaning in what they are asked to learn, we will continue to produce robots and underachievers. Correspondingly, until we provide more meaningful forms of assessment, learners will have little incentive to pursue any type of deep meaning. They'll simply skim a few facts off the top, pass the test and call that an education. If *that's* an education, then we're all in trouble; and we *are* in trouble.

In fact, the research shows that presenters who try to give learners as much facts as possible are doing both their learner and themselves a disservice. Studies were done on medical school participants. All of them were pre-tested, tested and post-tested two weeks later. When the professor gave fewer details and less trivia, but focused on a greater understanding and meaning of the material, exam scores went up. Here are the details on a graph, courtesy of Charles Jensen:

Mean Scores of Low, Medium, and High Density Groups

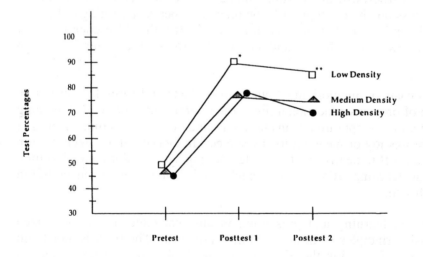

Russell, J., Hendricson, W., and Herbert, R. J. Effects of Lecture Information Density on Medical Student Achievement. J. Med. Educ. 59(1984):881-889.

Once learners have access to gathering the resources to get information, (computer, peers, personal experience, video, reading, CD-ROM, telephone, lectures, creative thinking, etc.), they'll still need to process it internally. Their way of understanding it means they have to find a way to make sense of it in their way, in their world. Learners do best when they get both: 1) exposure to many options for processing and 2) choice, often, but not always in how they make meaning out of it.

How To Boost Meaning
And Understanding

Some of the best brain-based strategies for increasing meaning and understanding are the following:

1. Spiral learning... Instead of linear instruction, where the learning is introduced once, then never again (unless as a review for the test), use "spiral" instruction. Introduce it lightly, drop it, come back to it again in more depth, drop it, come back again to activate the knowledge into meaning. A single topic might be brought up four or five times. This is often called "layered learning."

2. Storytelling... The same information can either be woven into a story by you or rewritten and retold as a story or turned into one by the participants. There are many, many fables, musical and folktales that offer a perfect framework for better understanding of material than the content by itself.

3. Peer presenting... Allow the participants time to think it out first, then make their own notes or mind-maps on it. Then give them time to teach their peers. You may want to make it fun by adding some special circumstances to it (like preparing another for a debate).

4. Model making... In some cases, participants can build a scaled-down or working-size model of the material. That can be particularly useful in developing understanding of the material when it is physical and involves steps or processes.

5. Performance... Some material, especially in literature, history and science, lends itself to being performed. Allow participants time to do a quality job, then make a fun "stage" for them to perform on.

6. Music... Most material can be set to music, written about in music, and performed as a rap or an opera. It can also be used as the words to re-write an already familiar song, and then performed as a musical.

7. Reflection... Many kinds of material can be better understood if participants simply have time to think about it. Casual, unstressed think time is rarely allowed in school and can be of great benefit. By letting participants generate some prior questions, they make better use of the time.

8. Myths... Some of the best learning comes from utilizing the great myths of history. It can bring knowledge to life and instill it at a very deep, profound level. Jean Houston and Joseph Campbell are particularly adept at using this strategy. You may want to explore some of their books.

9. Thematics... The brilliant educator Susan Kovalik has championed this important strategy for years. It means that an idea is explored as an interdisciplinary spider web, not an isolated fact. A class could invest a month on the color red (nature, literature, politics, art, biology, emotion, etc.) or the subject of money can be learned from a dozen viewpoints. Your learners could spend a day simply exploring the various angles to the word "*relationship*," or "*fraction*," or "*multiply*," or "*diamond*," or "*integrity*." Each of those could be explored from a historical, mathematical, sociological, or biological viewpoint. In fact, the more angles it's studied from, the more thorough the understanding.

10. Expert/reporter interviews... This is a simple role-play activity. One learner plays the role of the famous reporter for a famous newspaper. The other learner plays the role of a famous expert on the subject that has been studied. The "reporter" spends time preparing quality questions and the "expert" spends time preparing for the interview.

11. Drawing... Many types of material can be best understood in the form of a drawing. Give participants a large piece of paper and let them express what it means to them. You may be surprised at some of the great examples you get.

12. Journals... Sometimes a journal will provide the reflective time needed to make the necessary connections for maximum learning. Some presenters use variations of the journal idea in the form of "learning logs." These are journals specific to learning and participants answer questions about what and how they learned, add their own feelings and possible applications of the learning.

13. Sculpture... Some learning can be represented as a physical object or a sculpture. If it is appropriate, many participants would love to be able to let out their own "Michaelangelo" and express themselves.

14. Debates... These can come in many forms. Half of the value is in preparing for the debates, since the actual debate often goes by too fast for reflective thinking. A variation on the debate is to simply let participants choose sides on a topic. Then, pick a partner and make the best case you can for why your topic is the more important of the two.

15. Personal quests/personal life... Sometimes this form of exploration goes into family history, hobbies or personal growth. It can often be a project that meets other goals such as social ones. A learner might not be interested in history, but is interested in music and in particular, guitars. So the presenter asks him to trace the history of guitars from earliest primitive models. Then the quest has more personal relevance.

16. Presentations... Again, the planning is much of the value in these. Also, the more props, music and visual aids used, the more meaning the presentation may have. Keep them fun by providing choice in the topic selection and a low-risk peer support environment.

17. Mind-mapping™... These webbed, thematic, graphic organizers offer colorful peripheral thoughts organized around a key idea. They were popularized by Tony Buzan, Michael Gelb and Nancy Margulies. These provide an excellent vehicle for understanding relationships, themes and associations of ideas.

18. Game design... Learners know many games, most of them from their culture while growing up. Allow your learners to take any game, such as Simon Sez, Monopoly, Jeopardy, Wheel of Fortune, Concentration, Ball Toss, Poker and others, then re-design it using alternative content. The thinking process of remaking a game often provides the connections to better understand your material.

19. Montage/collage... This format provides a vehicle for collecting and assembling thoughts and ideas in art. It's actually a combination between a mindmap, a sculpture and a drawing. The more choice and freedom you offer your learners, the more likely you are to get something really innovative.

20. Open discussion... In a low-risk learning environment, where it's safe to say risky things and safe to be wrong or unpopular, a simple discussion can provide a great vehicle for understanding. To make this work, a presenter has to provide the role model for open ideas and non-directed answers. As soon as the learners sense that you are trying to get them to say the one "right" answer, the discussion will deteriorate to rote answers that they think you want.

21. Physical activities... Sometimes a simple game can really bring an idea to fruition and create that "Aha" that we enjoy eliciting. It could be a "new games" idea, a world game or win-win playground game. It could be as simple as a debate that gets explored with a managed tug-o-war game.

22. Multi-status... The more ways your learners hear something, from more points of view, the more likely it'll make sense. A great way to help your learners is to get tutoring, pairing, coaching or listening from another grade level, an adult, or play a new role where they teach and learn. In other words, placing the learner in a variety of roles will help him or her explore what's known and how to communicate it.

23. Apprenticeships... A more long-term approach is to provide an expert for your learners to learn from as a tutor. Obviously, this works best in learning skills, but there is always a great deal of philosophy and life skills needed for any learner growing up today.

Best Learning Makes Many Connections

So much of the traditional sense of learning has been dictated by a rigid and narrow assessment process. The question is often followed by a quick answer and "Voila!" Supposedly something has been learned. But researchers tell us that when optimal learning occurs, much, much more has happened. In fact, the best learning has occurred when the brain can "draw upon" many different programs. In other words, does a learner know only that blue is a color? Or, does the meaning of blue go beyond that? Is blue how people feel? A type of movie? Come in a thousand shades? Can it be painted, drawn, printed, etched, typed, molded, sculpted and lasered? What other words sound like it? What have been your experiences of the color, the word, the feeling, the sound?

The greater the number of associations that your brain elicits, the more firmly the information is "woven in" neurologically. This means it has more than simply a larger quantity of meanings, but it also has more associations and depth per meaning. This quality of knowledge can be found best when learning is:

- related to the learner's past learning
- learned through multiple contexts
- discovered in rich, thematic immersion environments
- learned with multiple strategies: visual, auditory & kinesthetic
- explained or taught by the learner

How You Can Follow Up: You may want to read *The ACT Approach,* by Lynn Dhority; or *A Different Kind of Classroom,* by Bob Marzano.

Brain Maps & Learning Patterns:
Pathways To Meaning Through Relationships

Edelman says, "[t]he brain constructs maps of its own activities, not just of external stimuli, as in perception...." The brain areas responsible for concept creation contain structures that categorize, discriminate, and recombine the various brain activities occurring in different kinds of global mappings.

Neuroscientist Karl Pribram states that the brain's way of understanding is more through pattern discrimination than singular facts or lists. "The initial stages of processing are largely parallel rather than serial, and feature analysis results from patterns matching rather than feature detection."

Brain pioneer Hart says, "It can be stated flatly... the human brain is not organized or designed for linear, one-path thought.... [T]he brain operates by simultaneously going down many paths. We identify an object, for example, by gathering information - often in less than a second - on size, color, shape, surface texture, weight, smell, movement...."

Hart describes the importance of presenting material in larger patterns first: "Once we begin to look critically at this notion of presenting in a logical sequence, we can see that usually a further giant - and utterly wrong - assumption has been made: that if a subject is fragmented into little bits, and the learner is then presented with the bits... the learner will be quite able to assemble the parts and emerge with the whole - even though never given an inkling of the whole!"

Researcher Nummela-Caine states the importance of patterns to learning. The neocortex is both a pattern-maker and pattern-detector. The ability to make meaningful sense out of countless bits of data is critical to understanding and motivation. Since the brain's craving for meaning is automatic, patterning occurs all the time. Each pattern that is discovered can then be added to the learner's "perceptual maps" and the brain can then leave that state of confusion, anxiety or stress. It "maximizes" again and is ready for more challenges.

Such structures in the brain, instead of categorizing outside inputs from sensory modalities, categorize parts of past global mappings according to modality, the presence or absence of movement and presence or absence of relationships between perceptual categorizations. They must be able to activate or reconstruct portions of past activities of different types of global mappings, for example, those involving different sensory modalities. They must also be able to recombine, repattern, reformulate or compare them.

Every pattern that the brain is able to create means that it can then relegate that new "blueprint" to the nonconscious. From a survival point of view, it is critical to create patterns as quickly as possible. The process of creating a pattern or perceptual map utilizes both the conscious and nonconscious brain.

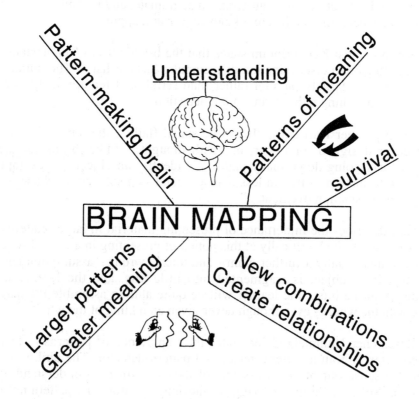

Pearce reminds us that neurons don't contain information, they simply translate, conduct and connect to others which resonate with its own frequency. All cells are simultaneously sending and receiving information. New information, which has no established patterns, or frequencies *must find uncommitted fields that are resonate*. Mapping can help trigger those fields. Fields can shift, rearrange and form new fields (neural mapping). In fact, the more fields it interacts with, the greater your depth of meaning, breadth of feedback and understanding.

In this process of establishing a neural, then mental map, the brain is less able to generate other parallel maps and is "thematically distracted." To the brain, there is a certain survival risk and vulnerability while a pattern is being created. But in the long term, that's what the brain must do and is best at doing. But do they really work?

Researchers who studied the use of
graphic organizers like mind mapping,
webbing or mindscapes have found that
they do, indeed, help learners understand
and recall information better
(But they have to be personalized!)

Armbruster found that participants who were taught and used mapping, boosted recall significantly. Some of the more interesting research was done by Chi on younger children, ages 4-8. But positive results were also found with adolescents and adults by Dansereau, Jones and Hagan-Heimlich.

Soloveichik reports on one of the most successful mathematics presenters in the world, Victor Shatalov. It seems that Shatalov has been using schematic organizers, like mind mapping, in his university level math classes for years. Students start the class by "mapping" what they understood from the previous class and then add to a new map as they learn the new concepts that day. Maps are color coded and revised to boost learning and retention.

In lectures around the former Soviet Union, Shatalov often would have overflow crowds of presenters, a thousand at a time, coming to hear him lecture on how he gets ordinary and previously failed participants, to excel. Perhaps the most amazing quality of his participants is their ability to perform complex and creative problems, often with great originality, indicating a true depth knowledge of the mathematics involved.

In mathematics, most participants have no concept of the "whole." All they get is an endless succession of facts, theorems and problems, each built on the previous ones. And none of them seemingly lead to a "whole" understanding of the subject. What's worse, if you miss any of the sequential steps, you lose out and are often lost for the term of the course because you can't pick up the understanding without a prior concept of the "whole."

In regard to patterns, there's much room for change. Maybe learning ought to consist less of the formalized start-a-topic and finish-a-topic format, and more of an informal, multi-level, pre-exposure with an on-going process of creating and eliciting maps. We could provide learners with patterns of the material to be learned in the early stages. There are many ways to provide more patterning for learners:

1) Days or weeks before actually starting a topic, pre-expose learners with oral previews, applicable games in texts/handouts, metaphorical descriptions, and posted mind-maps of the topic.
2) Before beginning a topic, give global overviews using overheads, videos/disks, and posters.
3) Help learners to form patterns during a particular topic by allowing them to discuss the material (unstructured talking), or putting them in teams to create models, mindmaps or pictures.
4) When you finish with a topic, make sure that you allow learners to evaluate the pros and cons, discuss the relevance, and demonstrate their patterning with models, plays, and teachings.

Many participants who have done poorly in the past may have simply needed a larger "map" of the material. In one study, two groups of college participants were given an essay-format post exam in a geology class. Those who had received instruction in conceptual mapping outperformed those who didn't.

A math presenter, Geoff Peterson, in New Zealand has tremendous success with his participants because he provides those conceptual global maps before learning the specific problems. You may want to provide large graphic, conceptual maps of the whole subject before you begin presenting or learning. Utilize videos, mind mapping, mindscapes, murals, field trips, excursions and other overviews.

> **What This Means To You:** Two things: 1) the importance of pattern-making and 2) the importance of tying into past and future learning. Past learning is part of the learner's perceptual maps. Therefore, the learner needs to integrate into the new learning what he or she knows, or it may not be "accepted."

A more random pattern style presentation and note-taking system may be the best for the brain and learning, suggests Dr. Howe from Exeter University. "Key word notes personally made" (vs. fill-in blanks or another's notes) scored highest in understanding and recall compared to other non-patterned note-taking systems. Use a note-taking style most like a spider's pattern, a visual landscape, a web or mind map, says brain expert Tony Buzan.

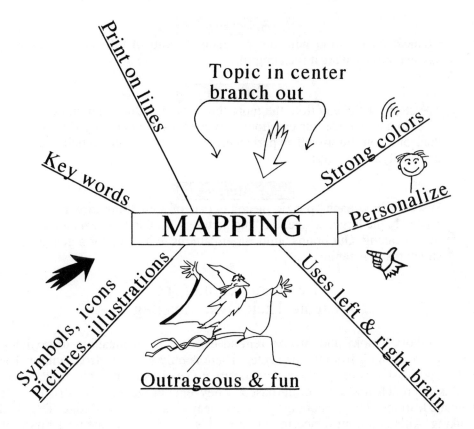

You can either have your learner's attention
or they can be creating meaning...
but never both at the same time

Getting attention is a precedent, a vehicle or precursor to the "meaning-making" process. Brain-based presenters know that they would never try to keep a learner's attention the whole time. That would prevent the learner from making meaning. How does our brain turn sensory information into something meaningful? That's a critical question to ask. Research tells us that three of the best ways to create meaning are:

Relevance

Connect information with other personally known information and associations to make it meaningful.

Emotion

The stronger the emotion, the more the meaning. Our brain and body react to and encode our emotional experiences dramatically different than our non-emotional experiences. This makes them much more personally meaningful.

Patterns

Discover how each "puzzle piece" is part of something larger... it's related to the larger whole, the "big picture." Isolated information has little meaning. Our brains build larger patterns to help us form genuine structures of meaning.

Learners Learning To Create Their Own Meaning

Authors Brooks and Brooks remind us there is no meaning in textbooks. There is no meaning from the presenter. There is only meaning from within. They make a persuasive point for the use of constructivist classrooms. The fundamentals of this approach are very brain-based. They encourage the use of integrated thematic learning. They encourage the use of learner's prior knowledge. They build thinking skills and confidence in learners. How? Two key strategies: First, they operate out of the context that learners *have to learn to create meaning for themselves* in what they learn. Second, this is done through problems, questions and projects that challenge the learners. Once again, the genius of this process is that the presenter gets out of the way of the learner so that the learner can create, from scratch real meaning in the learning.

How You Can Follow Up: *In Search of Understanding: The Case for Constructivist Classrooms* by Brooks and Brooks. Available through ACSD at (703) 549-9110. Also, *Making Connections: Teaching & The Human Brain,* by Caine and Caine; *Human Brain, Human Learning,* by Hart; *The Mind Map Book,* by Buzan. Resources on the "mapping" techniques: *The Mind Map Book,* by Buzan; *Mapping Inner Space* and "Maps, Mindscapes and More." See Appendix for details.

Multiple Programs Better For Understanding

Learning has much to do with the creation of meaningful patterns and programs of experience. For example, you have a regular routine (program) that you go through each morning as you get up and get ready for the day. But optimal learning occurs when your brain's sensory input challenges the student's brain to 1) "call up" the greatest number of appropriate programs, 2) expand an already existing program, and 3) develop new programs. In other words, a complex environment of challenge, novelty and relevancy.

Yet, all of this has to take place in an environment of low or no threat for the brain to be at it's best. In fact, the optimal circumstances for learning would have the following: 1) no threat 2) thoughtful orchestration of multi-dimensional presenting strategies 3) real-life experiences. To summarize the importance of patterns, Caine asks:

> *"Why, with our magnificent ability to detect patterns, make accurate approximations, speak multiple languages and create limitlessly, do we still break reality into bits and pieces... and fail to help learners understand the interconnectedness... into which the fragments fit?"*

Here's how it might work in your presenting situation: Have your learners develop an in-house consumer database of information about where to shop, find services, foods, movie reviews and engage in leisure activities. This project might take weeks and involve all seven intelligences. It is certainly relevant, challenging and novel.

What This Means To You: Many learners may have been underperforming because the learning environment was not optimal for the brain. Field trips and excursions followed by discussions and debriefings can be quite valuable. Larger, longer, complex projects that have immediate personal or practical value to the learners are also optimal.

The Power of Deep Meaning

One of the objectives in brain-based learning is to develop a sense of deeper meaning (as opposed to surface meaning). Deep meaning requires emotional investment by the learner. Deep meaning also means that multiple associations on multiple levels are made through the material. You can know about it in many ways, thematically and meaningfully. You have learned it both generally and specifically. You know it because you want to know it. It is in your long-term (not short-term, test-style) memory. You have thought about it and it's personally meaningful. The material also extends your natural knowledge of the world in a way that gives you richer meanings for the same vocabulary words.

One of the best ways to develop deeper meaning in learners is to understand the differences between typical classroom "learning" and "meaningful acquisition." The distinctions are best made by Dr. Steven Krashen. He made critical differentiation between the old formal way of "instructing" and the more useful way of allowing the learners to "acquire meaning." Krashen's research explains why, for example, most second language classes fail: they are full of formal instruction and woefully weak in the natural, subtle acquisition that the brain is used to using. They stress structure, grammar, rules and correctness, but they fail to allow participants to acquire learning the way they learned their own native first language. Here's a better way to put it:

Traditional learning	Meaningful acquisition
structured linear learning	non-linear, diverse input
knowing about a topic	having a feel for it
conscious, formal	non-conscious, informal
explicit test knowledge	implicit, intuitive knowledge
having it taught to you	simply picking it up
emphasis on knowledge	emphasis on meaning
extrinsic motivation	intrinsic motivation
perceived as work	joyful, curious & playful

The more schools become focused on structured goals, with countless measurable intermediate steps for participants using "outcome-based" learning, the less likely they are to achieve real learning. While it's important to be clear on what we all want, it's also valuable to be clear that *the brain doesn't learn very well by formal instruction or forcing outcomes.* Get the learners involved in setting goals. The brain is *least effective* when the learning is structured by rules, boxes, tests, structure and time limits. It learns extraordinarily well when the following five conditions are met:

- The environment is flooded with real-life experiences,
  rich visual, auditory & kinesthetic input.
- Learners have choice in how, when & what's learned,
  After initial exposure, the learning is driven by a natural curiosity
  to learn, not force-fed.
- The learning has enormous feedback without formal monitoring,
  a system that often induces threat, fear, anxiety and hesitation.
  Learning through activities, projects, games, peers, and discussion,
  mistakes corrected indirectly over time.
- Learners are never talked "down" to and they are able to learn
  any level of complexity at their own pace.
- The learner's needs are taken into consideration.
  Students feel safe, recognized, valued & inspired.

How can you help participants develop more "deep meaning?" Many times participants will develop it on their own. A favorite hobby can become deeply meaningful. While no single strategy guarantees success, there are many that can increase the odds. Here are several of them:

1. Do fewer, but more complex projects, especially lengthy multi-level projects, with sufficient time and resources.
2. Utilize the power of family history, stories, myth, legends and metaphors to help make the learning relevant.
3. Create more multi-status roles for participants: they teach, they learn, they coach, they observe, they assess, they discuss.
4. Utilize a variety of guest speakers on the same topic .
5. Help them find experts on a topic to learn from: they may be in the Yellow Pages, on a farm, a store, at a university or the parents of participants.
6. Widen the diversity of input: more use of peers, computers, journals, the neighborhood, the city and local businesses.
7. Use multi-grade, multi-age learning; go to another grade level and find out what they know or go to other presenters.
8. Make use of broader assessment forms so that participants are encouraged to use wider forms for learning. Allow more time for the learning.
9. Teach participants how to do on-going journals, charts, score keeping systems to self-assess so that they can better track their progress.
10. Allow the use of more meaningful subjects, and learner-selected themes.
11. Put high stakes in the learning through the setting of goals or the possibility of public presentations to evoke emotional investment.
12. Increase the use of simulations, dance, role play, multi-media, music.
13. Develop greater peer collaboration, make it a cooperative project.

14. Create immersion environments where the room has been re-designed or decorated as a city, new place or foreign country.
15. Encourage the use of more relationship-driven learning by providing apprenticeships with experts.

Learning Closely Linked With Emotions

Researchers have found critical links between emotions and the cognitive patterning needed for learning. Ornstein, Sobel, Lakoff and Rosenfield have documented how emotions influence learning in two ways: First, the "flavor" or "color" of our experiences are likely to make us either want more of it (it was pleasurable) or less of it (it was boring or painful). Second, positive emotions allow the brain to make better perceptual maps (O'Keefe and Nadel). That means that when we are feeling positive, we are able to sort out our experiences better and recall with more clarity. In fact, top endorphin (emotion hormone) researcher at the National Institute of Mental Health, Dr. Candace Pert, says,

*"The brain is just a little box
with emotions packed into it"*

How much do our emotions rule us? Just talk to anyone who is engaged in sales. Most salespersons will tell you the "buying decision" is usually emotional.

*The old model of learning was a very separate
mind, body and emotions. We now know differently.
Emotions are a critical part of your learner's
ability to think rationally and experience meaning*

For the moment, let's assume a learner arrives distraught over a domestic dispute, a lost article, or a lost game by a favorite team. The learner is irritable, moody and learns very little. He remembers the class as a waste of time and has a bad day. The opposite: a learner has just had a recent success or positive relationship encounter. The day is rosier, the birds are singing and he's happy. As a result, he learns better and has positive memories of the class. Here are some specific strategies you can use:

1) Make sure that the learner has a positive, safe way to "express out" any negative emotions. Suggestions include:
   • a mind-calming visualization or relaxation exercise
   • doing something physical: a walk, cross-crawl, stretching, or games
   • dialogue time: with partners, a small group, or sharing with the whole group
   • internal time: journal-writing, self-assessment, and goal-setting

200

• metaphorical rituals: put a "dumping box" near the door so learners can toss in any negative feelings, either on paper or symbolically.

2) Make sure that the learning engages positive emotions through:
   • use of role-play, theater, drama, mime and simulations
   • use of music, playing instruments, singing, chanting, cheers, and shouts
   • use of debate, controversial issues, personal stories, and improvisation
   • movement: dance, games, exercises, stretching, and play
   • excursions, guest speakers, trips, novel or challenging activities

> **What This Means To You:** We may want to pay much more attention to the emotional state of the learner. First, unless the learner is in a relaxed state of positive expectancy, very little of a constructive nature can happen. Second, as instructional leaders, we have the power to influence the emotional state with 1) activities that release stress or 2) increase bonding or 3) give the emotions a chance to be expressed.

How You Can Follow Up: Read *Pattern Thinking,* by Andrew Coward or *New Dimensions of Learning,* by Marzano available from ACSD at (703) 549-9110. Order a booklet: *How to Engage Emotions* or *99 Energizing Activities,* see Appendix for details.

Chapter Questions

1. What was novel, fresh and new? What was familiar or "old hat"?
2. In what ways do you already apply the information in this chapter?
3. What three questions can you now generate about this material?
4. How did you react emotionally to this information?
5. In what ways can you translate the key three or four theories and discoveries presented here into practical everyday useful ideas?
6. How did you react cognitively when you were reading the ideas of this chapter?
7. If these things are, in fact, true about the brain, what should we do differently? What resources of time, people and money could be redirected? In what ways do you suggest we start?
8. What was the single one (or two) most interesting or valuable insights you had?
9. Plan your next step, the logical practical application of what you've learned.
10. What obstacles might you encounter? How can you realistically deal with them?

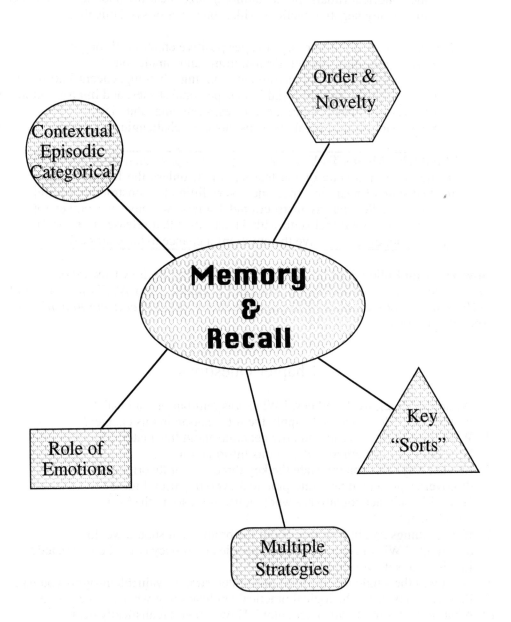

13
Memory & Recall

New Memory Models

How do your participants store and recall their learning? Surprisingly, there's no master filing cabinet; your brain does not store "pictures" of people, landscapes, memory libraries, films of scenes in our lives, soundtracks, microfilm, facsimiles. Damasio, Rose and Edelman verify that the brain does not "archive" information or memories. So, how do you remember? Your brain recreates those, "on the spot."

In fact, there is no specific place in the brain where you can get at them. When you think of an idea, hear your internal voice, get an image, recall music, see a color in your mind's eye, *you are reconstructing the original.* And as time goes by, our versions change. Our memories get more and more "recreated" and less and less true to the event. Your instant recreation of the original takes a split second (usually) and operates a bit like a volunteer fire department: there's no building, office or central system, but when a fire breaks out, the volunteers come from all over to one place and, (hopefully), put out the fire.

Calvin says that it's more important to *think process rather than location* in the brain. The process to increase memory might be the use of music, mnemonics, location triggers, intense sensory experiences, theater, motor manipulation or humor. Schacter suggests that *multiple memory locations and systems* are responsible for our best learning and recall. His research shows that different kinds of learning may require different ways to store and recall them, too.

> ***Any system utilizing two or more of the brain's
> natural memory processes is considered a complex and
> therefore successful, learning strategy***

In one study by Fabiani et al., learners were asked to use either rote or elaborate strategies to memorize words. Those using the rote method had higher forgetfulness ratios and a lower recall performance. The rote method involved simple repetition, also called "semantic" memory or "list-related" memorization. While this method is slow, requires review and often boring, it can be fairly accurate in isolated cases. Especially when compared to our episodic memory which some, including top neuroscientist Edelman, says is simply a memory of a memory. In other words, we usually are recalling our memory of what we remembered from our first (and heavily biased) impressions. If that sounds vague and inaccurate, that's what memory can be, at times.

Yet, we know that learners tend to remember much more when there is a field trip, a musical, a disaster, a guest speaker or a novel study location. Why? Multiple memory systems are activated.

> **What This Means To You:** Learners may seem to forget a great deal of what is taught, but the problem may be a reliance on singular memory system. If something is worth learning, it's probably worth remembering. Activate multiple memory systems with a variety of presenting activities, such as reading, listening to a lecture and seeing a video. Then follow up with projects, role-playing, at-home assignments, music, discussion, field trips, games, simulations or drama.

Brain Has Many Memory "Sorts"

There are many ways to classify memory (e.g., short-term & long-term, active and passive memory, surface and repressed, positive and negative, etc.). One of the most useful is to talk about contextual (episodic) and content (semantic or taxon) memory. O'Keefe and Nadel conducted their initial experiments on rats and later extended their findings to humans. They discovered a critical biologically-based difference between the two ways we deal with new information:

*Our brain sorts and stores information based on whether
it is heavily embedded in context or in content*

The difference between the two can be described quite simply: Information embedded in context ("episodic" memory) means it is stored in relationship with a particular location or circumstance. Information embedded in content is usually found in a book, computer, list or other information storage device.

Our spatial or contextual memory can be described as primarily based on *location and circumstances,* or context. Research discovered that it has unlimited capacity, forms quickly, is easily updated, requires no practice, is effortless and is used naturally by everyone (e.g., "What did you have for dinner last night?"). This natural memory is only context-dependent; it may be based on your movement, music, intense sensory experiences, sounds, puns, relationships and position in space and time.

Types of Retrieval Systems

Categorical/Semantic Memory
Also known as: semantic/taxon/declarative memory/linguistic
Short-term... working memory: < 15 seconds (unless rehearsed)
Works by association
Limited by chunks (1-7) & age (3-15)
Operating system: in our mind/using words
Requires higher intrinsic motivation
Examples: rhymes/mnemonics/peg words/similar content

Procedural Memory
Also known as body-kinesthetic learning/motor memory
Lasts for years
Works by association
Unlimited storage capacity
Operating system: in our body/in physiological states
Requires minimal intrinsic motivation
Examples: role play/riding a bike

Contextual/Episodic Memory
Also known as loci/spatial memory/episodic
Can last for years with moderate review
Works by association
Unlimited storage capacity
Operating system: space (location), time & circumstances
Requires minimal intrinsic motivation
Examples: "Where were you when...?"

Sensory & Synesthesia
Can be intense smells, tastes, feelings, pleasure, sights or sounds
Often lasts for years, may or may not need moderate review
Works by association/Unlimited storage capacity
Operating system: triggered by space (location) & circumstances
Requires minimal intrinsic motivation

The formation of natural memory is motivated by curiosity, novelty and expectations. It's enhanced by intensified sensory input (sights, sounds, smells, taste, touch). The information can also be stored in a fabric or weave of "mental space," which is a thematic map of the intellectual landscape, where learning occurs as a result of changes in location or circumstances, or the use of thematic presenting, storytelling, visualization and metaphors.

Information embedded in content is usually learned (or attempted to be learned, through rote and by following lists. "Semantic" is the type of list-oriented, sometimes rote, unnatural memory which requires rehearsal, is resistant to change, isolated from context, has strict limits, lacks meaning and is linked to extrinsic motivation. (e.g., She asks, "Remember that article you were reading last night? What was the name of the author?" He replies, "Gee, I don't remember. Why do you want to know?") This type of memory is unnatural and requires practice and constant rehearsal to keep fresh. That's why most people have the experience of "forgetting" so much trivia. The brain is simply not designed to recall that type of information.

Semantic memory is NOT "brain-compatible"- In fact, it's a very unnatural way to learn and remember things

This type of information gathering and memory of content without a context is difficult for the brain. This type of learning is typified by seated school work and homework ("Study for Friday's test by reviewing chapter six."). Information learned with the semantic method:

- is usually out of "real life" context, isolated and meaningless;
- is harder to update, change and revise;
- often requires extrinsic motivation.

A trip to China would provide our brain with heavy "embedding" in context. Millions of information bits, all in context, would be remembered for years. A two-week study session on China using a geography textbook is heavily embedded in content. And it all may be forgotten a day after the "big" test. Granted, the textbook is cheaper; but with some imagination, many presenters create much more "context" for the learning. It can be done with dress, language, food, environment and visitors.

For most presenters, planning time is short, so a simple alternative would work. Ask your participants to plan a trip to China. They might work in diversified groups. They would have to learn something about the geography, money systems, language, passports, weather, foods and customs. They could each present their

206

strategies to the rest of the class. A well-designed unit would remove the reliance on rote memory. It sure beats saying "Read and study chapter five for a test on Friday." All of the ideas are presented in this book *as an ideal* - you may not be able to implement every single one, especially at once! Do what you can, with the constraints you have.

> **What This Means To You:** There are profound consequences of applying this research. We may have been forcing many to learn in a very unnatural way. We have accidentally created generations of "slow" learners who easily forget what was taught. There may be a much better way to reach learners through the use of local memory, thematic mapping and interactive contextual learning.

Should we throw out "book learning?" No. Just because the brain is generally very poor at learning that way, we shouldn't discard the source. Semantic learning does have its place. When you ask for directions, for example, you want the shortest route from A to B. You don't want to drive all over the city to figure it out (although that would create a stronger "contextual map"). On the other hand, if you ask others what of significance they have learned in the last year, 90% of what they tell you will probably be contextually embedded information (vs. "rote" or "book learning").

There are dozens of implications of this research. It explains why we remember certain things and not others. Motor memory, often called "procedural" (e.g. riding a bicycle), musical memory (the melody of a favorite song) and sensory memory (smell of a flower) all fill the requirements of locale memory. More of these need to be used in presenting, training and learning. Linguistic and book work (lectures, reading, listening) are usually more semantic, although novelty, pattern changes and other variations can increase their impact.

For presenters concerned with discipline, there are significant implications (see also, "state-bound" learning). First, since participants remember very well the location and circumstances in which they are disciplined, all forms of "heavy discipline" from the front of the room carry dire consequences. A learner will remember how he felt and his brain's locale memory will link up that feeling with you, the classroom and the school. After only a few of these episodes, the learner walks in the door of a classroom and immediately his locale memory tells him, "I feel badly in this room." That can only continue for so long until he starts missing classes. That, in turn, invokes more discipline.

Then, if he is required to stay after school or come to "Saturday School," his brain links up bad feelings with school again. Soon, being on campus triggers bad feelings everywhere he goes. Naturally, he hates how he feels while he's in school and drops out. An administrator or presenter says, "He just wasn't motivated." But the brain scientists know better. He was a victim of a school that failed to understand how the brain really works. Attach embarrassment, revenge, pain and discomfort to being in school and most any learner will soon drop out just to avoid the pain.

This is a key concept of "brain-based" learning. It asks that you make a thorough analysis of your presenting and training to discover how much of what you do is "content embedded" and how much is "context embedded." Your own analysis may shock you. Contextually embedded learning is usually better.

Chances are, you'll want to reduce the amount of semantic memory required. Cut seat work by 90%. Give real world problems to solve in context. Give only homework which requires contextual learning, not lists, problems or pages of unrelated facts. The brain is not designed for textbook memory. In fact, to remember and to forget *are biologically balanced to prevent psychosis.*

Use whole language learning. Take advantage of the ease and thoroughness of the locale memory system to embed key ideas by using real life learning in real contexts, musicals, plays, role-play, real world excursions, on-the-job training, motor movement and intense sensory input. Use purposeful storytelling, thematic metaphors, directed visualizations and real-world problems. Be sure to review discipline policies. Eliminate any system that does behavior "score keeping." Stop actions which evoke the "Bad dog!" feeling in participants.

The Value of Context To Build Recall

Researchers at London University College tested two different groups of learners. The group who learned from print recalled much more than those who watched TV or videos, or who simply listened. Even for infants, when you provide the context (sounds & touch), they recall faces better than without them.

Boller and Rovee-Collier found that context dramatically improved memory. By learning about a subject in context, with a story, a map or something relevant, memory and recall improved. It also provided the framework for updating the memory by giving a kind of "revised edition" of the cognitive map. Calvin says that the active memory (a spatio-temporal pattern) is simply an organized pattern of synaptic strengths. But it needs an overall pattern to give it meaning. It works far better when you have established the context through patterns. Rose says, "...brains do not work with information in the computer sense, but with meaning...a historically and developmentally shaped process."

> **What This Means To You:** As a presenter and trainer, simply implement as many of these strategies and concepts as you can. It is unrealistic to expect yourself to use every single idea, every single class or course. Do what you can, avoid excessive use of semantic or taxon memory strategies. Instead of putting most of the emphasis on memorization and recall, it may be smarter and more efficient to place more emphasis on the context in which something is learned.
>
> Contextual learning simply provides more "hooks" and allows learners more time to make connections with what they consider to be important to them. Reading, hearing or experiencing the background on a topic aids understanding and recall. The placement of information being learned into a conceptual context, such as historical or comparative, boosts recall.

Memory Interplay With Emotions

MacLean reminds us that our emotions, hormones, and feelings all affect our learning. The role of the mid-brain in learning has been endlessly verified in studies on the memory of mammals. Studies by McGaugh and Introini-Collision with their teams of researchers verify the role of limbic area (mid-brain) hormones and the amygdala in long-term memory. The work of O'Keefe and Nadel was instrumental in establishing the role of the hippocampus (located in the mid-brain area) in emotions, indexing and learning.

Calvin reports that increased thalamic activity (engaging emotions) increases attention to what we learn. Our mental "gates" allow information either into or out of recent memory, never both at the same time. This has tremendous implications for classroom learning: You get either attention for memory or meaning derived from internal processing.

Hooper and Teresi document the work of "emotions pioneer" Dr. James McGaugh, psychobiologist at UC Irvine. McGaugh says that when emotions are engaged, the brain is activated. For example, when rats are injected with adrenaline, they remember longer and better. He says, "Arousal causes all these chemical cocktails - norepinephrine, adrenaline, enkephalin, vasopressin, ACTH - to spritz out. We think these chemicals are memory fixatives. They may work directly at the brain, but I think they exert most of their effects indirectly, through the peripheral nervous system... they signal the brain, 'This is important, keep this!'" McGaugh's research on emotions and hormones has consistently led him to conclude that they "can and do enhance retention...." The effects of hormones on memory is well-established. In fact, the rats injected with adrenaline remembered far longer than those who weren't injected.

Since our limbic area is responsible for both our emotions and our cognitive maps, how we feel about what occurs is important. Your brain "codes" every single incoming experience. The stronger the "emotional flavor," the more likely you are to recall it in the future. But, there's a catch: you are most likely to be able to recall it in that same state. Both Thayer and Maguire argue that each emotional state houses its own "library" of knowledge. During one success, you may recall another. During an argument, you're most likely to recall another argument.

What you probably remember most from your childhood was your lowest "lows" and your highest "highs." The same for presenters: you probably remember the worst and the best or the most outrageous. This applies across all areas of your life: the best and worst vacations, meals, dates, jobs, weather and so on.

> **What This Means To You:** The philosophy used to be: "Keep things under control. Don't let the participants get out of hand. Suppress emotions!" The new philosophy, based on the way the brain learns and remembers best, may well be: "Purposely and productively engage the emotions; make the learning personally compelling, deeply felt and real."

Make a purposeful strategy to engage positive emotions within the learner. Without it, the learner may not code the material learned as important. Long, continuous lectures and predictable lessons are the least likely to be remembered. Utilize the following: enthusiasm, drama, role-plays, quiz shows, music, debates, larger projects, guest speakers, creative controversy, adventures, impactful rituals and celebrations.

Other Influences On Recall

Research has verified that an easy way to remember something is to make it new and different. That's because our brains have a high attentional bias towards something which does not fit the pattern (novelty). Because it's immediately perceived by the brain as different and NOT fitting the pattern, the body's natural stress levels are raised. If it's perceived as a negative threat, the body may release cortisol. If it's perceived as a positive stress (challenge), then your body releases adrenaline. McGaugh et al. say that these chemicals act as memory fixatives.

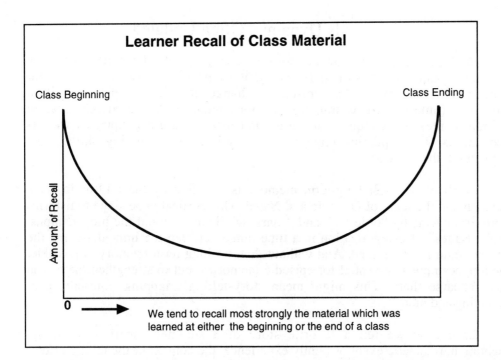

Learner Recall of Class Material

Class Beginning

Class Ending

Amount of Recall

0 →

We tend to recall most strongly the material which was learned at either the beginning or the end of a class

Once you have gone past the first item in a list or an experience, the novelty effect of it has eroded. So the brain treats it differently and is less likely to re-release chemicals into the body as a response to the change. This is why you remember the first and last moments of a learning experience more than the middle. Psychologists refer to this as the BEM principal, (Beginning, End and Middle), the order in which you are most likely to recall something. There is a distinctly different mental set at the beginning of an experience (anticipation, suspense, novelty, challenge, etc.) than the middle (continuation, more of the same, boredom, stability). The ending mental set is much different, too (new anticipations, emotions, etc.).

What This Means To You: Your participants may be able to remember much more of what happens if you provide more novelty (let them do much of it) and more beginnings and ends (and less middles). Introduce short modules of learning instead of long ones. Break up long sessions into several shorter ones. Have your participants provide surprise introductions to new topics.

How You Can Follow Up: Order *How to Boost Memory & Recall.* See Appendix.

Memory Is Dynamic, Often Updated

Edelman says that our memory is changing all the time with new information and changes in beliefs and circumstances. Because we change, our perceptions of the event's circumstances change in relationship to our lives. Ordinarily (unless there is trauma), memory requires "repeated rehearsal in different contexts." It requires updating and new categorical input, as well as associations. This updating engages our creativity and thinking skills. That originates in the neo-cortex.

Much of our best long-term memory is supplied by the mid-brain, says Edelman and the team of O'Keefe and Nadel. This cortical appendage transforms short-term events by "ordering" and "charging" them. Without the hippocampus, whole "suites" of categorization in a time range between the immediate and the forever could not be linked. And without that, no long-term memory is possible. The hippocampus is essential for episodic memories, but to strengthen them, you must rehearse them. This might mean story-telling, mapping, journals, peer presenting and more.

Each time we tell a favorite story of a summer vacation, wedding, celebration, traumatic event or family experience, the context of the telling affects how we tell it (who is there listening, what are the unique circumstances of that day). And we tell the story differently depending on our age, too. By telling the story, our memory increases. With our participants, once they learn the material, unless they continually create "dynamic maps" of the their understanding, the "replicative maps" lose meaning and repeating the material becomes much less powerful.

As good as it is, our episodic memory is still weak at recall compared to 100% accuracy. Psychologist Ulric Neisser did a study with his freshman psychology participants. He discovered that three years later their recall of a dramatic incident (he used the disastrous explosion and deaths from the space shuttle Challenger) was very different from what actually happened. He knew this because he had his participants record all the original details of each incident, plus the circumstances and other memories in their personal life. When compared with their original journals, 65% had memories which were partially true. *An amazing 25% of all participants were wrong in every single major fact.* And, *only 10%* had correctly recalled all of the key events.

As bad as this may sound (and it *is* bad if you're a defendant in court!), it's much better than the semantic memory. After the same length of time, the amount recalled by semantic memory would be less than 5%. Not good in either case. In order to recall things with consistency and clarity, multiple strategies are best.

> **What This Means To You:** Some participants say that as soon as a test is over, they've forgotten all that was on it. The so-called learning was simply replicative and not dynamic. There are many ways to keep the memory of learned information alive in your learners. Have participants do peer presenting and peer review on a weekly basis. Have participants re-create the material with mind maps, and then do presentations on it. Encourage the use of murals, mindscapes and learner projects. Continual revision, week after week puts the learning into more complex neural networking.

Brain-Based Methods
Insure Greater Memory & Recall

There are many, many ways for your participants to remember what they've learned. Some of them you can do "to them." Others are best learned by the participants so they can use them on themselves. Here are some of the best ways to help them recall learned material:

- Attach a strong emotion to it with a purposely designed intense activity
- Repeat it within 10 minutes afterwards, then 48 hours and then seven days
- Give participants or let them make a concrete reminder, like a token or artifact
- Act it out in a skit or do a fun, but engaging role play
- Use acrostics (first letter of each key word forms new word)
- Put it on a large, colorful picture or poster
- Chunk into groups of 7 or less to make each group of data easy

Since we just looked at seven ideas, let's reflect... which ideas from above do you plan to use more of? Which ones do you like the most? Why? Here's a few more ideas:

- Students identify key qualities & patterns of new information
- Personalize the lesson by using learner names, neighborhoods, etc.
- Both you and the learners summarize on paper and words
- Use a link system to link one idea to the next with action, absurdity
- Put it in greater context with trips, reading, discussion
- Use acronyms; the space agency in America is NASA
- Add more "What's in it for me?" to increase the incentive for the learner

Since we just did seven more ideas, let's pause again... which ideas would you now plan to use? When will you use them?

• Review in all five of our different senses; sight, sound, touch, etc.
• Implement the learning in some way, add it to your own personal life
• Use storyboards (like oversized comic strip panels) of key ideas
• Make a video or audio tape; the more complex the better
• Transfer it to your computer and use it often
• Use pegwords to link numbers or pictures to an idea for easy recall
• Create or re-do a song; re-write the lyrics of an old favorite, make a rap

Since we just did seven more ideas, let's pause again... which ones do you like the most? How might you implement them?

• Make up or use a childhood story with the info, then tell it
• Start with something exotic, then familiar, then unusual again
• Increase accountability: have a review check-up at regular intervals
• Real situation practice; go to the place where the learning occurs
• Hold unguided discussion on material; at least 5-15 minutes can work
• Make it more relevant & important by engaging more personal life
• Follow up with journal writing; give enough time for reflection

We just did another seven ideas... realistically, what can you use and how could you utilize them? Would you like more ideas?

• Build a working model that embodies the key elements of the idea
• Create or support learner study support groups
• Better nutrition: in several studies, the lecithin from wheat germ helped
• Create a positive association with the material; emotions are best!
• Partner to partner summary; make sure learners have choice
• Use dramatic concert readings; read key points with music backdrop
• Learners mindmap it, share their mindmaps, then re-do later in week
• Learners teach it to small groups of peers, or adults
• Follow-up a month later through video, writing, and discussion
• Learn contextually in different places so each location is a key clue

It's always good to get reality checks....We just did another chunk of ideas. You say you *already* use them? If so, good. By the way, you must really LOVE learning!)

How You Can Follow Up: *How to Boost Memory & Recall,* by Jensen; *Quantum Learning,* by DePorter; and *Power Learning,* by Lofland. See Appendix.

Chapter Questions

1. What was novel, fresh and new? What was familiar or "old hat"?
2. In what ways do you already apply the information in this chapter?
3. What three questions can you now generate about this material?
4. How did you react emotionally to this information?
5. In what ways can you translate the key three or four theories and discoveries presented here into practical everyday useful ideas?
6. How did you react cognitively when you were reading the ideas of this chapter?
7. If these things are, in fact, true about the brain, what should we do differently? What resources of time, people and money could be redirected? In what ways do you suggest we start?
8. What was the single one (or two) most interesting or valuable insights you had?
9. Plan your next step, the logical practical application of what you've learned.
10. What obstacles might you encounter? How can you realistically deal with them?

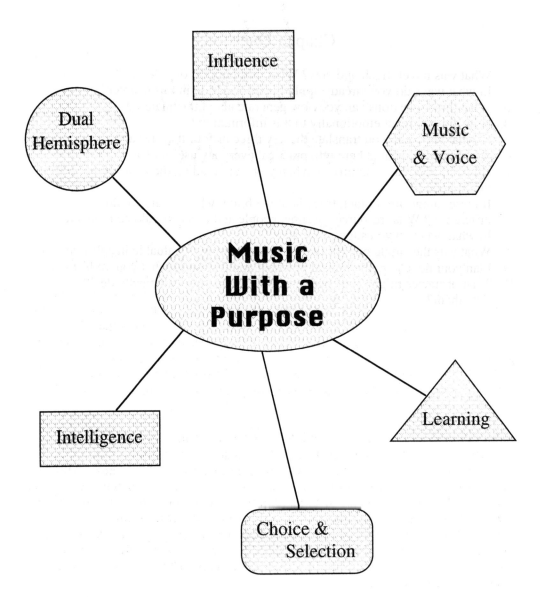

14
Music With A Purpose

Music Has Powerful Influence On Learners

The National Broadcasting Corporation produces "Dateline," a weekly TV newsmagazine. Airing on September 1, 1994, a special edition was devoted to the music of Mozart. Researchers say, listening to selected compositions of Mozart during either active or passive learning can measurably increase spatial learning, memory and reasoning. In studies done on pre-schoolers, secondary level and college level participants, another interesting thing was discovered. The computer-generated images of the brain activity *had striking similarities to the written score of Mozart-composed music.* Coincidence, or not? Could it be that Mozart activates the brain in a way that we are biologically receptive or programmed to think? More studies are needed.

At the Center for the Neurobiology of Learning and Memory at California's UC Irvine campus, a study measured the impact of listening to Mozart before taking a standardized test. The participants who listened for 10 minutes (Mozart's Sonata for Two Pianos in D Major), raised their test scores in spatial and abstract reasoning. On an intelligence test, the gain was *nine points after just ten minutes!* Although the effect in the brain is only temporary, the results can be duplicated with additional reactivation at any time. Those who listen only to a relaxation tape or had silence either improved only slightly or stayed the same. Researchers agree that more research is needed to discover the effects of other music, timing and other intelligence scores.

217

Certain music can boost attention,
learning, motivation and memory

Dr. Edrington and his colleagues did studies with willing college participants at Tacoma Community College. Using headphones, they were "fed" specially designed beat frequencies to create specific states for learning. Students in his classes scored significantly higher than those who tried to keep their own attention without the special "hemi-synch" music beat. Using statistical analysis, they discovered the odds of getting the results were less than one chance in 10,000. Also mentioned in *Supermemory,* author Ostrander found first graders who focused even better than adults when the special acoustic beat rhythms were used.

A 1987 National Music Educators Conference report says participants taking music courses scored 20-40 points higher on standardized college entrance exams. A college entrance examination board study discovered that participants who took four or more years of music classes scored higher on both verbal and math tests. Of the countries with the top-rated science and math results, all of them have a strong music and art programs.

Other researchers revealed insights about music and its effects on the body. Dr. Houston says music "raises the molecular structure of the body...." The body resonates at a stable molecular wavelength. Music has its own frequencies, which either resonate or conflict with the body's own rhythms. When both are resonating on the same frequencies, you feel powerfully "in synch," you learn better and are more aware and alert.

Music carries with it more than just feelings. It can be a powerful vehicle for information. Webb says, "Music acts as a premium signal carrier, whose rhythms, patterns, contrasts, and varying tonalities encode any new information...." The use of music as a partner, using point-counterpoint or riding the sound waves like a "sound surfer" can be a powerful way to carry a large volume of content. In fact, according to Lozanov, a "well-executed concert can do 60% of the presenting work in about 5% of the time."

How does music do this? It activates more than the right brain. It elicits emotional responses, receptive or aggressive states and stimulates the limbic system. The limbic system and subcortical region are involved in engaging musical and emotional responses. But more importantly, research has documented the limbic part of the brain is responsible for long-term memory. This means that when information is imbued with music, there's a greater likelihood that the brain will encode it in long-term memory.

Music and acoustic pioneer Dr. Alfred Tomatis says that sound provides an electrical charge to energize the brain. His research shows cells in the cortex of the brain act like small batteries to generate the electricity you see in your EEG printout. Amazingly enough, the brain's own batteries were not charged by metabolism, they were charged externally, through sound. Tomatis discovered that specific high frequencies sped up the brain's recharging process. This recharge affected posture, energy flow, attitude and muscle tone. The most powerful frequencies for this are in the 8000 hertz range. Prior research found that low frequency tones discharge mental and physical energy while the correct higher ones power up the brain. In other words,

The right sounds produce optimal learning
states as well as energizing the body for
maximum wellness and optimism

Dr. Robert Monroe, engineer and founder of the Monroe Institute, has produced audiotapes which use specific beat frequencies to create synchronized rhythmic patterns of concentration. He calls them "Hemi-Synch" and they are designed to help the left and right hemisphere of the brain work together for increased concentration, learning and memory. He has thousands of success stories, including a wide range of learners from first graders to college participants and professionals. Best results require a headset for the sounds, meaning that it's not yet practical for many school budgets. But things may change as educators discover the power of music and sound.

In Japan, one group of anesthetized surgery patients listened to music on headphones while another group did not. The "music" group had lower stress levels in the blood, which is positive. In your classroom, you may have found that when you play relaxing music, or Baroque in the major key, your participants tend to settle down and focus.

Halpern says, "Important new evidence shows that not only is the study of music beneficial in itself, but the introduction of [it] into a school's curriculum causes marked improvement in math, reading, and the sciences." He adds that the absence of art and music "can retard brain development in children." From his personal experience and exposure to others in the field, Halpern has become convinced of the necessity of music in learning. He says, "Ideally, sound and music should be used educationally throughout the curriculum." The benefits he cites are:

• Relaxation and stress reduction (stress inhibits learning)
• Fostering creativity through brain wave activation
• Stimulating imagination and thinking

- Stimulating motor skills, speaking and vocabulary
- Reducing discipline problems
- Focusing and aligning energy as a group
- Patterned concert readings (using music as a background to presentation)

Researcher King did experiments that were designed to determine if a particular selection could evoke a particular neurophysiological response. He says that there is no statistically significant difference between using Baroque and New Age music in the effectiveness of inducing alpha states for learning. King used music from "Duotones," by the artist Kenny G, but speculated that other similar music types may work as well. Multiple independent tests were performed for all samples, and King concluded that either New Age or Baroque music could be used to enhance learning.

Researcher Felix says that the following summary can be made about the role of music in presenting, training and learning:

"Significant positive effects of music during learning have been reported. Positive effects of music played during testing are not as consistently supported.... There are also a small number of studies which report no significant effect of background music during learning or testing .... Studies reviewed lend support to claims for the effectiveness of music from the baroque and classical periods.... [O]ther styles of music... may also be effective."

There's clear evidence that music affects brain waves and our physiological states. There is also an abundance of anecdotal and experiential evidence that the purposeful and well-planned use of music can positively impact learners. However, very little brain state research has been done using today's music.

What is the effect of rock music, heavy metal, rap or New Age music? Most of us only know that we like it or don't like it. Yet, you may have found that many types of music lead to enhanced states optimal for learning. Your participants may enjoy background or foreground music when used sparingly and appropriately.

When you use music in an educational or training environment, use it for a purpose. Instead of playing the radio or some "white noise" that you heard was good for learning, think about the specific physiological and emotional state that you'd like to evoke. Carefully choose the music that elicits that state.

What This Means To You: We may be under-utilizing music. We rely so much on our own voices to deliver meaning. Yet music is a terrific carrier of meaning and it is readily available for learning. The new research describing the "Mozart Effect" tells us that music may be a powerful way to build reasoning, memory and intelligence. If you're not using music in your presenting, it may be a good time to start. If you are already, it may be time to expand or enhance your collection.

How music is presented is as important as what music you select. Many educators have found that although the original music suggested by Bulgarian learning pioneer Dr. Georgi Lozanov works well, other selections also work. Many have successfully used Reggae, Latin, pop, jazz, New Age, big band, waltz, rap, rock, soul and other types for learning.

Use music in your learning situations. Since each type of music can elicit a different type of psycho-physiological state, use a variety. When your learners arrive, you may want to play music that creates a state of anticipation or excitement (grand movie themes, upbeat classical). For storytelling, use music that has built-in peaks and valleys and engages fantasy and emotion (classical or romantic). For background, you may want to use low volume Baroque.

Music should be used purposefully for best effect. Too much can create saturation to the listener, and it loses its effectiveness. As a general rule, include music in 30% or less of the total learning time, unless the class requires it by nature of its content (a music class).

How You Can Follow Up: *Introduction to the Musical Brain,* by Don Campbell; *How to Use Music in Teaching and Training, Trainer's Manual for Accelerated Learning with Music;* Send for **free** bulletin: "Thrilling Music Selections to Motivate Your Audience." See Appendix.

Music Affects Moods, Lowers Stress Levels

Scartelli reports on two ways to reduce learner tension: biofeedback and listening to calming music. When he combined the two in his research, however, he got the best results. There's an enormous difference in the types of music that can be used productively. You'll want to consider cultural factors, the physiological state of the learner and convenience factors.

Let's say you are listening to the radio. Maybe you're feeling so-so or a bit blah. Suddenly, on the radio, one of your all-time favorite songs is played. Maybe it is one you recall from a special time as a teenager or college learner. Or maybe it's a song that brings back special memories of a first love. Whatever the associations, you immediately feel better. Once again, music has worked its charms.

> **What This Means To You:** In learning contexts, music may be under-used. Music can be used as a mood enhancer to get learners in a better state of readiness for learning. With a world of possibilities for creating positive triggers and releasing endorphins in learners, it would be a shame to miss out. Get music which gives positive, upbeat messages. Make sure that it's in a major key. Use show business themes or music from the most popular epic motion pictures. Use local music that has a particular appeal just to your learners. Experiment a bit. Ask your learners what music they like to use when they want to get into a great mood.

Music Resonates Entire Body

Top music and brain expert Clynes explains how dramatically music can affect learners. The older, more traditional viewpoint was that music affected the non-dominant hemisphere. For example, a right-handed person is more likely to be left-hemisphere dominant. And that leads to using more of the right side of the brain for music. But Clynes says the following:

1) Both sides of the brain are involved in processing music.

2) The harmonic structure, interval quality, timbre, and the spatial, temporal, long-term patterns are recognized by our non-dominant hemisphere (in most of us, the right hemisphere). The short-term signatures, like rapidly varying volume, rapid and accurate pitch trajectory, pacing and words, are recognized by the dominant hemisphere (in most of us, the left).

3) Over the last hundred years, music has changed. Clynes says that the trend is toward "a gradual shift of the 'focal point' of musical processing from the minor hemisphere, in, say, baroque or classical music, to the dominant hemisphere of today's avant-garde music." In other words, today's music engages more of the brain.

4) The pulse of the body (heart rate) tends to synchronize with the beat of the music. The faster the music, the faster the pulse. In Clynes' words, "[A]n aspect of the transformation of sound pulse to motor pulse displays a tendency to follow the dynamic character of the sound pulse...."

Webb says that the effects of music on the mind and body are best summarized in these eight areas:

- the effects on muscular energy of tones and scales
- an increase in molecular energy
- the influence of rhythm on the heartbeat
- changes in metabolism, which affect physical energy
- a reduction of pain and stress and faster healing recovery in patients
- relief from fatigue and low energy
- the release of emotions, feelings and character
- the stimulation of creativity, sensitivity and thinking

Interestingly enough, a non-musician's and a musician's brain react differently to music. Dr. John Mazziotti measured blood flow and brain activity through brain scans while different learners listened to music. The right hemisphere "lit up" when music was played to a musical novice, but the musician's left side of the brain was more active when listening to the music. There was also more activity in the limbic system.

Presumably, this occurred because the processing for this kind of listener is much more analytical, even to the point of processing nonconsciously the tones, tempo and rhythm. At the Montreal Neurological Institute, Justine Sergent confirmed, once again, that the whole brain is involved in the processing of music.

Music affects all of us; its reputation as a universal language is well deserved. In a research study by Clynes, 40 Central Australian Aborigines of the Warlbiri Tribe scored high on recognition of musical sounds of joy, love, reverence, grief, anger, sex and hate. Their scores were equal to university participants at the University of New South Wales, MIT, and the University of California at Berkeley.

> **What This Means To You:** Since music is be used among many cultures, use a diversity of music to reach the minds of your learners. Experiment to find appropriate avenues for using music in learning. Use it for introductions, to set the mood, as an energizer, for background and for celebrations and closures.

Which Music Selections Most Benefit Learning?

Is one type of music better for learning than another? The research says that it depends on the individual and what effect you are trying to get. Clynes and Walker say that, to be safe, there is a greater consistency in the body's pulse response to classical music than to rock music. In other words, you will get more predictable, safer and more consistent responses. This doesn't mean that contemporary music cannot work; just that much of it elicits less predictable responses.

Lozanov says that it depends on what you're trying to do with the music. His research says that classical (circa 1750-1825) and romantic (circa 1820-1900) are better for introducing new information. He suggests Baroque (circa 1600-1750) as a passive review at the end of a session. Others (Webb & Webb) suggest that dozens of types of music can work for learning, as long as one understands the brain and the affects music has on it.

Lozanov suggests active concerts (speaking theatrically with musical interplay) for introducing new material. This is the process of delivering information in rhythm with music in such a way that one is "sound surfing." When the music is dynamic, loud or fast, you pause to let the music carry itself. When it is slower or pausing, your material is delivered with enthusiasm and drama. This process, he claims, can deliver about 60% of the content in 5% of the time. Suggested composers are Mozart, Beethoven and Hayden.

How does this work? Music is a powerful signal carrier; it activates emotions and long term memory and fully engages the brain's most receptive states. From some, you can expect powerful emotional reactions; from others, less obvious, but there nonetheless. Roederer says, "In other words, motivation and emotion can be triggered with no relationship to the instantaneous state of the environment and the actual response of the organism to it." He adds, "We must seek a lead toward understanding the emotional response to music...."

224

Examples are everywhere: The NBC Nightline special mentioned earlier, unveiled the "Mozart Effect." What powerful effects have you noticed? You may have learned the alphabet with a song or know of an advertiser's jingle that stays in your mind. Music alongside content is very powerful.

> **What This Means To You:** There may be many other ways that we could use music to carry messages into the minds of receptive learners. One is to use learner-generated songs. Have your participants select five songs that they already know well (like Jingle Bells, birthday songs, simple and traditional folk songs, etc.). Then re-write the song's lyrics with new words to be learned. Sing the song several times. The new lyrics will be more easily transferred into the minds of the learners. By the way, you learned the alphabet not by singing "the alphabet song," but by using the melody of "Twinkle, Twinkle Little Star" with re-written lyrics (the letters).

When you want to use music for dramatic introductions of content, use show music, movie themes or any other dramatic music. To deliver key content, classical or romantic music is best. For closed-eye review, Baroque is optimal. Many other forms of expression also work, from world music, to folk, jazz, country, gospel, traditionals, marches, pop and New Age. Experiment. Keep using what works, and change what doesn't.

How You Can Follow Up: For a *Free* Bulletin on "Thrilling Music Selections to Motivate Your Audience." See Appendix.

Engaging Both Hemispheres By Combining Music & Voice

While it's true that music can engage the brain, a combination of words and music can dramatically increase the results. A "concert reading" is the purposeful use of music in presenting or training with planned content interplay creating the effect more like a sound track for a movie, play or an opera. Lozanov discovered that well-delivered concerts can open gateways to learning, reach the subconscious, create better understanding of subject matter, activate long-term memory and reduce overall learning time. There are three types of concert readings in accelerated learning:

1. **Preview** This is the initial globalization. Use short, light, fun, intriguing, attention-getting music as a chorus, parable, chant, or poem. It builds confidence and anticipation. This should be done at the beginning of a new session when a fresh topic is introduced... length 3-7 minutes. Use dramatic, light or bizarre music to inspire.

2. **Active Concerts** To present detailed material, use dramatic presentation with classical or romantic selections; Beethoven or Hayden. This places new material in context. The material could be metaphors, reading of plays, scripts, dialogue or text. This can be used in the middle or next to last part of session, once every 5-10 hours of learning time. These are done for 5-15 minutes. Let music play for 10-30 seconds first... never compete with it. "Sound surfing" means you use the musical pauses, go silent during the louder, more active parts, then pick up pace again

3. **Passive Review** The subdued review of key points. The same material used for an active concert can be applied here, but with baroque selections instead. Students are relaxed, with eyes closed. These are done for 5-8 minutes at the end of a session

Performing in Concert With Music

1. Content Make sure that you know your own content well and are comfortable with the meaning of it. Tell the participants what you'll be covering; give them a short preview of the material verbally. Do this even when you are using handouts of the material.

2. Music Make sure that you have listened to your music many times so that you know it well. How long does the introductory movement last? Make sure you know that. When does it go up and back down again in volume? How about the pacing and tempo? Do you know when it happens?

3. Create the environment You may want to change the lighting a bit. Have the learners stand and stretch, do some deep breathing. Give positive suggestions of expectancy. Allow participants to sit comfortably.

4. Credibility Stand with authority. Announce the name of the musical selection; the composer and specific piece. This will prevent some listeners from being distracted during your reading trying to figure out which composer and selection it is.

5. Volume Make the volume loud enough to fill in the non-speaking parts and quiet enough so that you can talk during the "down" times.

6. Pause Get the attention of the audience. Create anticipation. Wait until the introductory movement of the selection is over before you begin. Usually it's from 5-35 seconds into it.

7. Dramatic Make large movements and gesture to emphasize key points. Think of yourself as a Shakespearean performer and enjoy making a show. Finish with a dramatic statement or final closing remark.

Experiment! Doing concert readings is a great way to have fun, be creative and embed some powerful learning. Repetition is the secret to comfort. And with comfort, you get confidence and competency.

How You Can Follow Up: *How to Use Music in Teaching & Training*. See Appendix.

Chapter Questions

1. What was novel, fresh and new? What was familiar or "old hat"?
2. In what ways do you already apply the information in this chapter?
3. What three questions can you now generate about this material?
4. How did you react emotionally to this information?
5. In what ways can you translate the key three or four theories and discoveries presented here into practical everyday useful ideas?
6. How did you react cognitively when you were reading the ideas of this chapter?
7. If these things are, in fact, true about the brain, what should we do differently? What resources of time, people and money could be redirected? In what ways do you suggest we start?
8. What was the single one (or two) most interesting or valuable insights you had?
9. Plan your next step, the logical practical application of what you've learned.
10. What obstacles might you encounter? How can you realistically deal with them?

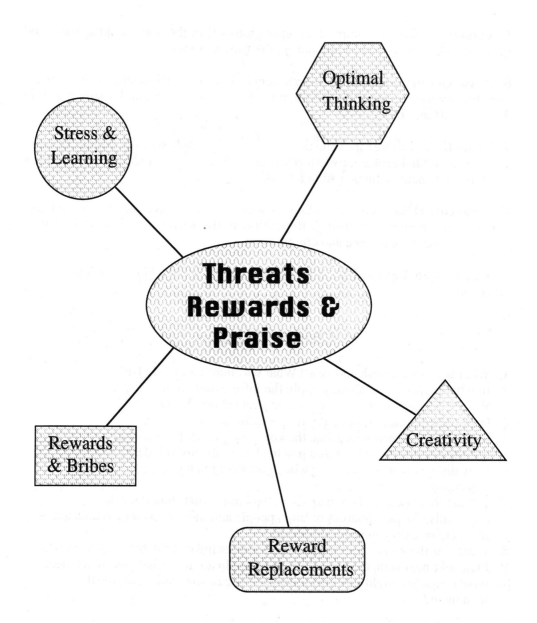

228

15

Threats, Rewards & Praise

Selected Words Can Affect Learner's Brain

How important are your responses to learners? It turns out that they're critical. Quite powerfully, the work of Rozanski suggests that criticism and put-downs trigger harmful heart abnormalities as significant as a heavy workout. It seems that negative language does, in fact, harm more than earlier thought. When presenters say harsh, negative things, the body reacts as well as the mind. Mind, body, mind-body, we keep seeing evidence of the undeniable link. It's a dramatic bit of research:

> *Studies demonstrate that sarcasm and*
> *put-downs can do measurable, physiological*
> *harm and should be avoided*

Kotulak has also reported that words can be just as powerful as prescription drugs in behavior modification. The work of UCLA psychiatrist Dr. Lewis Baxter has documented that carefully chosen words can activate the same areas of the brain as a highly-prescribed drug. The therapeutic value of language indicates that words can, indeed, heal.

In this particular case, Baxter and his colleagues studied the brains of obsessive-compulsive patients using PET scans (positron emission photography), which measures cell activity in various parts of the brain and creates a color photo of it. They found that the caudate nucleus was overactive in these patients and acted like a behavior "fixative" since it allowed for the repetition of unwanted behaviors. The prescribed drug, Prozac, raises the level of the brain's own sedative, serotonin, so that the behavior ceases. During the test cases of behavior therapy, the patients experienced identical changes in the caudate nucleus, calming down the patients as the drug did.

As an example, one of your learners is feeling depressed or upset. Your carefully-chosen words raise his spirits and help generate motivation. The learner thanks you.

> **What This Means To You:** Your effect may be much greater than you previously thought. Your potential for effecting change may also be far greater. The importance of choosing words carefully is underscored. Practice giving your learners encouragement and affirmation. Do this less as an exception, but more as long-term support and verbal definition of the learner's potential genius.

Learners Impacted By Two Different Stresses

Researchers O'Keefe and Nadel, Jacobs and Nadel, and Dientsbier discovered that the body has "good stress" and "bad stress." The positive forms of stress occur when we feel challenged and want to "rise to the occasion." In those cases, the body releases adrenaline and noradrenaline, which actually heighten our perceptions, increase motivation and even enhance physical strength. The circumstances for positive stress are particular. Positive stress occurs when we feel we have:

- desire to solve the particular problem
- the ability to resolve a problem
- some control over a situation
- sufficient rest between challenges
- perceived a solution to a problem

The negative form of stress ("distress") occurs when we feel stressed by some kind of threat, such as embarrassment, loss of prestige, being pressed for time or having lack of choice. It also occurs when we feel helpless because we:

- are forced to solve a problem we don't want to
- don't perceive a solution to a problem
- lack the resources to solve a problem
- have unacceptable risk levels involved in trying to solve it
- have little or no control over a situation

The body (adrenal glands) responds to negative stress by releasing moderate amounts of the hormone cortisol. While small amounts can feel good, too much depresses the immune system, tenses muscles and can impair learning. High levels of cortisol induce the despair we often feel when we are overwhelmed. Worse yet, it can "destroy hippocampal neurons associated with learning," says Sylwester. In addition, Vincent says even short term elevation of cortisol can create confusion and poor distinctions between what's important and what's not.

Research strongly suggests that stress strangles decision-making, judgment and impairs memory and learning

The area of the brain most affected is the hippocampus, which is very sensitive (reacting negatively) to this hormone. That weakens the brain's locale memory and indexing systems, and may narrow perceptual "mapping." The hippocampus is also the center of the body's immune system, so the release of cortisol weakens the body's ability to fight disease.

Learners in a state of fear or threat not only learn worse, their immune system is depressed and learning slows

Some people lead highly busy, tightly scheduled lives, working 10-12 hours a day, six days a week, and they are healthy, stress-free and happy. Others have routine, predictable jobs, working 30-40 hours a week, and they feel tired, stressed and unhappy. The differences in their feeling of well-being come from the two different kinds of stresses at work.

It's possible that some learners who are underperforming are simply under distress. It was either created by others or themselves, but they may not have the resources to recognize or change the stress level. They may not even know they are living under this stress if it's been with them all their lives. The stresses may be originating in the learner's home or work life, in the classroom or training room.

> **What This Means To You:** Insure that learners want to solve a problem or do an activity. Then, have the following conditions met: 1) they perceive a solution is possible 2) they have the resources to solve it 3) they have control over the situation 4) they have sufficient time to do the learning 5) they have the knowledge and skills to recognize and manage their own stress levels. Utilize exercise, hydration and "purposeful play" (learning games) to keep the learning stress low. It may also be up to the instructional leader to do relaxation training.

Threats Undercut Brain's
Optimum Thinking & Creativity

The work of Hart, Lozanov, Nadel, and Leonard has confirmed that the brain operates differently when any type of threat is perceived. Under threat, the brain uses less of the "higher order" thinking skills of the neocortex and resorts to using more of the fastest and most survival-oriented part of the brain, the "reptilian" brain stem.

Let's use this example: you're taking an important exam, the pressure is on, and you are having trouble thinking of an answer. But the moment you turn the test in and walk outside, the pressure's over and threat is gone. The answer pops into your head. But now it's too late.

Threats can be any stimulus that causes the brain to trigger a sense of fear, mistrust, anxiety or general helplessness in the learner. Threats can be defined as physical (harm from presenters, parents or other learners), intellectual (learner feels helpless, stressed for time, overmatched without needed resources or skills, challenged or mocked on the basis of expressed ideas) or emotional (embarrassed, humiliated, made fun of, disciplined publicly or made an example of through isolation or a "lesson" taught). The groundbreaking work of O'Keefe and Nadel has revealed that under any type of perceived threat, the brain:

- loses its ability to take in subtle clues from the environment
- reverts to the familiar "tried and true" behaviors
- loses some of it's ability to index, store and access
- becomes more automatic and limited
- loses some of its ability to perceive relationships and patterns
- is less able to do the "higher order" thinking skills
- loses some memory capacity
- tends to over-react to stimuli - in an almost "phobic" way

Examples of threats in learning are too numerous to mention. You may have heard another presenter say the following lines:

"Every minute you're late is going to cost you."
"You know what's going to happen if you don't, don't you?"
"I'll just stand here and wait until you're ready to quiet down."
"If you do that one more time, you're staying after."
"If I have to tell you again, we'll just stop everything."

The most common "threat line" starts with the words, "If you... " When learners hear those threats, their brain says, "Here we go again... " Similarly, the presenter suddenly calls a learner for an answer. The learner may or may not know the answer, but in the "moment of truth," while everyone else is watching and waiting, he forgets what he knows. The presenter then calls on another learner (another "victim" of the minimizing).

What This Means To You: Many learners may actually be much better thinkers, use more complex problem-solving skills, be more intelligent and less troublesome than previously thought IF the threats are removed from their environment. Make the learning environment a safe, relaxed environment. Eliminate reward systems which either are controlled by an outside agency (you, a business, the school, etc.).

Avoid calling on learners unless they volunteer. Eliminate discipline policies which work by threat, score keeping or embarrassment. Never threaten a learner by saying you'll send them to a higher authority, kick them out or call their parents. Give more time for classwork. Reduce the threat of grades by providing more frequent feedback. Make the assessments more genuine and meaningful by making them less stressful and less threatening.

How You Can Follow Up: *Punished by Rewards,* by Kohn; or *Eager to Learn,* by Wlodlowski.

Improperly Used or
Excessive Praise Found Harmful

Researcher Kohn says that we may want to be cautious in how praise is used. Children can become negatively dependent on it just as they can on any other external reward. This dependency can lead to lower self confidence, loss of the joy of learning and decreased self-esteem. The praise can also be interpreted as being manipulative. Brophy also suggests that the use of praise can easily backfire. This occurs for two reasons: the learner interprets the praise as 1) "You're controlling my behavior, and I resent it," or 2) "My current capabilities must be sub-par and in real need of improvement."

Case Western Reserve University researcher Roy Baumeister's experiments verified that heavy praise given to a learner can backfire. While intermittent praise can be positive, praise from authority figures can increase "pressure to perform" and result in performance anxiety. Subjects who were given praise right before a skills test consistently performed worse than those who did not receive praise. Students heavily praised became more tentative in their answers and gave up on their own ideas more quickly than those who were not.

As a common example, a presenter continually praises participants for doing homework or for sitting quietly in class. Soon, the learner discovers that it is the praise that he seeks, not the behavior that the presenter is attempting to reinforce.

> **What This Means To You:** The most striking and permanent interpretation of a positive judgment is that it's still a judgment. Reduce praise from you and increase peer feedback and support. That's much more motivating to the learner. Encourage rather than praise. Say, "You're on the right track," or "Let's give it a great effort."
>
> Give praise that is not contingent on performance. Encourage the learner to take risks. Provide affirmation, not back-slapping. When the task is completed, ask the learner what his or her assessment of the task is. That way the learner begins to develop a sense of quality about the learning or task instead of pressure to perform just to get it over with. Teach learners how to give supportive feedback to their peers.

How You Can Follow Up: Read *Punished By Rewards,* by Kohn.

Intellectual Poison:
Rewards & Other Bribes

In never-ending efforts to control, manipulate, manage and influence learners, some educators have been using rewards. Are rewards a smart thing to do, considering the brain's natural, operational principles? Absolutely not. First let's define a reward.

A reward is defined as
a compensation or consequence
which is both:
1) predictable and 2) has market value

If it's only predictable, but has no market value (e.g., a smile, a hug, a compliment, a long-delayed low-odds random item, an awards assembly, public approval, etc.), then it is simply an acknowledgment, not a reward. If it has market value, but absolutely **no** predictability (a spontaneous party, pizza, cookies, gift certificates, small gifts, trips, tickets, etc.), then it is a celebration, not a reward. If participants know that by behaving a certain way, there's a chance that they might get a prize, that's enough predictability to be called a reward. The determining criteria is simple:

***Did the learner change his behavior
in the hopes of getting the favor?***

If what you offer is a lottery ticket, then it is not a reward. In other words, the behavior of buying a lottery ticket does not have sufficient correlation to winning the lottery. It's true, your chances of winning are far better by purchasing a ticket than not getting one. But only the disillusioned or desperate would "behave better" in the hopes that "someone up above" will smile upon them with a winning number. For rewards, the compensation has to have market value (it sure does!) and be predictable (the lottery ticket is not).

If you offer something that has both of those qualities, you are, in fact, bribing the learner. You have a reward system, regardless of what you try to call it. Rewards carry an implicit and covert threat: "If you don't meet the criteria for the reward, some opportunities will be withdrawn from you."

How do you tell which is a reward and which is simply an acknowledgment or celebration? Once again, ask the important question: *"Did the learner change behavior based on the possibility of getting something for it?"* In other words, "Did the bribe accidentally or purposely influence or alter the learner's course of action?" As you can tell, the issue has a great deal to do with intent. And that's sometimes tough to read.

Rewards Impact Learners Negatively

In Amabile's work, the relationship between motivation and rewards is explored. In profound, far-reaching research on the creative process, she says, "extrinsic motivation inhibits intrinsic motivation." The ability to be creative is strongly linked to intrinsic motivation, since it gives the brain "freedom of intellectual expression," which fuels even more thinking and motivation.

A reward system prevents the establishment of intrinsic motivation because there's rarely an incentive to be creative - only to do the asked-for behavior. Creativity is rarely part of any reward system - in fact, the two are usually at far ends of the scale. You get either intrinsically motivated creative thinking or extrinsically motivated repetitive, rote, predictable behaviors.

Caine and Caine say it best: *"[A] system of rewards and punishments can be selectively demotivating in the long term, especially when others have control over the system"* (Sound like a school or business?). Their contention is that the existence of any behavior-oriented threats and anxiety, coupled with a lack of learner input and control, will "downshift" learner thinking, causing learners to prefer repeated, predictable responses to lower anxiety, and making presenters think the reward system is working. This makes it harder to initiate changes within the system - since any changes in the system will create "threat and anxiety" to both participants and presenters, meaning we will get more of the same.

As an example, in kindergarten, many learners get a smiley sticker for good work. By third grade, it's cookies or candies. By fifth grade, the reward is a pizza for a class that behaves well. By eighth grade a learner is being bribed by his parents. Is it any wonder that by the time a learner reaches eleventh grade, and the presenter wants him to do a research paper, the learner response is, "What do I get?" Or he may simply ask, "What for?"

Learners who have been bribed for either good work or good behavior find that soon the last reward wasn't good enough. A bigger and better one is wanted. Soon, all intrinsic motivation has been killed off and the learner is labeled as "unmotivated." Like a rat in a cage pushing a food bar, the learner behavior becomes just good enough to get the reward.

Some, like Kohn, might say that most all rewards are bad. But Ford argues that it depends on whether the reward creates a conflict with the learner's existing goals. The three most likely times this occurs are:

1. *If the learner feels manipulated by the reward*
   "You just want me to give up my guitar lessons."
2. *The reward interferes with the real reason the learner started*
   "Now that I'm getting rewarded for getting good grades, I care only about what's on the test, not real learning."
3. *The reward devalues the task and the learner feels bribed*
   "This class must be pretty bad if they're giving us a bribe just for attending it."

The three categories above cover most situations where the reward system might be used. It seems that there are few other situations where the need would arise. Let's use as an example, a school that is having problems with truancy and low attendance. The administrative staff decides, as an incentive, to reward those who come every day. Now, each learner gets a reward for having a 100% attendance month. The school has worked out an arrangement with local businesses. The reward is a free meal at McDonalds or a pizza at Pizza Hut.

Students immediately feel bribed for coming to school. They think, "This must be really bad for them to have to bribe us." But they still do the rewarded behavior. "It's stupid, but we'll play the game," they say. Now school is about "working the system," instead of learning.

Rewards May Perpetuate
The So-Called "Low Achievers"

The above headline can be inferred from the work of many researchers. The work of O'Keefe and Nadel was important because it demonstrated that in stressful situations, rat behavior becomes rigid and stereotyped with repeated, predictable responses, "completely eliminating the participation of the locale system." The locale system is the part of the brain that may be responsible for certain types of memory and spatial mapping. We know from research that the use of rewards increases learner stress.

Spielberger's work is profound because it links up the physiological states of anxiety, negative stress and threat with thinking and human performance. He says that anxiety:

1) reduces the ability to solve complex problems
2) reduces learner responsiveness to the environment
3) increases stereotyped, low-risk behavior
4) increases learner attentiveness to and reliance upon external systems of rewards and punishments

Deci says that there is evidence linking extrinsic motivation with work involving non-creative tasks, rewards and punishments, memorized skills and repetitive tasks. In order to get learners to be creative and have greater subject interest, higher self-esteem and the ability to be reflective, there must be intrinsic motivation. Reward systems prevent this. Make no mistake about it:

Learners who are experiencing stress and anxiety
in their environment will prefer external motivation,
meaning a system of reliable rewards

Paradoxically, *the worse the learner environment is for motivation, the more the learner seeks rewards.* The rewards are initially welcomed by the learner, where predictability and certainty are the trade-offs for lowered anxiety. Stressed, anxious learners *are* more likely to look to others for safe, predictable role modeling, to listen to others for goals and to increase their own stereotyped, lower-order thinking.

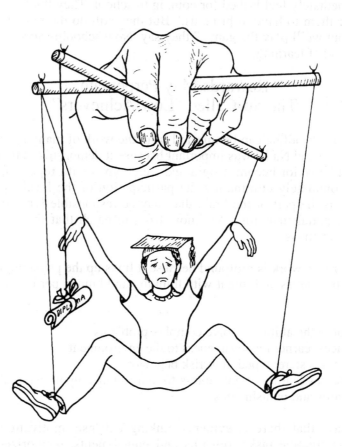

This creates a "Catch-22." Rewards, at a low level, work. The presenter continues their usage. The learner now is a victim of the "glass ceiling" principle: he learns to perform to the lowest level needed to get the reward. Caine says, "In effect, they prefer external forms of motivation and lose sight of internal motivation."

Let's use as an example, the learner who has been on a reward system, seems to like it and wants more; he complains when it is dropped and his performance goes down. The presenter uses this as evidence to say, "I know I shouldn't bribe him, but the system works!"

In the long run, rewards do more damage than good
towards motivating the so-called underachiever

The problem is that the system does work - too well. But then again, holding a gun to someone's head works, too! It will get them to do all kinds of things, but it's not good for the learner's brain (among other things). Rewards lead to learners who become preoccupied with "playing the game" and not really doing quality learning. Why? The ability to alter perceptual maps, to do higher-order thinking and to create complex thematic relationships with the subject is not available to the brain when it experiences the anxiety of a reward system.

The more you use a reward system, the more you evoke the "two-headed dichotomous dragon." That means: 1) the psychological anxiety of performance increases and 2) every reward carries with it an implied certainty of success or failure - but which one? The learner then wants to reduce the uncertainty, so he picks tasks that have a high degree of predictability (often boring, repetitive skills). The learner also is more likely to pick goals set by others instead of himself (even the goals he does pick are often the basic, overworked, media-reinforced, cliché types).

> **What This Means To You:** Replace rewards with positive alternatives. These include meeting learner goals, peer support, positive rituals, self-assessment, acknowledgments, love of learning role-modeling, enthusiasm, increased feedback, more options for creativity and learner control over the work.
>
> Rewards are doing more harm than good, encouraging results other than those originally intended. Phase out reward systems. It makes more sense to make school or work a worthwhile place to be than to try to bribe people to attend or perform. By using the brain-based strategies in this book, rewards will become totally unnecessary.

Creativity Stifled By Rewards

A study by Brandeis University researcher Teresa Amabile found that, in many areas, reward systems lower the quality of the work produced. She conducted more than two dozen studies over nearly 20 years with the same results: in the long run, rewards don't work. Among artists, creativity (as judged by their peers) dropped when they already had signed a contract to sell the work upon completion. The fact that they knew for sure that they were going to be paid for the work lessened their fullest expression.

Let's say that in reading, learners were offered rewards for getting the reading done and for remembering key bits of information. The results were devastating: learners not only had worse memory for the "key" information, but also the recollection of "incidental" information dropped to almost nothing.

> **What This Means To You:** The example above perfectly demonstrates the disadvantage of rewards. In terms of reading enjoyment, the incidental and peripheral information is often equally or more important than the key information. It is also considered essential to creativity and understanding because of the contextual base it provides. Reduce or eliminate the use of rewards; they are not worth the cost.

How You Can Follow Up: *Growing up Creative,* by Teresa Amabile; *Seven Kinds of Smart,* by Thomas Armstrong.

Rewarded Actions Lose Appeal

In research by Alan Kazden following a decade of post-reward analysis, the conclusions are clear: when the goodies stop, the behavior stops, too. Kazden, *who once was a proponent of rewards,* set up a token economy system in a health care institution. At first, he was excited about the behavior changes. In his first publication, *The Rich Reward of Rewards,* he talked about how much patient behavior had changed. And that's what people remembered the most. But ten years later, in *The Token Economy: A Decade Later*, he changes his mind. Kazden says,

> *"Removal of token reinforcement results*
> *in decrements in desirable responses*
> *and a return to baseline or near-baseline*
> *levels of performance"*

Every learner has his or her own bias which they bring to a particular context. The biases constitute personal beliefs, hopes, expectations, fears, values and emotions. These are what hold a behavior in place. In fact, Hart says, "To change the behavior, the biases must be changed, not the behavior directly." The rewards are designed to change the behavior, not the biases. Hence, any reward-driven activity is likely to fail in the long run.

We all know presenters often offer rewards for attendance, homework or discipline. Pizza Hut had a program designed to reward participants for reading by offering pizzas. The follow-up may show that the ones who read the most were the ones who were reading already. They just decided to play the game. Many of the readers who were not ordinarily reading before the promotion may not now be readers. Long-term follow up will tell.

> **What This Means To You:** Many learners could become very intrinsically motivated if given a chance. But as long as a reward system is in place, they'll play the game and undermine their own progress in the long-term. Reduce or eliminate all rewards. Use the alternatives of celebrations, increased variety and quantity of feedback.

Should You *Ever* Use Rewards?

If rewards are counterproductive in so many areas, is there a time and place for them at all? Yes, says Kohn. "If your objective is to get people to [temporarily] obey an order, show up on time and do what they're told," rewards can work, he says. But, he adds emphatically, rewards are simply changing the specific, "in the moment" behavior and not the "person." However, if your objective is to achieve any of the following, rewards simply don't work:

- *long-term quality performance*
- *becoming self-directed learners*
- *developing values of caring, respect and friendliness*
- *creativity and higher-order thinking skills*
- *honesty, integrity and self-confidence*
- *inner drive and intrinsic motivation*

In one study, fourth graders were asked what kind of reward they'd like for doing a simple classroom task. They were given that reward for doing it, as promised. Later, when it was time to do the task, *they performed more poorly on the task than the group that was not offered a reward.*

Here's an example of where a reward might be used. You have a bunch of chairs to move to another room. It's the end of the day, you're tired and hungry. You ask a couple of participants who stay after class if they'd be willing to help you move them. They say, "No, not really." But you're desperate. You say, "How about if I get you both a Coke?" They change their minds and decide it's worth it. The desks get moved. Everybody's happy. The reward was appropriate.

241

> **What This Means To You:** The reward had come to symbolize the presenter trying to get them to use or like the activity. As a consequence, the participants perceived that the task was intrinsically undesirable. A fundamental concept is: If the learner is doing the task to get the reward, it will be understood, on some level, that the task is inherently undesirable. Forget the use of rewards. Any that you are using now, phase out slowly. Use other strategies such as increased feedback, peer support, creativity and love of learning.

Alternatives Found To Bribery & Rewards

There are many powerful alternatives to bribing participants for better behaviors. This short-term narrow-minded Skinnerian approach has been found to do more harm than good. But are there realistic alternatives? Yes, there are. The first and most powerful one is this: make school meaningful, relevant and fun. Then, you won't have to bribe participants.

If you are using any kind of reward system, *let it run its course and end it as soon as you reasonably can.* If you stop it abruptly, you may get a rebellion. The learners will need a "de-tox" or "rehabilitation" time to get off the "reward drug." Remember, the research says:

Learners who have been on a reward system will
become conditioned to prefer it over free choice

Replacing rewards with alternatives gets a bit tricky in two cases. First, in schools, *the entire system of marking and grading is a reward and punishment system.* The rewards are good grades which leads to presenter approval, scholarships and university entry. How can an instructional leader work properly (without bribes and rewards) within a system that is so thoroughly entrenched? Use the options outlined above. What if other presenters use rewards, but you don't? The participants will soon discover that your way is not a bribe to learn or behave. Learners will be able to make the distinctions after some time and will prefer your way of learning. Be patient.

Secondly, there are many "gray areas." The getting of a certificate may be just an acknowledgment when you give it, but its role may become complicated. What if the learner takes it home and the parent rewards him with money? Then it becomes a reward in spite of your best intentions. The solution is to try to make parents aware of the destructive effects of rewards at an open house night or by letter. Naturally, schools have to be careful of this "step ladder" effect, where accumulated acknowledgments (certificates, etc.) can lead to a reward.

> **What This Means To You:** You can stop bribing learners! The brain loves to learn. This book is full of alternatives to bribery. At the earliest possible convenience, end the system and replace rewards with alternatives. Suggestions are listed below.

a) Acknowledgments: both verbal and non-verbal. Thank-you's, descriptive feedback, ceremony, praise and hugs, certificates, peer recognition all work!

b) Boost the quantity & quality of feedback: learners need consistent feedback, every single class session, even if it's simply a group choral recall, partner feedback, or team feedback. In the absence of feedback, learners want rewards - after all, it's just another form of feedback. Make it a point to insure every learner gets daily feedback.

c) Celebrations: small or large, spontaneous displays marking periodic success. These could be high-five's, bragging time, pointing out something they liked about another's work, an impromptu pizza, or a day trip.

d) Demonstrate and role model the joy of learning: every time you can, share your own excitement and enthusiasm over something you learned. That will give your learners the important message that learning, in and of itself, is valuable and rewarding.

e) Enhance relationships: sharing more of yourself, learning and caring more about the learners you work with, is critical. Often the single most important reason that learners like a subject has to do with the relationship they have with you, the instructional leader. Keep some professional distance, but be genuinely interested in your participants. Naturally, learner to learner bonding works great, too.

f) High need/high relevance: from a survival point of view, the brain is best designed to learn what it NEEDS to learn to survive. When the content of the material is perceived as being needed by the learner, motivation goes up. Or, if it's personally meaningful, the intrinsic rewards are highly likely to happen on their own. Extrinsic, gimmicky rewards are almost ludicrous compared to something personally motivating.

g) Choice & creativity: constant control and manipulation of the learner creates resentment and disempowerment. Offer ways that the learner can make choices about how the learning is done. A consistent stream of choice will provide a context for greater motivation. Input, suggestion boxes, learner presenting and teamwork can also contribute to a more motivated learner. This is one of the true secrets to motivation.

h) Rich, stimulating, positive environment: consisting of four parts: 1) water, food and exercise for the brain; 2) posters, sounds, and manipulatives that change every few weeks; 3) mistakes are welcomed; 4) learning is valued, discussed and debriefed by the participants.

The primary point to be made here is that you don't have to bribe learners to learn. The human brain loves to learn! Simply follow the "rules" for brain-compatible learning and learners will re-kindle their thirst and hunger to learn.

What the Reward Proponents Say

Educators usually fall into one of three camps. On the left are the humanists who believe that the best will come out of learners if you treat them right. Their basic approach is "educare" or draw out the intrinsic motivation. In the center are the cognitives who feel their job is to tell the learners what needs to be learned. They treat them as an empty vessel that needs to be filled. On the right are the behaviorists who operate from a control theory. In that paradigm, the way you get learners to learn is to first gain control, then control **what** they learn, **how** they learn it and if they aren't interested, simply bribe them. Those who are steadfast in their insistence on rewards usually defend them on the following grounds:

1. *Rewards are necessary. "After all, what's the intrinsic reward for computing the problem 4 + 4?"*
2. *The studies on intrinsic rewards are theoretical only.*
3. *Rewards are harmless.*
4. *The real world uses rewards.*
5. *Rewards are effective.*

Those who have discovered the power of alternatives know the answers already. But for the others, here are some comments about the five points raised above:

1. "Rewards are necessary." This is false. In the "control paradigm," participants *have been so conditioned,* that even simple learning begs for a motivating cue. That's because *their natural love of learning has been manipulated out of them.* But there are millions of participants who learn based on curiosity, joy and their natural love of learning. Learners who say they want or prefer rewards have simply been conditioned to want them.

2. "The studies on intrinsic rewards are theoretical only." This is false. Hundreds of studies on the follies of rewards have been done on real people in everyday situations. Out of the top twenty-five high schools in 1993 in America, only two of them use a reward system (aside from grades). Twenty three of them rely on quality, real-life learning. One of the most innovative programs for over a dozen years, SuperCamp, *uses no rewards* and its results have been reported in doctoral dissertations, on over 200 radio and television stations and hundreds of newspapers worldwide.

244

3. "Rewards are harmless." False. Consistent studies have documented that, under the context of a reward, the brain operates differently. The behaviors become more predictable, stereotyped, rigid and narrow. In other words, you can get a behavior, it's just very limited. And it's not the best from your participants.

4. "The real world uses rewards." In some cases, yes, in many cases, no. Critics say that everyone gets rewards for their work, but that's not true. Many, many people work only because they love their job. The majority of presenters went into their profession because they liked the satisfaction of helping others grow and succeed, not the money. Other jobs pay much more. Working hard doesn't guarantee a lifestyle of the rich and famous. In fact, most of the rich and famous got to the top by doing what they love to do and **not** focusing on any reward.

5. "Rewards are effective." In rote, repetitive tasks, *yes, for a while;* but then the novelty of the reward wears off and the performance drops. Remember, someone can hold a loaded gun to your head and get you to do almost anything. It's effective, isn't it? But that's a bad criteria. The real-world research demonstrates consistently that behaviors which are rewarded, then not rewarded, cause a drop off in quality and productivity. The rewarded behavior rarely continues, whether it's for a reading program, to behave, to write a book report or whatever. In short, those who did the behavior for rewards, not the intrinsic, will quit once the rewards are gone. Those who did the behavior whether there was a reward or not, will continue to do it, even after the reward is gone.

Humanistic	Cognitive	Behaviorist
ask	tell	reinforce
elicit	transmit	strengthen
intrinsic motivation	options	ext. motivation

How to Replace Rewards in Learning

When you are ready to remove all of your built-in rewards, don't expect a standing ovation. Research has shown that many learners will prefer rewards. even though it is counter-productive to their learning. Why? It's predictable. Take your time to slowly phase out the rewards. Do it with the participants, in partnership. First, let any existing system expire on its own. The potential uproar over a change may not be initially worth it. Then, participants should be notified about the change. Presenters who make unilateral decisions about classroom operations are ignoring learner input and reinforcing a sense of learner powerlessness. Presenters, at the earliest years appropriate, should engage the participants in an active, unguided discussion about the real cost of rewards and ask the participants to talk, too.

Second, you must replace the rewards with greater choice and learner empowerment. Removing the rewards does not assure the presenter that genuine, authentic, intrinsic learning will take place. That is achieved through a complex set of orchestrated, interactive, empowered learner choices. Learners must choose to learn something for their own reasons, and that's more likely when presenters openly talk about it. It's based on perceived needs, values, belief systems, emotions and goals. Unless those needs are addressed, the removal of a reward system will only address a small part of the problem you want solved.

Third, you'll need to increase the frequency of feedback in other ways. Once you have set up a dozen other ways for participants to get meaningful feedback (see the chapter on profound assessment), then the rewards will become meaningless. The role of testing, grades, scholarships and working for rewards must be brought into significant discussion. It is an ongoing systemic process to get rid of reward systems. It takes time, careful attention and cooperative planning. Do it right. Make sure that all who are involved in and affected by the decisions are a part of the process.

How will you know when the final ill effects of rewards have been eliminated? It's simple. You will never, never again hear participants ask

"Is this going to be on the test?"

If you hear that, they are really saying to you, "I've had the love of learning bribed out of me by unknowing presenters. So, since I don't think learning is any fun, I want to have a reason to learn this or be compensated for my effort. Therefore, do I really have to do this? Otherwise, I don't want to learn it for its own sake."

How You Can Follow Up: Read *Punished by Rewards,* by Kohn.

Chapter Questions

1. What was novel, fresh and new? What was familiar or "old hat"?
2. In what ways do you already apply the information in this chapter?
3. What three questions can you now generate about this material?
4. How did you react emotionally to this information?
5. In what ways can you translate the key three or four theories and discoveries presented here into practical everyday useful ideas?
6. How did you react cognitively when you were reading the ideas of this chapter?
7. If these things are, in fact, true about the brain, what should we do differently? What resources of time, people and money could be redirected? In what ways do you suggest we start?
8. What was the single one (or two) most interesting or valuable insights you had?
9. Plan your next step, the logical practical application of what you've learned.
10. What obstacles might you encounter? How can you realistically deal with them?

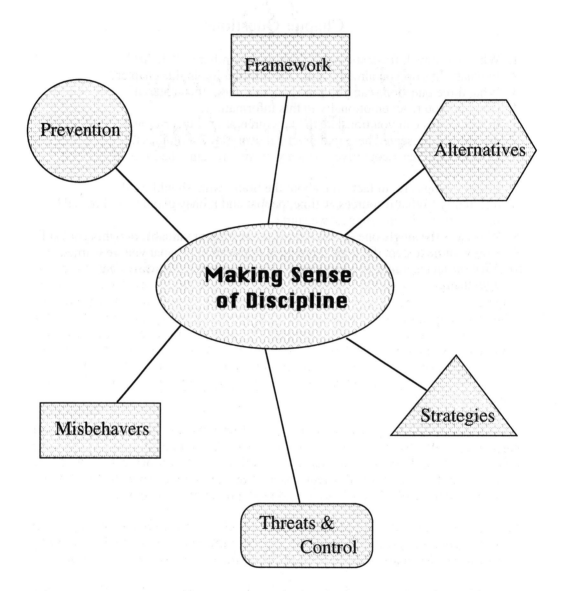

248

16
Making Sense of Discipline

A Realistic Discipline Philosophy

A more brain-based discipline policy takes into consideration what we now know about the brain and learning. It accepts the natural tendencies we have and responds more sensibly to problems. Primary sources of discipline problems include a poor learning environment filled with threat, stress, lack of choice, inappropriate learning styles and multiple intelligences used or not used. The primary biological source for discipline problems is the mid-brain area. That's the part of the brain that deals with attention, arousal, boredom, emotions and motivation. The more we understand how this part of our brain functions and what we can do about it, the fewer our discipline problems. We'll return to the role of emotions in a moment. Chapter two also gives you a good background; you may want to review it now.

First, when dealing with discipline, all of us have "mental models" about our participants. We formed them many years ago. They may or may not be very functional. Regardless, these models are the primary decision-makers for us. These frameworks, these cause and effect propositions are either useful or they're not. Here's an example of a NON-brain-based model regarding discipline:

Presenter gets control >>> by suppressing emotions >>> so presenter can teach >>> so supposedly participants can learn >>> suppressed emotions hurt learning >>> then they learn less >>> presenters coerce them more >>> to pass the test.

Some presenters would argue that the above scenario is absolutely necessary for running "a tight ship." The problem is, you may get a tight ship, but you'll also get forced or impaired learning from cautious low-risk learners. What would a model, a framework or philosophy be like that was more brain-based?

That's what this chapter is about. There are many components. The shorthand of the model might look something like this:

emotions have appropriate outlets >>> so learners feel good >>> learners learn more >>> discipline problems diminish >>> more choice is offered >>> more learning is fostered >>> less direct instruction needed >>> now everyone wins.

In a bit more detail, here are the six brain-based fundamentals for establishing a better climate for learning with fewer discipline problems:

1. Disruptions are a normal part of living

Regular disruptions are part of school, life and part of our reality. Some can be prevented at school, but some are inevitable. Life is chaotic, if we are to make schools more relevant, we must learn to treat most non-emergency disruptions as enjoyable challenges and sources of curiosity. It is easier for **you** to adapt than to try to change the world to meet your point of view. Disruptions are going to happen. Ask yourself, "What are the two or three most common disruptions and how can I deal with them positively and proactively?" *Message to participants: "School is real life."*

2. The classroom is a "learning environment"

Within this learning environment, occasional discipline takes place. The classroom is *not* a well-disciplined class in which learning *better occur* or else! That sounds more like a correctional facility. Student presenters are often taught: *first,* you get control, *then,* you teach (and supposedly *they* learn). But that's *all backwards.* The worst environment for learning is high fear, high stress. The optimal learning state is low stress, high challenge. Get engaged learning going on and the discipline problems will disappear fast. *Message to participants: "What we are about is learning."*

3. Students are all basically good

Students are just trying to manage their everyday lives. Students rarely wake up in the morning, planning or plotting, with the sole intent to "get you." But they do have normal concerns for expression, control, attention and love. Some of the ways they express their needs are inappropriate for a classroom. One of your strategies is to provide productive outlets for their frustration and need for control and attention. At the same time, you may want to teach them how to do that for themselves, too. *Message to participants: "You are a human being, I respect you."*

4. The best discipline is the kind nobody notices

It's crazy to formally discipline every learner "mistake." The less participants *know* they are being disciplined, the better. Keep "learning" as the "class event" by observing learner states and creating constant engagement, novelty, challenge and diversity. The more outraged you become about discipline problems, the more they occur. (If *you're* upset, who's in control?) Remember this: "Where the attention goes, the energy flows!" Keep your attention more focused on the joy and excitement of learning. Use the presenting and learning strategies outlined in the other chapters. *Message to participants: "Presenter has things handled."*

5. Discipline problems are simply feedback to you
Most problems are "in the moment" reactions. Respond non-verbally (with actions, not words), non-traditionally (no lecture) to most discipline problems. After all, most problem-behaviors originate from the reptilian, limbic or right brain, not the left-side of the brain. Make your responses appropriate to where the learner is *really at.* Save the lectures, the left-brain discussion of rules as a last resort response. *Message to participants: "I know exactly where you're at."*

6. Prevention solves 95% of the problems
By keeping participants engaged and positively expressive, they'll have the outlets they need without causing you a headache. Keep participants in the appropriate states for learning. Avoid unplanned "transition" or "down time." Do "behind the scenes" work with certain participants who need it. The best presenters have virtually no discipline problems *not* because they have participants who are already well-behaved, but because they create the conditions for optimal learning. Message to participants: *"Focus on the important things."*

How to Prevent Discipline Problems

1. Limit the amount of focused learning time before switching to some kind of diffusion activities. Suggested time amount: use the age of the participants in minutes (up to 25 min. maximum).

2. Use baroque music in the background (at low level to soothe & inspire) for some of the time, maybe at other times, environmental music like waterfalls, oceans, forest birds, etc.

3. Create more "W-I-I-F-M" (What's in it for me?) for the participants: **ask them** to elicit good reasons for themselves to do things... more relevance! Start with their needs and goals. The more the learning meets their goals (instead of someone's else's, the more engagement you'll get).

4. Make rules fair, clear and enforceable... the fewer the better. Make sure that participants know the reasons behind every rule you have. Post the rules.

5. Put participants in cooperative groups or teams for part of the time. Keep teams accountable. Use teams as a source of fun, socialization and positive peer pressure

6. Make positive eye contact with each of your participants within the first minutes of class. Also connect with parents as early in the year as you can (if it's appropriate), by open house, phone or notes, if possible.

7. Boost ways participants can have more input into their classroom. Install a suggestion box... read all, respond to them in writing or actually do it!

8. Provide ample auditory outlets for expression. Learn to deal with emotions. Ways to teach, buzz time, partner affirmations, group time, discussion, teams, sharing. This gives learners time to de-stress and gain secondary social goals.

9. When you present rules, let participants play the "what if" game to find exceptions, then brainstorm solutions, make rules concrete.

10. Make the classroom more interesting to be a learner in and change it often. Make it busy, colorful, fresh, challenging, wild and relevant.

11. Anticipate, read and respond swiftly to learner states. Frustration usually leads to apathy, anger or revenge. Do prevention of problems.

12. Make rapport-building a part-time job.... Start with the kids you relate to least & do it verbally and non-verbally. If it's broken, repair it ASAP. Know the tendencies of auditory learners who tend to talk a lot and mismatchers who accidentally disrupt class in an attempt to learn. They're often pointing out what's "off, different, missing or wrong."

13. Keep the physical body moving many times per hour or the brain can switch off. Use movements, stretching, or switch activities.

14. Keep your own stress levels low. "Download" each work day. Take care of your physical body. Enjoy "mindless" relaxing play.

15. Work on your areas of concern like parent communications or improving administrative policies or communications to staff.

16. Give clear, mobilizing directions. Do it in this order: why, when, who, what, re-check for understanding, then congruent call to action. Be consistent, so participants become conditioned to listen carefully.

17. Give participants more control through choosing ways to do things. Use suggestion instead of threats. Let them pick 10 of 15 problems, choose either this or that topic, or this or that time priority. Choices work!

18. Get parents involved in your discipline program from the beginning. Send home the plan, the reasons, the excitement and get agreement.

19. Have lunch with a learner to create, build or maintain a relationship.

20. Teach using the multiple intelligences. Make sure that when you plan out your week, you have covered all of them.

21. Provide outlets for participants to talk about the things that are important to them. Discussion time, sharing circles, partner or buddy time.

22. Students write a weekly or monthly letter to presenter and get response.

23. Role play discipline problems and rehearse positive reactions.

24. Shared pairs - participants pair up and help monitor each other in class

25. Students give the presenter evaluations - the input helps improve presenting and reduce likelihood of problems.

26. Eliminate threats, rewards and demands.

27. Let participants know you care by attending some kind of outside class activity that they may be involved in: a play, city event, sports, etc.

Over-Controlling Learners Can Backfire

Often, presenters want to quickly change learner behavior for conformity or expediency. But research by Ford makes an important distinction: one-time short-term vs. multiple long-term strategies. He says,

"Highly controlling motivational strategies such as real or implied threats, strong punishments, compelling rewards and forced competition are sometimes effective... however, they are likely to produce negative developmental consequences if they are repeated across many different behavioral episodes"

In other words, by consistently using controlling means on your learners, you'll undermine their overall success. In fact, Ford says, "there is compelling literature on the motivational consequences of controlling experiences that indicates people lose interest in activities when they feel coerced or manipulated to engage in those activities, even when the motivational strategies used were intended to be positive and motivating." Additional research by Deci, Lepper, Deci and Ryan, Ryan and Stiller, and Kohn confirms this.

In most cases, school starts off being fun and motivating with high initial interest. By later years, that enthusiasm has been replaced with resentment, complacency and avoidance. Controlling strategies, lack of creativity and choice, and parental pressure have killed intrinsic motivation for another year.

> **What This Means To You:** We may have much more to do with the behaviors of our learners than we previously thought. Hold a staff meeting. Get everyone aligned on this issue. Develop a policy that everyone can buy into. Eliminate rewards; replace them with the alternatives of choice, creativity, enthusiasm, multi-context learning and celebration.

Constant Subtle Threats Harmful

Presenters who pause and say with a stern voice, directly to the class, "I'll just wait until you're ready to learn" may be doing more harm than good. This threat ("I'll withhold my presenting as long as you are withholding your good behavior") is a simple example of the continual threats that pervade a typical classroom. Research now tells us that threatening learners may foster more of the same behavior that we are trying to avoid.

A threat is any stimulus that causes the brain to trigger defensiveness or a sense of helplessness in the learner. An example of a subtle threat to the learner is when an assignment or project is given, and the learner lacks the resources to carry it out. The brain sits in a state of stress. In some cases, the threat may be perceived as indirectly aimed at one's self-esteem, confidence and peer acceptance.

According to Jaques and Leonard, threats adversely affect one's ability to plan for the long-term and to stay engaged at a task for a long period of time. These abilities are critical for learners: some evidence links success with the ability to postpone immediate gratification and go for the long term. Caine says that threats, even if occurring indirectly through rewards, may hinder our ability to tolerate ambiguity and to delay gratification, and that it may be "among the most important and devastating of all consequences."

In many cases, a learner is told that if he solves a problem (or has good behavior, perfect attendance, etc.) he will get a sticker, token, food or other reward. With every reward, there is an implied lack of reward (punishment) for a contra-behavior. Spielberger states that learner dependence on "flocking behaviors" (social conformity) and reliance on extrinsic rewards (bribes, stickers, etc.) actually increases with threat.

Many presenters have difficulties with learners diagnosed as ADHD (attention deficit hyperactivity disorder). These individuals can be a tremendous discipline problem with restless, unfocused and impulsive behaviors. Many researchers say ADHD is partially caused by specific neurotransmitter deficiencies in the brainstem and limbic areas. In some cases, properly prescribed drugs such as Ritalin™ and Cylert™ can make dramatic improvements in learner's behavior. However, other alternatives ought to be explored first, leaving medication as a last resort.

Another example can be seen with a learner who is constantly disciplined because of his inability to stay engaged in a task or his inability to delay gratification. The discipline may actually create a "state of threat" which perpetuates the problem.

> **What This Means To You:** We may need to redefine what we consider to be threats in a learning environment. We may need to utilize alternative forms of motivation. Any system of learning which uses heavy authority, position, laws, threats, rules, punishments and rewards will, over the long run, perpetuate the very behaviors it is trying to eliminate. The techniques may work initially, but soon the learner behavior will become rote, minimized and stereotyped.

Learners who feel picked on and threatened by adults are least likely to change behavior because the part of their brain that deals with "perceptual mapping" and complex behavior change is unable to be engaged. Both adults and teenagers stay in peer groups for identity and safety. So-called "low achievers" who are constantly threatened, disciplined and bribed with rewards may be unable to work for delayed gratification. The part of their brain they need to use, the frontal lobes, are less likely to be engaged under a system where others have control and they feel pressured to perform like a rat in a cage.

This may explain many of the common behaviors of gangs, so-called "low-achievers" and the drifting learners who seem unmotivated. The more they are threatened, the more behaviors they'll have which demonstrate a lack of higher-order thinking skills and increased short-term thinking.

> **What This Means to You:** Identify substandard learner behaviors. Identify areas of threats, both implied and explicit. As much as possible, remove threats from the learning environment and introduce alternative forms of motivation, such as novelty, curiosity, positive social bonding and relevant content. Avoid reliance on extrinsic rewards.

Brain-Compatible Discipline Strategies

There are usually special circumstances around the disciplining of an individual learner. Either the learner has a sordid past, a clean past, is upset, or someone made him or her misbehave or some other story. *Stay out of the story business.* Keep the focus on learning. When a learner is misbehaving, remember, he is NOT a problem. He usually has no problem; **you are the one** who is upset. He is simply acting inappropriately... just like you have in your life, too. Short term, you simply want to change the learner's state into a better one. Long-term, you want the learner to learn to manage his or her own behaviors better.

Most discipline problems are inappropriately
expressed emotions...find more productive outlets
for them and you'll reduce discipline problems dramatically

Based on what we know about the brain, the mid-brain area is most responsible for discipline problems. Since it regulates arousal thresholds, attention cycles and learning biases, some steps are obvious. First, we ought to accept that the brain has an attentional bias for contrast, novelty and emotion. When we ignore this, many learners get bored and restless. The way things are taught can keep learning interest high - more complex, detailed in the morning, more global, physical in the afternoon. Our brain's focus-diffusion cycles mean that we might keep learner interest for about their age (in minutes). The internal-external shifts mean that we might allow more time for learners to process things alone, in reflective time. As mentioned earlier, the concept of "on task" is totally irrelevant. The brain does not work like a machine - it cannot be forced to focus.

There are many "levels" of discipline. *Someone who is doing bodily harm or property damage needs immediate and different strategies* than someone who's talking too much. In general, your first approach is to simply stop the problem behavior with as little notice and fanfare as possible. In other words, *keep the solution "invisible" while you continue presenting.* Here are some possible responses when a problem occurs, listed from least severe to most severe.

Level 1 - Invisible: "Nobody knows but the presenter"

Focus on changing the state of the learner, not the behavior. When the state changes, the behaviors automatically change. It's indirect, it keeps the focus on learning and it works like a charm. Many things can change the physiological state of the learner. 1) switch activities 2) have them take in a slow deep breath 3) switch tonality of your voice 4) make a new gesture in the room to a new location 5) attention drawn away from the person with a comment 6) use a change of music 7) step out of room for a second, 8) lead participants in stretching or Simon Sez game, 9) have participants do oral partner affirmations quickly 10) give learner a special class job 11) your proximity.

Some suggestions may include just a bit more "notice" of the behavior and are less "invisible." 12) name dropping; use the names of three or more participants in a sentence 13) use "shhh" more creatively like "You sssssshhhhould find this interesting" 14) use gestures or a gentle touch 15) change your facial expression 16) use a change of state ritual you've used before 17) shout out the door 18) yell to an object 19) ask a team or group leader to start an activity among participants 20) send learner on an errand 21) admonish the object of noise making instead of the learner... "Bad pencil! If it doesn't quiet down, I'll have to put it in the bad pencil box."

Level 2 - Minor attention drawn: "No big deal"

Be direct and light. Use no or low-threat consequences to succeed. 1) Use eye contact, ask learner to choose A behavior or B action. "Brian, can you keep it down? I'd really appreciate that." Or, 2) "Kim, you're a responsible person - so here's your choice: hold it down for the next 10 minutes or we've got to have a talk after class." Or, 3) "Kenny, by keeping your hands to yourself, we can finish without any more interruptions and get out on time." Tonality, intent, congruency and consistency will make this work most of the time.

Use no threats, follow through on all consequences and avoid keeping a learner after school. For most kids, it simply helps them hate that classroom or school even more. They get bad associations about school when they can sit and brood about mistakes.

Level 3 - Patience is gone: "I'm serious now!"

Sometimes just one person or a few are causing trouble. No need to disrupt everyone. If you have just a single learner or very few that are causing the disruption, continue talking to the whole class. Interject a story quickly about a dog or kid that you once had to yell at loudly. In the story, turn to the noisy kids and say you got so mad, you had to tell the dog to "Quiet down!" Continue with your story. The behavior will stop. There are many other statements you can make in the context of a story. But that usually gets their attention and helps them quiet down.

If you want to discipline the entire group (or most of them), never get "heavy" from the front of the room where you teach. That "contaminates" your creative presenting area. Grinder recommends you use a consistent "Hot Spot" for disciplining large groups of class. Go to a special area in the room, that you only use for discipline, away from the front of the room, the door, your desk. Stand there and use your "heavy" voice and strong disciplining eye contact and gesture (there are also other options besides being "heavy").

Get the class's attention and give your message. You can state the word "Courtesy!" or "Boys and Girls!" or "Ladies and Gentlemen!" if you want to yell. Then leave the spot, go back to your presenting area. Change your voice, tonality and facial expression back to normal. Ask the participants to take in a deep breath, just to change their state to a better learning state, and continue presenting. No lecture on discipline, no recital of the rules, no more heavy talk. You got what you wanted: the noise was stopped and they all got your disapproval. So now you can go back to presenting.

Level 4 - Time to talk serious. "What's really up?"

Before you get to this stage, ask yourself if you've done everything you can to make class interesting, relevant and provided constant choice in how to learn. Are you using many learning styles and multiple intelligences? If you've done all you can, then we want to have the learner take on responsibility for his behavior.

Time to have a meeting with the learner, preferably outside of class time, first alone. Ask questions and listen to the story without blaming. First learner-presenter, then if needed, add parents, principal, etc. 1) Allow for emotions to be expressed and gain rapport 2) Discover and meet each other's concerns 3) Create new agreements each is willing to keep 4) Put something "at stake" for the learner, something he or she has to lose if the agreement is broken. Set up a way to monitor or manage the plan.

Some Misbehavers May
Actually Be Good Learners

Rosenfield says that, in its search for meaning, our brain is constantly sorting out incoming data to find patterns. This pattern-detecting allows the brain to make cognitive maps. O'Keefe and Nadel says that our brain needs to register something familiar and yet is simultaneously motivated and intrigued by novelty. James says that the brain either "matches" up with (familiar) data or it "mismatches" (differentiates, finds exceptions) with it (and combinations in-between).

What does all this mean? A learner may learn by similarities (familiarity) or differences (novelty) in varying amounts. Virtually no one does either type of learning 100% of the time, but there are tendencies. James says that 50% of Americans match and mismatch evenly - they do both with the same frequency. He adds that 10% of the population mismatches constantly and that 40% are habitual "matchers." The matchers work at the same job for years, keep the same friends, eat at the same restaurants and do many of the same activities year after year. They use generalizing phrases like "everyone, always, we, never, all." They make generalizing patterns quickly.

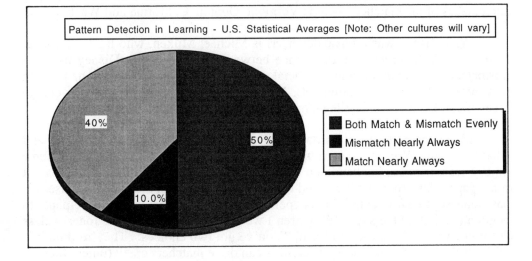

Pattern Detection in Learning - U.S. Statistical Averages [Note: Other cultures will vary]

40%

50%

10.0%

■ Both Match & Mismatch Evenly
■ Mismatch Nearly Always
▨ Match Nearly Always

The "mismatchers" tend to prefer change over sameness. They try out new things, go to different restaurants, take a new route home, and experiment more. They find exceptions to the rule, they use phrases like, "but..." and "not always..." If a sign says "NO Trespassing," a matcher will obey. A mismatcher will wonder "What's in there?" Mismatchers are distinctly different from:

1) divergent thinkers (who tend to be more exploratory and creative, but not as contrarian)
2) skeptics (who tend to question things consistently but are either closed minded or impossible to sway
3) age-related "phases" (almost all two-year-olds say "NO!" to nearly everything, but that's a developmental stage)
4) delinquents (who simply want to be "bad" because of domestic problems, peer pressure, low self-concept, etc.)

The degree to which a nation's population or particular culture (urban, rural, men, women, etc.) matches or mismatches is entirely culturally reinforced. In some cultures, like Japan, it's simply bad etiquette to mismatch, so you have a nation which has a higher percentage of matchers. In Israel, the culture encourages asking questions, finding exceptions and mismatching. Australia has a higher percentage of mismatchers than most countries, to a small degree, because it was used as a penal colony by England. More importantly, it has what is known as the "California greener grass syndrome." That means those who emigrate are often self-selected as being "different thinking" and wanting a change. That's partly what makes-up self-selected California's diverse population. In America, more matchers live in the Midwest than any other part of the country. States with relatively high percentages of mismatchers include Vermont, Oregon, California and Washington.

Walt Disney was a mismatcher, as is Michael Milken, who made an illegal fortune on Wall Street. The difference between the two is that Disney used his mismatching to break the rules of social conformity and establish what he thought was missing (family entertainment). Milken used his mismatching tendencies to break the rules also, but for illegal trading on Wall Street.

Mismatchers in the classroom tend to focus on differences, exceptions and what is missing. You say to a group that you'll be done in ten minutes. After some time, a learner raises his hand and says "It's been eleven minutes." You pass out some paper. A learner, having found the only misspelling on the handout, raises his hand and says, "How come this is spelled wrong?" You ask your participants to begin an activity. One says, "Why aren't we doing this the way Mr. Jones's class did it last year?" If you say to them, "You've got two choices." They're thinking, "What's the third?" And those differences can drive matchers crazy (unless they've read this, first).

Most participants respect the classroom rules, but perhaps one learner keeps breaking them, almost as if he is obsessed with trying to find out the answer to the question, "I know the rule, but is there an exception to it?" This kind of response is typical of that made by a mismatcher. Pull that learner aside and tell him that you think, "Creativity is wonderful, but if you are creative in other areas than discipline, it'll keep us both happy and you out of trouble."

Again, rarely is anyone a total "matcher" or "mismatcher." Usually, you'll have learners who "match generally, with some mismatching," or "mismatch generally with some matching." The whole point is to realize that these learners are sorting patterns their way in order to learn. You can easily recognize learners as generally more "matchers" and "mismatchers."

Those who are matchers tend to:

- agree with you more often
- prefer the familiar, tried and true
- be uncomfortable with novelty
- follow rules, stay with the group
- learn by similarities
- do what is expected by others

Those who are mismatchers tend to:

- disagree more often
- prefer novelty, change, a bit of risk
- sometimes ignore rules and boundaries
- need differences to understand

To deal with those who are mismatching:

1) Don't try to "fix" them; they're not broken.
2) Appreciate and respect their alternative point of view ("Thanks for pointing that out. I hadn't thought of that.").
3) Make sure that they follow the same rules as everyone else. Avoid labeling any learner, since they may vary preferences, depending on stress levels or circumstances. It's best to use "matcher" and "mismatcher" as active, flexible verbs e.g., "He was mismatching me again," or, "Good mismatch."

What This Means To You: We may have labeled countless learners as troublemakers when, in fact, the way they learn is simply by trying to establish a pattern for meaning. Think of the question, "Is this person filling the mold (matching) or trying to break the mold (mismatching)?" The next time a learner says, "Hey you misspelled a word on this worksheet," say "Thanks for finding that. If you'd like, you can be in charge of always finding any typos or misprints." Learn to appreciate that mismatchers love to learn, they simply learn by differences, not similarities.

How You Can Follow Up: *Insider's Guide to Learning Styles,* a booklet or *How to End Discipline Problems in 30 Days.* See Appendix for details.

Chapter Questions

1. What was novel, fresh and new? What was familiar or "old hat"?
2. In what ways do you already apply the information in this chapter?
3. What three questions can you now generate about this material?
4. How did you react emotionally to this information?
5. In what ways can you translate the key three or four theories and discoveries presented here into practical everyday useful ideas?
6. How did you react cognitively when you were reading the ideas of this chapter?
7. If these things are, in fact, true about the brain, what should we do differently? What resources of time, people and money could be redirected? In what ways do you suggest we start?
8. What was the single one (or two) most interesting or valuable insights you had?
9. Plan your next step, the logical practical application of what you've learned.
10. What obstacles might you encounter? How can you realistically deal with them?

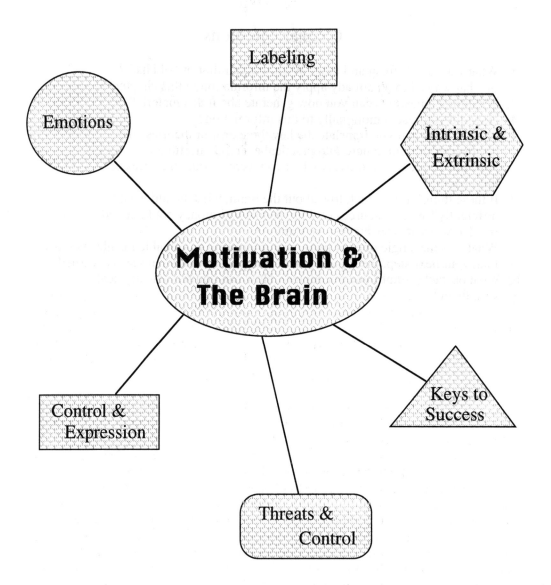

17
Motivation &
The Brain

The Controlling vs. Expression Paradigm

An all-too-common question often asked is "How do you motivate participants?" The answer is both simple and complex. First of all, even the question shows a misunderstanding of the real nature of motivation. *The human brain loves to learn.* In fact, its survival depends on learning. Learners have already motivated themselves for much of their life. Their brains have hungrily absorbed information, integrated it, made meaning out of it, remembered it and used it at the appropriate moment thousands of times. Therefore the question, "How do I motivate participants," says more about the asker than the participants.

One thing it says about the asker is, that their context for asking is not learning, *it's control.* The question they are really asking is, "How can I control their behavior?" The truth, the real answer, *will make no sense in the paradigm or context of control.* You have to leave the paradigm to get an answer that makes sense. Is your paradigm that your job is to be a learning catalyst (one who lights a fire for learning) or that of a "presenter" (one who stands and delivers - once the participants are under control)? In the paradigm of a presenter, there are many ways to "motivate"... temporarily. In the paradigm of a learning catalyst, it's a moot question. After all, in a brain-based learning environment, the learners are already motivated - just the way they already were before walking to class. Management guru Dr. Deming said that "All human beings are born with intrinsic motivation." They don't need someone to stand over them and motivate them (unless they have a brain-antagonistic environment).

The Folly of Labeling Learners

The unmotivated learner is a myth. Rarely are the most motivating conditions for learning met in a typical context. This may explain why so many have been labeled as "underachievers" or uninterested. To even arrive at business or a classroom requires some sort of motivation. It may be positive or negative, but it has gotten them there. Once the learner is in the seat, either they are bringing a new strong motivating attitude with them, or the presenter needs to elicit one. The demotivated learner's negative beliefs and behaviors are usually triggered or reinforced by an artificial, unresponsive school environment. Identifying, classifying, grouping, labeling, evaluating, comparing, and assessing these demotivated learners has done little to solve the problem.

There is no such thing as an unmotivated learner.
There are, however, temporary unmotivated states
that schools, presenters or the participants
themselves can trigger

Each learner is either motivated from within (intrinsic) or from the outside (extrinsic). *All of the following de-motivate learners and drive out of them any possibility of intrinsic motivation:*

- Coercion, control and manipulation
- Weak, critical or negatively competitive relationships
- Infrequent or vague feedback
- Outcome-based learning (unless learners generate outcomes)
- Inconsistent policies and rules
- Top-down management & policy-making
- Repetitive, rote learning
- Sarcasm, put-downs and criticism
- The perception of irrelevant content
- Boring, single-media presentation
- Reward systems of any kind
- Teaching in just one or two of the multiple intelligences
- Systems that limit reaching personal goals
- Responsibility without authority
- Hopelessness in achieving academic success

Most presenters use both intrinsic and extrinsic forms of motivation. As a result, much of the good things that are done by a presenter are undermined by themselves or others. The obvious choice is to have your learners motivated mostly from within. To do that, it takes a more brain-based approach. The research on motivation is both powerful and persuasive:

266

The school environment, for most learners,
is quite antagonistic towards the brain. Educators would
literally be astonished by the motivated learning accomplished
in a brain-compatible environment

Should the environment be all smiles, hugs and easy grades? **Absolutely not.** The brain thrives on challenges and variety. Stanford biologists separated amoebae cultures into three petri dishes. One was the control, the other gave the amoebae an abundance of food, light and heat. The third gave the amoebae enough of each, but not excessive. In fact, the amounts were randomly varied. You might guess the results: the third amoebae culture developed the strongest and lived longest. Can you apply that to our own environment? Maybe: don't punish the participants excessively or make everything so easy they never grow. When learners are required to figure it out, to earn what they get and develop themselves, they'll grow more.

Intrinsic vs. Extrinsic Motivation

Much of the extrinsic motivation characteristics originate in the home life: Feuerstein says extrinsically-motivated learners tend to "...avoid dissatisfaction by focusing on the ease, comfort, safety and security afforded in non-task conditions." Each of those factors has been identified as being "culturally responsive." Translated this means, "they were brought up that way." While we have little influence on those factors, we can influence others. Organize learning around the way the brain naturally likes to learn. Researcher Bishop makes the distinction very well:

"Young people are not lazy. In their jobs after school and on the football field, they work very hard. In these environments they are part of a team where individual efforts are visible and appreciated by teammates. Competition and rivalry are not absent, but they are offset by shared goals, shared successes and external measures of achievement... On the sports field, there is no greater sin than giving up, even when the score is hopelessly one-sided. On the job, tasks not done by one worker will generally have to be completed by another...."

When a learner drops out of school, he's not unmotivated; he just wanted a more responsive environment, *which the world outside of school promises.* But if we can make dramatic, positive alterations in the school's climate, policies, presenter methodologies and systems, we can keep the focus on learning and hook learners in for a lifetime.

Let's say a learner seems unmotivated all week long. Presenters say that he has no motivation or concentration. But on Saturday, he has his guitar lessons. He practices for hours without any bribe or external motivation. This activity makes quite a statement about how much the brain loves to learn.

There is a great deal of disagreement among researchers regarding what promotes intrinsic motivation. In fact, an interesting question is, "Should 100% intrinsic motivation even be desired?" Many would say no. Regardless, here are characteristics of intrinsically motivated learners. They:

> • **seek to exercise control over their environment**
> • **seek stimulation, activity and incongruities**
> • **have little or few feelings of inferiority**
> • **have high self-concept and contextual beliefs**
> • **prefer challenge, problem-solving & novelty**
> • **have high expectations of success**
> • **get satisfaction from responsibility & achievement**
> • **have strong self-efficacy to maintain**
>   **feelings of competence and self-determination**

This list can suggest many strategies for developing greater motivation. But other conditions can be developed in a learning context, many of which are relatively simple to do. This is important to realize, especially since "actual ability is relatively independent of motivational determinants of achievement," says Feuerstein. Drawing from the combined work of the authors Singer, Glasser, Lozanov, Hart, Wlodlowski, Murphy and Donovan, we can outline what the brain needs for optimal motivation:

Conditions & Strategies For
Eliciting Intrinsic Motivation

1. Meet perceived needs & goals

The brain is designed biologically to survive. It will learn what it NEEDS to learn to survive. Make it a top priority to discover what needs your learners have and engage those needs. If participants need what you have, they're interested. If the content relates to the student's own personal life, they're interested. For example, six-year-old participants have higher needs for security, predictability and presenter acceptance than a 14-year-old learner. Their needs are more likely to be peer acceptance, a sense of importance and hope. An 18-year-old learner is more interested in autonomy and independence. Use what's appropriate for the age level of your participants.

2. Provide control & choice

Creativity and choice allow the learner to express & feel valued. The opposite of this is manipulation, coercion and control. Control and choice lowers stress and draws out what the learner really wants to do and learn.

3. Positive social bonding

This comes in many forms: a presenter they like, a classmate they like or partners and teams they like. Again, this reduces helplessness and stress.

4. Curiosity

We all know that inquiring minds want to know, that's the nature of the human brain... keep engaging curiosity - it works! Newspaper tabloids and electronic tabloids have played off our curiosity for years. Witness all the stories about Elvis, aliens, Charles and Diana, O.J. Simpson, celebrities and UFOs.

5. Engage strong emotions

Engage emotions productively with compelling stories, games, personal examples, celebrations, role-play, debates, rituals, music. We are driven to act upon our emotions because they are compelling decision-makers.

6. Nutrition

Better nutrition means better mental alertness. Learn about how we think, learn and want to improve. Write up a list of suggestions, give to participants or parents or both. Suggest specific brain foods (eggs, fish, nuts, leafy dark green vegetables, apples, bananas and others mentioned elsewhere in this book).

7. Use multiple intelligences

They can really hook learners in: spatial, bodily-kinesthetic, interpersonal, verbal-linguistic, intrapersonal, musical-rhythmic, mathematical-logical. We are particularly motivated when we can do something in an area that we have already developed as one of our seven intelligences.

8. Success stories

How have past participants done? What obstacles have they overcome to succeed? Any famous? Any who have made a major contribution? These stories form structure that creates a mythology of success. Just walking on to the campus of a famous university like Oxford, Harvard, Stanford, Wharton or Notre Dame can elicit feelings of motivation.

9. Acknowledgments

These include assemblies, certificates, group notices, team reports, peers who give compliments, presenters who praise appropriately. These give the brain positive associations which continue to fuel further actions.

10. Frequency of feedback

Make it your part-time job to make sure learners get far more feedback each class, use peers, charts, discussion, peer presenting, projects, role-play. The all-time best way to motivate the brain is with information; immediate and dramatic.

11. Physiological states

Learn to read and manage states. There is no such thing as an unmotivated learner, only unmotivated states. Elicit anticipation and challenge states. Learn to manage your own states to get the best out of yourself.

12. Provide hope of success

Learners need to know that's it's possible for them to succeed. Regardless of the obstacles or how far behind, hope is essential. Dr. Gelenberg of the University of Arizona and Dr. Jerome Frank of Johns Hopkins strongly believe that hope works like a powerful drug and is essential to restoring demoralization. Every learning context must provide some kind of hope.

13. Role model joy of learning

Since over 99% of all learning is non conscious, the more you get excited about learning, the more motivated your learners are likely to be excited.

14. Celebrations

These include peer acknowledgment, parties, food, hi-five's, cheers, etc. These create the atmosphere of success and can trigger the release of endorphins that boost further learning.

15. Physically & emotionally safe

The environment should be emotionally safe to make mistakes and physically safe from hazards or other participants. Safe to ask any question and safe to make contributions. Physical needs met for lighting, water, food, movement and seating.

16. Use learner's learning style

Provide both choice in how learners learn, and diversity in what you offer. By appealing to the learner's best strategies, you'll make it more accessible.

17. Positive Beliefs (capability & context)

Reinforce to learners that they can succeed and can do this particular task. Discover what those beliefs are as soon as possible and work to affect them positively.

All of the items mentioned above cost nothing (no rewards or bribes needed) and they work. It is certainly more preparation and work initially, to create a climate of intrinsic motivation, but it pays off in the long run. Presenters who rely on extrinsic motivation may be vastly underestimating three things: 1) the power of their influence 2) the desire of the learner to be intrinsically motivated 3) the long term ease in doing it.

```
+--------------------------------------------------+
|               Provide control & choice           |
|            Meet perceived needs & goals          |
|               Positive social bonding            |
|                     Curiosity                    |
|                Engage strong emotions            |
|                      Nutrition                   |
|                Use multiple intelligences        |
|                    Success stories               |
|                   Acknowledgments                |
|                  Frequency of feedback           |
|                  Physiological states            |
|                 Provide hope of success          |
|                 Role model joy of learning       |
|                     Celebrations                 |
|               Physically & emotionally safe      |
|                Use learner's learning style      |
|           Positive Beliefs (capability & context)|
+--------------------------------------------------+
```

Combining these, an example might be: learners working on a team, with no academic grades as a threat, with members they like (and feel safe to dialog with), choosing how to solve a problem on a larger personally meaningful project (that they originally chose), with a moderate, but not constricting, time deadline in a rich, stimulating environment.

Much Learning Occurs As a By-Product of Another Activity

In research by Wentzel, it was found that optimal learning does not necessarily require massive motivation. Often, when participants who would not ordinarily be engaged, focus on their own self-determination, learning becomes

271

the positive by-product. Ford says that multiple social contexts provide greater opportunities for learner goal attainment and satisfaction. In fact, the argument is made that the learner's brain is in a better state for learning when traditional "learning" is disguised. In other words, in areas where the learning is a "by-product" of the activity, the learner may excel the most. Multiple contexts for learning are also powerful. Lozanov utilized games, role-play and peripherals to immerse the learner in an environment in which the learning was usually only a by-product of all else that was going on.

Emotions Are Essential Key to Motivation

Utilizing the whole brain approach, acknowledging both left and right hemisphere learning, says Levy, "respects the inseparability of cognition and emotion." She adds that by purposefully engaging your learners in meaningful emotional processes, you'll tap into more of the student's brain.

A top researcher on emotions, N. H. Fridja says that understanding learner emotions is one of the keys to motivation. Although the presence of emotions doesn't guarantee the content of the problem, it tells the brain, "This is important, pay attention!" Emotions influence:

- selective attention
- event interpretation
- motivation
- prediction
- recall
- decision-making
- problem-solving
- learning

When strong emotions are engaged, they so flavor the human experience that the learner is unable to bring anything else to conscious attention. Unlike a typical cognitive thought, once emotions are fully engaged, they cannot be hidden or made non-consciously without a great degree of effort. In other words, while some learners may be able to temporarily ignore a powerful emotion for a few minutes, it does need to have a form of expression. How often are learners distracted from learning by previous arguments in the halls, at home or in the school playgrounds? Suppression only defers the learner's engagement to a few moments later. Emotions require contexts for expression or they will disable a learner within minutes.

Emotions run the brain most of the time, not our cortex. Let's say that you know that you should do an errand, or make a phone call or pay a bill. You have all the reasons to do it. But you still put it off. For how long? Until you _feel_ like doing it. Damasio says that emotions and logic are so interwoven, we shouldn't even attempt to "untangle them." His research suggests that it's a biological survival function to use the emotions to pursue better decision-making strategies.

Choice Remains Critical to Maintaining Motivation

Should learners be told what to do, or should they be given choice? The answer partly depends on the age of the learner. Regardless of age, however, most learners are given little choice in their learning situations, which are organized, routed, facilitated and structured for them by others. That's not good, according to the research teams of Deci and Ryan, and Deci, Vallerand, Pelletier and Ryan.

When participants are given control over the content and process of their learning, motivation goes up, say Mager and McCann. But to motivate learners, it is important to allow them to make choices "about personally relevant aspects of a learning activity." Students need to be able to align self-determined goals with instructional goals.

In addition, learners who tend to focus more on fun and friendships may be able to be engaged when there are ample opportunities for self-determination and peer interaction, says Wentzel. These provide ways to meet personal goals and, to some, degree, instructional goals. In other words, the more ways the goals can serve the learner's own agendas, the better.

There are ways to tap into learning, excitement and participation levels for many learners who appear to be unmotivated. Help learners to become more aware of their own personal, academic, health, social, athletic and career goals. A learner is often willing to work on a team project because there's another person on the project that he likes and would like to get to know better.

What This Means To You: Design instructional experiences that allow for more ways for learners to meet their own goals. They need ways to show off, meet new people, be an expert in something, grow, get in shape or become well-respected. Implement as many of the optimal motivating conditions possible as much of the time as possible. Avoid labeling any learner as a "low" or unmotivated learner until he has had the consistent experience of optimal conditions and a chance to prove himself.

Qualities of Learning Experiences
(Listed in order, from least to most motivation required)

The Real Thing
Being there, on-location learning; excursions, a field trip.
Requires minimal extrinsic motivation.
Engages maximum contextual memory.

Immersion
Simulated on-site, a richly constructed environment.
Purposeful, multi-sensory, "another world,"
such as a room designed as a foreign country.

Interactive Concrete Learning
Off-site; hands-on; using skills, materials & tools.
Sports, arts, personal coaching, role play, and training,
best followed by debriefing.

Interactive Abstract Learning
Teaching & learning using representations, not the real thing.
Tutoring, distance learning, **CD-ROM, INTERNET.**
Minimal contextual memory engaged**.**
(Virtual reality will soon make this "the real thing")

Second Hand Learning
Distance learning, video, book, lecture.
Requires substantial intrinsic motivation to make it active; thinking,
discussion, mapping, etc.

How You Can Follow Up: *The Little Book of Big Motivation* by Jensen, *Eager to Learn,* by Wlodlowski; *45 Student Motivational Strategies; or SuperTeaching,* by Jensen. See page Appendix.

Chapter Questions

1. What was novel, fresh and new? What was familiar or "old hat"?
2. In what ways do you already apply the information in this chapter?
3. What three questions can you now generate about this material?
4. How did you react emotionally to this information?
5. In what ways can you translate the key three or four theories and discoveries presented here into practical everyday useful ideas?
6. How did you react cognitively when you were reading the ideas of this chapter?
7. If these things are, in fact, true about the brain, what should we do differently? What resources of time, people and money could be redirected? In what ways do you suggest we start?
8. What was the single one (or two) most interesting or valuable insights you had?
9. Plan your next step, the logical practical application of what you've learned.
10. What obstacles might you encounter? How can you realistically deal with them?

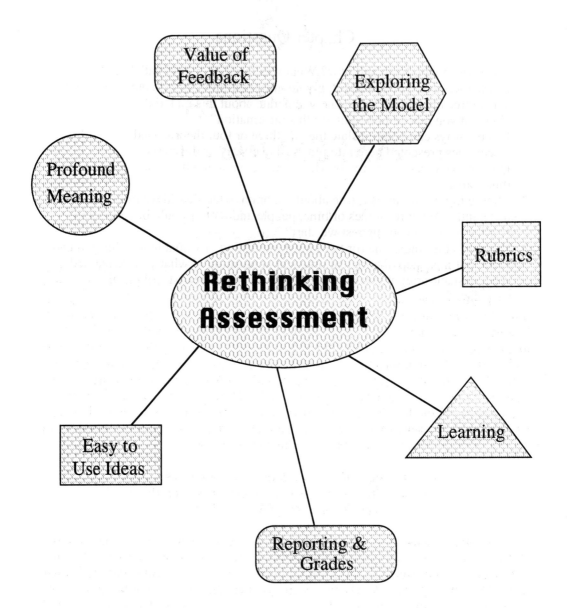

Value of
Feedback

Exploring
the Model

Profound
Meaning

**Rethinking
Assessment**

Rubrics

Easy to
Use Ideas

Learning

Reporting &
Grades

276

18
Rethinking Assessment

What is Learning and How Do We Measure It?

Many educators think they measure learning everyday. After all, the dictionary definition of learning is simple: it's related to knowledge and understanding. Yet, many of the world's top neuroscientists would have a tough time defining learning. Why? *Much of what is important cannot be measured.* Example of the "hard-to-measure" include our so-called "mental models" of how things work, our values, our capability beliefs, the degree of personal transference and levels of depth of meaning. Outcome-based education where there are specific, defined, measurable outcomes would be brain-antagonistic unless the learners have a say in them. It still operates out of the "demand model" of learning. If even the outcome-based models have some difficulty, is there an easy answer? No, you simply cannot measure, with current technology, at this time in our neurobiological history, most of the truly important learning the brain does.

> *Biologically, the best, most valuable and deepest learning does not produce any tangible results for a considerable time*

In other words, most assessment is off course. Certainly you can measure if a learner can create and manipulate prose arguments or summarize what the presenter has said. But is that the only thing we want? What will serve the learner in a competitive global society where the greatest advantage may be in learn-to-learn skills, teamwork, model-building, problem-solving, systems thinking and communication skills? The vast content knowledge base will be accessible to anyone who has a computer, television, phone or fax. Should we ask that an

277

increasingly larger body of knowledge be memorized and replayed at test time? It depends on what you call learning.

In Chinese, the definition of learning is made up of two symbols: One is for studying, the other for practicing constantly. In other words, you cannot say, "I've learned that," as so many traditional presenters and participants are proud to announce. You can only say, "I've introduced myself to it and am practicing it." In the classroom, we have to ask hard questions about what kind of learners we want to create: those who can replay data or those who are true learners. A true learner is a practicing learner. Here's the Chinese symbol for learning:

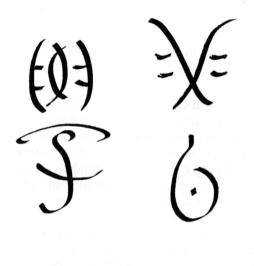

1. Why is learning specific to the learner? In brain-based learning, all learning is in-process and related to the on-going lives of the learners. Top neuroscientist Edelman says learning is behavior that leads to synaptic changes in global mapping that satisfy "set points" (translated: when we connect two ideas to something personally relevant). Top learning systems analyst Senge explains, "Learning is about enhancing capacity to produce results that really matter to you." The bottom line is, learning has to become personally relevant.

2. What is deemed important by the "stake-holders" in the system?
Another question we ask is "Which learning is relevant?" A "stake-holder" is any one person or group of persons who have a vested interest in the outcome of an educational system. The most commonly listed ones are: parents, the government, district offices, employers, community members, school boards, presenters, administrative staff, relevant union workers, state agencies, and participants. Naturally, the participants are usually given very little choice over what is offered, what is selected and what assessment will be given. The "stake-holders" should all have input over what's offered. But participants, starting at the first year of schooling, are also old enough to make some decisions about choices in learning.

3. How do we know when we have learned something?
We often don't know. It's one thing to acquire knowledge; our brain acquires and processes thousands of things per day nonconsciously. Just getting to 4 levels of learning school each day fills minds with images, experience and sound. This

4 Levels of Learning

Unconscious
Competency
*("I am unaware
of the process
while doing it")*

Conscious
Competency
*("I am aware of
doing it while
in the process")*

Conscious
Incompetency
*("I realize what
I don't know")*

Unconscious
Incompetency
*("I don't know what
I don't know")*

question is powerful because, in a brain-based learning environment, your learners will be learning far more than either they or you can keep track of or assess. But is our learning about acquisition or the more consciously applied learning that is asked for on a test? The answer is, we must find ways to give participants credit for both.

Ultimately learning is judged by someone who expects tangible, measurable results. The problem is that *the best learning takes time.* Over and over again I have witnessed participants who seemed to vehemently resist ideas, programs and disciplines only to have them emerge years later as far wiser and better rounded than those who got the highest marks on the spot. And we all know the opposite: a learner who does what's expected, fills in all the boxes perfectly and graduates with little skills for living in the real world. The perfect metaphor from nature is: If you keep pulling up your newly planted fruit tree to see how it's growing, two things will happen: first, checking it won't tell you how it's doing in the medium to long-term and second, the plant will never grow like it's supposed to grow.

4. What is appropriate to know and demonstrate at a specific age and for the brain's development?
Your learners can have as much as *a three year difference* in the development of their brains. It's unrealistic to hold each learner to a specific standard or group norm that ignores what we know from neuroscience.

> *Comparing one learner to another*
> *is one of the most irrelevant and damaging*
> *assessment strategies ever devised*

What one learner is doing academically is totally separate and unrelated to another learner. Their brains can be as much as three years apart! Their background can be a world apart. Out with the bell-shaped curve! One learner may have no morning nutrition or a poor breakfast each day. A curve or any rating system is unfair and irrelevant. The only thing that really matters is "How is that learner doing compared to that same learner earlier?" Each learner should not be competing against other learners, but rather him or herself. Lastly, the brain is most interested in learning to survive. As humans we only want to be better than another if we feel threatened (economically, emotionally, intellectually, socially or physically) or our survival is at stake.

5. How can we make the learning personally meaningful?
If we make a distinction between knowledge (usually surface knowledge) and meaning (something of value or something that helps our own world make sense, or that extends our existing natural knowledge) then it is clear that *we are after meaning* in our participants, *not just knowledge.* The surface knowledge will be

forgotten shortly after any test given and what lasts is the meaning. Presenters, schools and districts who compare participants against one another are doing a disservice. Also, if in fact, all learning is personal, how then can you compare the personal meaning of one person with that of another?

The learners ought to be able to talk about how the learning has become personally meaningful and the specific links to their own life. This is the learning that is going to last. It is the learning that makes school and education rewarding, rich and timeless. It's also the kind of learning that spurs the intrinsic motivation to learn. Surface knowledge often requires some form of external motivation. The less of it, the better.

6. How do we instill a notion of quality in our learners?
There are many ways to increase the quality of work that your learners produce. First, and foremost, they must know what quality is. You can help by defining exactly what it is through constant daily examples. Ask your learners what they think quality is. Ask them to bring in two products; one of poor quality and one of excellent quality. Ask them to describe or list the differences.

Secondly, schools must model the quality as an organization. This means that quality is chosen as a value over expediency or short-term gain. It means that quality is promoted and modeled by the staff and management. It means that the school understands what quality is, values it and promotes it.

Third, the presenter models quality. The more that a presenter "lives it," the more the participants get the message it's important. This can be modeled in the planning of activities, dress standards, vocabulary, room set-up, materials and behavior. Since over 99% of all learning is non-conscious, the message that learners get from the presenter is either quality counts or it doesn't.

7. How can this learning, if at all, be used in other ways?
Certainly the whole issue of contextualization and generalization comes into play. Now that you have learned ABC, how can you apply it to DEF or HIJK? This process takes the learning from one domain and asks the learner to map it onto another domain.

Sternberg and Wagner say that intelligence is very related to the ability to generalize learning to perform in novel contexts. To do that, they say, it requires, "... the use of widely applicable performance components." That requires planning, metacognition and both inductive and deductive reasoning. While presenting participants about thinking and learning, we are also providing them with the framework to succeed off on their own in the productive work world.

281

Sometimes the best way to find this out is simply a conversation, other times it may be demonstration. In either case, it's important for learners to be able to ask questions and formulate thinking about what they know, how they know it, and where it fits in their life. Asking more or fewer questions is irrelevant; it's the quality of the question that counts. *One single question may reflect more profound understanding than twenty surface-level questions.*

What Kind of Learning is Really Going On?

Here's the crux of brain-compatible assessment: Most of time when we think we are assessing learning, we are merely *getting feedback on the learner's ability to play the testing game."* Most of what is easily assessed is biologically and personally irrelevant to the brain. Authentic assessment is an incremental improvement over traditional formalized testing. Broad-based assessment using the multiple intelligences is better than a strict pencil and paper test.

Let's not kid ourselves. Most of what is important to the brain, that which truly shapes our understanding, our thinking, our meaning and character lives is *very difficult to assess.* In order to decide if your assessment is on the mark, or if it misses the real learning, use these seven categories to decide. Here are the ways in which the humans brain can "evidence" learning:

1. **As data or information...**the learner can replay the data back to the presenter, but it rarely has meaning... the learner still needs to sort it out and make relevant connections until the learner does sort it out, it's meaningless

2. **As meaning...** information is transformed by the learner... here the learner discovers, for him or herself, the patterns, the relationships, the themes, useful tie-ins or the interdisciplinary connections

3. **As a new or better working model...** a system...a conscious or non-conscious set of organizing principles of how something works ("democracy is run by special interest groups" or "democracy works when...")

4. **Specific, useful "how-to" strategies** and skills...these are usually embedded as procedural memories and are often called "body learning" ...examples would be playing an instrument, building a model, hitting a baseball, working a microscope, etc.

5. **Attitudes,** perceptual bias & opinions have changed; these open or close the "gates" of learning...how you feel about a topic or subject is quite critical... Do you feel positive about the topic, like it or want to learn more?

6. **Observable behavior changes**...many neuroscientists would say that unless there is a corresponding change in physical behavior, we cannot say that biologically, something has been learned. In other words, cognition or auditory descriptions of content understanding is not integrated until the whole body is involved in learning

7. **Internal...** how this learning affects you personally and also implications for your past, present & future. The more connections you make, the greater the neural mapping

Valuable Distinctions For Presenters

There's a difference between assessment, testing, feedback, reporting and grades. At each layer, the subjectivity increases and so does the stress. At the start, is the simplest system; feedback, clean and pure. By the time we get to the lower layers, it's gotten pretty controversial. The layers might be characterized as the following:

1. Feedback:	is specific sensory information
2. Testing /Assessment:	a subjective way to gather information
3. Reporting:	subjectively communicating the information
4. Grading:	evaluating & communicating the subjective assessment

As mentioned before, there are many, many approaches to take for nearly every topic in education. This book takes the point of view or position of "What's good for the brain and learning?" You may have another position called "What's in vogue, what's politically correct?" But there is considerable evidence that doing things the way the brain learns best will reduce your problems in the long run. Increase the frequency and quality of learner feedback to get better learning.

Comparing Scores
Among Learners

Does it matter whether some cultures or races consistently test lower than another? In a controversial book, *The Bell Curve,* authors Herrnstein and Murray say blacks test out at a consistently lower IQ than whites. A moot point, since Asians outscore Anglos in math and science. Native Americans outscore Hispanics in spatial approximation. We know learning and meaning is all culturally carried. That's been common knowledge for years. But comparing scores is irrelevant for many other reasons.

One, intelligences may be culturally preferred, but, they can also be developed, say Howard Gardner and Robert Sternberg. Second, Herrnstein's and Murray's evidence is based on traditional IQ scores and socio-economic correlates, not the more updated multiple intelligences profiles from Howard Gardner. It also does not include the research of Diamond, Greenough, Jacobs and Ramey on the effects of enriching environments on the brain.

Brain-based schools make it a point to offer learning in many learning styles and multiple intelligences. Presenters should offer a challenging curriculum to *all* learners. They would be surprised how many would then be re-labeled as gifted or talented. In New York, at the Hostos-Lincoln Academy, an inner-city population of high-schoolers are being transformed from "written off" and labeled "drop out" to excellent "scholars." These are the smart new, restructured schools: small neighborhood fast-moving ones with high feedback, strong relationships and very high presenter and learner expectations.

Presenters trained in brain-based learning believe in the real potential of the brain in every learner AND they live it. They understand the power of suggestion, implications, and covert language. They know the influence of expectations. In short, they simply make sure that all learners are given equal opportunity to learn and use the strategies necessary to make it happen. There's no distinction between "low or high" learners.

The Brain Thrives On Feedback
Because It Needs It For Survival

Grades are, too often, used for comparisons and have little functional place in brain-based learning. By contrast, feedback and reporting **do** have a very legitimate role. The brain loves feedback because simply, it gives it the information needed to survive. Feedback makes for better brains and learners.

Our biological brain thrives on
feedback for growth in learning,
intelligence and survival

Not only is feedback important to the brain, the reporting of the feedback is important to the learner, his or her parents, the school staff and the community. After all, they are the "stakeholders" in the system and they have a legitimate vested interest in knowing the progress of that learner. The brain thrives on feedback.

* **the more often, the better**
* **the more immediate, the better**
* **the greater the specificity, the better**
* **the more appropriately dramatic, the better**
* **the longer feedback is delayed, the less useful**

What This Means to You: To optimize learning, make it a rule that you provide your learners feedback every 30 minutes or less. This is simple to do when you consider that you have many forms of feedback. It can come from you, but that's the most inefficient. Utilize pre-established criteria from which learners can self-assess, use partners and classmates or simply use the whole group to provide feedback. Engage all of your options: you can hold a class discussion where learners get ideas validated or shaped; you can use peer presenting, debates, ask learners to make mind maps with partners, observations, team discussions or a show of hands. Feedback comes in a thousand easy and useful forms!

Why We Dislike Most
Forms of Testing and Assessment

Most of us, and the learners we work with, dislike testing. It's stressful and often irrelevant. It can make, on any given day, even the best prepared learners, feel stupid. It rarely lets us "shine" as learners. All of these problems arise because of the traditional academic testing model. Both formal and informal testing has been around for a long time. The old model of academic testing in schools around the world is quite simple:

1. A presenter or bureaucracy decides what is to be learned
2. The presenter teaches and makes up the test
3. The participants study what they think will be on the test

4. The participants take the test
5. The presenter grades the test, based on what he or she decided was important
6. The participants usually forget what they studied a few hours/days after the test
7. The cycle repeats itself

Typically, assessment can cause narrowed learning simply to "make the grade." Particularly stressful is any grading system which has enormous delays and high stakes. You don't need to be a rocket scientist to realize the stress of the system above. The presenter makes all the choices and the learner narrows the learning to exactly what's predicted to be on the test. Then, of course, to get school achievement scores higher, many presenters are encouraged to teach directly to the test. Not good. It's a manipulated system of control, with fixed outcomes and narrowed learning. And it is certainly a poor assessment model for preparing our citizens for the next century.

You'll rarely find someone neutral about grades. Around the world, people either love them or hate them. Obviously, grades are used for several reasons. Most of them don't fit with a more brain-based learning approach. The proponents of grading systems say:

1. Grades help motivate learners. This is false. Hundreds of educational and social studies have suggested that extrinsic motivation reduces internal motivation. The motivation, if any, that grades provide is more often based on the fear of doing poorly. That means it is more often used to manipulate learners as a form of extrinsic reward or punishment.

2. Grades are a form of feedback. This is false; feedback is useless unless it's immediate, specific and in the form the learner needs for correction. Typically, grades are given after months of learner "performance" and they are represented by a single letter or number.

3. Grades help us get the best out of our learners. This is false; countless studies demonstrate that when we are being evaluated, we find the subject less interesting, say Grolnick and Ryan. Researchers Butler and Amabile say creativity dropped and learners took easier, less challenging paths, say Kage. Learners who become obsessed with how they are doing tend to do just what is needed to get the grades.

4. Grades help us sort and evaluate learners. This is false; grades bear little relationship to talents, abilities, intelligence or predictors of future success. Presenters are heavily influenced by the personality of the learner, influenced by other participants, the school standards and in short, are very subjective in their analysis. Blind studies suggest that if learner work has the name of a learner who has scored high earlier ("the halo effect"), that, even if you switch it with the lesser work of another, it will be scored higher if the "good" name is on it. There is also grade inflation (pressure to raise or lower grades) and such a variety of standards, that a top grade in one class or school means something very different than a top grade in another. In short, grades are a poor system for doing the job we really want done.

5. Grades show learner responsibility. This is false; they are often a displacement of responsibility. The traditional model is that each learner "earned" a high grade or "deserved" a poor grade. This model infers that each learner is offered the resources and support necessary at the appropriate times to compete with others for an often limited supply of "goodies." It implies that, with all the school offered, the learner simply "chose" to do well or poorly. In many cases, this is true, but in many more, it's not. Often, what the learner is good at, is not tested or reported.

In reality, learners are rarely given the brain-based environments, rarely offered the skills and information outlined in this book. That model also infers that it's the learner that is *solely* responsible for their learning. What about learners who have presenters who criticize, who poorly orchestrate the learning, who have low expectations of them? Over 80% of all presenters give participants sarcastic remarks, which we know cause stress, resentment and even heart fluctuations. They follow a "demand" model that Kohn says is designed around blame and deflecting responsibility. "We *demand that you do better*" is the frame around most school philosophies.

> *Demands reduce choice and quality of work.*
> *Traditional schools demand more of their participants;*
> *Brain-based schools foster intrinsic motivation*

We all know that learner responsibility is critical to their success. But responsibility cannot be assigned. How did you feel when someone said you were responsible for something that you didn't even care about? Responsibility must be "taken on" willfully by the learner *when the time is right.* Our role as educators is to provide the resources so that our learners can, on their own volition, be responsible, not for us to demand it (or else!). It's a difference of a "demand model" versus a "support model."

Unfortunately, many are going in the other direction. Schools which do any of the following practices are, in the long run, undermining sound educational practices. They are ignoring critical research and proven, sound educational strategies about how the brain learns best. Here are some of the most counter-productive practices to learning:

Use of rewards, bribes or incentive systems
The comparing of grades or making them public
Limited or premature forms of assessment
Lack of consistent, frequent classroom feedback
Tests results which take more than 72 hours
Presenters (not participants) only ones with input on assessment
Grading on a curve, comparing learners to others

By reducing those unsound educational practices, schools will go a long way in increasing learning, motivation and success. But obviously, a replacement is needed. What would work better?

Alternatives to Assessments
& Performance Reviews

We know feedback is good for learning. Reporting is essential. Assessment will go on for quite some time. And, there are obviously some strong disadvantages to grades. Even most presenters dislike having to prepare, give and defend them. But what are the alternatives in a brain-based school? Here are eleven simple ones:

* **Increase feedback; both the form and quantity**
* **Students have input on curriculum**
* **Use grades only as final report at the end of a term**
* **Students taught to self-assess**
* **Assess the real learning that is going on (see list)**
* **Use multiple forms of reporting and assessment**
* **Avoid rewards of any kind, for effort or results**
* **Individual assignments get substantive comments, not grades**
* **Students have input on criteria for assessment**
* **Utilize a wider variety of evidence of learning**
* **Grade on mastery, not a bell-shaped (or any shape) curve**
* **Discuss with stakeholders (parents, community) the system you're using, how and why it works & what's expected of each**

Many schools are currently moving towards this model. They are doubling and tripling the quantity of feedback given participants. And they are getting the learners involved in setting criteria for assessment. Many major universities are relying less on the standardized achievement tests, less on rigid once-a-term testing and more on feedback and other, more useful factors.

The difference, has to do with the model you use. Out of the old "demand model," presenters set higher standards, schools set higher standards and districts set higher standards and use outcome-based learning where the learners have little input on the outcomes. Even society sets higher standards ("*Goals 2000: What we will learn or do by the year 2000*") and all *insist* that the participants do better. We demand, demand, demand, when they don't deliver, we punish them with disapproval and lower grades.

Your model is either based on demand or based on enrichment and support

Another model, the "enrichment model," asks, "How do we encourage learning the way the brain is best designed to learn?" In this model, districts, schools and presenters make the changes to create enriched learning environments, not prisons of coercion. In this model, our collective on-going goals are to bring out the genius in every single learner. Is this just another bit of fanciful thinking? Absolutely not. At schools around the country and world, significant strides are being made in developing a more brain-based structure. One of the best changes has been in presenting and assessment using multiple intelligences, introduced in Chapter 11. This is a way to focus on strengths, not deficiencies. The greater the variety of brain-based assessment methods, the higher the percentage of participants who will succeed. Why? A brain-based approach means we identify and assess the learning in our participants based on the newer wider definitions of intelligence.

In 1983, Dr. Howard Gardner, Professor of Graduate Education at Harvard University proposed that there are seven major groupings of intelligences. The existing model had defined just two of them. Gardner defined intelligence as the ability to: 1) use a skill, 2) fashion an artifact, or 3) solve a problem in a way that is valued by the particular culture of that individual. He says that each of us has our own unique combination of these intelligences and that they can and do change over a lifetime.

Teaching and assessing to the seven (multiple) intelligences does two things: 1) It insures that a greater percentage of learners will be reached and succeed; 2) it develops the latent abilities that might not emerge otherwise. Here are the seven intelligences: Logical-Mathematical, Spatial, Interpersonal, Bodily-Kinesthetic, Verbal-Linguistic, Intrapersonal and Musical-Rhythmic. The way to assess using each of the intelligences is fairly simple. The next seven steps will give you some strong choices.

How to Assess Learning
More Accurately, More Often

1. Use observation in problem-solving. Give participants a problem to solve which can be solved many different ways. For example, the one about the man and the woman starting out walking from the same place. The man takes two steps for every three the woman takes. They start out together, and immediately lose synchronization. After how many steps will they be back in "sync" again? That problem can be solved using just about every one of the seven intelligences. But which one is chosen by the participants?

2. Give participants a choice in activities and games to play and watch. Discover which ones they pick: Pictionary, Monopoly, crossword puzzles, manipulative puzzles, charades, music recognition, etc. Then observe what they do during that game.

3. Use discussion, and reflection after a play, movie or musical. After participants watch one of these, ask which parts struck them most and were really memorable - was it the music, the action, the relationships, etc.?

4. Watch the type of learning and intelligence used the most. Students tend to do what they like or are most successful at doing. Find out who are the questioners, the noise and music-makers, the artists, doodlers, the active learners, the talkers, the loners, etc.

5. Your observation in inventions & model-building. Give participants a chance to design, build and use some kind of a physical representation of the topic learned. Observe what parts of the task they like and excel in most easily. You'll learn a great deal about how each learner learns.

6. Allow for the use of music and sounds. Students create jingles or songs about a unit. They create a song and sing or perform it. They could re-do the lyrics to a song with the new key words.

7. Other Choices. Use any of the choices below for ways to understand what's being learned and the quality of the learning.

   • Student uses self-assessment.
   • Give participants a choice on type of assessment
   • Journal or diary with reflections and personal growth
   • Get credit for community or business work
   • Produce a videotape (or audio tape)

- Peer assessment (with your established criteria)
- Build working models that demonstrate knowledge
- Student interviews with you
- Make a chart of progress in the course
- Write a story or article
- Perform a play, musical or dance
- Create artwork, a painting
- Graphic organizers like Venn diagrams
- Make an advertising flyer for the course/subject
- Produce a large mind map
- Self-assessment using personal or course goals

Feedback on the Path
To Mastery Learning

Remember, choice and variety is the key for motivation and learning. Those are just some of the possible ways to assess participants. The form of assessment that could be used is unlimited. Many staff and administrators have developed better benchmarks and criteria to measure each through mastery level in learning. While some will argue that *just one* of the criteria below is most important, all three really are equal. You'll want to find a way to provide feedback on:

1. **Product.** What is it that participants are creating? What kind of quality is it?
2. **Process.** Many educators feel that the journey, the process of how the learner got to the product is as, if not more important, than the product.
3. **Progress.** This is often referred to as the "improvement gain." The question is more how far has the learner come, given the circumstances?

Keeping in mind that much of what's *really* important cannot be measured, at least some progress has been made. The basic value of this is not for the schools to be able to compare participants, but for learners to have feedback on the milestones in their learning. You might have three categories:

☐ **EN**...Entry level; this means the learner has *just started learning* in an agreed-upon area or discipline. No progress yet.
☐ **DEV**...Developing; this means that the learner is *in process of developing* the key skills and information needed for basic competence. This has stages, so that progress can be noted.
☐ **EX**...Extending; means that the learner has *already met the criteria* for learning in that particular subject or skill and is exploring it further.

In primary and secondary schools, this means that every single unit will need to have each of the above three categories detailed. It is a time-consuming process, but it will provide more stability, fairness and accuracy in the long run. It insures that when a learner switches from one school to another, the assessment will help accurately determine where the learner is really at, not solely a subjective opinion. The district-wide arithmetic criteria for Ann Arbor, Michigan, at the kindergarten level, is listed below.

Not Yet:	Developing	Achieving	Extending
counts 1-5	counts 1-10	counts 1-20	Counts 20+
skips #s	errors at 11-20	forward only	counts
needs help	needs prompt sometimes	oral or written	backwards

Is this better than a letter grade? It certainly provides more information. It certainly is less judgmental. It certainly provides a more standard understanding of a learner's progress. Yes, it is better than just a letter grade, as long as it is used properly. Remember, the learner's brains may be as much as three years apart, developmentally, and still be normal. There is no allocation in this assessment for that. As long as it is used for feedback and presenter information, not for comparison, it's acceptable.

A rubric is simply a matrix which lists the criteria for measuring what you want. It's an attempt to get more objective about the "subjective." By itself it is neither good nor bad. A rubric is only brain-based IF it answers these critical brain-based questions:

1. **Immediacy:** Feedback is only useful to the brain when it's immediate. Students must get it the very same hour. When feedback is delayed, its value drops dramatically.
2. **Criteria Used:** Are you using the factors that truly assess learning? Here are some examples mentioned earlier: *Relevancy/Meaning* - How is the learning personally meaningful? *Mental models revealed* - The learner must show HOW they think this concept works - *Perceptual bias* - How does the learner feel about it? How strongly? Why? *Reality check* - What has changed? What behaviors are different?
3. **Student Input:** Unless participants help set the criteria, this form of assessment is more of the same "demanding" that has been causing the original core problems.

To create your own rubrics for assessment, you might take these seven steps:

- **Explore & gather ideas from other rubrics**
- **Find work samples and explore the range of quality**
- **Discuss the qualities & characteristics of excellent work**
- **Prioritize the list of qualities**
- **Make a sample rubric**
- **Test it with a sample of learner work**
- **Revise as needed**

The idea of a rubric is simple: Take all the those ideas, intuitions, beliefs and opinions about what is excellent and do your best to objectify them. Many presenters find that the use of rubrics can make the assessment easier, even when you're using such diverse methods. A rubric is simply a criteria-based grid which uses specific and defined guidelines to assess learning evidence. It might look like a box with 5 lines across and 5 high. Everything your participants submit for assessment ought to have clearly defined ways for participants to succeed. No more "presenter's intuition" or a vaguely defined opinion about what is or is not quality. It's time to invite learner input on what they think constitutes quality. While your first rubric for assessment may be quite rough, it will evolve over time to become a better way to discover what learners know, feel and can do. Below is an example of a rubric used for a research document.

Sample Performance Rubric

Criteria for Quality: Rating from 1-5

Completeness... *5*
Personal Meaning... *3*
Accuracy.. *5*
Bias Defended... *1*
Mental Models Explained................................. *3*
Creativity... *2*
Overall Presentation.. *5*

Comments: *Overall look of project was great, suggest a closer review of basics and clarity in communication.*

Work together with the learner to rate him or her. By making your criteria very specific, you get better quality work from your participants. You can set an arbitrary standard, from one to five, All 5's on a project would be the highest possible. A "1" might be for work turned in late or the wrong assignment completed. "2" can be on time, accurate content and sloppy throughout. A "5" might be on time, visually appealing, the right topic, in-depth, meaningful and reflective. It's up to you and the participants (if age appropriate). You can create a more objective set of standards for what is seemingly a subjective learner effort.

Does a rubric system solve the assessment dilemma? No, it doesn't. Brain-based learning says that the underlying structures of how the brain learns must be addressed. The rubric provides us with *a system* for assessing. However, it doesn't tell us *what criteria* we are using to assess. If we use the old criteria, the results will simply be more time-consuming and more disappointing. The old criteria was presenter-directed content. Many learners discovered that even with rubrics, it's still the "same game" of learning for the test. One strategy you can use to take away the "game" that learners play to get the better grade is personal relevance.

The Role of Personal Meaning

It may be that the best form of assessment is to ask ourselves what will be the most personal and lasting model for the brain. We know this much: when it is personally meaningful, it's bound to last longer. Why? Multiple memory maps, engagement of emotions and larger number of synaptic connections insure more thorough, more easily recalled and more enthusiastic learning.

The concept of meaningful assessment is simple: *the highest priority is that the demonstration of the learning has to be related to one's own life.* In short, it is not a question of information, *it has to integrate personal meaning into it.* Only when the learning becomes woven into the fabric of one's own life does it become genuinely, internally, meaningfully learned; and it will last! Here are the criteria important to this concept:

Examples of Criteria
1. Evidence of progress towards multiple learning goals - a timeline. Learners use personal goals to demonstrate progress.
2. Ability to transfer the subject knowledge to other subjects.
3. An indication of transfer of learning from school to life. Discussion, written evidence or demonstration of this.
4. Evidence of self-reflection and self-awareness on a topic. Might be in the form of a journal or interview.
5. Understanding the basics of that topic as well as details or trivia.
6. Relevance and meaning of that topic in a local or global context.
7. Demonstration of use of a related skill, problem-solving or ability to produce a model or an artifact in that topic.

Meaningful assessment virtually guarantees that
the learning will come alive for the learner and that it
will be a part of his or her life for the long term

Meaningful assessment is more than just one more way to test. It's a comprehensive approach to the whole process. It's very delicate because you never want learners to learn "just for the test." But you do want them to know that they are accountable.

The concepts behind meaningful assessments are simple: 1) the learning must be related to the students' personal life and be found to be an extension of everyday naturally-acquired knowledge; 2) the learner always gets a choice in which of the 20 mediums can be used for assessment; 3) each level of assessment requires that participants use a greater number of options available for demonstration; 4) participants are not graded on a curve or compared to other participants; 5) grading is done both by the presenter and the participants, using criteria for mastery that has been agreed upon by both presenters and the participants. It insures that the following will occur:

1. Students will have a way to express what they know, in the way that they know it best.
2. Students will be measured by consistent standards, ones on which they had some input.
3. All learners will have equal chance to succeed.
4. Learners will be encouraged to learn in a meaningful way.

How do you use everyday learning opportunities as forms for profound assessment? First, set up activities that allow you time to observe and listen. Second, involve the participants in self-assessments. Third, you may want to find alternative time management strategies to free up time for more productive assessing. For example, once a week or once a month, can you double up with another presenter at your grade level? Can you utilize volunteer support staff to free up your time? This will allow you to be more thorough in the support of learner learning. Here are some ways that participants can be learning while you are observing.

Learning & Feedback Strategies

1. Newspaper article Let participants create their own mock-up front page of some learning topic. They take many points of view and each has to be related to their own life. That way it could be covered from personal, financial, sociological, historical, literary or scientific aspects.

295

2. Community projects. Students can bring in the results of work that they have done in the community. It could be social, ecological or work done with a business.

3. Commercials Students take their subject matter and turn it into a commercial. It could be a written one for the print media, a tape to be played on the radio or a video. Make it personal to the student's interests.

4. Student presenting Allow the participants time to think it out first, then make their own notes or mind-maps on it. The more props, music and visual aids used, the more meaning the presentation may have. Keep them fun by providing choice in the topic selection and a low-risk peer support environment. Then give them time to teach it to the class.

5. Model-making In some cases, participants can build a scaled-down or working-size model of the material. That can be particularly useful in demonstrating their understanding of the material when it is physical and involves steps or processes.

6. Performance Let participants do drama or theater on the material. Some material, especially literature, lends itself to being performed. Allow participants time to do a quality job, then make a fun "stage" for them to perform on.

7. Music Most material can be set to music, written about in music, performed as rap or opera. It can also be used as the key words to re-write an already familiar song, and performed as a musical.

8. Interview Many kinds of material can be assessed if participants simply have time to talk freely about it. Casual, unstressed discussion-interview time is rarely used and can be of great benefit. The ability to formulate questions and to extrapolate hypothetical answers becomes important here.

9. Artwork/Drawing Let participants have a chance to express themselves in art. Many types of material can be best understood in the form of a drawing. Give participants a large piece of paper and let them express what it means to them. You may be surprised at some of the great examples you get.

10. Journals/Learning Logs For participants that are more private and intrapersonal, you may learn much about what the learner knows through this reflective medium. In these journals, the content is specific to learning and participants can create or answer questions about what and how they learned, add their own feelings and possible applications of the learning.

11. Sculpture Some learning can be represented as a physical object or a sculpture. If it is appropriate, many participants would love to be able to let out their own "Michaelangelo" and express themselves.

12. Debates These can come in many forms. Half of the value is in preparing for the debates. You may want to make your criteria for assessment very specific, so that they know how they'll be appraised.

13. Mind-mapping Let participants create huge, poster-sized maps of what they know. These webbed, thematic graphic organizers offer colorful peripheral thoughts organized around a key idea. They were popularized by Tony Buzan, Michael Gelb and Nancy Margulies. These provide an excellent vehicle for understanding relationships, themes and associations of ideas.

14. Game design Learners know many games, most of them from their culture of growing up. Allow your learners to take any game, such as Simon Sez, Monopoly, Jeopardy, Wheel of Fortune, Concentration, Card games, Ball toss, Poker and others, then re-design it using alternative content.

15. Montage/collage This format provides a vehicle for collecting and assembling thoughts and ideas in art. It's actually a combination between a mind map, a sculpture and a drawing. The more choice and freedom you offer your learners, the more likely you are to get something really innovative.

16. Multi-media Students can make a video, cassette tape or CD. Insist that it be quality and help provide access to the necessary resources. Your rubric will help you and your participants evaluate these so-called "subjective" mediums.

17. Students write test Let participants figure out what's important and what's not. Then ask them to create their own test. You can set some basic criteria, but keep plenty of room for creativity.

18. Timelines, Diorama These can be a great way to demonstrate an idea. The idea comes alive in a chronological graphic description. The goals, processes, resources and players are included along with the content learned.

19. Personal Goals Checklist Students set original learning goals, interim goals, then they revise them as time goes on. Goals are self-assessed: if reached, when reached, how reached and when re-assessed. Each learner shares this analysis with the presenter.

20. Attitudinal Surveys You design them, participants fill them out. Use both box-checking and short essay. Ask questions such as "how did you feel about this subject when we first started?" Then ask progressive ones to find out if the learners have changed their feelings about it.

21. Plan & Produce a Mini-Party or Conference Students plan an "experts" gathering on the topic. They gather up speakers, plan the talks, organize the logistics and put it on. Can either be just planned or actually carried out.

22. Prepare an encyclopedia, journal, book, album or yearbook Brainstorm possibilities. Research the topic. Gather articles, photos, create drawings. Prioritize ideas, plan and produce.

23. Create a wall-sized mural Can be done as a school or civic project. The planning, producing and documentation of this project can bring tremendous results.

24. Create story boards Disney cartoonists pioneered the concept of storyboarding: start with a sequence of roughly drawn pictures that capture each key moment. Put them up on a wall to create and trace the history of the project.

25. Write a story The story could be either fiction or non-fiction. The point of it would be to make the information personally meaningful to the creator of the project and the other learners.

26. Student Choice Allow the learner to select an example, process or product for evaluation. It could be something that was originally developed outside of class time like an organizing system, a hobby or unusual collection. This can work only if you provide the acceptable criteria for it in advance.

All of the above choices could be used for feedback or assessment. For short updates, quizzes, etc., participants get to choose any of the forms listed above to demonstrate their learning. For mid-terms and moderate level assessment, participants choose any two of the above. For major assessment and final exams, Allow participants to choose for any three (or 2 or 4 or 5) of the 26 strategies (or any others you've selected).

What This Means to You: With variety and choice, you can now have a model which honors and respects all of your learner's gifts. You can focus less on "how smart" a learner is and focus more on "how is he or she smart?" By using the concept of profound assessment, your learners are more likely to feel fairly treated and fairly assessed. They'll be more willing to submit their learning to you or their peers for review.

How You Can Follow Up: Read *Graduation by Exhibition,* by McDonald, Barton, Smith, Turner & Finnery; *Assessing Student Outcomes: Performance Assessment Using the Dimensions in Learning Model,* by Marzano, Pickering & McTighe; *A Practical Guide to Alternative Assessment,* by Herman, Aschbacher and Winters. Available from ACSD at (703) 549-9110.

Chapter Questions

1. What was novel, fresh and new? What was familiar or "old hat"?
2. In what ways do you already apply the information in this chapter?
3. What three questions can you now generate about this material?
4. How did you react emotionally to this information?
5. In what ways can you translate the key three or four theories and discoveries presented here into practical everyday useful ideas?
6. How did you react cognitively when you were reading the ideas of this chapter?
7. If these things are, in fact, true about the brain, what should we do differently? What resources of time, people and money could be redirected? In what ways do you suggest we start?
8. What was the single one (or two) most interesting or valuable insights you had?
9. Plan your next step, the logical practical application of what you've learned.
10. What obstacles might you encounter? How can you realistically deal with them?

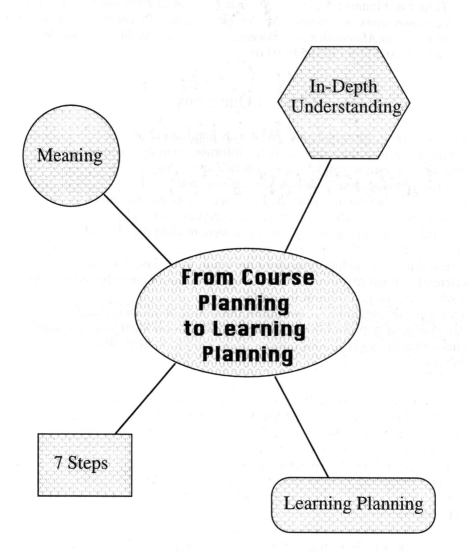

In-Depth
Understanding

Meaning

**From Course
Planning
to Learning
Planning**

7 Steps

Learning Planning

19

From Course Planning to Learning Planning

From Covering the Content to Uncovering the Learning

The old paradigm was: plan what there is to **present**, then present it. In the new paradigm, the thinking is "What is there to **learn** and **how** can it be **learned** best?" After all, there are many, many "formats" suggested to presenters about the "right" way to teach. But where are the formats and plans that talk about how the learners will learn it best? You won't find them in a traditional school of education.

In brain-based learning, the lesson planning is done backwards: we start with the learner, not the content. The organization of the lesson is based around creating conditions optimal for the best natural learning. The brain *rarely learns in a one-at-a-time sequence like, "Introduce unit A, learn it, take test on it. Now go to Unit B..."* It learns by immersion: jumping into the middle of life-like Unit K, then participants introduce real diversions "A, D & G." Then moving ahead and backwards, more like spiral than a straight line. That's how we learn and survive in most of what we call "real life."

Closed quarter learning, in training rooms and schools, does require some structure. One of the best brain-compatible formats was developed by Susan Kovalik. Before it is introduced, here is a brief contrast between traditional lesson planning and the more brain-based, thematic interdependent approach. It can provide us with a real awakening.

301

Old Style Planning

The old way of presenting was to take any subject like math, science or history and divide it into smaller chunks called units. Then sub-divide the units into daily and weekly lesson plans. Then, each day, present a micro chunk of the whole. It sounds logical. But is it? Imagine yourself as a three or four year-old once again. You get your first bicycle for your birthday. You're all excited and you want nothing more than to jump on it and go! But your parents have decided that you should learn to ride a bicycle the proper way, in the right "order." They will teach you how to ride a bicycle by instructing you in the following units of content:

A. Safety
    Personal safety
        Bike hazards
        Defensive attitude
    Neighborhood safety
        Possible hazards
        Neighborhood culture
    Sidewalk and Road safety
        Laws, customs

B. History of the bicycle
    Original inventors
    Purchase price & replacement costs
        New vs. used/pros & cons
        Contingency plan for frame or mechanical damage
    Transportation niche
        Advantages and disadvantages of usage
        Comparisons with other modes
    Mechanical & product specifications

C. The Skills of Riding
    The mental approach
        The first steps
    Proper use of training wheels
        Body positioning
    Advanced riding skills

D. Everyday Use
    Storage of bicycle (locks, garage, etc.)
    Permission (when, length of time, etc.)
    Extras (Horn, basket, etc.)

Naturally, before your parents have completed presenting you unit "A," you have lost interest and gone on to do something else. The brain is far more capable than the list above indicates. Obviously, a more typical child's approach is to get a few bits of important information, then hop on a bike and give it a try.

The brain learns best in real-life, immersion-style
multi-path learning... fragmented, piecemeal presenting can
forever kill the joy and love of learning

Amazingly enough, most kids learn to ride a bike just fine. But if you think about it, that's how you learned some of the most complex things in your life. Your native language, for example. Did you learn rules of grammar first? Did you get classes in it? Did you take tests in it? Of course not! You were never formally taught your native language. You "picked it up."

Is it possible that our brain can "pick up" other subjects? Is it possible to learn science, history, geography, math, life skills, literature and the arts by just "picking them up?" Of course it is! That's the way our brain is designed to learn: multi-path, in order or out of order, many levels, many presenters, many contexts and many angles. We learn with themes, favorite subjects, issues, key points, questions, trial and error, and application. That is thematic learning.

> *Thematic learning is a process*
> *closer to the way the human brain*
> *is naturally designed best to learn*

The underlying principle is that our world is an integrated whole, and that one of the greatest gifts you can offer your participants is the connectedness of classroom education to the real world. The thematic approach urges you to follow threads that weave throughout your student's world instead of a single subject or textbook. Textbooks are not only often out of date, but more importantly, they present a single viewpoint or approach which the authors have chosen. In this fast-moving information age, your preferred sources of information should be the student's real life experience, magazines, computers, videos, television, journals and libraries.

An Interdependent Thematic Approach

The theme approach was designed by master presenter Susan Kovalik and explained in *The ITI Model.* The basic components of it are as follows:

Year-long Theme: This is a year (or semester) long organizational structure consisting of a basic theme (with a real grabbing title). If it's unknown by the kids, it's a poor cognitive organizer. Pick a topic that you can work with for a year.

Examples might be: The Zoo (grade 1-2). "What Makes it Tick?" (3-5th grade) The Mississippi River (4-6th grade) or "Parasites" (science class, grades 7-8). In business, the theme might be sports, an amusement park, a Shakespearean play a TV show or hundreds of others.

The theme should have the following qualities: your excitement, learner understanding and excitement, worthy of extensive time invested, plenty of materials and resources available for it, has application to student's real world, has a clear pattern and the rationale is compelling for learners.

Components: The physical locations and the human issues. Use situations, events, contributions by participants.

Examples from the themes above: "The Zoo" (geography of world zoos, animals, systems to run a zoo, economics of a zoo, endangered species, colors of animals, foods eaten, the food chain, etc.)

"What Makes It Tick?" (clocks of the past, the world as a clock, geologic time, famous clocks, making watches, timers, body clocks, calendars, mechanisms, computers, etc.)

"The Mississippi River" (inhabitants, who it affects, geology, stores & businesses, the folklore, the uses of water, the name itself, fishing, changes in river paths, flooding, agriculture, weather, maps, etc.)

"Parasites" (as meant in nature, the molecular world, society, personal relationships, economics, medicine, law, history of the word, English, etc.)

Topics: A specific aspect of the location or human issues will be studied, about one per week.

Suggestion: Use the newspapers, television, kid's examples and school issues to tie into each of the components.

Key Points: Concepts, skills, knowledge, attitudes, values, models & patterns.

Suggestions: Brainstorm the essential things you'd like participants to learn. Identify your resources: physical locations, CD-ROM's, library, school sites, guest speakers, computers, etc. Your goal is a real hands-on immersion. Study your districts scope and sequence of curriculum mandates. Integrate the child's points of curiosity; what are their "whys" and "wherefores?" You become a learner all over again and experience the joy of learning.

Inquiries: These are the specific applications of the key points. You may want to use the various levels of Bloom's Taxonomy and integrate the learning into Gardner's Multiple Intelligence.

Examples: The Zoo (Knowledge: list & describe all the animals in the zoo. Comprehension: group them in to categories & discuss why and how. Application: build a model lion enclosure that lions would like. Analysis: write and sing a rap about the daily life of animals; what it is like from their point of view. Evaluation: create a checklist of desirable enclosure qualities, visit your own zoo, and evaluate the quality of life for 10 zoo animals. Synthesis: Using what you've learned from ideal zoo environments, pretend visitors from another world came to earth and wanted to make a zoo full of humans. What do you think a zoo for humans would be like? Work in groups and draw it out on a huge piece of paper. Discuss and describe to the class.

Thematic Learning in a Nutshell

To understand it conceptually, picture a spider web. The title is in the center (your year-long theme). If you have nine months, you'd have nine branches coming out from the center of the web, much like spokes of a wheel. Those are the monthly components. On each of the spokes, you'd have weekly topics, four of them. Certainly you can vary it as situations may arise to alter your plans. This thematic style of presenting and learning has been demonstrated far more effective than the traditional unit, chunk, unit chunk, all unrelated and piecemeal.

The classroom becomes a living, learning laboratory. The learning is connected and the themes are relevant. Think of the classroom possibilities for discussion, projects, plays and writing! Give your participants a list of at least ten addresses where participants can write for free information. Include U.S. Government agencies, the Chamber of Commerce as well as state agencies. Help them discover for themselves, how to locate addresses, phone numbers and contact persons for each unit. This is a terrific way for them to become a lifelong learner.

The Everyday Format

The purpose of the upcoming format is simple: it's designed to make learning planning easy. While it's true that the presenter is the #1 influence in the classroom, and the learning climate makes all the difference, you can do a great deal with brain-compatible formats. Most other lesson plans ignore the simple principles from this book that the brain requires for best learning. This one uses what's been presented earlier in this book as a foundation. You provide the intangibles.

There is an enormous difference
between presenting and learning

There are some strategies that will encompass the wide range of principles that help encourage the brain to absorb, process and store experiences and information meaningfully. What's presented here next is not a lesson plan, but rather a reminder of what usually makes learning work. Under each of the seven steps, select the strategies that are appropriate for your learner's age, subject, circumstances and experience level.

Brain-Based "Learning Planning"

1. Preparation

Do as many of these as are appropriate:
- Pre-expose learners to topic - (can be done hours, days and weeks in advance: this helps the brain build better conceptual maps)
- Offer learn-to-learn skills

- Teach brain nutrition and offer coping, self-esteem & life skills
- Create a strong immersion learning environment; make it interesting!
- Your own credibility and prestige is reinforced often
- Plan best time of day for learning each item based on brain cycles and rhythms
- Discover students' interests & background - they set their own goals
- Make sure your environment has many colorful peripherals posted
- Provide brain "wake-ups" (cross-laterals or relax-stretching)
- State strong positive expectations; allow learners to voice theirs, too
- Create relationships, strong positive rapport
- Read audience states and make any adjustments before beginning

2. Globalization

Do as many of these that are appropriate:
This is where you create the curiosity or excitement
It's similar to the "anticipatory set" but goes farther to prepare the learner
- Provide the context for learning this topic and background
  (can be in the form of an overview first - this is the classic "big picture")
- Elicit from learners what possible value & relevance it has to them
  learners have to feel connected to the topic before you begin
  let them express how they feel it's relevant, not just you telling
- The brain learns particularly well from concrete experiences first!
  can you provide something real, physical or concrete?
- Create the themes, the interdisciplinary tie-ins to today's session
- Optimum "hook" is one with novelty that meets strong personal learner needs
Note: the Globalization is one of the most critical parts of a plan. It is what connects the learner to the learning. Make sure you include it.

3. Initiation

Do as many of these as are appropriate:
- Immersion in the topic: Flood with content! Instead of the singular, lock-step, sequential, one-bite-at-a-time information, there's an initial virtual overload of ideas, details, themes and meanings. Allow a sense of temporary overwhelming in learners: it'll be followed by anticipation, curiosity, and a determination to discover meaning for oneself. Over time it all gets sorted out, by the learner, brilliantly. If that sounds like the real world of learning, outside the classroom, you're right.
- This can also be the time to provide concrete learning experiences. It can be problem-solving, a field trip, interviews or hands-on learning. Learners may have some choice in how to do this. Ideally it employs all the senses: visual, auditory, kinesthetic, olfactory & gustatory.
  - It could be a group or team project to build, find, explore, or to physically design, etc.
  - Learning is best when it's based on discovery, need and themes; allow them to discover something new they're interested in, help the learners make it important and needed, and make it thematic...
  - Learners could attend theater, put on a skit, a commercial, or make a newspaper, etc.

306

This step offers enough choice to engage many learning styles. It is *not* "go home and read chapters four and five." This step provides the source of discussion since it's experiential. The key here is that since all do it, it puts all learners on equal ground
- A well-designed computer program can work here (like HOTS)

4. Elaboration

Do as many of these as are appropriate:
This is the processing stage; it requires genuine thinking. It may be an open-ended de-brief of the previous activity. This is the time to make intellectual sense out of the learning.
- Tie things together thematically, like a jigsaw puzzle making sense
- Learners can write, ask or design questions, go into data bases
- One option is for the learners to read up on the topic or watch a video
- Restate questions, write a test, hold peer discussions
- Learners can sort, analyze or make mind-maps of the material
- Can be a forum; can be done in a group or team
- Presenter can answer learner questions or elaborate on ideas
- Students can play presenter role and ask, interpret questions & ideas

5. Incubation

Do as many of these as are appropriate:
The brain is most effective in learning over time, not all at once
- This critical time is for unguided reflection, "down time"
- It is appropriate to have at least several hours, several days away from the topic. That way the brain gets time to subconsciously sort, process & connect ideas. Great for intrapersonal time.
- It could be a day off, a recess, silent time, journal writing time, relaxation time or simply a change of subjects.

6. Verification

Do as many of these as are appropriate:
This step is for the learner as much as the presenter. Using the ideas in this book on assessment, learners demonstrate what they know. It has to be made personally relevant. Learning occurs best when a model or metaphor is made by the learner about the new learning. There are dozens of ways to do it including:
- a presentation, with presenting tools, using peer presenting
- learner designs questions for a test, presenter interviews the learner
- a written assessment and verbal assessment
- a learner project - a working model, a mind map, a video, a newsletter, etc.
- learner presents a role-play or lesson to the class

7. Celebration

Do as many of these as are appropriate:
This step provides for the all-important self-convincers. See chapter two for rationale. These are best provided primarily by peers, secondarily by a presenter. Reinforcement needs modality (V-A-K), frequency (repeat it) & duration (time).

- Students who use a rubric to evaluate their work can tell each other how they did. Celebration needs to engage emotions also; have a toast with juice!
- It's bragging time, it's time to peer share, it's time to show others a demonstration of your work. It's a time to share success & give acknowledgments to peers. Make it fun, light and joyful.
- Music, streamers, horns and compliments can be part of the celebration
- It can be as simple as giving a classmate a "high-five"; or as complex as a class-designed and produced celebration party.
- This step create the all-important love of learning. Never miss it!

> **What This Means to You:** It's critical that we begin to ask more and more questions about what learning is. Since even neuroscientists have a tough time explaining it, we might want to have a wider, broader platform on which to express it. Learning planning is a way of focusing on learning instead of on presenting. It follows brain-compatible principles. The primary change for you is to create a more thematic, integrated, interdisciplinary curriculum. You may want to use it for a year as a experiment and review the results.

Long-Term Learning Goals:

In this chapter there are long-term *content* planning (thematic learning), and the short-term daily *process* (seven steps of a lesson). Now we move to the long term *process* of learning. There are five stages for learner understanding and meaning. In general, they tend to happen in order, as the brain develops greater neural mapping in the subject area.

#1. Content: information or acquisition (unrelated content).
Process: learner has no awareness of process at this stage.
#2. Content: thematic mapping, greater content associations.
Process: learning how to learn the skills of learning.
#3. Content: able to relate it to self, community, planet.
Process: processing the process; metacognition.
#4. Content: peer mastery, deep meaning, expert learner.
Process: Re-contextualizing it; generalization.

#5. Content: new insights & ability to think "outside the box," new themes, a paradigm-creating pioneer... Process: systems mastery, skills to empower local and global learning organizations.

You might want to keep mental notes of where your learners are at. Your goal is to move them from the introductory level as far as possible. In some cases, getting to level two or three will be a major victory. In other cases, your goal and the learner's goal might be to get to level five.

How You Can Follow Up: *ITI: The Model* (Integrated Thematic Instruction) by Susan Kovalik, *Planning Integrated Curriculum,* by Susan Drake. Available from ACSD at (703) 549-9110. *The ACT Approach,* by Dhority or *Accelerated Learning* by Rose. See Appendix.

Chapter Questions

1. What was novel, fresh and new? What was familiar or "old hat"?
2. In what ways do you already apply the information in this chapter?
3. What three questions can you now generate about this material?
4. How did you react emotionally to this information?
5. In what ways can you translate the key three or four theories and discoveries presented here into practical everyday useful ideas?
6. How did you react cognitively when you were reading the ideas of this chapter?
7. If these things are, in fact, true about the brain, what should we do differently? What resources of time, people and money could be redirected? In what ways do you suggest we start?
8. What was the single one (or two) most interesting or valuable insights you had?
9. Plan your next step, the logical practical application of what you've learned.
10. What obstacles might you encounter? How can you realistically deal with them?

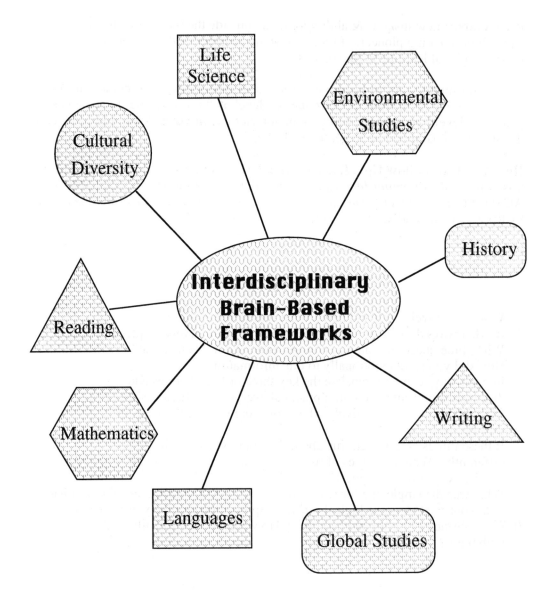

Life
Science

Cultural
Diversity

Environmental
Studies

History

Reading

Interdisciplinary
Brain-Based
Frameworks

Writing

Mathematics

Languages

Global Studies

20
Interdisciplinary Brain-Based Frameworks

Simple, But Not Easy

The new frameworks are so obvious when you think of the brain. How do you learn? You learn all levels at all times, from easy to hard. You learn all subjects, at all times, from the most immediate to the most distant. You integrate what you can, at the level you can, every day. There is no separate curriculum for every single subject in your real life. It is not my intention here to provide a complete framework for all levels of brain-based learning curriculum. However, you will get some specific examples of how you can extend your existing curriculum. Then, over time, you can make more dramatic brain-based changes.

The Reality of Brain-Based Curriculum

How does your brain learn curriculum? It doesn't. Our brain is constantly integrating all subjects across the curriculum at all times. No more compartmentalized, contrived learning. As an example, at the grocery store you learn about more than just food: you use transportation to get there, psychology to interact, global studies to meet people of other cultures and you need mathematics to figure your bill. Your new brain-based curriculum changes must: 1) connect with many other subjects 2) be based in reality - the learner's everyday life 3) be generated by the learner and 4) have sufficient time to truly explore topics in-depth. As these changes are implemented in your school, you find, dramatic changes in learner motivation and quality of understanding.

311

The classroom will extend, 24 hours a day, to the home, work, recreational areas and the non-stop electronic university. We'll see fewer and fewer textbooks. Laptops, wall-sized televisions, distance learning and virtual reality will all make learning more accessible, more impactful and more interwoven into our life's daily patterns. Instead of physically taking your children to a formalized, accredited, private school every day, it will be available (for a price) over cable channels. Learning through television, cable, phone and computer will become more common.

At schools, you'll see more age and grade *clustering,* not specific ages or grades each year. As we have seen earlier, all six or ten or fifteen year olds are likely to be at different neurological developmental stages. It's unlikely they will want to perform at the same level academically, physically or socially. Statewide curriculums and frameworks which include specific year-by-year grade-level performance standards are inappropriate and will be phased out. All 13-year-olds may not be neurologically ready for algebra or geometry. While the human brain is capable of an enormous amount, unless the groundwork has been laid or the presenter has extraordinary flexibility, the learner may simply become frustrated. What's developmentally appropriate for learners to know or do, has a range of years. For example, "All learners from ages four through about six ought to be able to know or do the following..."

We'll be seeing the reduction of special education and gifted classes soon. The pendulum will be swinging back the towards the center. The fact that a four-year-old can perform certain behaviors that a six-year-old can, does not make the four-year-old a prodigy or genius. While it is reasonable to expect some general academic milestones for learners, it is unreasonable to label those who are "ahead or behind" as either gifted or slow learners. They may be completely normal. Schools with time-flexible (and high!) standards are more likely to have their participants succeed. Why? The brain is designed to survive and succeed, as long as you give it a chance.

You'll be seeing more attention to time blocks and subject scheduling. Developmentally, the primary school brain learns best in shorter units of learning time (30-40 minutes in K-2 and 40-60 in grades 3-5) or on whole day blocks. The middle and high school learner is ready for, and needs, class lengths in 90-150 minute blocks. This allows presenters and learners to better develop individual ideas, themes and use more of the multiple intelligences with them. More importantly, it allows for the presenter-to-learner, mentor-to-apprentice relationship that research and intuition have proven so valuable.

Evolving Mathematics

You'll see mathematics presented more often as real life problems to solve. Remember earlier in this book we talked about the brain as being biologically wired to survive? The brain learns, in order to survive. Most mathematics can be learned by your participants IF the perception is that the content or processes are needed. In fact, you can't stop youngsters from learning arithmetic when it comes to counting up money for video games, clothes or candy bars. They learn it very fast - it's "survival math." The old days of solving the irrelevant "problem" of two trains, going at 60 miles an hour, leaving the station at the same time from opposite cities that pass each other after how many minutes? - those days, fortunately, are long gone.

Why do participants do math problems in a class? It's not insight, illumination or deep personal meaning. It's to find the answer, of course! The one that's usually in the back of book. On the average, between 70-85% of all secondary participants dislike math. What does that tell us about the way it's been taught? There has to be a better way.

An excellent brain-compatible program was developed in the Netherlands called *Math in Context*. It's being pioneered by many innovative schools with the cooperation of the University of Madison, Wisconsin. The program establishes what skills are appropriate for developmental levels. Then, it offers math units that consist of project-style, challenging, real-life problems. The projects engage learner teams who then need to learn the mathematics in order to solve the problems. The old way was: math is an end unto itself. Learn to do this problem because it's good for you. The new way is different: The learning of math is *a by-product on the way to solving the real problems of everyday life.*

Let's say it's an algebra class. The learner problem regards the potential purchase of two plots of land. One is zoned single-family and the other is zoned multi-dwelling. Each costs a different amount, each is on the same size acreage. They have a 10 day purchase option on each of them. Given potential costs, potential revenues, license, taxes, city ordinances, trends in housing, projections of land values, your personal cash flow, your family needs, environmental issues and interest rates, which one makes better financial sense and why? That's a very complex problem that requires the use of formulas, graphs, estimates, interviews and projections. The participants may interview real estate agents, bankers, city council persons, consult their teammates, use calculators, go to text books, use computers or ask the presenter for help. To draw some conclusions, they'll have just 10 days. Projects like these are engaging and motivating. Most important, they're real life. It's brain-based learning.

313

Implementation starts with one unit over a two week period. Then each term, additional units are added, as the presenter comfort level grows. Soon, everyone is so used to it, its the only way to go. Total implementation of this new framework will take about two years. Some presenters are fearful that their old way of "stand and deliver," is being threatened. It is, and it's about time! Textbooks are being abandoned in droves by up-to-date presenters. Suddenly, more presenters are acting more like a catalyst and coach instead of an all-knowing presenter or professor.

For math to be more brain-based, it has to tie into the rich lives of the learners. Many geometry presenters introduce cubes or parallel lines as if they were some new concept. How ridiculous! Take your participants outside the classroom and stand and look around. There are cubes (buildings, boxes, etc.) everywhere! Take them to the street corner. There are parallel lines everywhere! It's almost that simple! Math is no strange new language. It's everywhere!

Languages the Brain-Based Way

The new biology of the brain tells us that children are born with a pre-wired understanding of how language works. An infant may not know what the word for table is, but he or she sure knows that it is a thing, an object. In fact, research has demonstrated that when a parent or presenter says "This is a table," children understand that the presenter is referring to the larger object, not the COLOR of the object, or the MATERIAL it is made out of and certainly not THE ACT of pointing out a table. The child seems to intuitively know the general and specific details of what the presenter means. Now, this may not seem very important or relevant, but it is.

Human beings have the genetic storage for the systems of language. We don't know all the vocabulary words, but we do, genetically, understand syntax. Point to a cat drinking milk, and say "cat." The child knows you are referring to the cat, not the act of a four-legged furry mammal drinking milk. In fact, even the best scientists have failed to build a language-learning robot that can understand all the "rules" that a 3-year-old knows. The point is, we don't need to teach language structure when we teach our native languages. So why do we do it in a foreign language class, when in many cases, it's the same as our own language? It's time to take into consideration how the brain learns languages best. Languages are learned through acquisition, not formal instruction. Steven Pinker, linguist and researcher, says:

"It is in the detailed analysis of grammar that evidence is provided for the deep biological nature of language... Nowhere does the old idea of tabula rasa fall on its face with such force. Children reveal to us that huge aspects of the mind are built-in"

Language learning is universal, from native to "foreign" languages. Using brain-based principles, every one of us can learn virtually any language on earth. How? We are wired to genetically understand them. All we need is the NEED to learn it. There are, of course, better times to learn it than others. As we mentioned earlier, foreign languages are best when learned from ages 3-10. Waiting until middle school or high school is NOT brain-based and an enormous waste of learner potential. Using the brain-based approach, presenters are most likely to do the following:

- A complete immersion environment simulating a foreign country complete with music, posters & dress
- All mistakes pointed out indirectly, emphasis on using the skills, save the grammar for later at the advanced levels (learn it the way we all learned our native language)
- Absolute minimum of grammar, syntax and rules (save it for highest level)
- Use of music, role-play and celebrations
- Real-life situations, no textbook learning; learning is thematic everywhere
- Use of alternative characters: puppets, assumed identities participants take on full characters and roles
- Multiple contexts for memory embedding: inside and outside the classroom, a restaurant, a civic event, a festival

At the University of Massachusetts, Dr. Lynn Dhority has been using this philosophy and these strategies presenting German for years. Instead of the old way of language, starting with sentences and vocabulary, using singular, lock-step, sequential, one-bite-at-a-time lesson planning, initially Dhority uses a virtual overload of ideas, details, themes and meanings. Lozanov created a temporary chaos in the learner's mind. The explosion of ideas is followed by curiosity and intrigue. It prompts the learner to discover meaning for him or herself. Dhority consistently floods his participants with more German than they can possibly grasp. Over time it all gets sorted out, by the learner, brilliantly. If that sounds like the real world of learning one's own native language, you're right.

Dhority has been consistently one of the most effective language instructors anywhere. His accelerated language programs have been used by the national defense department and analyzed in great detail. He was an honored faculty

315

member at Harvard and his participants consistently emerge with top marks for language acquisition. He is one of many presenters who embodies a more brain-based approach.

In learning a native language, participants can learn everything from origins of grammar, to writing skills and literature in a more brain-based way. Here's an optimal place for thematic, patterned learning. The secret is to keep the threat low, expression high and the use of peers strong. Use theater works for learning about literature. Use teams to learn small amounts of more rote, repetitive information. Avoid all rewards in the expression of creativity and writing skills. Employ greater use of videos, guest speakers and outreach projects.

Many reading programs work well. New Zealand's excellent reading programs are models worldwide. The Whole Language reading programs are usually designed to be brain compatible. So is the Reading Recovery Program. Quality reading programs employ the use of theater, voice, tonal shifts, attentional biases, search for meaning, and they reach visual, auditory and kinesthetic learners.

In thinking skills and problem solving, the HOTS (Higher Order Thinking Skills) program is one of the best. It's a computer-based program developed by Stanley Pogrow out of the University of Arizona. It uses questions to stimulate thinking, language, learning and problem-solving skills. One of the best testimonials of the program is the participants - most of them really enjoy it!

Lively Life Sciences

Here, the participants get an opportunity to learn about how sciences affect their own lives. The study of biology can be as boring or as engaging as a presenter makes it. Students can learn about biology through discussions of alcohol, drugs, pregnancy, AIDS or other STDs. Or, they can decide whether to build a human helper-robot, a "droid." This means they would need all the knowledge of biology (and more!). They could understand how others around them develop Parkinson's or Alzheimer's Disease. A real-life project might be this: you find out your mother or father is getting Parkinson's Disease. Find out what causes it, how it affects your parent. What are the traditional treatments and what alternatives can you locate? When offered as an opportunity to fill needs (like love, health, thinking, parent bonding or sex) this course becomes a high interest priority to the learner's brain.

Global Studies/Geography

Once again, the philosophy of brain-based learning is being carried out in this subject by presenters worldwide. The structure varies dramatically from classroom to classroom, but the results are always the same: motivated learners who gain an authentic, in-depth understanding of the material. Some of the characteristics are:

- Students have some choice in how they learn: computer, video, phone, teams, partners or by themselves
- Learning is thematic - tied together with larger meaning patterns
- Large, consuming projects are developed:
  - learners develop economic/social aid packages
  - participants develop communication /satellite companies
- Travel plans in detail are developed for round-the-world trips including visa, passports, ticketing and packing lists

A group or team project to learn the geography of the Unites States might be an early settler challenge. Class teams pretend they have just immigrated to America (or any other country) in the year 1850. They arrived from Europe in Virginia and want to go to California. There are two families. What season of the year might they travel? Consider the following: weather, Indians, bandits, transportation modes, food supplies, money available, skills, geography, health, etc. What path would they take? What obstacles are realistic? What cities would not even be started in 1840? What documentation is there available? What would the trip be like? Plan it out in complete detail. What would the equivalent trip be like today? For six graders, this might be a 4-week project. In a science class, your class could plan a trip to Mars. Think of the math, astronomy, biology, global studies, language, and science required to make THAT happen!

Gifted and Talented Programs

You'll see fewer and fewer GATE, TAG and special education programs in the next few years. In brain-based learning, there is no ability grouping. Why? The only way you could ability group is to first compare participants. And a comparison of two participants is one of the most irrelevant activities an institution can perform. How Karen compares to Diane is absolutely immaterial. Karen's brain may be as much as three years ahead or behind Diane's in development. Karen has an entirely different multiple intelligences profile than Diane. Karen may have a miserable and unacceptable home environment which, sadly, impairs learning and provides constant stress and dramatic undernutrition. The only

317

relevant bit of data about Andrea is "How is Andrea doing today compared to Andrea's performance of a week ago or a year ago?" Now that's useful data!

The Key School is a public elementary school in Indianapolis, Indiana. When it embraced the multiple intelligences model several years ago, the school policy became "Every learner is gifted." *And they have discovered it.* Ordinary children act and perform like those in the special schools for the gifted. What does this say about the so-called gifted programs? It says that they are for all participants. What made the difference at the Key School? Many things, but the presenters have an attitude that everyone is gifted and they skillfully use the multiple intelligences.

Brain-based learning says gifted and talented programs are, at their best, ignoring what we now know about the brain. At worst, they are very elitist and damaging. Why? The whole presumption about who is gifted and who is not *is based on an outdated model.*

Early & False Assumptions About Gifted Learners

1. It's false that giftedness can be measured or predicted (The majority of society's greatest contributors were NOT identified as gifted in school).
2. It's false that so-called average (or below average) participants would not benefit from an enriched gifted program (Research suggests that **all** learners benefit).
3. It's false that there are only a few truly gifted learners. (Master Japanese violin presenter Suzuki discovered he could teach competent-level violin playing to **any** child) Glen Doman discovered he could teach reading and math to babies.
4. It's false that special talents and abilities are fixed and cannot be taught. Anyone can learn to do most anything with competence, though certainly not at the level of highest mastery.
5. Some say that there's *something special* about gifted learners. Yes, this is true in a strange way. At the primary school level, those who are more visual learners are more often mislabeled as the "talented and gifted." Visual learners are often quieter, read better, focus longer and pay attention to the presenter. Among many presenters, having a learner like that is a real "gift" in your class! At other levels, often those thought of as "gifted" have developed abilities in other areas such as music, dance, art or reflection. These are simply a few of the multiple intelligences that are often ignored in traditional classes. If you have an ability, and it's ignored, you're unlikely to develop it.

The fact is, we have been ineffective at predicting those who will make the greatest impact in our society. Here's a list of those who were "slow" or problem participants: physicist Steven Hawking, poet Maya Angelou, producer/director Steven Spielberg, Walt Disney, Broadway genius Martha Graham, Martin Luther King, Albert Einstein, musician Stevie Wonder, business whiz Bill Gates, Sam Walton, writer W.E.B. DuBois, personal computer inventors Steven Jobs and Steven Wozniak, activist Caesar Chavez, singer Ray Charles, astronomer-writer Carl Sagan, producers Spike Lee and Quincy Jones. It reads like a "Who's Who!" Each one has made a significant contribution to our generation. In addition, there are countless others, females, immigrants, slow learners and others who have made critical contributions but are not "household" names. Maybe it's time to bring our assessment of what's "gifted" into the **real** world.

Having said *there is no place for so-called "gifted and talented" learners in a brain-based program,* what about the other end of the spectrum? Should there be pullout programs for participants with special needs? Yes, but only a certain kind of program. There's a difference between presenting content and process. Many pullout (special education) programs teach primarily content. They simply teach it slower, using more flexibility and stronger relationships. By itself, that's not bad. But in the larger context of education, it may be more of a disservice unless it's done right. The bad part is that participants get stigmatized as "slow learners" and their self concept can be destroyed.

Doing it "right" means that all pullout programs should be presenting process and values, not content. Don't teach the spelling words, teach the brain-based system of HOW to spell. Don't just put them in a good "state" for learning, teach them HOW to manage their own states. Teach them about eye accessing cues, learning style profiles, learn-to-learn skills, graphic organizers, communication skills and social skills. Give them self-confidence through skills not content. These participants should be back in regular classes as soon as possible.

When regular presenters are trained in brain-based presenting and learning strategies, their participants learn more effectively and efficiently. More of their participants learn better and they retain the learning longer. Self-confidence is up and so is love of learning. This means you'll have fewer problems and fewer participants who need special attention or special skills from a pullout program.

Special Services

The policy of inclusion is gaining acceptance after two decades of being politically incorrect. Regardless of the motives, the effects are the same. More and more participants who had previously been separated from others in "pullout" programs are now being mainstreamed. Is this a smart move? In general, yes, though there are some obvious exceptions.

In 1992, over 10% of all learners in America aged 6-21 received some type of special education services. Approximately one-half were diagnosed with some kind of "learning disability." Of the remaining participants (25%) were labeled as either speech or language impaired or (25%) more severe (autism, dystrophy, retardation, etc.).

If you counted all the participants that have been diagnosed with attention-deficit disorder, hyperactivity, special education, learning disorders, emotional problems, developmentally delayed, ESL and other learning problems, the number would be huge. How big, depends on the school; but in many areas, the number would be as high as 40% of the school population. Why are so many labeled as "different?"

Part of the answer is funding, part of it is political correctness and part of it is ignorance. More funding is an incentive for many schools to identify anyone who is different. Fear of special interest criticism leads many to tout their special programs. Ignorance about the brain often allows many presenters to offer a watered-down, snail's-pace curriculum. Yet, research strongly suggests that the brain thrives on novelty, challenge and enrichment. We will find that many of the so-called "slow" learners become articulate and engaged when they are given the type of environment that's best for the brain. Overdoing the special education classes places an enormous drain on resources. There is a better way to go.

Now, in this same community, implement brain-based schools. Allow for more differences in male and female brain development. Allow for more differences for individual same-sex brain development. Start second and third language presenting at all elementary levels. Serve better brain food for school supported breakfast and lunch programs. Put more nutritious food in vending machines. Utilize more learning styles in the instructional process. Allow for down-time, use graphic organizers. Reduce stress, threat and inappropriate discipline programs. Get the parents on your side. Teach and assess using the multiple intelligences. After doing this for two years, count how many participants are diagnosed with problems. About 1-3% will need to be separated because they are exceedingly disruptive. The remaining percentage is more likely to stabilize at near 2-5%. Now, that's something a school can work with more easily.

How You Can Follow Up: Read *How to Untrack Your School,* by Paul George. Available from ACSD at (703) 549-9110.

Culturally Different or
Culturally Deprived?

In a brain-based school, diversity is valued. What makes a program of cultural diversity more "brain-based?" Each person has, and of course, each culture promotes, their own unique "map" of "how things are." Honoring these maps is the easiest way to encourage learning and meaning to that person's brain or culture. The relationship between cognition and culture has been well explored by many researchers (including Feuerstein) and need not be repeated here. An example of "brain-antagonistic" education he uses is too-often repeated around the world in real life.

Throughout the history of the American government, there has been an attempt to use education to "westernize" the Native Americans (over 700 different tribes). The government-run schools viewed the Indian language and culture as an impediment to the Indian's future. The schools were an attempt to "convert" the "backward Indian" into a American white man. The efforts were on saving the person, and ignoring the culture. The failure record of these schools was monumental. But there are some positive solutions.

Each of us has our own lifetime of rich experiences, either in our own imagination or real life. All our experiences can be used positively, in some way, for learning. Brain-based presenting with cultural diversity means using the culture of the people as a strength, not a detriment. Dr. Henry Levin's Stanford program called Accelerated Schools is built around using each student's qualities as strengths instead of analyzing and evaluating them to discover the most trivial "deficiency." Here are some examples of how to use the existing culture to teach. Many Native Americans commonly orient better with the following.

<u>Learning Strategies</u>
1. Graphic organizers for relationships and meaning
2. More references to sacred symbols and meanings
3. Better integration of whole-parts-whole learning
4. The development of comparisons and contrasts
5. Greater emphasis on spatial orientation
6. Stronger use of non-verbals, family involved
7. Purposeful use of existing ritual and ceremony

Presenters who use the strategies above are more successful. The good news is that times are changing. In 1975, laws were passed which give more responsibility and authority of the structure and process of the Native American education back to the those who are being educated. But biases remain worldwide. The solution? Change the biases, and the process will begin.

In the early 80's, at a black university, UWC in Cape Town, South Africa, the pass rate among participants was a mere 17% in the Faculty of Science. Research showed that black participants were extremely motivated and curious. So why the high failure rate? Follow-up research verified the following characteristics:

1. Most were unable to form & keep strong mental pictures
2. Greater preference to approximation vs. literal data collection
3. Higher reliance on coaching, partners and group work
4. A lack of both short-term and long-term goals

Analysis from a cultural perspective would tell us they were rich with background, but weak in the skills needed for science success. There's a happy ending to the story: the intervention programs that recognized the real problems and dealt with them have been quite successful among the participants at UWC. Are those different from the norm, "culturally different" or "culturally deprived?" Operating from the second choice, we'll fail; from the first, we'll all have a better chance to succeed.

One successful model is the MLE (Mediated Learning Experience) process, developed by Feuerstein. It places a mediator in between the learner and the world of structured stimuli. The mediator regulates the frequency, content, order and intensity in a way that promotes meaning to the learner. In a way, that's what a special education presenter does. The three criteria for success?

1. intentionality & reciprocity (the learner needs to know how much you care and to have a mutually respectful relationship
2. meaning (the learning has to have meaning in the lives of both)
3. transcendence (the real goal is to move beyond the learning at hand and into the personal life of the learner and the needs of society)

Much attention lately has been focused on how to motivate the apathetic, disinterested, discouraged learners or the "at-risk" group. But Kagan says that existing *"...factors within classrooms and schools transform participants at risk into a discrete subculture that is incompatible with academic success."* These participants are consistently demoralized by what Ford calls negative *"...social comparisons with 'smarter' peers, lack of school-initiated peer support for achievement, and an emphasis on avoiding failure, or avoiding 'hassles,' rather than on learning...."*

Many are said to have a lack of curiosity (one of the prime ingredients of intrinsic motivation). Yet that's a normal part of the brain's activity. In other words, the context (circumstances or people) can actually *drive out the curiosity* from a learner's brain. In short, the school climate may well be contributing to the problems as much as anything. What can be done about it? As our next chapter reveals, a great deal can be done.

> **What This Means to You:** All topics can now take on a more brain-based approach. The old days of stand, teach, test and pray are over. Using the principles outlined about the brain in the earlier chapters of this book, you can design and implement approaches to learning that participants really enjoy AND they learn more.

How You Can Follow Up: *Mathematics Education for a Changing World* by Steven Willoughby. *The Evolving Multicultural Classroom* by Rose Reissman. *Mediated Learning Experience,* by Reuven Feurstein; *Planning Integrated Curriculum,* by Susan Drake. Call ACSD at (703) 549-9110. *The ACT Approach,* by Lynn Dhority. Available by catalog. See Appendix.

Chapter Questions

1. What was novel, fresh and new? What was familiar or "old hat"?
2. In what ways do you already apply the information in this chapter?
3. What three questions can you now generate about this material?
4. How did you react emotionally to this information?
5. In what ways can you translate the key three or four theories and discoveries presented here into practical everyday useful ideas?
6. How did you react cognitively when you were reading the ideas of this chapter?
7. If these things are, in fact, true about the brain, what should we do differently? What resources of time, people and money could be redirected? In what ways do you suggest we start?
8. What was the single one (or two) most interesting or valuable insights you had?
9. Plan your next step, the logical practical application of what you've learned.
10. What obstacles might you encounter? How can you realistically deal with them?

Seven Steps

Big Picture

Building a Learning Organization

Distinctions

Key Principles

21
Building a Learning Organization

The Bigger Picture

Most of the school reform and restructuring strategies that are suggested, mandated or implemented are doomed. Why? Based on recent brain research, outdated reform ideas will only exacerbate the problem, not solve it. How important is it to develop cross-curricular, interdisciplinary, systemic change? It's critical! Research by Ryan, et al., Paris, Ryan and Stiller, and Covington all suggest that *educational leaders may want to reconsider these fatal paths:*

- 100% curriculum mandates (removes learner choice & buy-in)
- high stakes testing (creates presenting to the test and causes student's brains to "minimize") - instead create more frequent assessment
- short-term assessment (much short-term learning is useless - instead provide a rich and constant source of learner feedback)
- outcome-based learning that focuses only on assessment of immediate results or on measurable results (many of the brain's best learning cannot be measured) instead of learning HOW to learn with joy & passion.
- outcome-based learning which excludes learner input (the "demand model")
- annual testing standards for what is "average" or "normal." (better to have wider standards; brains may be from 1-3 years apart & still be normal)
- rigid performance evaluations of presenters (causes presenters to perform according to the assessments; discourages creativity)
- strongly controlling classrooms (creates resentment, apathy)
- "stand & deliver" presenters who lecture, lecture and lecture
- special programs for so-called gifted and talented learners or, for the "at-risk" (they need the enrichment of the "gifted")
- controlling, bribery and punitive systems and tactics (school can be made to feel more like a prison when using bribes & rewards for simple behaviors)

If you want learning to go up and your participants to change, influence the factors you have the most control over. When participants get a more responsive environment, their behaviors change, say Edmonds and Kagan. In spite of all the educational restructuring and reform, there is one single change that would do more to motivate learners than any other:

Make school more real and less artificial.
Learning is best when it's rich with real-life
situations, problems and solutions

Schools and businesses can change all they want, but until they make the true distinctions between what motivates learners in "real life" and what is going on in their own environments, it's all going to get the same result: good, curious, motivated people who are demotivated, and then branded as lazy.

Involving The
Learners in Reform

The research shows that the following approaches will work:

First, provide participants with consistent choice in the reform process.

1) Reorganize tasks and activities so that all of the routines involve some kind of team and partner work.
2) Elicit genuine short-term academic goals from all participants and align school goals **with** students' own lives and social and personal goals.
3) Provide an environment which is responsive to learner goals.
4) Infuse learner learning with emotion, energy and enthusiasm.
5) Utilize learner values, such as autonomy, peer approval and responsibility, to provide maintenance structures for school systems.
6) Create a new model of presenter-presenter support so that every presenter knows every other presenter's best ideas.
7) Establish a "bottom-up" administrative approach wherein participants experience that their beliefs, goals, and values are consistently integrated into school design.

*For brain-based learning to work school-wide,
the approach must be for long-term, personal, systemic and organizational
change - anything less is doomed to fail.*

Schools who use the brain-based learning methods outlined in this book are consistently more successful than those who don't. What is meant by successful? There are fewer dropouts, the children enjoy school more, they are willing to take risks, think for themselves, and be creative. They understand how they learn and love to do it. But it's more than just applying a few techniques. A school must become a learning organization. Pulling from the works of *Ten Steps to a Learning Organization* and *The Fifth Discipline Fieldbook,* you may want to follow the following sequence of steps for transforming a school into a learning organization:

1. Assess the Existing Learning Culture
Do this both formally and informally, both individually and organizationally. Be sure to make it safe for others to tell the truth about their organization. Through discussion and genuine dialogue, understand the mental models of each employee... these are the paradigms that shape their decision-making on a daily basis. Find out how they think the system works, how presenting or learning works. Sometimes this step can create despair at the results uncovered. Only after the truth (and sometimes, despair) is revealed, can the real work begin.

2. Build a Collective Vision
Do this through discussion, through reflection, through safe dialoging, develop shared images of a successful organization. Map out the vision and post it visually. Make it collective, huge, vivid and fun to look at. Develop the values and principles which will guide the organization on its path. Avoid seeking specific strategies at this time.

3. Establish a Learning Climate
Identify, encourage and promote the positive and good practices which help the organization stay on its vision. Continually discover and share what's working. Reward risk-taking with acknowledgments and celebrations. Allow for mistakes; celebrate the lessons learned and move on. Make this policy for both participants and faculty. The questions are: "Do you continually test your experience? Are you producing knowledge? Is it something your organization has not done before and values?"

4. Encourage Personal Mastery

Unless each member of an organization is practicing what is being preached, it creates an uncomfortable dissonance. Support each member to create a personal vision, guiding life principles and both long and short-term personal goals. Provide sourcebooks from authors like Steven Covey, M. Scott Peck or Anthony Robbins. Provide videos on these topics and let staff share their personal quests with the others with an in-house, in-service. Offer learn-to-learn skills for the faculty. Make sure that everyone knows how to learn successfully in their way. By being a great role model as a learner, the participants will be more likely to become one also. If you believe it, live it!

5. Design and Promote Learning as a Team

Through discussion, commitment and regular, purposeful reflection and meeting time, each learner absorbs and shares what is learned with others. Help others become resources for each other by making it easier on everyone to get what they need. The organization is now "sideways." It's not bottom-up, top-down, but it's participatory at all levels. Encourage all of the following: cooperation, shared ideas, strategies, learning plans, research, classroom supplies, guest speakers, videos and community support resources. Your question is, "Do you share the knowledge you gain with others, consistently?"

6. Systems Thinking is Everyone's Business

Discover what systems are in place that encourage the fulfillment of the collective vision and which ones do not. Understand the key relationships that make your organization a success. Make the systems make sense and make them simple. Ask the questions, "Why?" over and over until you find out what investment the organization has in keeping a particularly useless policy?

7. Nourish the Dream

All the planning and "seed planting" in the world will produce nothing unless you nourish the dream. Create a fun and dramatic metaphor for the change. Discover what the key statistical indicators in your school are for quality of learning. Be satisfied with small, continuous improvement. If you discover your key indicators were the wrong ones, find new ones. "Kaizen" is a Japanese word that means never ending improvement. Make this your 25-year theme. Create public scorecards so everybody knows how every team and the whole organization is doing. Most importantly, learn from your in-house statistics and commit to improving them, forever!

*The number one thing that successful
learning organizations do well is
support people to embrace change*

How do you know if your school is a learning organization? It's easy. Ask yourself the answers to these questions: Does the staff act differently around management than other staff? Does the staff act differently around "certain staff" than others? Are they afraid to speak their mind to others or to management? Can they try out new ideas without any fear of repercussion? Do the members of this school feel generally satisfied in their work? Are there discussions commonly held about educational practices or is it mostly about gossip, problems? These questions allow you to find out what kind of a learning climate exists. In general, you'll find that your school is a learning organization when the following things are happening:

1. The school's vision often emerges in discussion, artifacts and practices that are being used at the school.

2. The staff feel that their work is meaningful and makes a difference.

3. The staff seems much smarter when working together instead of dragging each other down or working better alone.

4. Staff are encouraged to find out how others do their job so they know how they influence others (systems thinking).

5. Learners, staff, management and others feel free to inquire about other's biases and assumptions. There are very few (if any) "sacred cows" (topics off limits for discussion).

6. There's a great respect for the differences, the experience and concerns of others at the school.

7. Everyone in the organization is growing, stretching and becoming more of the person they want to.

Learning organizations will succeed well into the 21st century for many reasons. One of them is NOT that they will successfully know or predict or anticipate the future and prepare for it. Why would that NOT happen in a learning organization? Even if we knew the future, we would: 1) not agree on how to interpret it 2) have differing theories of how to deal with change 3) have varying value systems that might conflict. What WOULD happen in a learning institution would be that they would *learn their way into the future.* They would, literally, learn HOW to succeed as needed. Where would they start? First, they would begin the steps to becoming a brain-based school.

Defining A Brain-Based Organization

Can one define a brain-based school? An automotive engine can have many things wrong and still work. It can have many things right about it and still not work. Brain-based schools are not perfect. They have not solved all problems. How they are different is simple: it's like the manager-executive difference. The manager does things right, the executive does the right things. The brain-based school does *most of the right things and usually does them the right way.*

There are several ways you can tell immediately. As you walk around your campus, what do you see? Do you see participants who are enjoying being at school? Do they work together in groups outside of class? Do they do extra work on their own? Do they bring things to school from their personal life, without being asked? Do they make it to class on time? Is attendance high? Are presenters highly regarded and spoken of well in private? Brain-based schools have a different "feel." There are hundreds of schools who have begun to embody the principles of this book. What else makes the difference?

Presenters think of themselves as "learning catalysts" instead of presenters. After all, *presenters* teach. The old definition is basically *more of the same,* top-down, "me in power, you are lesser." However, a learning catalyst *changes the role to promoting learning in whatever form is appropriate.* They are fully skilled in the use of multiple intelligences and learning styles. They more than "talk the talk," they are living the model. Remember,

If you don't "live it"
you don't believe it

They are skilled at reading learner states and managing them appropriately. They utilize and integrate technology, mind mapping, accelerated learning, peripherals, music and art across the curriculum. They give learners choice and variety, with plenty of feedback. And more importantly, they've not only had exposure to these methods, *they use them consistently and with confidence. The next page gives you some (reproducible)* distinctions and examples.

Summary of Brain-Based Learning

Not Brain-compatible	**YES:** Brain-Based
Low emotional impact	Appropriately high emotional arousal
Fragmented, sequential only	Global, unified, thematic, real life
Standard boring illustrations	Colorful, abundant memory maps
Suppressing learner energy	Utilizing & expressing energy
Lecture, more didactic	Multiple intelligences served
Emphasis on content	Emphasis on context, meaning & value
Resigned to the learner's state	Positively conditions the learner & states
Mistakes recognized directly	Mistakes noted indirectly or re-framed
Learner association with failure	Use of alter-ego, other fun characters
Subjects taught separately	Subjects learned interdisciplinary
Emphasis on quiet learning	Often rich with talking, music, activity
Belief that learning is difficult	Attitude is: it's easy, fun & creative
Creates tension & stress to learn	Keeps stress low and enjoyment high
Learning as only mental/cognitive	Learning also as action, movement
Quest for a single answer	Search for questions
Forced learning driven by grades	Intrinsic motivation evoked with need
Central focused stimuli	Use of significant peripheral stimuli
Extended presenter lecture time	Alternate focus & diffusion activities
Assumes authority from role	Creates constant respect & credibility
Finish when time's up	Finish with celebration
Subtle or obvious threats, helplessness	Remove threats; focus on support
Focus on learning in classrooms	Real world, simulations, trips
Institutional boring rituals	Positive, purposeful rituals
Infer, tell, demand	Suggest, ask & tell
Insistent focus on conscious learning	Use of strong non-conscious learning
Minimal open & closing time	Longer open & close, shorter middle
Delayed, indefinite vague feedback	Immediate, dramatic feedback
Teach for the test, with stress	Learn for the joy of learning & real life
Sit at desks & limit interactions	Mobility, face each other, partners, groups
Abrupt exposure to content	Purposeful & consistent pre-exposure
Introduce topic, forget it	Multiple exposure & activation at 1-3 days
Outcome-based mandated learning	Our best learning is NOT measurable
Constant use of negations: many "don'ts"	Use of totally positive language
Use of bribes, rewards, gimmicks	Intrinsic motivation elicited
Starve the brain for stimulation	Enriched: music, sights, aromas, movement
Disciplined, ordered, quiet, repressive	Expressive, changing, noisy, music
Single topic only by presenter choice	Learner input on topics

Principles of Brain-Based
Organizations

• **Learning is the top priority** Simple, but powerful words. Students are excited about learning and school. Remember *the brain naturally loves to learn.* In brain-based schools, learn about life, they learn from each other, they learn what is in the curriculum and they are ready to become lifelong learners willing to contribute to society. But this takes a purposeful effort by the school.

Beginning in the 50's and 60's, schools were asked to become carriers of social policies. As a result, their ability to focus on learning became diluted and scattered. In fact, social and business expert Peter Drucker says,

"... making the school the organ of social policies has,
without any doubt, severely impaired its capacity to do its job."

What is it's job? Drucker says America formally transitioned from being an industrial-based economy into a knowledge-based economy in 1990. He says learning-to-learn skills are absolutely critical to success. How universal are they and how often are they reinforced at your school? Let's examine them.

• **Teamwork** To make it work, the staff has its own compelling, collective vision. The school has a well-defined purpose and mission. The values are clearly stated. Students have input. The faculty dresses well, enjoys their jobs and speaks highly of their colleagues and the participants. The staff works as a team, role modeling cooperative behaviors for participants. The faculty plans lessons cooperatively, works with each other in collegial support groups and solves problems as a team. They trade classrooms often, team-teach at times and double up on classes to give their colleagues time for staff meetings or planning time.

At larger schools (500+ participants), break the learner body into smaller clusters of 100-250 participants. Students and presenters all have partnerships that last for however long that learner is at school. All participants work with presenters, in partnership, to achieve mutual goals. Every learner has an adult advisor and meets with them on a scheduled basis.

• **Mastery of time** This includes the three biggest needs in schools: 1) the need to free up time blocks for greater relaxed planning and collaboration time for presenters. 2) Block learning: K-2 participants about 40-60 minutes, grades 3-6 in blocks of 60-90 minutes and secondary level 7-12 participants in time blocks of about 90-120 minutes. Naturally, you offer stretch and diffusion breaks within each of those blocks. 3) The option to rotate subjects, so no subject always gets a certain time slot. No learner should be stuck having to learn math always at two in the afternoon. In general, offer literal subjects early, physical ones midday and global and relation ones later.

• **An atmosphere of celebration** If you want to inspire love of learning in participants, you must role-model it. Celebrate all learning as a joyful process, not a directed means to the tested end. Celebrate each learner equally, regardless of knowledge, skill, race or age. Celebration of learning has to occur often, on a daily or weekly basis. Celebrate even the mistakes. In fact, the only sin is not recognizing or learning from our mistakes. A "Brain-based" school has a goal of discovering what is good and positive in the learning, not emphasizing the mistakes.

• **Majority of learning contextually embedded** The old way of presenting was to "Stand and Deliver." The brain is actually very poor at learning large amounts of material from books. It is naturally good at learning in the locations and circumstances of everyday life. It learns quickly and easily when it can associate or "code" the learning with a novel experience, in a novel location, or a strong feeling, a theme, an event, a date, or a hook of some kind that ties it in with the content.

• **Minimized discipline** Parents, participants and faculty have worked together to create a clear system for dealing with severe misbehavior where *everyone has a part* in the decision-making. It means the classroom *is focused on learning, not maintaining control.* Is this some liberal, new age attitude? NO. When learning is joyful and empowering, discipline problems go down. The discipline policy is supported by learner peers, powered by peer pressure and rarely needed. Faculty members are respectful of participants as desire to be respected in return. Presenters know that they may have authority over the learners, but it's a two-way street. Learners have a right to be respected and provided with an opportunity to learn. All presenters are well versed in the brain research on discipline.

In a fully-implemented brain-based learning approach, the reason problems rarely occur is because participants are fully engaged, curious, engrossed, challenged and excited about learning. Eliminate boredom and frustration and most discipline problems vanish.

• **Intrinsic motivation** Learning based on curiosity, need and relevance. Eliminate classroom or school-wide rewards systems - No bribes for performance, no bribes for attendance, no bribes for being good in class. No coupons, cards or certificates that say "I caught you being good." Top schools simply make school worth going to so they don't have to bribe their kids; they make it the "best party in town."

• **Take brakes off learning**   Avoid the constant group instruction trap. Use diverse learning centers, interest grouping and mastery learning pacing. Allow learners to work, learn and grow at their pace, not the presenter's. Allow each to move as quickly as he or she is able, without strong pushing. Respect creative ideas that do not fit "the box." The presenter is the producer of the student's "play." Allow for new and different ways to solve problems without the traditional limits.

• **Learners hunt for meaning** There's a natural need to create meaning in every learner. The right process is to get out of the way of that hunt for meaning. Supply the resources that enable learners to figure out how to make something make sense. Information can be fragmented or meaningful. The learning is geared towards usefulness and productivity. English and spelling is learned in order to do something with it; make signs for a school play or for an upcoming conference.

• **Accountability**   Students are responsible for their own learning. Students have input in the school, the classrooms and with presenters (learning catalysts). Students have many ways to choose what they want to learn (within limitations) and how they can learn it (choice of using their own learning styles). Staff get written feedback weekly by participants so they can use the feedback to improve their approach. Every learner has a single presenter (a guide) who interacts through brief, but private talks once a month.

• **Patterns, connections & thematic learning**   Learn and develop the integrated curriculum model offered by Kovalik. Focus on patterns of meaning, not isolated "math facts," names, dates and capitals. Use mindmaps to discover what participants know, use them at the end of a lesson, unit or term to help participants put the information into a huge contextual visual map. Use thematic presenting, where a single theme for a day or a week is used to cut across the curriculum to develop meaning and relevance.

As an example, let's say the word is *"season"* (learning opportunities for this can be found in: weather, clothes, people's attitudes, food, advertising, etc.). Or, let's say the word is *a particular color* (learning opportunities for this can be found in: people, clothing, cars, nature, food, books, plants, animals, etc.). Or, let's say the word is *"grateful"* (learning opportunities for this can be found in: health, sports opportunities, family, weather, etc.). The word might be *"multiply"* (learning opportunities for this can be found in: animals, science, TV, crime, prices, nature, ideas, etc.)

334

• **Assessment of participants, of staff, of administrators**   The primary form is best when it is quality self-assessment. A healthy organization is constantly giving itself useful feedback. For participants, make it in many types of meaningful forms that are authentic, based on the diverse and multiple learner intelligences. Informal assessment in some form of feedback ought to occur for participants at least once an hour, every single class session.

I co-founded one of the world's most successful learning programs, SuperCamp. We asked all participants to give the staff *daily evaluations*. Why? If something wasn't working, we wanted to know right away, not when the class is over. Feedback is king and with immediate feedback, and time to self-correct, presenters can be among the best anywhere. Students ought to be taught, along with the staff, to self-assess and get sufficient feedback, coaching and support to make the corrections.

• **Multiple goals met**   Insure that the school allows participants to meet their own needs, dreams and goals. Provide opportunities for them to learn about career options, brain foods, conflict resolution, how their brain works, self-confidence and social skills. When a school helps learners grow in these ways, it becomes a "win" for everyone. There's no reason that it should be a forced, unilateral autocratic agenda thrust on learners who get little input.

• **Encourage & design discussions about learning**   Metacognition, thinking out loud, making learning popular is the key to success. Create opportunities for participants to share ideas, theories and discoveries. All that is learned is open for discussion with no material off limits or considered a "sacred cow." The mind works just like a parachute - when it's open!

• **Examples set**   The school staff promotes and role models learning and the love of it. Any signs, cards, banners, posters or cartoons that mock, ridicule, joke about or otherwise infer that learning or school is other than fantastic, are removed. That means get rid of all cups, posters and signs like: *"Homework causes brain damage... School is something we sandwich in between weekends... TGIF... Presenter's three favorite words are June, July & August... School is Hell... Underachiever and proud of it.... Hang in there... You want it when?... Tell me again, why am I here?"*   They are all negative and should be removed.

• **Brain-respectful**   Respectful of the brain's biological needs in learning... Make water available in the classroom, insure adequate diet and nutrition for learning, have longer two-hour blocks at the secondary level, use movement, activities and games to keep the body active. Respect the brain's natural timetables. Use more

335

complex, new and difficult material in the morning, more thoughtful, interactive and global learning later on. Limit lecture time to the student's age in minutes, allow for reflection and discussion time afterwards.

• **Aesthetics**   The physical campus is pleasant, clean and attractive to attend. Individual classrooms are rich, stimulating immersion learning environments full of color. They may also include positive posters, sights or signs, mobiles, pets, manipulatives, reading material, technology, natural lighting, water, comfortable chairs and flexible seating.

• **Immersion**   Presenters at a brain-based school don't just introduce participants to units. They immerse them in the unit and all related units, themes and global patterns. The classroom immersion can happen from a physical point of view: it must extend the real world, the hallways, the lawn, the buildings, the neighborhood, the videos and when all that is exhausted, the classroom is transformed. It can be turned into a space station, another country, a rain forest or a courtroom.

The classroom must also be an immersion in content. Instead of the singular, lock-step, sequential, one-bite-at-a-time lesson planning, there's an initial virtual overload of ideas, details, themes and meanings. Originally, Lozanov discovered this does not create chaos in the learner's mind. Instead, it's a sense of temporary overwhelming followed by curiosity, intrigue and a determined quest to discover meaning for oneself. Dhority, one of the best accelerated learning language presenters, consistently floods his participants with more German than they can possibly grasp. Over time it all gets sorted out, by the learner, brilliantly. Just like the real world of learning one's own native language.

• **Choice**   Students can design their own styles and process for learning. This encourages efficiency, creativity and happier learners. Students can choose another coach or presenter (learning catalysts) if they are having a tough time with one. While it's true that participants want and need choice for optimal use of their minds, it's also important for the school to provide the essential structure for a sound educational experience.

• **Healthy lifestyles taught**   Instead of health instruction only being a separate and distinct part of the curriculum, it's also on-going. Students should be taught to be drug-free, tobacco-free and encouraged to eat proper "brain-enriching" foods.

• **Presenters**   Must be provided with quality staff development with time to ask questions and implement changes. All encourage a hunt for meaning, not a force-feeding of information. The participants are encouraged to find personal meaning, class & school meaning and a larger, global contextualization. The emphasis is on meaning, not repeating back answers.

• **Cooperative learning as an alternative to tracking**   It is common practice among far too many schools to track and group participants by ability level. More often than not, the lower-tracked groups end up getting dull, repetitive instruction. This leads to bored and discouraged learners with lower self-confidence and self-esteem. Cooperative learning, when done well, allows participants who may not understand a concept to get immediate tutoring by a peer. The additional social context and self-confidence rubs off in other areas.

• **Creativity**   Students can enjoy learning, feel challenged and really look forward to coming to school. There is clear evidence of learner expression, creativity and personal quests for meaningful learning. Students will often stay after class and stay at school when they really enjoy it. They'll often participate in volunteer, extra-circular activities. School is simply a great place to be!

Schools around the world are changing to a more brain-based approach. In the book, *The Learning Revolution,* the authors tell of hundreds of successful schools that you may want to contact (and learn what they have learned).

What This Means to You: You may want to share this book with others on your staff. Start a conversation about brain-based learning and discover what the interest level in promoting it may be. Start up a list of suggestions centering around the brain-based learning research found in this book. Discuss ideas with others. Set up deadlines. Get support. Get others excited about them. Implement positive changes in your presenting methods and learning environment right away. You have little to lose and much to gain. There are already schools around the world which exemplify many or all of the above items. Check the resources below. You may also want to network with other schools through the brain-based learning networks.

What are the key priorities to start work on at your school? The six critical ones are listed on the next page. The schools that are successful pick just one or two areas, then implement it fully before moving on. Which of these areas are you and your staff ready to start with? When will you start?

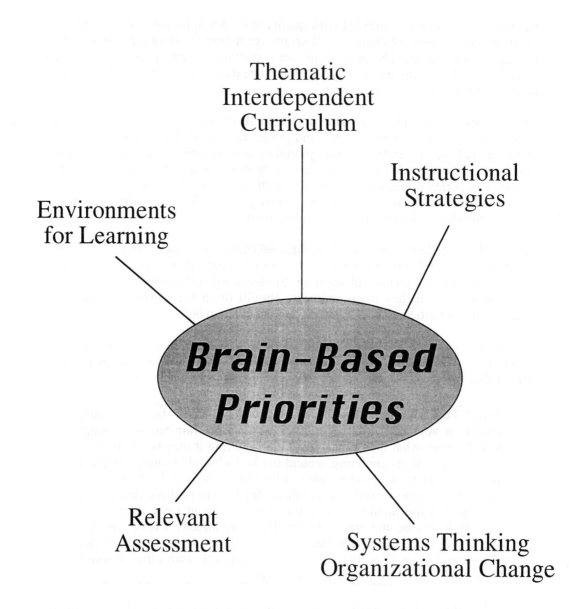

Thematic
Interdependent
Curriculum

Instructional
Strategies

Environments
for Learning

Brain–Based Priorities

Relevant
Assessment

Systems Thinking
Organizational Change

Suggested Follow-up: You may also be interested in purchasing *Ten Steps to a Learning Organization* or *School Success: The Inside Story,* by Peter Kline and Lawrence Martel; *Mindshifts* by Caine, Caine and Crowell. *The Learning Brain,* by Jensen; *The Learning Revolution,* by Dryden & Vos; or *Making Connections: Teaching & The Human Brain,* by Caine & Caine. See Appendix for details. For consulting services, you may want to contact the author, Eric Jensen by fax at 619-546-7560 or phone 619-546-7555.

Chapter Questions

1. What was novel, fresh and new? What was familiar or "old hat"?
2. In what ways do you already apply the information in this chapter?
3. What three questions can you now generate about this material?
4. How did you react emotionally to this information?
5. In what ways can you translate the key three or four theories and discoveries presented here into practical everyday useful ideas?
6. How did you react cognitively when you were reading the ideas of this chapter?
7. If these things are, in fact, true about the brain, what should we do differently? What resources of time, people and money could be redirected? In what ways do you suggest we start?
8. What was the single one (or two) most interesting or valuable insights you had?
9. Plan your next step, the logical practical application of what you've learned.
10. What obstacles might you encounter? How can you realistically deal with them?

Family
Support

Business

A Systems
Approach:
A Learning
Community

Publicity

Community
Support

22
A Systems Approach: The Learning Community

Develop Local Support

A more brain-based approach can be applied successfully to everything from on-the-job training to work environments. You might bring up the topic of the brain and learning to parent groups, social clubs, support groups, service groups and special interest organizations. Find ways to encourage community involvement. Make learning-to-learn a community priority. Bring the school out to the community by making it a real year-round learning center. Offer courses during evenings and weekends, to parents, participants and others. Increase multi-status, multi-age and multi-cultural presenting. Students teach each other, grandparents teach and tutor, community leaders, scientists, writers, artists, engineers, designers, retailers and attorneys speak.

Getting the Word Out

Offer to appear on talk shows. Get on cable interview shows. Draw attention to positive things happening at your school to get media coverage. When TV stations have editorial opinions, make sure yours are heard, too. Be a caller on radio talk shows. At conferences and conventions, make sure brain-based learning references are offered. Sponsor or attend district or state or even school conferences on the brain and learning. At bookstores and presenter resource shops, ask for more brain-based books. Contribute articles to local, regional and state-wide newsletters. Videotape local presenters using more brain-based approaches and share the video with other presenters.

Business Interventions

At your spouse's business and at your own, encourage more brain-compatible practices. Encourage "stand and stretch" breaks more often. Ask for better snacks and lunches, either from vending machines or the counter. Reduce criticisms and promote positive peripherals. Write letters to the editors of the business newsletter. Contribute a column or article on the brain and how to encourage better learning. Promote learn-to-learn skills at work. Educate about gender differences in a positive way that avoids stereotypes and discrimination. Make the written memos and longer communications more user friendly. Promote the use of graphics, better use of color, negative ionizers, plants and natural lighting. Encourage better chairs for better posture, more mobility and movement. Help promote multi-age, multi-status work groups to encourage peer learning. These are just a few of the hundreds of suggestions in this book that apply to business.

Encourage Support From the Family

Research is conclusive on the value of family support in academic success. What can you tell parents about how the brain learns best? If the brain could talk and have a point a view, the home environment would be labeled as either a positive "Yes!" or an emphatic "No!" There's not much in between. Children who are raised in homes where basic rules of the brain are respected, are more likely to grow up happier, be more creative, more responsible, are able to be better learners and are even healthier. How can this be?

The brain learns best in a sensory-rich immersion environment, rich with positive suggestion (a creative, affirming "can-do" attitude) and with loving parents who provide feedback, opportunities for exploration and managed risk. Parents who delay feedback, give negative feedback (the average parent gives a 5-1 ratio of negatives to positives) or provide only conditional support, will disadvantage their offspring.

While you might say, "If every parents uses these negatives, what's the big deal?" Keep in mind that there are parents who do all the right things and the results are astounding. Many parents who say, "I've done all the right things and I still have trouble with them" often ignore the role they really play in affecting their children. While it's true that there are many other influences on the family (TV, peers, school, organizations, music, magazines, etc.), it's also true that the family is the number one influence.

342

Parent Checklist for Learning

1) Do you share something wondrous and exciting every day with your children that you personally learned during the day? Do you ask them? If so, that contributes to a positive role model of the value of learning.

2) Do you take your children to events that are designed specifically for learning? These things provide the critical opportunities to develop learning skills.

3) Do you speak of school and your job as a joyful adventure or do you more often refer to the headaches, unmotivated learners, the late hours, the "TGIF" attitude where there's a countdown until Friday, the next holiday or summer?

4) Is your home a rich, positive learning environment, full of challenge, novelty and ways to learn such as a computer, games, toys, cards, art, and music?

5) Do you avoid sarcasm, negative remarks, criticism? Do you believe 100% in the potential of your children? Do you daily affirm their gifts, their genius?

6) Do you provide affection, warmth and other signs of your love for them? Are genuine compliments given? Or, do they get an occasional pat on the back?

In many of these cases, you might think that these are simply "good parenting" tips. In a way, you're right. Many parents have been doing these things all along, but not knowing how important they are for the brain itself, as a learning organ. There are some more questions to ask yourself. In fact, you may want to print this checklist for the parents of the children at your school.

7) Is the television used sparingly, as much for learning as for entertainment? Or, has it become just a babysitter, full of craziness, violence and empty sitcoms packed with put-downs? What is really learned from it?

8) Do you take your children with you on trips, in the car, by bus or plane? Do you explore, discover and get excited about life, animals, plants, and people?

9) Have you eliminated the use of threats in your family? Or, do your kids do what they have to do because the alternatives are "Or else!?"

10) Do you recount, revise, and review family activities? Do you encourage your children to do the same? This builds strong positive memories. Do you offer your kids a choice (whenever appropriate) in things to do and & how to do them? Is there always hope? Do you talk positively about the future and its options?

11) Are your children getting adequate, stress-free rest, feeling safe & secure?

12) Is the daily food good for the brain? Do you insure you children have protein for breakfast, eat apples, eggs, bananas, wheat germ, lean meats, leafy green vegetables, and a diet low in polyunsaturated fats (no saturated ones)?

As a parent, you may want to become more aware of the things that contribute to growing a better child, from the developmental point of view. You might start a simple checklist on the refrigerator with just one, two or three things that, as a family, you'll work on. In time you can create a superb family environment.

How to Influence Parents at Your School

It is dramatically in our best interest to influence parents. They are a primary source of influence on the participants at school. They also can make the difference between a program working at school or failing. Here are ways to influence the parents of your learners.

1. Mailings/flyers. Make the flyer colorful, simple, easy to read, interesting and valuable. Give parents suggestions on nutrition, ways to provide an enriching home environment, how to reduce stress and help with learning. Provide suggested reading lists and even offer to make those books available at school.

2. Open house. Parents visit the school on a special day or night. One of the most under-used opportunities. Make it into a time for real discussion. Make it fun! Use music. Have suggested books on hand for browsing. Have parents do a mind map on their child's background and interests.

3. Through the newspaper (with positive articles on specific, effective programs).

4. Community Relations. School or presenters participate in school-school, school-business community events where you have contact with other presenters. Or, have the presenters come to an event at the school. A fair, forum, project, etc. Publicize it!

5. Organizations. Speaking at Rotary, PTA, Kiwanas, Toastmasters, etc., can all be a forum for influence.

6. Local television. Often local cable TV companies or public access stations will welcome a half hour to an hour on a topic like "What every parent should know about their child's education."

7. Through schools acting as a community learning center. One of the best ways to influence parents is by sponsoring community classes. Invite parents or parents and participants on such topics like discipline, parenting, learning styles, crafts, finances, art, sexuality and music. The better the topics, the more the attendance. The more catchy and provocative the class titles and descriptions, the greater the attendance.

8. Invitations to visit. Offer parents a chance to visit the classroom or attend a "special for parents" curriculum meeting. Help them understand the challenges and goals that you face in your work.

9. Produce a video, audio or play for parents. The more parents and kids it involves in the production and marketing, the more you'll have want to desire to visit. Take an existing play and re-write the script to make it fit a particular slant or agenda (like one on the brain!).

10. Community events. A local conference, meeting, press conference, a fair, forum or other form of community dialog can bring people together. Views can be shared, questions answered and concerns met.

> **What this means to you:** It's time to be pro-active. It's time to map out a specific set of strategies for reaching parents on a continued basis. Make up a plan, designate staffing & follow through.

How You Can Follow-up: *The Fifth Discipline Fieldbook,* by Senge. *Awakening Your Child's Natural Genius,* or *Seven Kinds of Smart,* by Armstrong. Your *Child's Growing Mind,* by Healy.

Chapter Questions

1. What was novel, fresh and new? What was familiar or "old hat"?
2. In what ways do you already apply the information in this chapter?
3. What three questions can you now generate about this material?
4. How did you react emotionally to this information?
5. In what ways can you translate the key three or four theories and discoveries presented here into practical everyday useful ideas?
6. How did you react cognitively when you were reading the ideas of this chapter?
7. If these things are, in fact, true about the brain, what should we do differently? What resources of time, people and money could be redirected? In what ways do you suggest we start?
8. What was the single one (or two) most interesting or valuable insights you had?
9. Plan your next step, the logical practical application of what you've learned.
10. What obstacles might you encounter? How can you realistically deal with them?

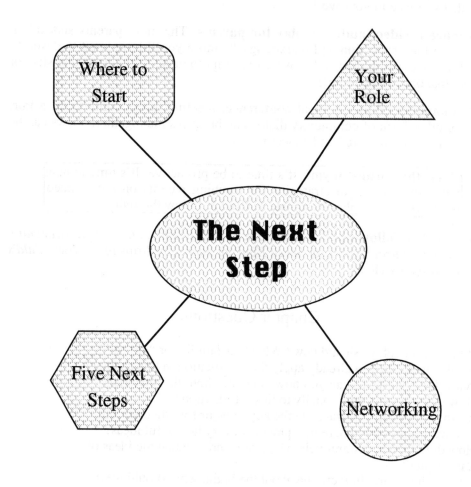

346

23
The Next Step

The Best Place to Start

There's no better place to start than with ourselves. Learn this information, integrate it and make it yours. Read, try it out. Talk over, try it out. You may want to attend a workshop on this material. A six-day training for becoming a brain-based facilitator is described in the appendix.

Gather information   Learn the basics of brain-based learning. Read about it and ask questions. This book is the beginning of your knowledge base. You may want to order *The Learning Brain* or *SuperTeaching,* both mentioned in the Appendix or Recommended Reading List. There are others that are recommended in the bibliography.

Make connections   Use thematic mapping, greater content associations and learning how to learn the skills of learning. Now your learning will begin to make more sense, through more associations. Make mind maps, discuss these ideas. Find related ideas and share them, too. Integrate these ideas in your work and personal life. Unless you make the learning personal, it will lack potency and value.

Expand your learning and associations   Relate it to self, community, planet. Your content learning has now become related, on-a-bigger-scale, learning. It makes sense to you on a larger scale - yourself, the environment. This is often referred to as "natural knowledge." Form support groups, hold meetings, and sponsor activities. Write newsletters and get involved in the brain-based networks.

Become a local expert   Speak on this topic. Make sure you role model these principles. Speak at your school, your district and the community. Write materials for the classroom or school that apply these important principles. It's also re-contextualizing & using generalization. In content, your peers may now acknowledge you as an expert. Begin to develop learning organizations.

New applications Over time, and with reflection, you'll gain new insights and ability to think "outside the box," with new themes, as a paradigm-creating pioneer. You'll discover novel and innovative applications for the brain-based frameworks. Create new learning and systemic models based on current brain research.

Your Next Step

There are many, many ways to get started with a more brain-based school and community approach to learning. Nobody has the one, single answer for you because the answer needs to be derived from a consensus. But you might be interested in a year-long study of successful schools. It was found that all successful transformations had the following characteristics:

SEARCH - "What else is out there?"

1. The staff searched near, far and wide for successes and solutions. Read, network, call other schools, attend conferences, check out books, buy newsletters and hold discussion groups.

CONSOLIDATE - "What do we have so far?"

2. Analyze & modify the solutions for your own needs & culture. Commit to building on existing strengths.

UNIFY - "Can we all agree on what we want?"

3. Get complete input and "buy-in" for the vision and steps to take. Develop a complete staff unity of purpose.

SOLIDIFY - "If this is good, then let's make it policy"

4. Make your ideas into *policy*, not just another good idea. Willingly assume responsibility, but with corresponding amounts of authority to act on what was needed at the time.

COMMIT - "If we believe in it, let's stick with it!"

5. Commit to staying with it until it works. No excuses. Emphasize the positives and celebrate the successes. Learn to communicate what isn't working and fix it. Take on reform as a permanent on-going process, not some one or two year gimmick to quiet critics. Quality is an endless process.

> **What This Means to You:** It's not easy, but it's simple. Take the first step and start walking. Get support and turn your good ideas into a movement. We can have learning work for everyone. And it can begin with you taking action, right now.

How you can follow up: You may want to get a catalog of brain-based resources. Networking opportunities are listed below. You may want to get copies of this book in bulk for others at your school.

For inservices, consulting or conference speaking, contact the author, Eric Jensen, at: (619) 546-7555 or fax (619) 546-7560.

For a free catalog of over 100 Brain-Based Resources or for most of the books mentioned in this book, contact the publisher at:

Turning Point, Box 2551
Del Mar, CA 92014, USA
Phone (619) 546-7555 or (800) 325-4769
Fax (619) 546-7560

Appendix

Brain-Based Resources:

Here are the products listed in the sections called "How You Can Follow Up." These are available by mail order. Order using the toll-free number below.

Title:	*Author:*
4-Mat System	Bernice McCarthy
12 Brain-Booster Posters	Eric Jensen
Accelerated Learning	Colin Rose
Brain Gym	Paul & Gail Dennison
Brain States	Thomas Kenyon
Brain-Based Learning & Teaching Video	Eric Jensen
The ITI Model	Susan Kovalik
The Creative Brain	Ned Herrmann
The Everyday Genius	Peter Kline
Human Brain & Human Learning	Leslie Hart
If the Shoe Fits	Carolyn Chapman
Introduction to Accelerated Learning	Eric Jensen
The Learning Brain (book, tapes & video)	Eric Jensen
Learning & Teaching Styles	Kathleen Butler
Learning Modalities	Eric Jensen
Learning Revolution	Dryden & Vos
Learning Styles of the 1990's	Eric Jensen
Little Book of Big Motivation	Eric Jensen
Making Connections: Teaching & the Human Brain	Nummela Caine & Caine
Managing Your Mind & Mood Through Food	Judith J. Wurtman, Ph.D.
Mapping Innerspace	Nancy Marguiles
Mind Food & Smart Pills	Ross Pelton
Multiple Assessments for Multiple Intelligences	Carolyn Chapman, et al.
Power of Color	Dr. Morton Walker
Punished by Rewards	Alfie Kohn
Righting the Educational Conveyer Belt	Michael Grinder
Rhythms of Learning	Campbell & Brewer
School Success	Kline & Mart
Seeing with Magic Glasses	Launa Ellison
Seven Ways of Teaching	David Lazear
Super Teaching	Eric Jensen
Ten Steps to a Learning Organization	Kline & Saunders
Thirty Days to Bs and As	Eric Jensen

Overnight and 2nd Day delivery available. Call 800-325-4769 or fax 619-546-7560. FREE catalog included. Unconditional satisfaction or money-back guarantee. For further brain-based information, contact the resources below:

•**SuperCamp Program for Teens, or Quantum Learning**
Learning Forum, 1725 South Hill Street, Oceanside, CA 92054-5319

•**ASCD'S Brain-Based Learning Network, CARE** (attn: Dr. Joan Caulfield)
Rockhurst College, 1100 Rockhurst Road, Kansas City, MO 64110-2561

•**The Brain Store** (Turning Point's website)
http://www.tpbrain.com

Bibliography &
Further Readings

Ackerman, Sandra. *Discovering the Brain* (1992) Washington, D.C.: National Academy Press.

Alkon, Daniel. *Memory's Voice* (1992). New York: Harper-Collins.

Allen, C. K. (1990). Encoding of Colors in Short-Term Memory. *Perceptual and Motor Skills* (71.1, 211-215).

Amabile, Teresa (1989).*Growing Up Creative.* New York: Crown Publishing.

Amabile, T. & Rovee-Collier, C. (1991, October). Contextual Variation and Memory Retrieval at Six Months. *Child Development,* 1155-66.

Ames, Carole. Children's Achievement Attributions and Self-Reinforcement: Effects of Self-Concept and Competitive, 345-55.

Ames, Carole. (1981). Competitive Versus Cooperative Reward Structures: The Influence of Individual and Group Performance Factors on Achievement Attributions and Affect. *American Educational Research Journal* 18, 273-87.

Ames, Carole. (1992). Achievement Goals and the Classroom Motivational Climate. *Student Perceptions in the Classroom.* (Ed. Dale Schunk and Judith Meece). Hillsdale, NJ: Erlbaum.

Ames, Carole. (1992). Classrooms: Goals, Structures, and Student Motivation. *Journal of Educational Psychology* 84, 261-71.

Ames, Carole. (1987). The Enhancement of Student Motivation. *Advances in Motivation and Achievement.* Eds. Maeher and Kleiber (Vol. 5, pp.123-148). Greenwich, CT: JAI.

Anderson, R. C., & Pearson, P. D. (1984). A Schema-Theoretic View of Basic Processes in Reading Comprehension. *Handbook of Reading Research.* (Pearson, Ed.) New York, NY: Longman.

Annette, M. (1973). Handedness in Families. *Annals of Human Genetics* 37, 93-105.

Apacki, Carol. (1991). *Energize!* Granville, OH: Quest Books.

Armbruster, B. and Anderson, T. (1980). "The Effect of Mapping." *Center for the Study of Reading* 182735th ed. Urbana, IL: University of Illinois.

Armstrong, Blake. (1991, June 12). "Studying and Television." *Bottom Line Personal.* Report of research at University of Wisconsin, 9.

Armstrong, Thomas. (1987). *In Their Own Way.* Los Angeles, CA: Jeremy Tarcher Publishing.

Asbjornsen A., Hugdahl, K., & Hynd, G. W. (1990). The Effects of Head and Eye Turns on the Right Ear Advantage in Dichotic Listening. *Brain and Language* 39.3, 447-58.

Backman L., Nilsson, L. G., & Nourp, R. K. (1993). Attentional Demands and Recall of Verbal and Color Information in Action Events. *Scandinavian Journal of Psychology* 34.3, 246-254.

Bandler, R. (1988). *Learning Strategies: Acquisition and Conviction.* (Videotape). Boulder, CO: NLP Comprehensive.

Bandura, A. (1986). *Social Foundations of Thought and Action: a social cognitive theory.* Englewood Cliffs, NJ: Prentice-Hall.

Barden, R. C., & Ford, M. E. (1990). *Optimal Performance in Golf.* Minneapolis, MN: Optimal Performance Systems.

Barkley R. (1988, September). *Attention-Deficit Hyperactivity Disorder.* (Lecture at conference) The Many Faces of Intelligence. Washington, D.C.

Barrett, Susan. (1992). *It's All in Your Head.* Minneapolis, MN: Free Spirit Publishing.

Baumeister, R. F. (1984). Choking Under Pressure: Self-Consciousness and Paradoxical Effects of Incentives on Skillful Performance. *Journal of Personality and Social Psychology* 46, 610-20.

Baumeister, R. F. (1992). Of humor, Music, Anger, Speed and Excuses: Reflections of an Editorial Team After One Year in Office. *Cardiovascular Research* 12, 1161-3.

Baumeister, R. F., Heatherton, T. F. & Tice, D. M. (1993). When Ego Threats Lead to Self-Regulation Failure: Negative Consequences of High Self-Esteem. *Journal of Personality and Social Psychology* 64.1, 141-56.

Becker, Robert. (1986).*Cross Currents.* Los Angeles, CA: Jeremy Tarcher, Inc.

Bennett, E.L., Diamond, M.C., Krech, D., & Rosenzweig, M. (1964). Chemical and Anatomical Plasticity of the Brain. *Science,* 146, 610-619.

Benton, D., & Roberts, G. (1988). Effect of Vitamin and Mineral Supplementation on Intelligence of a Sample of Schoolchildren. *The Lancet,* 140-143.

Bergin, D. (1989). Student Goals for Out-of-School-Learning Activities. *Journal of Adolescent Research* 4, 92-109.

Bergland, Michael. (1985).*The Fabric of Mind.* Ringwood, Vic.: Penguin.

Berliner, D. C. (1984). The Half-Full Glass: A Review of Research on Teaching. *Using What We Know About Teaching.* (Hosford, P.L., Ed.). Alexandria, VA: Association for Supervision and Curriculum Development.

Biggee, Al. (1982). *Learning Theories for Presenters* (4th ed.). New York, NY: Harper & Row.

Black J. E., et al. (1990, July). Learning Causes Synaptogenesis, Whereas Motor Activity Causes Angiogenesis, in Cerebral Cortex of Adult Rats. (Proc. of a conference of the National Academy of Sciences). 87.14, 5568-72.

Black J. E. (1989). Effects of Complex Experience on Somatic Growth and Organ Development in Rats. *Developmental Psychobiology* 22.7, 727-52.

Blackman, et al. (1982). Cognitive Styles and Learning Disabilities. *Journal of Learning Disabilities* n2 15, 106-115.

Blakemore, Colin. (1977). *Mechanics of the Mind.* New York, NY: Cambridge University Press.

Blakemore, Colin. (1990).*The Mind Machine.* (with Richard Hutton & Martin Freeth). London, England: BBC Books.

Block R. A., et al. (1989). Unilateral Nostril Breathing Influences Lateralized Cognitive Performance. *Brain and Cognition* 9.2, 181-90.

Bloom, et al. (1988).*Brain, Mind and Behavior.* W. H. Freeman and Co.

Boller, K. & Rovee-Collier, C. (1992). Contextual Coding and Recoding of Infant's Memories. *Journal of Experimental Child Psychology* 53.1, 1-23.

Botella, J. & Eriksen, C. W. (1992). Filtering Versus Parallel Processing in RSVP Tasks. *Perception and Psychophysics* 51.4, 334-43.

Bourre, J. M., et al. (1993). Function of Polyunsaturated Fatty Acids in the Nervous System. 48.1, 5-15.

Bourre, J. M., et al. (1993). *Brainfood.* Translated from French. Boston, MA: Little, Brown & Co.

Bower, G. H. & Mann, T. (1992). Improving Recall by Recoding Interfering Material at the Time of Retrieval. *Journal of Experimental Psychology* 18.6, 1310-20.

Bower, G. H., Mann, T.D., & Morrow, G. (1990). Mental Models in Narrative Comprehension. *Science* 247.4938, 44-8.

Bracha, S. (1987). Circling Behavior in Righthanders. *Brain Research* 411, 231-235.

Braun, C. M. (1992). Estimation of Interhemispheric Dynamics from Simple Unimanual Reaction Time to Extrafoveal Stimuli. *Neuropsychological Review* 3.4, 321-65.

Breier, A. Noise and Helplessness. (1988). *American Journal of Psychiatry* 144, 1419-25.

Brewer, C. and D. Campbell. (1991). *Rhythms of Learning.* Tucson, AZ: Zephyr Press.

Bricker, William, McLoughlin & Caven. (1982). Exploration of Parental Teaching Style: Technical Note. *Perceptual & Motor Skills* n3 Pt. 2 55, 1174.

Brophy, J. (1981). Presenter Praise: A Functional Analysis. *Review of Educational Research* 51, 5-32.

Brophy, J. (1987). Socializing Student's Motivation to Learn. *Advances in Motivation and Achievement* (Maeher & Kleiber. Eds.) Vol.3, pp. 181-210. Greenwich, CT: JAI.

Brown, J.S., & VanLehn, K. (1980). Repair Theory: A generative theory of bugs in procedural skills. *Cognitive Science* 4, 379-426.

Buckley, R. & Hawley, C. (1977). Hyperkenesis and Dye Sensitivity. *Journal of Orthomolecular Psychiatry* 2, 129-137.

Burton, L. A. & Levy, J. (1989). Sex Differences in the Lateralized Processing of Facial Emotion. *Brain and Cognition* 11.2, 210-28.

Birren, Faber. (1959). The Effects of Color on the Human Organism *American Journal of Occupational Therapy.*

Butler, R. (1988). Enhancing and Undermining Intrinsic Motivation. *British Journal of Educational Psychology* 58, 1-14

Butler, R., & Nissan, M. (1986). Effects of No Feedback, Task-Related Comments, and Grades on Intrinsic Motivation and Performance. *Journal of Educational Psychology* 78, 210-216.

Buzan, Tony. (1993). *The Mind Map Book: Radiant Thinking.* London, England: BBC Books.

Caine, G., Caine, R.N., & Crowell, S. (1994). *Mindshifts.* Tuscon, AZ: Zephyr Press.

Caine, G., & Caine, R.N. (1990). Downshifting: A Hidden Condition That Frustrates Learning & Change *Instructional Leader* VI 3, 1-3, 12.

Caine, G., & Caine, R.N., Eds. (1993). Understanding a Brain-Based Approach to Learning and Teaching. *Educational Leadership* 48: 2,66-70.

Caine, G., & Caine, R.N., Eds. (1994). Making Connections: *Teaching and the Human Brain.* Menlo Park, CA: Addison-Wesley.

Calvin, William & Ojemann, George. (1994). *Conversations with Neil's Brain.* Reading, MA: Addison-Wesley Publishing Co.

Campbell, D. (1983). *Introduction to The Musical Brain.* St. Louis, MO: Magnamusic.

Campbell, D. (1992). *100 Ways to Improve Your Teaching Using Your Voice & Music.* Tucson: Zephyr Press.

Campbell, D. Ed. (1992). *Music and Miracles.* Wheaton, IL: Quest Books.

Carbo, M. (1980). An Analysis of the Relationship Between the Modality Preferences of Kindegartners and the Selected Reading Treatments as they Affect the Learning of a Basic Sight-Word Vocabulary. *Dissertation* St. John's University.

Carbo, M., Dunn, R., & Dunn, K. (1986). *Teaching Students to Read Through their Individual Learning Styles.* Englewood Cliffs, NJ: Prentice-Hall.

Cardinali, R. (1991). Computer Hazards: Real or Imaginary? *Health Care for Women International* 12.3, 351-8.

Carpenter, G. & Grossberg, S. (1993). Normal and Amnesic Learning, Recognition and Memory by a Model of Corticohippocampal Interactions. *Trends in Neuroscience* 16.4, 131-7.

Carper, Jean. (1993). *Food: Your Miracle Medicine.* New York, NY: Harper Collins Publishers.

Carruthers, S. & Young, A. (1980). Preference of Condition Concerning Time in Learning Environments of Rural versus Eighth Grade Students. *Learning Styles Network Newsletter* 1.2, 1.

Centerwall, B. S. (1992). Television and Violence: The Scale of the Problem and Where to go From Here. *Journal of the American Medical Association* 267.22, 3059-63.

Chapman, Carolyn. (1993). *If the Shoe Fits.* Palatine, IL: Skylight Publishing.

Cherry, C., Godwin, D., & Staples, J. (1989). Is The Left Brain Always Right? Sydney, Australia: Hawker & Brownlow.

Chi, M. (1985). Interactive Roles of Knowledge and Strategies in the Development of Organized Sorting and Recall. *Thinking and Learning Skills.* (Chipman, S.F., Segal, J.W., & Glaser,R.) Vol 2. Hillsdale, NJ: Lawerence Erlbaum & Assoc.

Christianson, S. (1992). Emotional Stress and Eyewitness Memory: A Critical Review. *Psychological Bulletin* 112.2, 284-309.

Chugani, H. T. (1991). Imaging Human Brain Development with Positron Emission Tomography. *Journal of Nuclear Medicine* 32.1, 23-6.

Clark, D.L., Kreutzberg, J.R., & Chee, F.K.W. (1977). Vestibular Stimulation Influence on Motor Development on Infants. *Science* 196, 1228-1229.

Clynes, Manfred, Ed. (1982). *Music, Mind and Brain.* New York, NY: Plenum Press.

Clynes, Manfred, Ed. (1982). Neurobiologic Functions of Rhythm, Time, and Pulse in Music. *Music, Mind and Brain.* New York, NY: Plenum Press.

Cohen, E.G. (1990). Treating Status Problems in the Cooperative Classroom. *Cooperative Learning: Research and Theory.* (Sharan, S., Ed.) New York, NY: Praeger Press.

Condry, J., & Chambers, J. (1978). Intrinsic Motivation and the Process of Learning. [In *The Hidden Costs of Rewards: New Perspectives on the Psychology of Human Motivation.*] (Lepper, M.R., & Greene, D., Eds.) Hillsdale, NJ: Lawrence Erlbaum & Associates.

Connors, Keith. (1980). *Food Additives and Hyperactive Children.* New York, NY: Plenum Press.

Connors, Keith. (1989). *Feeding the Brain.* New York, NY: Plenum Press.

Cook, N.D. (1984). Callosal Inhibition: The Key to the Brain Code. *Behavioral Science* 29, 98-110.

Cook, N.D. (1984) The Transmission of Information in Natural Systems Journal of Theoretical Biology. 108, 349-367.

Corballis, M. (1983). *Human Laterality.* New York, NY: Academic Press.

Coren, S., & Halpern, D.F. (1991). Left-handedness: A Marker for Decreased Survival Fitness. *Psychological Bulletin* 109, 90-106.

Coren, S. & Porac, C. (1981). *Lateral Preferences in Human Behavior.* New York, NY: Springer-Verlag.

Cotton, M.M., & Evans, K. (1990). A Review of the Uses of Irlen (tinted) Lenses. *Australian and New Zealand Journal of Ophthalmology* 18.3, 307-12.

Covington, M.V. (1991). Motivation, Self-Worth, and the Myth of Instensification. (Paper presented at annual meeting of the American Psychological Association). San Francisco, CA.

Coward, Andrew. (1990). *Pattern Thinking*. New York, NY: Praeger Publishers.

Crick, Francis. (1994).*The Astonishing Hypothesis: The Scientific Search for the Soul*. New York, NY: Charles Scribner and Sons.

Csikszentmihalyi, M. & Isabella. (1990). *Flow: The Psychology of Optimal Experience*. New York, NY: Harper & Row.

Czeisler, C. A. (1986). Arousal Cycles Can Be Reset. *Science* 233, 667-71.

Damasio, Antonio. (1994) *Descartes' Error.* New York, NY. Putnam & Sons.

Dansereau, D. F. (1985). Learning Strategy Research. *Thinking and Learning Skills.* (Chipman, S.F., Segal, J.W., & Glaser, R.) Vol 1. Hillsdale, NJ: Lawerence Erlbaum & Assoc.

Dartigues, Jean-Francois. (1994, February). Use It or Lose It. *Omni.* p. 34.

Davidson, R.J. (1992). Anterior Cerebral Asymmetry and the Nature of Emotion. *Brain and Cognition* 20.1, 125-51.

Dean, W., Morgenthaler, J. (1990). *Smart Drugs and Nutrients.* Santa Cruz, CA: B&J Publications.

Dean, W., Morgenthaler, J., & Fowkes, S. (1993). *Smart Drugs II: The Next Generation.* Menlo Park, CA: Health Freedom Publications.

DeBello, T. (1985). A Critical Analysis of the Achievement and Attitude Effects of Administrative Assignments to Social Studies Writing Instruction Based on Identified, Eighth-Grade Students' Learning Style Preferences for Learning Alone, With Peers, or With Presenters. *Dissertation.* St. John's University.

DeBono, Edward. (1970). *Lateral Thinking.* New York, NY: Harper & Row.

Decety, J., & Ingvar, D.H. (1990). Brain Structures Participating in Mental Stimulation of Motor Behavior: A Neuropsychological Interpretation. *Acta Psychologica* 73.1,113-34.

Deci, E. (1978). Application of Research on the Effects of Rewards. *The Hidden Costs of Rewards: New Perspectives on the Psychology of Human Motivation.* (Lepper & Greene, Eds.) Hillsdale, NJ: Lawerence Erlbaum & Assoc.

Deci, E., et al. (1982). Effects of Performance Standards on Teaching Styles: Behavior of Controlling Presenters. *Journal of Educational Psychology* 74, 852-59.

Deci, E. (1980). *The Psychology of Self-Determination.* Lexington, MA: DD Heath.

Deci, E. (1985, March). The Well-Tempered Classroom. *Psychology Today.* pp. 52-53.

Deci, E. and R. M. Ryan. (1985). *Intrinsic Motivation and Self-Determination in Human Behavior.* New York, NY: Plenum.

Deci, E., et al. (1992). Autonomy and Competence as Motivational Factors in Students with Learning Disabilities and Emotional Handicaps. *Journal of Learning Disabilities* 25, 457-71.

Deci, E., et al. (1991). Motivation and Education: The Self-Determination Perspective. *Educational Psychologist* 26, 325-46.

Dekaban, A. (1970).*The Neurology of Early Childhood.* Baltimore, MD: Williams and Wilkins.

Della Valle, J. (1984). An Experimental Investigation of the Relationship(s) Between Preference for Mobility and the Word Recognition Scores of Seventh Grade Students to Provide Supervisory and Administrative Guidelines for the Organization of Effective Instructional Environments. Dissertation. St. John's University.

Della Valle, J., et al. (1986). The Effects of Matching and Mismatching Student's Mobility Preferences on Recognition and Memory Tasks. *Journal of Educational Research* 79.5, 267-72.

Dennison, Paul, & Dennison, Gail. (1988). *Brain Gym.*. (Presenter's Ed.) Ventura, CA: Edukinesthetics.

Dhority, Lynn. (1992). *The ACT Approach. The Use of Suggestion for Integrative Learning.* Philadelphia, PA: Gordon & Breach Science Publishers.

Diamond, Marian. (1988). *Enriching Heredity: The Impact of the Environment on the Brain.* New York, NY: Free Press.

Dienstbier, R. (1989). Periodic Adrenalin Arousal Boosts Health, Coping. *Brain-Mind Bulletin* 14.9A.

Dixon, N. (1981). *Preconscious Processing.* New York, NY: Wiley.

Doll, W.E.J. (1989). Complexity in the Classroom. *Educational Leadership* 47.1, 65-70.

Domino, G. (1970). Interactive Effects of Achievement Orientation and Teaching Style on Academic Achievement. *ACT Research Report* 39, 1-9.

Dossey, Larry. (1993) Healing Words. San Francisco, CA: HarperCollins Publishers

Douglass, C.B. (1979). Making Biology Easier to Understand. *American Biology Presenter* 41.5, 277-99.

Drucker, Peter. (1994, November).The Age of Social Transformation. *Atlantic Monthly,* 274,(5) pp. 53-80.

Dryden, Gordon & Vos, Jeannette. (1994). *The Learning Revolution.*. Rolling Hills, CA: Jalmar Press.

Dunn, R. & Dunn, K. (1978). *Teaching Students Through Their Individual Learning Styles: A Practical Approach.* Reston, VA: Reston Publishing Co.

Dunn, R. & Dunn, K. (1987). Dispelling Outmoded Beliefs About Student Learning. *Educational Leadership* 44.6, 55-61.

Dunn, Kenneth & Rita. (1992). *Bringing Out The Giftedness In Your Child,* New York, NY: John Wiley.

Dunn, R., et al. (1985). Light Up Their Lives: A Review of Research on the Effects of Lighting on Children's Achievement and Behavior. *The Reading Presenter* 38.9, 863-69.

Edelman, G. *Bright Air, Brilliant Fire.* (1992). New York, NY: Basic Books.

Efron, R. (1990).*The Decline and Fall of Hemispheric Specialization.* Hillsdale, NJ. Lawerence Erlbaum and Associates.

Ehret, C. (1981). From Report by the National Argonne Laboratory. Lemont, IL.

Ellison, Launa. (1993). *Seeing With Magic Glasses.* Great Ocean Publishers, Arlington, VA.

Emery, Charles. (1986, October). Exercise Keeps the Mind Young. *American Health.*

Engel, A. K., et al. (1992). Temporal Coding in the Visual Cortex: New Vistas on Integration in the Nervous System. *Trends in Neurosciences* 15.6, 218-26.

Epstein, H. (1974). Phrenoblysis: Special Brain and Mind Growth Periods. *Developmental Psychology* 7, 207-24.

Eysenck, Michael. (1994).*The Blackwell Dictionary of Cognitive Psychology.* Oxford.

Fabiani M., Karis, D., & Donchin, E. (1990). Effects of Mnemonic Strategy Manipulation in a Von Restorff Paradigm. *Electroencephalography and Clinical Neurophysiology* 75.2, 22-35.

Feingold, D. (1985). *Why Your Child is Hyperactive.* New York, NY: Random House.

Feldman, R.G. & White, R.F. (1992). Lead Neurotoxicity and Disorders in Learning. *Journal of Child Neurology* 7.4, 354-9.

Felix, Uschi. (1993).The Contribution of Background Music to the Enhancement of Learning in Suggestopedia: A Critical Review of the Literature. *Journal of the Society for Accelerative Learning and Teaching* 18.3-4, 277-303.

Feuerstein, Reuven, Klein, Pnina, Tannenbaum, Abraham. (1991). *Mediated Learning Experience.* London, UK: Freund Publishing House Ltd.

Fiske, S.T., & Taylor, S.E. (1984). *Social Cognition.* Reading, MA: Addison-Wesley.

Fitch, R.H., Brown, C.P. & Tallal, P. (1993). Left Hemishere Specialization for Auditory Temporal Processing in Rats. *Annals of the New York Academy of Sciences* 682, 346-7.

Ford, Martin. (1992). *Motivating Humans.* Newbury Park, CA: Sage Publications.

Ford, R.N. (1969). *Motivation Through the Work Itself.* New York, NY: American Management Association.

Fox, N.A. (1991). If It's Not Left, It's Right. Electroencephalograph Asymmetry and the Development of Emotion. *American Psychologist* 46.8, 863-72.

Fox, N.A., Sexton, M. & Hebel, J.R. (1990). Prenatal Exposure to Tobacco: Effects on Physical Growth at Age Three. *International Journal of Epidemiology* 19.1, 66-71.

Frederiksen, N. (1984). Implications of Cognitive Theory for Instruction in Problem-Solving. *Review of Educational Research* 54, 363-407.

Freeley, M.E. (1984). An Experimental Investigation of the Relationships Among Presenter's Individual Time Preferences, Inservice Workshop Schedules, and Instructional Techniques and the Subsequent Implementation of Learning Style Strategies in Participant's Classroom. *Dissertation.* St. John's University.

Friedman, R. C., & Downey, J. (1993). Neurobiology and Sexual Orientation: Current Relationships. *Journal of Neuropsychiatry and Clinical Neurosciences* 5.2, 131-53.

Frijda, N.H. (1988). The Laws of Emotion. *American Psychologist* 43, 349-58.

Fuchs, J.L., Montemayor, M., & Greenough, W.T. (1990). Effect of Environmental Complexity on the Size of Superior Colliculus. *Behavioral and Neural Biology* 54.2, 198-203.

Gadow, K. D., & Sprafkin, J. (1989). Field Experiments of Television Violence With Children: Evidence for an Environmental Hazard? *Pediatrics* 83.3, 399-405.

Galin, D., & Ornstein, R. (1974). Individual Differences in Cognitive Style: Reflexive Eye Movements. *Neuropsychologia,* 12, 367-376.

Garai, J.E., & Scheinfield, A. (1968). Sex Differences in Mental and Behavioral Traits. *Genetic Psychology Monographs* 77, 169-229.

Gardner, Howard. (1985). *Frames of Mind.* New York, NY: Basic Books.

Gardner, Howard. (1993). *Multiple Intelligences: The Theory in Practice.* New York, NY: Basic Books.

Gazzaniga, M. (1992). *Nature's Mind.* New York, NY: Basic Books.

Gelb, Michael. (1981). *Body Learning.* New York, NY: Delilah Books.

Gelb, Michael. (1988). *Present Yourself.* Rolling Hills, CA: Jalmar Press.

Glasser, William. (1981). *Stations of the Mind.* New York: Harper & Row.

Glasser, William. (1985). *Control Theory.* New York, NY: Harper Collins.

Gleik, J. (1987). *Making a New Science.* New York, NY: Viking.

Goldman, J., et al. (1986). Behavioral Effects of Sucrose on Preschool Children. *Journal of Abnormal Child Psychology* 14, 565-78.

Gordon, H.W. (1978). Left Hemisphere Dominance for Rhythmic Elements in Dichotically Presented melodies. *Cortex* 14, 58-76.

Gouchie, C., & Kimura, D. (1990). The Relationship Between Testosterone and Cognitive Ability Patterns. *Research Bulletin* 690. University of Ontario, London, Canada.

Gratton, G., Coles, M. G., & Donchin, E. (1992). Optimizing the Use of Information: Strategic Control of Activation of Responses. *Journal of Experimental Psychology* 121.4, 480-506.

Green, K.P., et al. (1991). Integrating Speech Information Across Talkers, Gender and Sensory Modality: Female Faces and Male Voices in the McGurk Effect. *Perception and Psychophysics* 50.6, 524-36.

Greenough, W.T., & Anderson, B.J. (1991). Cerebellar Synaptic Plasticity: Relation to Learning Versus Neural Activity. *Annals of the New York Academy of Science* 627, 231-47.

Greenough, W.T., and B. Anderson. (1991). Cerebellar Synaptic Plasticity. *Annals of the New York Academy of Sciences* 627, 231-47.

Greenough, W.T., Withers, G. & Anderson, B. (1992). Experience-Dependent Synaptogenesis as a Plausible Memory Mechanism. *Learning and Memory: The Behavioral and Biological Substrates*. (Gormezano, I. & Wasserman, E., Eds.) Hillsdale, NJ: Erlbaum & Associates. pp. 209-29.

Grinder, Michael. (1989). *Righting the Educational Conveyor Belt*. Portland, OR: Metamorphous Press.

Grinder, Michael. (1993). *Envoy*. Battle Ground, WA: Michael Grinder & Associates.

Grolnick, W.S. & Ryan, R.M. (1987). Autonomy in children's Learning: An Experimental and Individual Difference Investigation. *Journal of Personality and Social Psychology* 52, 890-898.

Grunwald, L., & Goldberg, J. (1993, July). Babies Are Smarter Than You Think. *Life Magazine,* 45-60.

Gur, R.E., Gur, R.C., & Harris, L.J. (1975). Cerebral Activation as Measured by Subjest's Eye Movements. *Neuropsychologia,* 13, 35-44.

Hagan-Heimlich, J.E., and S.D. (1984). Pittelman. Classroom Applications of the Semantic Mapping Procedure in Reading and Writing. *Program Report* 84.4.

Halpern, D.F. (1990). Hand Preference and Life Span. (Unpublished manuscript).

Halpern, S. (1985). *Sound Health*. New York, NY: Harper & Row.

Hampden-Turner, Charles. (1981). *Maps of the Mind*. New York, NY: Macmillan Publishing.

Hampson, E. & Kimura, D. (1988). Reciprocal Effects of Hormonal Fluctuations on Human Motor and Perceptual Spatial Skills. *Behavioral Neuroscience* 102.3, 456-9.

Harmon, D.B. (1991). The Coordinated Classroom. Grand Rapids, MI: [In Liberman, Jacob, *Light: Medicine of The Future*] Santa Fe, NM.

Harper, A.E., & Peters, J.C. (1989). Protein Intake, Brain Amino Acid and Serontonin Concentration and Protein Self-Selection. *Journal of Nutrition* 119.5, 677-89.

Harper, C., & Kril, J. (1990). Neuropathology of Alcoholism. *Alcohol and Alcoholism* 25.2-3, 207-16.

Harper, C., & Kril, J. (1991). If you drink your brain will shrink. *Alcohol and Alcoholism*. (Supplement) 1, 375-80.

Hart, Leslie. (1975). *How the Brain Works: A New Understanding of Human Learning*. New York, NY: Basic Books.

Hart, Leslie. (1983). *Human Brain and Human Learning*. White Plains, NY: Longman Publishing.

Harter, S. (1978). Pleasure Derived form Challenge and the Effects of Receiving Grades on Children's Difficulty Level Choices. *Child Development*. 49, 788-799.

Harter, S. (1980). The Perceived Competence Scale for Children. *Child Development* 51, 218-35.

Harter, S. (1982). A Developmental Perspective on Some Paremeters of Self-Regulation in Children. *Self-Management and Behavior Change: From Theory to Practice.* (Karoly, P., & Kanfer, F. H., Eds.) New York, NY: Pergammon Press.

Hassler, M. (1991). Testosterone and Musical Talent. *Experimental and Clinical Endicrinology* 98.2, 89-98.

Hayne, H., Rovee-Collier, C., & Borza, M.A. (1991). Infant Memory for Place Information. *Memory and Cognition* 19.4, 378-86.

Healer, Janet. (1977). Microwave Towers May Affect Brain. *Brain/Mind Bulletin* 2.14E.

Healy, Alice & Lyle Bourne. (1995) *Learning and Memory of Knowledge and Skills.* Thousand Oaks, CA. Sage Publications.

Healy, J. (1990). *Endangered Minds: Why Our Children Can't Think.* New York, NY: Simon and Schuster.

Healy, J. (1987).*Your Child's Growing Mind.* New York, NY: Doubleday.

Healy, J. (1993). Why Kids Can't Think. *Bottom Line Personal* 13.8, 1-3.

Herbert, Nick. (1993). *The Elemental Mind.* New York, NY. Dutton Books.

Hermann, D.J. & Hanwood, J.R. (1980). More evidence for the Existence of the Separate Semantic and Episodic Stores in Long-Term Memory. Journal of Experimental Psychology: Human Learning and Memory 6 & 5, 467-478.

Herrmann, Ned. *The Creative Brain.* Lake Lure, NC: Brain Books, 1988.

Herrnstein. (1994). A Bell-Shaped Curve. New York, NY: The Free Press.

Hirsch, A. (1993). Floral Odor Increases Learning Ability. Presentation at annual conference of American Academy of Neurological & Orthopedic Surgery. Contact: Allan Hirsch, Smell & Taste Treatment Foundation, Chicago, IL.

Ho, Kevin. (1988, March). The Dimensionality and Occupational Differentiation of the Hermann Brain Dominance Instrument. Department of Educational Psychology, Brigham Young University.

Hobson, J.A. (1989). *Sleep.* New York, NY: W.H. Freeman.

Hodges, H. (1985). An Analysis of the Relationships Among Preferences for a Formal/Informal Design, One Element of Learning Style, Academic Achievement, and Attitudes of Seventh and Eighth Grade Students in Remedial Mathematics Classes in a New York City Alternative Junior High school. *Dissertation.* St.John's University.

Hodges, Jeffrey. (1992). *Learn Faster Now.* Toowoomba, Queensland, Australia: Down Under Publications.

Hoffer, A., Walker, M. (1994). *Smart Nutrients.* Garden City Park, NY: Avery Publishing Group.

Hofman M.A., & Swaab, D.F. (1991). Sexual Dimorphism of the Human Brain. *Experimental and Clinical Endocrinology* 98.2, 161-70.

Hooper J., & Teresi, D. (1986). *The Three Pound Universe: The Brain, from Chemistry of the Mind to New Frontiers of the Soul.* New York, NY: Dell Publishing.

Hopfield, J., Feinstein, D., & Palmer, R. (1983, July). Unlearning Has a Stabilizing Effect in Collective Memories. *Nature.* pp. 158-59.

Horn, G. (1991). Learning, Memory and the Brain. *Indian Journal of Physiology and Pharmacology* 35.1, 3-9.

Horne J. (1989). Sleep Loss and Divergent Thinking Ability. *Sleep* 11.6, 528-36.

Horne J. (1992, October 15). Human Slow Wave Sleep: A Review and Appraisal of Recent Findings, with Implications for Sleep Functions and Psychiatric Illness. *Experientia* pp. 941-54.

Horowitz, L., & Sarkin, J.M. (1992). Video Display Terminal Operation: a Potential Risk in the Etiology and Maintenance of Tempromandidibular Disorders. *Cranio* 10.1, 43-50.

Houston, Jean. *The Possible Human: A Course in Enhancing Your Physical, Mantal and Creative Abilities.* Los Angeles, CA: Jeremy Tarcher, 1982.

Huchinson, Michael. (1986). *Megabrain.* New York, NY: Beech Tree Books.

Huttenlocher, P.R. (1990). Morphometric Study of Human Cerebral Cortex Development. *Neuropsychologia* 28.6, 517-27.

Hynd, G.W. (1992). Neurological Aspects of Dyslexia: Comment on the Balance Model. *Journal of Learning Disabilities* 25.2, 110-2, 123.

Hynd, G.W., et al. (1991). Attention-Deficit Disorder Without Hyperactivity: A Distinct Behavioral and Cognitive Syndrome. *Journal of Child Neurology* 6, S37-43.

Hynd, G.W., et al. (1991). Corpus Callosum Morphology in Attention Deficit-Hyperactivity Disorder: Morphometric Analysis of MRI. *Journal of Learning Disabilities* 24.3, 141-6.

Iaccino, James. (1993). *Left Brain-Right Brain Differences: Inquiries, Evidence, and New Approaches.* Hillsdale, NJ: Lawrence Erlbaum & Associates.

Introini-Collision, I.B., Miyazaki, B. & McGaugh, J.L. (1991). Involvement of the Amygdala in the Memory-Enhancing Effects of Clenbuterol. *Psychopharmacology* 104.4, 541-4.

Isaacs, K.R., et al. (1992). Exercise and the Brain: Angiogenesis in the Adult Rat Cerebellum After Vigorous Physical Activity and Motor Skill Learning. *Journal of Cerebral Blood Flow and Metabolism* 12.1, 110-9.

Jacobs, B. Serotonin and Behavior: Emphasis on Motor Control. *Journal of Clinical Psychiatry* 52, 17-23. (Suppliment).

Jacobs, B., Schall, M. & Scheibel, A.B. (1993). A Quantitative Dendritic Analysis of Wernicke's Area in Humans: Gender, Hemispheric and Environmental Factors. *Journal of Comparitive Neurology* 327.1, 97-111.

Jacobs, W.J., & Nadel, L. (1985).Stress-Induced Recovery of Fears and Phobias. *Psychological Review* 92.4, 512-531.

James, Tad. (1989). *The Secret of Creating Your Future.* Honolulu, HI: Advanced NeuroDynamics.

James, T., Woodsmall, and Wyatt. (1988). *Timeline and the Basis of Personality.* Cupertino, CA: Meta Publications.

Jaques, E. Development of Intellectual Capability. *Essays on Intellect.* (Link, F.R., Ed.) Alexandria, VA: Association for Curriculum and Development.

Jauchem, J. (1991). Alleged Health Effects of Electromagnetic Fields: Misconceptions in the Scientific Literature. *Journal of Microwave Power and Electromagnetic Energy* 26.4, 189-95.

Jauchem, J., & Merritt, J.H. (1991). The Epidemiology of Exposure to Electromagnetic Fields: An Overview of the Recent Literature. *Journal of Clinical Epidemiology* 44.9, 895-906.

Jauchem, J., & Frei, M.R. (1992). Heart Rate and Blood Pressure Changes During Radiofrequency Irradiation and Environmental Heating. *Comparative Biochemistry and Physiology* 101.1, 1-9.

Jenkins, D.J., et al. (1989). Nibbling Versus Gorging: Metabolic Advantages of Increased Meal Frequency. *New England Journal of Medicine* 321.14, 929-34.

Jensen, Eric. (1995). *SuperTeaching.* Del Mar, CA: Turning Point Publishing.

Jensen, Eric. (1993) *Thirty Days to Bs and As.* Turning Point. Del Mar, CA.

Jensen, Eric. (1994).*The Learning Brain.* Del Mar, CA: Turning Point Publishing.

Jensen, Eric. (1995).*The Little Book of Big Motivation.* New York, NY: Ballantine.

Jernigan, T.L., & Tallal, P. (1990). Late Childhood Changes in Brain Morphology Observable with MRI. *Developmental Medicine and Child Neurology* 32.5, 379-85.

Johnson, M. H., et al. (1991). Newborns' Preferential Tracking of Face-Like Stimuli and its Subsequent Decline. *Cognition* 40.1-2, 1-19.

Kagan, D. M. (1990). How Schools Alienate Students at Risk: A Model for Examining Proximal Classroom Variables. *Educational Psychologist* 25, 105-25.

Kage, M. (1991). The Effects of Evaluation on Intrinsic Motivation. (Paper presented at the meeting of the Japan Associaiton of Educational Psychology). Joetsu Japan.

Kandel, M. & Kandel, E. (1994, May). Flights of Memory. *Discover Magazine,* 32-38.

Kandel, E. & Hawkins, R. (1992, September). The Biological Basis of Learning and Individuality. *Scientific American* pp. 79-86.

Kanter, R.M., Clark, D.L., Allen, L.C., & Chase, M.F. (1976). Effects of Vestibular Stimulation on Nystagmus Response and Motor Performance in the Developmentally Delayed Infant. *Physical Therapy,* 54:(4), 414-21.

Kaplan, R. (1983). Reader's Visual Fields Increase with Color Therapy. *Brain Mind Bulletin* 8.14F.

Karkowski, W., Marek, T., & Noworol, C. (1989). Stimulating Work Found to Boost Pain Perception. *Work and Stress* 2, 133-37.

Kavet, R., & Tell, R.A. (1991). VDT's: Field Levels, Epidemiology, and Laboratory Studies. *"Health Physics"* 61.1, 47-57.

Kenyon, Thomas. (1994). *Brain States.* Naples, FL: U.S. Publishing.

Khachaturian, Zaven. (1991). Mental Decline As We Grow Older. *Bottom Line Personal* 12.23, 9.

Khalsa, D., Ziegler, M., & Kennedy, B. (1986). Body Sides Switch Dominance. *Life Sciences* 38, 1203-14.

Kim, I.K. & Spelke, V. (1992). Infants' Sensitivity to Effects of Gravity on Visible Object Motion. *Journal of Experimental Psychology: Human Perception and Performance* 18.2, 385-93.

Kimura, D. (1985, November). Male Brain, Female Brain: The Hidden Difference. *Psychology Today.*

Kimura, D. (1986, October). How Different Are Male and Female Brains? *Orbit.*

Kimura, D. (1987). Are Men's and Women's Brains Really Different?" *Canadian Psychology* 28.2.

Kimura, D. (1989, November). Monthly Fluctuations in Sex Hormones Affect Women's Cognitive Skills. *Psychology Today* pp. 63-66.

Kimura, D., & Hampson, E. (1990, April). Neural and Hormonal Mechanisms Mediating Sex Differences in Cognition. *Research Bulletin* 689. Dept. of Psych. University of Ontario, London, Canada.

Kimura, D. (1992, September). Sex Differences in the Brain. *Scientific American* pp. 119-25.

King, Jeff. (1991). Comparing Alpha Induction Differences Between Two Music Samples. Abstract from the Center for Research on Learning and Cognition, University of North Texas, TX.

Klein & Armitage. (1979). Brainwave Cycle Fluctuations. *Science* 204, 1326-28.

Kline, Peter. (1990). *Everyday Genius: Restoring Your Children's Natural Joy of Learning - And Yours, Too.* Arlington, VA: Great Ocean Publishers.

Kline, Peter & Martel, Laurence. (1992). *School Success: The Inside Story.* Arlington, VA: Great Ocean Publishers.

Kline, Peter & Saunders, Bernard. (1993). *Ten Steps to a Learning Organization.* Arlington, VA: Great Ocean Publishers.

Klivington, Kenneth, Ed. (1989). *The Science of Mind.* Cambridge, MA: MIT Press.

Klutky, N. (1990). Sex Differences in Memory Performance for Odors, on Sequences and Colors. *Zeitscrift fur Experimentelle und Angewandte Psychologie* 37.3, 437-46.

Kohn, A. (1993, September). Choices for Children: Why and How to Let Students Decide. *Phi Delta Kappan,* 8-20

Kohn, Alfie. (1994, October). Grading: the Issue Is Not How But Why. *Educational Leadership* Volume 52, 2, 38-41.

Kopera, H. (1980). Female Hormones and Brain Function. *Hormones and the Brain.* (de Wied & Van Keep, Eds.) Lancaster, England: MTP Press. pp. 189-203.

Kosmarskaya, E.N. (1963). The Influence of Peripheral Stimuli on Development of Nerve Cells. [In The Development of the Brain and its Disturbance by Harmful Factors, Klosovski, B.N., Ed.] New York, NY: Macmillian Publishing.

Kotulak, Ronald. Unraveling Hidden Mysteries of the Brain. (1993, 11-16 April).*Chicago Tribune.*

Krashen, Steven. (1982). *Principles and Practice in Second Language Acquisition,* New York, NY: Pergamon Press.

Krashen, S. & Terrell, T. (1983). *The Natural Approach.* San Francisco, CA: Alemany Press.

Krimsky, J.S. (1982). A Comparitive Analysis of the Effects of Matching and Mismatching Fourth Grade Students With Their Learning Styles Preferences for the Environmental Element of Light and Their Subsequent Reading Speed and Accuracy Scores. Dissertation. St. John's University.

Kohn, Alfie. (1987). *No Contest: The Case Against Competition.* New York, NY: Houghton-Mifflin.

Kohn, Alfie. (1993). *Punished by Rewards.* New York, NY: Houghton Mifflin.

Kroon, D. (1985). An Experimental Investigation of the Effects on Academic Achievement and the Resultant Administrative Implications of Instruction Congruent and Incongruent with Secondary Industrial Arts Student's Learning Style Perceptual Preferences. Dissertation. St. John's University.

Lakoff, G., & Johnson, M. (1980). *Metaphors We Live By.* Chicago, IL: University of Chicago Press.

Lande, R.G. (1993). The Video Violence Debate. *Hospital and Community Psychiatry* 44.4, 347-51.

Lavabre, Marcel. (1990). *Aromatherapy Workbook.* Rochester, VT: Healing Arts Press.

Lavond, D.G., Kim, J.J. & Thompson, R. F. (1993). Mammalian Brain Substrates of Aversive Classical Conditioning. *Annual Review of Psychology* 44, 317-42.

LeDoux, J., & Hirst, W. (1986). Attention. *Mind and Brain: Dialogues in Cognitive Neuroscience.* New York, NY: Cambridge. pp. 105-85.

Leff, H. & Nevin, A. (1994).*Turning Learning Inside Out.* Tucson, AZ: Zephyr Press.

Lepper, M.R. (1981). Intrinsic and Extrinsic Motivation in Children: Detrimental Effects of Superfluous Social Controls. [W.A. Collins, Ed.] Aspects of the Development of Competence: The Minnesota Symposium on Child Psychology. Vol 14. Hillsdale, NJ: Lawerence Erlbaum. pp. 155-214.

Levine, S.C., Jordan, N.C., & Huttenlocher, J. (1992). Development of Calculation Abilities in Young Children. *Journal of Experimental Child Psychology* 53.1, Ú72-103.

Levinson, H. (1991). Why Johnny Can't Pay Attention. *Bottom Line Personal* 12.20, 11.

Levinthal, C. (1988). *Messengers of Paradise: Opiates and the Brain.* New York, NY: Doubleday.

Levy, J. (1983). Research Synthesis on Right and Left Hemispheres: We Think With Both Sides of the Brain. *Educational Leadership* 40.4, 66-71.

Levy, J. (1985, May). Right Brain, Left Brain: Fact and Fiction. *Psychology Today.* p. 38.

Lewicki, P., Hill, T., & Czyzewska, M. (1992). Nonconscious Acquisition of Information. *American Psychologist* 47.6, 796-801.

Lieberman, H.R., Wurtman, J.J., & Teicher, M.H. (1989). Circadian Rhythms in Healthy Young and Elderly Humans. *Neurobiology of Aging* 10.3, 259-65.

Lingerman, H. (1983).*The Healing Energies of Music.* Wheaton, IL: Theosophical Publishing House.

Livingstone, M., et al. (1991, September). Physiological and Anatomical Evidence for a Magnocellular Defect in Developmental Dsylexia. *Proceedings of the National Academy of Science* 88, 9743-7947.

Lloyd, Linda. (1990). *Classroom Magic.* Portland, OR: Metamorphous Press.

Locke, E.A. & Latham, G.P. (1990). Work Motivation and Satisfaction: Light at the End of the Tunnel. *Psychological Science* 1, 240-46.

Lozanov, Georgi. (1979). *Suggestology and Outlines of Suggestopedia.* New York, NY: Gordon & Breach.

Lozanov, Georgi. (1991). On Some Problems of the Anatomy, Physiology and Biochemistry of Cerebral Activities in the Global-Artistic Approach in Modern Suggestopedagogic Training. *The Journal of the Society for Accelerative Learning and Teaching* 16.2, 101-16.

Luiten, J., Ames, W., & Ackerson, G. (1980). A Meta-Analysis of the Effects of Advance Organizers on Learning and Retention. *American Educational Research Journal* 17, 211-18.

MacLean, Paul. (1978). A Mind of Three Minds: Educating the Triune Brain. *77th Yearbook of the National Society for the Study of Education.* Chicago, IL: University of Chicago Press. pp. 308-42.

MacLean, Paul. (1990). *The Triune Brain in Education.* New York, NY: Plenum Press.

MacMurren, H. (1985). A Comparative Study of the Effects of Matching and Mismatching Sixth Grade Students With Their Learning Style Preferences for the Physical Element of Intake and Their Subsequent Reading Speed and Accuracy Scores. *Dissertation.* St. John's University.

Mager, R.F., & McCann, J. (1963). *Learner-Controlled Instruction.* Palo Alto, CA: Varian Press.

Maguire, J. (1990). *Care and Feeding of the Brain.* New York, NY: Doubleday.

Malloy, John. (1975). *Dress for Success.* New York, NY: Warner Books.

Malone, T., & Lepper, M. (1987). Making Learning Fun: A Semanticomy of Intrinsic Motivations for Learning. *Aptitude, Learning and Instruction III: Cognitive and Affective Process Analyses.* (Snow & Farr, Eds.) Hillsdale, NJ: Lawerence Erlbaum & Assoc. pp. 223-53.

Mandler, G. (1983). The Nature of Emotions. *States of Mind.* (Miller. J., Ed.) New York, NY: Pantheon Books.

Mandell, A., (1980). Toward a Psychology of Transcendence: God in the Brain. [In Davidson, J.M. & Davidson, R.J., Eds.] *Psychology of Consciousness.* New York, NY: Plenum Press.

Mark, Vernon. (1989). *Brain Power.* Boston, MA: Houghton-Mifflin.

Marzolla, Jean & Lloyd, Janice. (1972). *Learning Through Play.* New York, NY: Harper & Row.

Martin, R.C. (1993). Short-Term Memory and Sentence Processing: Evidence from Neuropsychology. *Memory and Cognition* 21.2, 176-83.

Marzano, Robert. (1992). *A Different Kind of Classroom.* Alexandria, VA: ASCD.

McCarthy, B. (1990). Using the 4MAT System to Bring Learning Styles to Schools. *Educational Leadership* 48.2, 31-37.

McCarthy, Michael. (1991). *Mastering the Information Age.* Los Angeles, CA: Jeremy Tarcher.

McGaugh J.L. (1989). Dissociating Learning and Performance: Drug and Hormone Enhancement of Memory Storage. *Brain Research Bulletin* 23.4-5, 339-45.

McGaugh J.L., et al. (1990). Involvement of the Amygdaloid Complex in Neuromodulatory Influences on Memory Storage. *Neuroscience and Biobehavioral Reviews* 14.4, 425-31.

McGee, M. (1979). Human Spatial Abilities: Psychometric Studies and Environmental, Genetic, Hormonal and Neurological Influences. *Psychological Bulletin* 86.5, 889-918.

McGuiness, D. (1976). Sex Differences in Organisation, Perception and Cognition. *Exploring Sex Differences.* (Lloyd, B., & Archer, J.) London, England: Academic Press. pp. 123-55.

McGuiness, D. (1985).*When Children Don't Learn.* New York, NY: Basic Books.

McNamara, R.K., & Skelton, R.W. (1993). The Neuropharmacological and Neurochemical Basis of Place Learning in the Morris Water Maze. *Brain Research Reviews* 18.1, 33-49.

Meese, J.L., Wigfield, A., & Eccles, J.S. (1990). Predictors of Math Anxiety and its Influence on Young Adolescents' Course Enrollment Intentions and Performance in Mathematics. *Journal of Educational Psychology* 82, 60-70.

Meleges, F.T., & Hamburg, D.A. (1976). Psychological Effects of Hormonal Changes in Women. *Human Sexuality in Four Perspectives.* (Beach, F.A., Ed.) Baltimore, MD: Johns Hopkins University Press. pp. 269-95.

Messant, P.K. (1976). Female Hormones and Behavior. *Exploring Sex Differences.* (Lloyd, B. & Archer, J.) London, England: Academic Press. pp. 183-211.

Michaud, E., & Wild, R. (1991). *Boost Your Brain Power.* Emmaus, PA: Rodale Press.

Milich, R., & Pelham, W.E. (1986). The Effects of Sugar Ingestion on the Classroom and Playgroup Behavior. *Journal of Consulting & Clinical Psychology* 54, 1-5.

Mills, R.C. (1987, April). Relationship Between School Motivational Climate, Presenter Attitudes, Student Mental Health, School Failure and Health Damaging Behavior. (Paper at Annual Conference of the American Educational Research Association). Washington, D.C.

Mills, L. & Rollman, G.B. (1980). Hemisphereic Asymmetry for Auditory Perception of Temporal Order. *Neuropsychologia,* 18, 41-47.

Mitler, Merrill, Carskadon, M., Czeisler, C., Dement, W., Dinges, D., & Graeber, R. Curtis. (1988). Catastrophies, Sleep and Public Policy: Consensus Report. *Association of Professional Sleep Societies, Committee on Catastrophies, Sleep, and Public Policy, Sleep* 2 (1), 100-109. New York, NY: Raven Press.

Miura, I.T. (1987). A Multivariate Study of School-Aged Children's Computer Interest and Use. (Ford, M.E., & Ford, D.H.) *Humans As Self-Constructing Living Systems: Putting the Framework to Work.* Hillsdale, NJ: Lawerence Erlbaum & Assoc. pp. 177-97.

Miyamoto, R.T., et al. (1989). Comparison of Sensory Aids in Deaf Children. *Annals of Otology, Rhinology and Larynology* 142 (Supplement) pp. 2-7.

Miyamoto, R.T., et al. (1991). Comparison of Speech Perception Abilities in Deaf Children With Hearing Aids or Cochlear Implants. *Otolaryngology and Head and Neck Surgery* 104.1, 42-6.

Miyamoto, R.T., et al. (1992). Longitudinal Evaluation of Communication Skills of Children With Single or Multichannel Chochlear Implants. *American Journal of Otology* 13.3, 215-22.

Moeller, A.J. & Reschke, C. (1993). A Second Look at Grading and Classroom Performance. *Modern Language Journal* 77, 163-169.

Moir, Anne, & Jessel, D. (1991). *Brainsex.* New York, NY: Dell.

Morgan, Brian, & Morgan, Roberta. (1987). *Brainfood.* Los Angeles, CA: Price, Stern, Sloan.

Morgan, M., & Granger. (1989). Electric and Magnetic Fields from 60 Hertz Electric Power: What Do We Know About Possible Health Risks? *Dept. of Engineering and Public Policy.* Pittsburg, PA: Carnegie Mellon University.

Morgane, P.J., et al. (1993). Prenatal Malnutrition and Development of the Brain. *Neuroscience and Biobehavioral Reviews* 17.1, 91-128.

Murphy, M. & Donovan, S. (1988). *The Physical and Psychological Effects of Meditation.* San Rafael, CA: Esalen Institute.

Murrain, P.G. (1983). Administrative Determinations Concerning Facilities Utilization and Instructional Grouping: An Analysis of the Relationship(s) Between Selected Thermal Environments and Preferences for Temperature, an Element of Learning Style. *Dissertation.* St. John's University.

Nadel, L. (1990). Varieties of Spatial Cognition. Psychobiological Considerations. *Annals of the New York Academy of Sciences* 608, 613-26.

Nadel, L., Wilmer, J. & Kurz, E. M. (1984). Cognitive Maps and Environmental Context. *Context and Learning.* (Balsam and Tomi. Eds.) Hillsdale, NJ: Lawerence Erlbaum & Assoc..

Nadler, J.V., et al. (1990). Kindling, Prenatal Exposure to Ethanol and Postnatal Development Selectively Alter Responses to Hippocampal Pyramidal Cells to NMDA. *Advances in Experimental Medicine and Biology* 268, 407-17.

Nakamura, K. (1993). A Theory of Cerebral Learning Regulated by the Reward System. *Biological Cybernetics* 68.6, 491-8.

Needleman, H.L., et al. (1979). Deficits in Psychologic and Classroom Performance of Children with Elevated Dentine Lead Levels. *New England Journal of Medicine* 300, 689-695.

Neisser, Ulric & Harsch, Nicole. (1992). Phantom Flashbulbs: False recollections of hearing the news about Challenger. [In *Affect and Accuracy in Recall: Studies of "flashbulb" memories*] Cambridge University (Winograd, E. & Neisser, U., Eds.)

Nelig, A., Daval, J.L., & Debry, G. (1992). Caffeine and the Central Nervous System: Mechanisms of Action, Biochemical, Metabolic and Poststimulant Effects. *Brain Research Reviews* 17.2, 139-70.

Neve, C.D., Hart, L., & Thomas, E. (1986, October). Huge Learning Jumps Show Potency of Brain-Based Instruction. *Phi Delta Kappan* pp. 143-8.

Nisbett, R.E. & Ross, L.D. (1980). *Human Inference: Strategies and Shortcomings of Social Judgement.* Englewood Cliffs, NJ: Prentice-Hall.

Novitt-Moreno, Anne D. (1995). *How Your Brain Works.* Emeryville, CA: Ziff-Davis Press.

Nummela, R., & Rosengren, T. (1986). What's Happening in Student's Brain's May Redefine Teaching. *Educational Leadrship* 43.8, 49-53.

Nummela, R., & Rosengren, T. The Brain's Routes and Maps: Vital Connections in Learning. *NAASP Bulletin* 72: 83-86.

Oakhill, J. (1988). Time of Day Affects Aspects of Memory. *Applied Cognitive Psychology* 2, 203-12.

Obler, L.K. & Fein, D. (1988). *The Exceptional Brain.* New York, NY: Guilford.

O'Keefe, J., & Nadel, L. (1978). *The Hippocampus as a Cognitive Map.* Oxford, England: Clarendon Press.

Olds, James. (1992). Mapping the Mind onto the Brain. *The Neurosciences: Paths of Discovery.* (Worden, F., Swazey, J., & Adelman, G., Eds.) Boston, MA: Birkhauser.

Olney, J. (1982). The Toxic Effects of Glutamate and Related Compounds in the Retina and the Brain. *Retina* 2.4, 341-59.

Orlock, Carol. (1993). *Inner Time*. New York, NY: Birch Lane Press, Carol Publishing.

Ornstein, Robert. (1984). *The Amazing Brain*. Boston, MA: Houghton-Mifflin.

Ornstein, Robert. (1986). *Multimind*. Boston, MA: Houghton-Mifflin.

Ornstein, Robert. (1991). *The Evolution of Consciousness*. New York, NY: Simon & Schuster.

Ornstein, Robert & Sobel, D. (1987). *The Healing Brain and How It Keeps Us Healthy*. New York, NY: Simon & Schuster.

Ornstein, Robert, & Thompson, Richard. (1986). *The Amazing Brain*. Boston, MA: Houghton-Mifflin.

Osberger, M.J., Maso, M., & Sam, L.K. (1993). Speech Intelligibility with Cochlear Implants, Tactile Aids or Hearing Aids. *Journal of Speech and Hearing Research* 36.1 186-203.

Ostrander, Sheila & Schroeder, Lynn. (1991). *SuperMemory.*, New York, NY: Carroll & Graf Publishers.

Paris, S.G., et al. (1991). Developmental Perspective of Standardized Achievement Testing. *Educational Researcher* 20, 12-20.

Parker, Kenneth. (1982). Effects of subliminal symbiotic stimulation on academic performance: Further evidence on the adaptation-enhancing effects of oneness fantasies. Journal of Counseling Psychology, Vol. 29 (1).

Pearce, Joseph Chilton. (1992) *Evolution's End*. San Francisco. HarperCollins.

Pelton, Ross. (1989). *Mind Food & Smart Pills*. New York, NY: Bantam Doubleday.

Petty, R.E., & Cacioppo, J.T. (1984). Motivational Factors in Consumer Response Advertisement. (Green, Beatty, & Arkin, Eds.) *Human Motivation: Physiological, Behavioral and Social Approaches*. Boston, MA: Allyn & Bacon. pp. 418-454.

Pfurtscheller, G. & Berghold, A. (1989). Patterns of Cortical Activation During Planning of Voluntary Movement. *Electroencephalography and Clinical Neurophysiology* 72, 250-58.

Pintrich, P.R., & Garcia, T. (1991). Student Goal Orientation and Self-Regulation in the College Classroom. *Advances in Motivation and Achievement*. (Maeher & Pintrich, Eds.) Vol. 7. Greenwich, CT: JAI. pp. 371-402.

Pizzo, J. (1981). An Investigation of the Relationships Between Selected Acoustic Environments and Sound, an Element of Learning Style, as They Affect Sixth Grade Students' Reading Achievement and Attitudes. *Dissertation*. St. John's University.

Popper, K.R. (1972). *Objective Knowledge*. Oxford, England: Oxford University Press.

Prasad, A.N., & Prasad, C. (1991). Iron Deficiency; Non-Hematological Manefestations. *Progress in Food and Nutritional Science* 15.4, 255-83.

Price, G. (1980). Which Learning Style Elements are Stable and Which End to Change? *Learning Styles Network Newsletter* 4.2, 38-40.

Prigogine, I., & Stengers, I. (1984). *Order Out of Chaos*. New York, NY: Bantam.

Prince, Francine & Harold. (1987). *Feed Your Kids Bright*. New York,NY: Simon and Schuster.

Prinz, R.J., Roberts, W.A., & Hantman, E. (1980). Sugar Consumption and Hyperactive Behavior in Children. *Journal of Consulting and Clinical Psychology*. 48, 760-69.

Pulvirenti, L. (1992). Neural Plasticity and Memory: Towards an Integrated View. *Functional Neurology* 7.6, 49-57.

Redfield, D.L. & Rousseau, E.W. (1981). A Meta-Analysis of Experimental Research on Presenter Questioning Behavior. *Review of Educational Research*. 51.2, 237-45.

Restak, R. (1988).*The Brain*. New York, NY: Warner Books.

Restak, R. (1988). *The Mind.* New York, NY: Bantam Books.

Restak, R. (1991). *The Brain Has a Mind of its Own.* New York, NY: Harmony Books, .

Restak, R. (1994). *Receptors.* New York, NY: Bantam Books.

Restak, R. (1994) *The Modular Brain.* Charles Scribner's Sons. New York, NY.

Rice, R. (1975). The Effects of Tactile-Kinesthetic Stimulation on the Subsequent Development of Premature Infants. (Unpublished doctoral disseration) University of Texas at Austin. *Dissertation Abstracts* 35(5): 2148B.

Robin, D.E., & Shortridge, R.T., (1979). Laterization of Tumors of the Nasal Cavity and Paranasal Sinuses and its Relation to Aetiology. *Lancet* 8118, 695-696.

Roederer, Juan. (1981). Physical and Neuropsychological Foundations of Music. *Music, Mind and Brain.* (Clynes, Manfred, Ed.) New York, NY: Plenum Press.

Roland, P., et. al. (1990). Functional Anatomy of Storage, Recall and Recognition of a Visual Pattern in Man. *Neuroreport: An International Journal for the Rapid Communication of Research in Neuroscience* 1.1, 53-6.

Rose, Colin. (1986). *Accelerated Learning.* New York, NY: Dell Publishing.

Rose, F., Davey, M., & Attree, E. (1993). How Does Environmental Enrichment Aid Performance Following Cortical Injury in the Rat? *Neuroreport: An International Journal for the Rapid Communication of Research in Neuroscience* 4.2, 163-6.

Rose, Steven. (1992). *The Making of Memory.* New York, NY. Anchor/Doubleday.

Rosenberg, B.A., (1980). Mental Task Instruction and Optokinetic Nystagmus to the Left and Right. *Journal of Experimental Psychology: Human Perception and Performance*, 6, 459-472.

Rosenfield, I. (1988). *The Invention of Memory.* New York, NY: Basic Books.

Rosenfield, M., & Gilmartin, B. (1990). Effect of Target Proximity on the Open-Loop Accomodative Response. *Optometry and Vision Science* 67.2, 74-9.

Rosenfield, M., & Gilmartin, B., & Ciuffreda, K.J. (1991). Effect of Surround Propinquity on the Open-Loop Accomodative Response. *Investigative Ophthalmology and Visual Science* 32.1, 142-7.

Rosenthal, R. & Jacobsen, L. (1968). *Pygmalion in the Classroom.* New York, NY: Rinehart & Winston.

Rosenzweig, M.R., Love, W. & Bennett, E.L. (1968). Effects of a Few Hours a Day of Enriched Experience on Brain Chemistry and Brain Weights. *Physiology and Behavior* 3:819-825.

Rosenzweig, M.R., Krech, D., Bennett, E,L. & Diamond, M.C. (1962). Effects of Environmental Complexity and Training on Brain Chemistry and Anatomy. *Journal of Comparitive Physiological Psychology* 55(4): 429-437.

Rossi, A.S., & Rossi, P.E. (1980). Body Time and Social Time: Mood Patterns by Cycle Phase and Day of the Week. *The Psychobiology of Sex Differences and Sex Roles.* (Parsons, J.E., Ed.) London, England: Hemisphere. pp. 269-301.

Rossi, A.S., & Rossi, P.E. (1986). Hemisphereic Dominance Switches.

Rovee-Collier, C., et al. (1993). Infants' Eyewitness Testimony: Effects of Postevent Information on a Prior Memory Representation. *Memory and Cognition* 21.2, 267-79.

Ross, E.D. (1984). Right Hemisphere's Role in Language, Affective Behavior and Emotion. *Trends in Neuroscience* 7, 342-345.

Rozanski, Alan. (1988, April 21). Mental Stress and the Induction of Silent Ischmia in Patients with Coronary Artery Disease. *New England Journal of Medicine* Vol 318, 16. pp.1005-12.

Rush, D., Stein, Z., & Susser, M. (1980). Prenatal Nutritional Supplementation. *Pediatrics* 65, 683-97.

Ryan, R.M., Connell, J.P., & Deci, E.L. (1985). A Motivational Analysis of Self-Determination and Self-Regulation in Education. *Research on Motivation in Education*. (Ames, C. & Ames, R., Eds.) Vol.2. Orlando, FL: Academic Press. pp. 13-51.

Ryan, R.M., & Stiller, J. (1991). The Social Contexts of Internalization: Parent and Presenter Influences on Autonomy, Motivation, and Learning. *Advances in Motivation and Achievement*. (Maeher, M.L., & Pintrich, R., Eds.) Vol. 7. Greenwich, CT: JAI. pp. 115-49.

Salthouse, T. (1986). A Cognitive Theory of Aging. Berlin, Germany: Springer-Verlag.

Samples, Bob. (1987). *Open Mind/Whole Mind*. Rolling Hills, CA: Jalmar Press.

Santostefano, S. (1986). Cognitive Controls, Metaphors and Contexts. An Approach to Cognition and Emotion. *Thought and Emotions: Developmental Perspectives*. (Bearson, D.J. & Zimilies, H., Eds.) Hillsdale, NJ: Erlbaum & Associates.

Scartelli. (1984). *Journal of Music Therapy* 21, 67-78.

Schacter, D.L. (1992). Understanding Implicit Memory. *American Psychologist* 47.4, 559-69.

Schatz, C.J. (1990). Impulse Activity and the Patterning of Connections During CNS Development. *Neuron* 5.6, 745-56.

Schatz, C.J. (1992, September) The Developing Brain. *Scientific American*. pp. 60-7.

Schatz, C.J. (1992, October). Dividing Up the Neocortex. *Science* 9, 237-8.

Scheele, Paul. (1993). *The PhotoReading Whole Mind System*. Wayzata, MN: Learning Strategies Corporation.

Scheibel, Arnold. (1994, November 1). You Can Continuously Improve Your Mind and Your Memory. *Bottom Line Personal* (15) 21, pgs 9-10.

Schiffler, Ludger. (1992). *Suggestopedic Methods and Applications*. Philadelphia, PA: Gordon & Breach.

Schneider, M.L., & Coe, C.L. (1993). Repeated Social Stress During Pregnancy Impairs Neuromotor Development of Primate Infant. *Journal of Developmental and Behavioral Pediatrics* 14.2, 81-7.

Schneider, W. (1993). Varieties of Working Memory As Seen in Biology and in Connectionist/Control Architectures. *Memory and Cognition* 21.2, 184-92.

Scholz, J. (1990). Cultural Expressions Affecting Patient Care. *Dimensions in Oncology Nursing* 4.1, 16-26.

Schunk, D.H. (1990). Goal Setting and Self-Efficacy During Self-Regulated Learning. *Educational Psychologist* 25.1, 71-86.

Schwartz, J & Tallal, P. (1980). Rate of Acoustic Change May Underlie Hemispheric Specialization for Speech Perception. *Science* 207, 1380-1381.

Segal, J., Chipman, S., & Glaser, R. (1985). *Thinking and Learning Skills*. Vol. I. Hillsdale, NJ: Lawrence Erlbaum & Associates.

Seligman, Martin. (1992). *Learned Optimism*. New York, NY: Pocket Books.

Senge, Peter. (1992). *The Fifth Discipline*. New York, NY: Random House.

Senge, P., Kleiner, A., Roberts, C., Ross, R. & Smith, B. (1994). *The Fifth Discipline Fieldbook*. New York, NY: Currency/Doubleday.

Shea, T.C. (1983). An Investigation of the Relationship Among Preferences for the Learning Style Element of Design, Selected Instructional Environments, and Reading Achievement of Ninth Grade Students to Improve Administrative Determinations Concerning Effective Educational Facilities. *Dissertation*.

Shields, P.J., & Rovee-Collier, C. (1992). Long-Term Memory for Context Specific Category Information at Six Months. *Child Development* 63.2, 245-59.

369

Shipman, V. & Shipman, F. (1983). Cognitive Styles: Some Conceptual, Methodological, and Applied Issues. (Gordon, E.W, Ed.) *Human Diversity and Pedagogy.* Westport, CT: Mediax.

Silver, E.A., & Marshall, S.P., (1990). Mathematical and Scientific Problem Solving: Findings, Issues, and Instructional Implications. [In *Dimensions of Thinking and Cognitive Instruction* (Jones, B.J., & Idol, L., Eds.) Hillsdale, NJ: Lawerence Erlbaum & Assoc.

Silverman, K., & Griffiths, R.R. (1992). Low-Dose Caffeine Discrimination and Self-Reported Mood Effects in Normal Volunteers. *Journal of the Experimental Analysis of Behavior* 57.1, 91-107.

Silverman, K., et. al. (1992). Withdrawal Syndrome After the Double-Blind Cessation of Caffeine Consumption. *New England Journal of Medicine* 327.16, 1109-14.

Silverman, L.H. A Comprehensive Report of Studies Using the Subliminal Psychodynamic Activation Method. *Psychological Research Bulletin.* Lund University 20.3, 22.

Silverstein, Alvin, & Silverstein,Virginia. (1986). *The World of the Brain.* New York, NY: Morrow Jr. Books.

Singer, J. (1977). *Ongoing Thought: The Normative Baseline for Alternative States of Consciousness.* (Zinberg, N.E.,Ed.) New York, NY: Free Press.

Singer, W. (1993). Synchronization of Cortical Activity and its Putative Role in Information Processing and Learning. *Annual Review of Physiology* 55, 349-74.

Sirevaag, A.M., & Greenough, W.T. (1991). Plasticity of GFAP-Immunoreactive Astrocyte Size and Number in Visual Cortex of Rats Reared in Complex Environments. *Brain Research* 540.1-2, 273-8.

Smith, A.P., Kendrick, A.M., & Maben. (1992). Effects of Caffeine on Performance and Mood in the Late Morning and After Lunch. *Neuropsychobiology* 26.4, 198-204.

Smith, B.D., Davidson, R.A., & Green, R.L. (1993). Effects of Caffeine and Gender on Physiology and Performance: Further Tests on a Biobehavioral Model. *Physiology and Behavior* 54.3, 415-22.

Soloveichik, Simon. (1979, May). Odd Way to Teach, But It Works. *Soviet Life Magazine.*

Sperry, R. (1968). Hemisphere Disconnection and Unity in Conscious Awareness. *American Psychologist* 23, 723-33.

Spielberger, C.D., Ed. (1972). *Anxiety: Current Trends in Theory and Research* Vol. 1 & 2. New York NY: Academic Press.

Squire, L. (1992). Memory and the Hippocampus: A Synthesis from Findings with Rats, Monkeys and Humans. *Psychological Review* 99.2, 195-231.

Sternberg, Robert. *Beyond I.Q.: A Triarchical Theory of Human Intelligence.*

Sternberg, R., & Kolligan, J. Jr., Eds. (1990). *Competence Considered.* New Haven, CT: Yale University Press.

Sternberg, Robert & Wagner, Richard. (1994). *Mind in Context.* New York, NY: Cambridge University Press.

Stone, C.L. (1983). A Meta-Analysis of Advance Organizer Studies. *Journal of Experimental Education* 54, 194-9.

Strasburger, V.C. (1992). Children, Adolescents and Television. *Pediatrics in Review* 13.4, 144-51.

Sullivan, R.M., McGaugh, J.L. & Leon, M. (1991). Norepinphrine-Induced Plasticity and One-Trial Olfactory Learning in Neonatal Rats. *Brain Research* 60.2, 219-28.

Sutter, Alice. (1991, January). VDT Noise Causes Stress. *Issues in Human Resources.*

Swabb, D.F., Gooren, L.J. & Hofman, M.A. (1992). Gender and Sexual Orientation in Relation to Hypothalmic Structures. *Hormone Research* 38 Supplement 2, 51-61.

Swanson, James. (1980). Contact: Research Institute, HSC, Toronto, Ontario, Canada. M5G 1X8.

Spielberger, C.D., Ed. (1972). *Anxiety: Current Trends in Theory and Research.* Vols. 1-2. New York, NY: Academic Press.

Sylwester, Robert. (1993, December - 1994, January). What the Biology of the Brain Tells Us About Learning. *Educational Leadership.* pp. 46-51.

Sylwester, Robert. (1994, October). How Emotions Affect Learning. *Educational Leadership* Volume 52, 2, 60-65.

Sylwester, Robert. (1995) A Celebration of Neurons. ASCD. Alexandria, VA

Sylwester, R. & Cho, J. (1993 January). What Brain Research Says About Paying Attention. *Educational Leadership.* pp. 71-5.

Tallal, P. (1991). Hormonal Influences in Developmental Learning Disabilities. *Psychoneuroendocrinology* 16.1-3, 203-11.

Tallal, P., Ross, R., & Curtiss, S. (1989). Unexpected Sex-Ratios in Families of Language/Learning-Impaired Children. *Neuropsychologia* 27.7, 987-98.

Tallal, P., Miller, S., & Fitch, R.H. (1993). Neurobiological Basis for Speech: a Case for the Preeminence of Temporal Processing. *Annals of the New York Academy of Sciences* 682, 27-47.

Taylor, E. (1988). *Subliminal Learning.* Salt Lake City, UT: Just Another Reality Publishing.

Taylor, H.L., & Orlansky, J. (1993). The Effects of Wearing Protective Chemical Warfare Combat Clothing on Human Performance. *Aviation Space and Environmental Medicine* 64.2, A1-41.

Thal, D.J., & Tobias, S. (1992). Communicative Gestures in Children with Delayed Onset of Oral Expressive Vocabulary. *Journal of Speech and Hearing Research* 35.6, 1281-9. '

Thal, D.J., & Tobias, S., & Morrison, D. (1991). Language and Gesture in Late Talkers: A 1-Year Follow-Up. *Journal of Speech and Hearing Research* 34.3, 604-12.

Thayer, R. (1986). Time of Day Affects Energy Levels. *Brain-Mind Bulletin* 12, 3D.

Thayer, R. (1989). *The Biopsychology of Mood and Arousal.* New York, NY: Oxford University Press.

Thompson, Richard F. (1993). *The Brain: A Neuroscience Primer,* 2nd ed. New York, NY: W.H. Freeman and Company.

Tonge, B.J. (1990). The Impact of Television on Children and Clinical Practice. *Australian and New Zealand Journal of Psychiatry* 24.4, 552-60.

Torrance, P. & Ball, O. (1978). Intensive Approach Alters Learning Styles in Gifted. *Journal of Creative Behavior* 12, 248-52.

Trautman, P. (1979). An Investigation of the Relationship Between Selected Instructional Techniques and Identified Cognitive Style. *Dissertation.* St. John's University.

Treisman, A. & Gormican, S. (1988). Feature Analysis in Early Vision: Evidence from Search Asymmetries. *Psychological Review* 95, 15-48.

Trevarthen, Colin. (1972). Brain Bisymmetry and the Role of the Corpus Callosum in Behavior and Conscious Experience. [In *Cerebral Interhemispheric Relations*] Bratislavia, Czechoslovakia: Publishing House of the Slovak Academy of Sciences.

Trevarthen, Colin. (1990). Growth and Education of the Hemispheres. *Brain Circuits and Functions of the Mind: Essays in Honor of Roger W. Sperry.* (Trevarthen, Colwyn, Ed.) New York, NY: Cambridge University Press.

Tryphonas, H., & Trites, R. (1979). Food Allergy in Children with Hyperactivity. *Annals of Allergy* 42, 22-7.

Uhl, F., et al. (1990). Cerebral Correlates of Imagining Colors, Faces and a Map - Negative Cortical DC Potentials. *Neuropsychologia* 28.1, 81-93.

Unger, Georges. (1976). Biochemistry of Intelligence. *Research Communications in Psychology, Psychiatry & Behavior* 1.5-6, 597-606.

Urban, M.J. (1992). Auditory Subliminal Stimulation: A Re-examination. *Perceptual and Motor Skills* 74.2, 515-41.

U.S. Department of Education. (1986). *What Works.* Washington, DC.

Van Dyke, D.C., & Fox, A.A. (1990). Fetal Drug Exposure and its Possible Implications for Learning in the Pre-School and School-Age Population. *Journal of Learning Disabilities* 23.3, 160-3.

Vasta, R., & Sarmiento, R.F. (1979). Liberal Grading Improves Evaluations But Not Performance. *Journal of Educational Psychology* 71, 207-211.

Verlee Williams, Linda. (1983). *Teaching for the Two-Sided Mind.* New York, NY: Simon & Schuster/Touchstone.

Vincent, J-D. (1990). *The Biology of Emotions.* Cambridge, MA: Basil Blackwell.

Virostko, J. (1983). An Analysis of the Relationships Among Academic Achievement in Mathematics and Reading, Assigned Instructional Schedules, and the Learning Style Time Preferences of Third, Fourth, Fifth and Sixth Grade Students. *Dissertation.* St. John's University.

Vos-Groenendal, Jeannete. (1991).An Accelerated/Integrative Learning Model Program Evaluation: Based on Participant Perceptions of Student Attitudinal and Achievement Changes. *Unpublished Dissertation.* Flagstaff, AZ: ERIC & NAU.

Vygotsky, L.S. (1985). *Thought and Language.* Cambridge, MA: MIT Press.

Wade, John. (1990). *SuperStudy.* Dellasta. Mount Waverley, Victoria, Australia.

Walker, Morton. (1991). *The Power of Color.* Avery Publishing, Garden City   Park, NY.

Wallace, C. S., et al. (1992). Increases in Dendritic Length in Occipital Cortex After 4 Days of Differential Housing in Weanling Rats. *Behavioral and Neural Biology* 58.1, 64-8.

Ward, C., & Jaley, Jan. (1993). *Learning to Learn..* New Zealand: A&H Print Consultants.

Webb, D., & Webb, T. (1990). *Accelerated Learning with Music.* Norcross, GA: Accelerated Learning Systems.

Webster, J.S., et al. (1992). A Scoring Method that is Sensitive to Right-Hemispheric Dysfunction. *Journal of Clinical and Experimental Neuropsychology* 14.2, 222-38.

Weil, M.O., & Murphy, J. (1982). Instructional Processes. *Encyclopedia of Educational Research.* (Mitzel, H.E., Ed.) New York, NY: The Free Press. pp. 892-893.

Weinstein, C.E., & R.E. Mayer. (1986). The Teaching of Learning Strategies. *Handbook of Research on Teaching.* (Wittrock, M.C. Ed.) 3rd edition. New York, NY: Macmillian Publishing. pp. 315-27.

Wenger, Win. (1992). *Beyond Teaching & Learning.* Singapore. Project Renaissance.

Wentzel, K.R. (1989). Adolescent Classroom Goals, Standards for Performance, and Academic Achievement: An Interactionist Perspective. *Journal of Educational Psychology* 81, 131-42.

White, R.T. (1980). An Investigation of the Relationship Between Selected Instructional Methods and Selected Elements of Emotional Learning Style Upon Student Achievement in Seventh-Grade Social Studies. *Unpublished Dissertation.* St John's Univeristy.

Whitleson, S. (1985). The Brain Connection: the Corpus Callosum is Larger in Left-Handers. *Science* 229, 665-8.

Whitleson, S. Sex Differences in the Neurology of Cognition: Social, Educational and Clinical Implications. *Le Fait Femenin.*

Wicker, F., et al. (1978). Reframing Problems: A Bigger Boost to Insight than Visualization. *Journal of Educational Psychology* 70, 372-7.

Williams, Linda Verlee. (1983). *Teaching for the Two-Sided Mind.* New York, NY: Simon & Schuster.

Wilson, D.A., Willnre, J., Kurz, E.M., & Nadel, L. (1986). Early Handling Increases Hippocampal Long-Term Potentialtion in Young Rats. Behavioral Brain Research, 21, 223-227.

Wittrock, M.C., Ed. (1977). *The Human Brain.* Englewood Cliffs, NJ: Prentice-Hall.

Wlodkowski, R. (1985). *Enhancing Adult Motivation to Learn.* San Francisco, CA: Jossey-Bass Publishers.

Wolfe, Patricia & Sorgen, Marny. (1990). *Mind, Memory & Learning.* Fairfax, CA: Self-Published.

Wolman, B., Ed. (1973). *Handbook of General Psychology.* Englewood Cliffs, NJ: Prentice-Hall.

Wree, Andrea. (1989). Sexes Differ in Brain Degeneration. *Anatomy and Embryology* 160, 105-19.

Wurtman, J. *Managing Your Mind & Mood Through Food.* New York, NY: Harper/Collins, 1986.

Wurtman, J. (1988). *Dietary Phenyalanine and Brain Function.* Boston, MA: Birkhauser. p. 374.

Wurtman, R.J. (1990). Carbohydrate Craving. *Drugs* Supplement 39.3, 49-52.

Wurtman, R.J., & Ritter-Walker, E. (1988). *Dietary Phenylanine and Brain Function.* Boston: Birkhauser.

Wurtman, R.J., Ritter-Walker, E., & Wurtman, J.J. (1989, January). Carbohydrates and Depression. *Scientific American,* 68-75.

Wurtman, R.J., et al. (1989). Effect of Nutrient Intake on Premenstrual Depression. *American Journal of Obstretrics and Gynecology* 161.5, 1228-34.

Wynn, K. (1990). Children's Understanding of Counting. *Cognition* 36.2, 155-93.

Wynn, K. (1992, August). Addition and Subtraction by Human Infants. *Nature* 27, 749-50.

Yeap, L.L. (1989). Hemisphericity and Student Achievement. *International Journal of Neuroscience* 48, 225-32.

Zalewski, L.J., Sink, & Yachimowicz, D.J. (1992). Using Cerebral Dominance for Education Programs. *Journal of General Psychology* 119.1, 45-57.

The Author

Eric Jensen is a former teacher who has taught elementary, middle school, high school level students. He remains deeply committed to making a positive, significant, lasting difference in the way the world learns. He received his B.A. in English from San Diego State University and M.A. in Psychology from the University of California. He has taught as adjunct faculty at the University of California at San Diego, National University and the University of San Diego. He's listed in "Who's Who Worldwide" and is a former Outstanding Young Man of America selection.

Jensen was the co-founder of SuperCamp, the nation's first and largest brain-based learning program for teens. He authored the best-selling *Student Success Secrets, The Little Book of Big Motivation, B's and A's in 30 Days, The Learning Brain* and *SuperTeaching.*

He was a key part of one of the largest (over 4,000 teachers trained) brain-based teacher training programs in the world. Trainers from AT & T, Disney, IBM, Digital, GTE, Hewlett-Packard, ICA, Motorola, Burroughs, Atlantic Bell, SAS and three branches of the military have used his methods. Jensen provides successful trainings for conferences, schools, organizations, and Fortune 500 corporations, and is an international speaker, writer and consultant.

Your Feedback to the Author

All feedback is welcomed. If you have any comments, corrections, additions or suggestions for the next printing of this book, please fax or write to the author at the address and phone number below. Also, if your school is currently in the change process, contact us, we can support your efforts.

For a speaker or trainer, contact the author: For brain-based training, conference speaking, consulting, corporate training, district or school in-services and workshops or for a *free* catalog of Brain-Based Learning Products for Teaching and Training, call (800) 325-4769 or (619) 546-7555, fax (619) 546-7560 or mail your name and address to: **Turning Point**, P.O. Box 2551, Del Mar, CA 92014 USA

Distributor and Overseas Inquiries Welcome: If you distribute a catalog, do workshops, or if you are a publisher overseas, your audience may be interested in learning more about these practical brain-based strategies. To offer a catalog and earn additional income, contact our publishing office for distributor price list. Call (619) 546-7555 or mail your name and address to: Turning Point, P.O. Box 2551, Del Mar, CA 92014 USA.

Exciting 6-Day Workshop: Brain Based Learning

- **Six exciting days, $675**
- **For all levels of teachers, trainers & administrators**
- **Learn new teaching, training & staff development skills**
- **Practical applications of new brain research**
- **Great for staff who want to redesign their school**
- **Integrate brain-based approaches in all areas**
- **Learn over 100 specific and useful ideas**
- **Increase your market value and income**
- **Discover potent new ways to boost learning**
- **Boost your own self-confidence & self-esteem**
- **Make a bigger difference & feel good about it**

If you enjoyed this book, you may want to take the training that goes with it. Are you a teacher, trainer or administrator? Do you now, or would you like to make your living as a presenter? Would you like to master the art of using all these brain-based strategies? Would you like to be able to consistently get audience participation, engage meaning and motivate for lasting changes? You would? Good, then keep reading. You're about to learn why taking a 6-day brain-based training may be one the best things you can possibly do for yourself (and your audience).

- Upgrade your skills for the 21st century
- Boost attention, learning, recall & usage
- 100% satisfaction guaranteed

There's a surging tidal wave sweeping the country and some say, the world. It's not just a trend. It's a virtual explosion in neuroscience discoveries. In the last few years, maverick researchers have uncovered astonishing details about the brain and learning, and they're already being implemented in technology, medicine and business. Learn how to apply them now, and you'll possess rare, powerful and highly marketable 21st century skills that can transform the very foundations of the educational system. You will become more than a contributor, you'll become a "key player" to global learning transformation. *As we move towards the next century, you'll either be part of the new learning revolution or left behind wondering "What happened?"*

As a former classroom teacher, a world-wide staff developer and corporate trainer with over 15 years of successful brain-based training experience, I have successfully trained over 5,000 teens and 15,000 adults. I've been a key part of two of the largest brain-based programs in the world. This has been my passion for years and I love to share it. Wouldn't you want to tap into that kind of experience? I'll bet you would.

Would you like to know what we cover? I'll bet you're curious like me. Just for fun, read the course items below that you'd like to learn & experience:

- How to design and conduct a workshop or training based on the brain
- The 12 super-essentials to know about the brain
- Better curriculum strategies (with tons of examples)
- How this wave of the future will be impacting your work

If you could successfully do those things, would your work be easier, more effective? Of course. Yet, why take my word for it when you can get it straight from past course participants:

"Simply mind-boggling... learned more in 6 days than in twenty years in education" P. Kohlbacher, IL

"You've planted the seeds and the harvest will be a bumper crop!" P. Park, MA

"Never been to a course that gave me so many ideas that were so specific." K. Norman

"I wish I had learned this stuff in college... it should be a graduate requirement." J. Murphy

"One of the best workshops I've taken in 25 years in the field of education... and the most fun by a mile!" L. Miller, Supervisor of Instruction, DE

I could give you countless testimonials. But let's get back to the curriculum of the six-day San Diego course. You can also expect to learn the answers to these topics:

- How to get the whole staff to "buy into" this process
- What is the perfect learning and thinking diet
- How to translate information into "deeply felt" meaning
- How to build and maintain high-performance teams

Those are just some of the more powerful skills and ideas which you can expect to learn. What happens when you implement the results of this course? I can cite you example after example of how participants from my courses have gone on to become highly requested speakers, presenters and even experts in their field. Sometimes I smile when I see conferences with two, three and in one case *four* professional speakers, all trained by me. But please, don't get me wrong. The participants did all the hard work to get good. But I do have a knack for lighting a professional fire and opening up minds.

"Get ready for a mind explosion like you've never had before" S. Robertson, CA

"Your workshop positively and dramatically changed my teaching forever... I have so many parents coming to me and telling me what the difference I've made in their children's lives." I. Forber.

There are more; I'll save them for later. Since you're probably an insatiable learner like myself, you might be interested in what else is offered in this workshop:

- Ingenious rituals which boost learning and maintain optimal states
- How to specifically teach the brain as a learning organ
- Which types of music are best for learning and when to use them
- The 5 secrets to permanently eliminating discipline problems

You may be wondering how in the world can we do all of those things in just 6 short days. The answer is simple. Using the powerful strategies of accelerated learning, we'll be able to enhance absorption, speed up the pace and still absorb far more than you ever believed possible. This methodology, combined with the sizzling cutting-edge neuroscience discoveries will help you learn faster. These breakthroughs will help you discover:

- The real learning differences between males and females
- The 7 secrets to boost concentration and attention in learning
- How to guarantee that your audience will recall & use what they learn
- The 3 types of memory (& which one to reduce the use of dramatically)
- The most amazing new discoveries about the brain you *must* know

In addition, you'll learn through one of the all-time best methods ever: my role-modeling. The workshop is meticulously planned so that you get a real experience of *how* all these brain-based strategies actually work. To put it bluntly, I am one of the few that actually practice what I preach.

As you can tell, I'm not shy about asking you to enroll. Why should I be shy? It's the best investment you can make in yourself and your future. You've got a satisfaction or money back guarantee. After this workshop, the first paid presentation you make, will probably return your investment immediately. And your referral business will astonish you. By the way, are there any other reasons you might want to enroll? Of course!

- Network with "like-minded" people
- Gain new professional skills & confidence
- Discover the 50 best brain-based resources
- Get ready for the 21st century

Let's take care of the details. The course takes place at a beautiful location with relaxing scenery and great food nearby. The location and dates vary each year, so call for this year's location. You can walk from your hotel to the training, no rental car needed. We'll also provide a virtual supermarket of the best set of brain-based resources *anywhere* on this planet. This is going to be some kind of special event! You *are* planning on being a part of it, aren't you?

The tuition costs $675. Can you afford it? It just may be a case of "Can you afford *not* to register?" If you've read this far, you *know* it's for you. Get your school or district to pay for it. Put it on your credit card, use your savings or get a grant. It's a tax deduction. But move fast. You and I know, if you want anything badly enough, you'll find a way.

The demand for brain-based presenters is growing faster than the supply! This can be for your school, business or your next career. So, go for it. You've got a satisfaction or money back guarantee. The registration form is on the following page. Fill it out, copy, mail or fax it. today. While it's fresh in your mind, and there are still spaces left in this sock-hopping, idea-packed, transformational training, go ahead and register. Your future is important and this can positively and fundamentally alter its course. Do it now. You'll be glad you did. That's a promise....

Registration

✔ **YES!** *I'd like to register. Here's my $95 deposit on the $675 tuition.*
Tuition includes course workbook, certification, all special activities and supplies.
Remember...transportation to the event, meals and lodging are extra. Send me
confirmation, travel, lodging, course details and confirmation kit by first class mail.
Held several times each July in San Diego, California. June and August locations
usually include the East Coast, Midwest or Texas. Call for this year's exact dates and
locations. *(Prices and locations valid thru September 1997)*

Circle Payment Form: VISA/MC   wire transfer   check   purchase order
I understand the complete balance ($580) is due no later than 2 weeks prior to event.
Free! With my $95 deposit, send me the amazing, exclusive book "Brain Facts."
Credits: SDSU extension credits available for an additional fee.
Hotel: Call the hotel direct for reservations. We'll give you that information when you call.
We'll suggest an affordable hotel within walking distance. Register early, rooms go fast!

Name (print)

School or Company Name   Role/Title

Home Address   City

State & Zip Code   Country

Phone (include area code)   Fax (include area code)

VISA or Master card number   Expiration date

*Group Discounts: Group price for schools, businesses and other groups of three (3) or more. Details
available by phone or in registration kit. Sorry, no group discounts allowed on registration day
(the first day of the course)*

*Cancellation Policy: All monies paid are refundable except a $25 registration fee. To qualify, you must
contact us by phone, fax or letter prior to course start date.*

*Guarantee Policy: You can be assured of a first-class workshop. After completion of the six-day course,
if you don't feel you got your money's worth, you may request & receive a refund (minus the $95 materials
and registration fee). Refund requests honored up to, but not exceeding 90 days following the course.*

---

call: **1 (800) 325-4769 or (619) 546-7555**
fax: **1 (619) 546-7560**
mail: **TURNING POINT, Box 2551 Del Mar, CA 92014**

Brain-Based Learning & Teaching
Video Staff Development

✔ Get others excited about learning   ✔ Save time & money
✔ Build enthusiasm & support   ✔ Cut learning time
✔ Reach large groups at a time   ✔ Make your job easier

For a staff of 50, this breakthrough $99 staff development program costs less than $2 a teacher. If you're hoping for miracles at your school, they may be closer than you think. As a top international consultant for the last 10 years, the travel schedule has been taking a toll on home and family time. So, although I still do some work, I'm cutting back. How does that affect you?

I'm on a mission to share difference-making principles of brain-based accelerated learning! And while I may not be able to do it in person, I sure can give you the best video training possible. I'm outraged by other school videos selling for $500-800. You *can* save a fortune and still get first-rate quality. Through the magic of video, I'll walk your staff through a meaningful one-hour or half-day in-service. The video covers all the key areas in this book:

- Physiology/Biology
- Timetables/Rhythms
- Memory & Recall
- Intelligence
- States/Attention
- Stress/Threats

- Emotions in Learning
- Strategies & Styles
- Different Learners
- Discipline Strategies
- Music/Environments
- Motivation & Rewards

See it in action! Enjoy state-of-the-art-virtual reality. Get specific classroom examples, graphics and colorful research-proven ideas. You get a lock-step "cookie-cutter" fail-safe video presentation, complete with step-by-step facilitator guide. It's guaranteed & risk-free. The topic is "Brain-based Accelerated Learning" and it is impacting education around the world. It can boost motivation, learning, attendance and help your staff consistently reach ALL of your learners. With spectacular special effects, the video highlights the key research in this book, making a persuasive and motivating case for the use of brain-based learning.

Use this video to provide a clear, concise and compelling case for why you do what you do. It uses state-of-the art virtual reality, classroom examples, graphics and interviews with administrators, teachers and trainers who use these strategies. Use it for staff development. Use it as an exciting tool for train-the-trainer programs.

How do you know this video will fit your needs? Four good reasons: 1) *It's based on this book.* If you like this book, you'll like the video. 2) *It's got a satisfaction, money-back guarantee.* 3) *It's got a fool-proof guidebook.* Keep your worries low and help make your presentation job easy. 4) *It's proven;* here's what others have said: *"Absolutely outstanding..couldn't take my eyes off it."* Mary Francis, N.J. *"I can't say enough good things... all my expectations were met & exceeded...."* T. Johnson, Principal, NJ *"The whole course was so valuable & enlightening, I can't wait to start using it."* Staff Developer, Austin, TX. You can easily lower stress, save money, bring fresh ideas in and get motivated. Encourage and enthuse staff members with this exciting product. Next-day and 2-day delivery service available. Here's what to do...

How To Order:

✔ **YES!** *I'd like the $99 Budget Staff Development Package.*
Includes facilitator's Manual for conducting a terrific staff development session. Two exciting 38 min. color sessions which can be used as a 2-hour to full-day in-service.

Item #801 only $99

✔ **YES!** *I'd like the $375 Deluxe Staff Development Package.*
It's a budget-stretching $500 value: It's a fail-safe, lock-step staff-development kit in a box. You get the two-part, 76 min. video, a facilitator's guidebook, overheads, handouts, posters for the faculty lounge and two of the best "Brain-Based Learning" books ever written.

Item #802, well worth $375

Name (print)

School or Company Name   Role/Title

Shipping Address   City

State & Zip Code   Country

Phone (include area code)   Fax (include area code)

VISA or Master card number   Expiration date

Circle Payment Form: VISA/MC   wire transfer   check   purchase order

Video Format Requested: VHS   PAL

Shipping & Handling, U.S. Orders add $7.95. Fast 2-day and express overnight delivery available. Overseas orders add $35 for shipping (U.S. funds only). **Total Enclosed: $_____**

call: **1 (800) 325-4769 or (619) 546-7555**
fax: **1 (619) 546-7560**
mail: **TURNING POINT, Box 2551 Del Mar, CA 92014**

Index

Notes

Notes

Notes

Notes

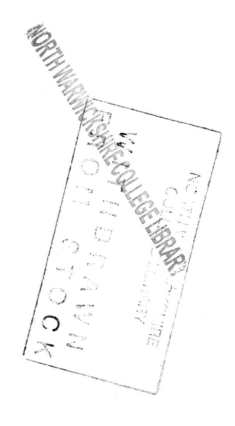